CW00864682

Critical Issues on Islamic Banking and Financial Markets

Islamic Economics, Banking and Finance, Investments, Takaful and Financial Planning

BY

SAIFUL AZHAR ROSLY

authorHOUSE™

1663 LIBERTY DRIVE, SUITE 200
BLOOMINGTON, INDIANA 47403
(800) 839-8640
WWW.AUTHORHOUSE.COM

© 2005 SAIFUL AZHAR ROSLY.
All Rights Reserved.

No part of this book may be reproduced, stored in a retrieval system, or transmitted by any means without the written permission of the author.

First published by AuthorHouse 02/03/05

ISBN: 1-4184-6930-0 (sc)

Library of Congress Control Number: 2004098487

Printed in the United States of America
Bloomington, Indiana

This book is printed on acid-free paper.

To my wife, Faridah and my children

Anas, Nur Iman, Ameen, Ariff and Nur Ilham

PREFACE

A llocation of scarce resources among competing uses remains the central focus of modern economics today. Economics as a study of choice looks at the behavior of people in managing scarce resources. To manage them well should require sound knowledge. When decisions are made by sheer guesswork and conjecture, an efficient way to allocate resources is hard to come by. As resources are not available in abundance, it should be allocated with care, i.e., efficiency.

Although economic science deals with efficiency, the equity criteria must not be overlooked. Doing so will put the meaning of life and its existence into oblivion as economics may succeed to address the need of the animal instinct in him but ignoring the higher order of life.

How man succeeded to fulfill the efficiency and equity criteria in resource allocation, will depend much on the value system he subscribes to when making choices. Values concerns what is right and wrong, good or bad. The question now is: What values should man adopt to help him make the correct choice?

The mobilization and allocation of capital is usually made on the basis of the system of belief or truth that one holds. In capitalism, truth is deeply rooted on reason and sense experience and the marketplace is where truth lies. In the marketplace, the demand for and supply of capital determined its rate of return. Thus, in capitalism, deriving income and profits from interest-bearing instruments is only rational, since what is right and wrong is measured by one's utility, something explainable by reason and sense experience.

The Islamic approach to capital mobilization and allocation requires one to observe values ordained by God. Here the Quran and Sunnah constitute two main sources of revealed values. While not denying the role of reason and sense experience in making economic decisions, Islam helps man to best harness these two powers in determining the best solutions for remedies.

This book is intended to demonstrate the interlinking network of values derived from revelation and reason-senses in resources allocation, particularly capital. It deals with variant issues invoking philosophy and ethics, history, economics, banking and the capital market. It is unique in the sense that the articles were written on practical ground, dealing with practical issues of the day. Islamic economics and finance are discussed by way of examples and problems faced by Islamic financial institutions, particularly in Malaysia. It hopes to present Islam to the business community in a dynamic way. It is a layman version of the Islamic financial markets.

My approach is both practical and critical, with a hope to invite debates and discourses among discerning observers. As an economist, my job is to dissect the inside and see what is going on. This is the scientific method. By way of observation, I have explained most of the existing financial instruments and policies in Malaysia and other Muslim countries as well. Critical observers who are curious how the Islamic financial markets operate in Malaysia will find this book helpful.

My critical comment is based on Islamic traditions that no stones should be left unturned in the quest for knowledge and truth. My sheer displeasure on current practices making profits by virtue of time value without an equivalent counter value ('iwad) is only obvious. And there are many others who share this view.

Certainly, this book is meant for public reading. Those who specialize in Islamic banking and finance may find this book quite elementary. It is written for the layman. But many people should find this book useful. The first group will obviously be the university and college students. There are numerous topics in this book they can use in preparing project papers and dissertations on Islamic banking and finance. My critical but positive outlook will make their study even more challenging and inspiring

The second group constitutes the legal practitioners who are now making some contacts with the *Shariah* and Islamic commercial law (*fiqh muamalat*) in dealing with legal documentations of Islamic financial instruments. This book will give them a helicopter view of the Islamic financial market in Malaysia and the underlying principles on which Islamic insturments are structured..

Financial planners, i.e., the third group, will find this book quite helpful. In order to give advice to prospective Muslim clients, they are expected to know the fundamentals of Islam, Islamic economics and financial transactions. Information on Islamic financial instruments such as Islamic deposits, shares, bonds, unit trusts, *takaful,* and inheritance (*fara'id*) will come in handy.

The fourth group must be financial practitioners themselves. Some may not agree with my views, but many have been supportive. This book can help further intensify research and development in their respective banks and Islamic banking divisions.

The last group shall consist of businesses, academics, and policy-makers. My fellow lecturers and colleagues who are looking for a comprehensive reference on Islamic financial markets will find this book as a good supplement to their reading list. This book is also useful for aspiring politicians who desire to sacrifice their life to help the Malaysian people live a better life. To do so, they are expected to equip themselves with knowledge. Knowledge on Islamic economics and finance is equally important.

Most of the articles in this book are taken from my research column articles written for the *SUN Daily, Zoomfinance Portal,* and the *Investors Digest,* the Kuala Lumpur Stock Exchange (KLSE) business magazine. It provides a critical view of current practices of Islamic banking and finance in Malaysia, going through the booms and busts between 1995 and 2004. Some of the data are not updated to reflect prevailing issues then. To some extent, this book is about the history of Islamic banking and finance in Malaysia. It is not an outdated piece of work as the principles underlying issues and problems investigated then are divine in nature.

The book is divided into ten sections. In Section One, the underlying principles of Islamic banking are examined followed by a critical look at Islamic financial products in Section Two, Three, and Four. The study of Islamic financial markets will be meaningless without examining its macroeconomic impacts. This is given in Section Five. This is followed by a brief look at the legal aspects of Islamic banking and finance in Section Six. An extensive analysis of the Islamic equities market is given in

Section Seven. In Section Eight, issues on the the Islamic bond market are highlighted with rigor. The book will leave a vaccum without examining the *takaful* industry, which is given in Section 9. More specific issues are discussed in Section 10.

The Government of Malaysia should be congratulated for its noble and strong support of the Islamic banking and financial market activities. Several laws on Islamic banking and *takaful* were enacted to make way for a competitive market environment under a dual financial system framework. In achieving the objective of positioning Malaysia as an Islamic financial center, the Capital Market Masterplan (CMP) listed thirteen recommendations, one of which recommended that efforts to increase the pool of Islamic capital market expertise be enhanced through training and education.

In similar fashion, the International Islamic University of Malaysia (IIUM) has placed Islamization of knowledge as the focal point of education and training in its academic programs. Research and teaching on Islamic economics as the mother knowledge of business, banking and finance has been intensively pursued to make the university a global leader in the field of Islamic economics and financial markets.

The ball is now at the feet of the practisioners, whether they desire to apply the true conception of Islamic commercial contracts or to adopt the shortcut route under an Islamic label. A global outlook would require them to recognize that differences in opinion on *Shariah* matters cannot be downplayed and ignored. An isolationist policy would not be good for Malaysia's quest to become a leading Islamic financial center in the world. The government must see that integration and consolidation with fellow Muslim countries in the field of Islamic banking and finance be pursued with rigor and wisdom. It is the intention of this book to highlight issues and problems that can further strengthen economic and business cooperation among Muslim countries towards the creation of an Islamic common market. Islamic markets must exist to see that policy decisions and market forces can actually stimulate desires of the Muslim people for the quest of self-reliance and economic freedom.

Saiful Azhar Rosly
International Islamic University Malaysia

TABLE OF CONTENTS

xi

SECTION ONE

ISLAMIC BANKING PRINCIPLES

One
Islamic Economics

Islamic economics as a subject is relatively new in Malaysian universities but practically unknown in corporate business. People may have heard about Islamic banking and finance, but there has been limited discussion on Islamic economics and many may think that these two are the same.

To some extent, there are similarities because economics is the mother knowledge of business and finance. The same is true for Islamic economics. But Islamic economics as a discipline is still a baby. It has relied a lot on Islamic commercial law (*fiqh muamalat*) with its undue emphasis on the prohibition of *riba* (usury) and the implementation of the *zakat* system. It is, thus, not surprising that Islamic economics is sometimes labeled as capitalism minus *riba,* plus *zakat.*

Focus on the monetary side of the economy has been overwhelming. It is normal to see discussions on Islamic economics to revolve around financial issues. Islamic banking and finance seemed to have overtaken other focus areas like economic methodology, the problem of the consumer and the firm, market structures, factor markets, public finance, poverty, and economic development.

But Islamic economics is not about financial institutions alone. It seeks to examine the behavior of man in the marketplace, his likes and dislikes and how these tendencies have impacted his way of conducting economic activities.

The problem at hand is, how is Islamic economics defined? Or how to best understand Islamic economics as field of study. One way is to take a look at the concept of scarcity. This is where the study of economics begins.

Islam has no objection to the concept of scarcity because scarcity is a fact of life. It exists when the necessary resources for producing things are not enough to satisfy all wants. Scarcity to an economist is like gravity to a physicist. It is a fundamental principle in the study of economics. Economists say that scarcity arises when available resources are not sufficient to fulfill human wants. In other words, economists have made two general assumptions about the universe and mankind, namely:

a) Assumption about the universe – Limited resources

b) Assumption about man – Unlimited human wants

Islam does not see the above assumptions are false and evil. In fact, Islam recognizes scarcity as nature's way arising from the two inherent conflicts between wants and ability. The limited resources assumption is made to show that man's ability to exploit resources is limited by his knowledge. In this manner, economics looks at relative scarcity and not absolute scarcity. The same applies to Islamic economics. There is no absolute scarcity in Islam, because the Quran says:

"It is Allah Who hath created the heavens and the earth and sends down rain from the skies, and with it bringeth our fruits wherewith to feed you; it is He who hath made the ships subject to you, that they may sail through the sea by His Command; and the rivers (also) hath He made subject to you. And He hath made subject to you the sun and the moon, both diligently pursuing their courses; and the Night and the Day hath He (also) made subject to you. And He giveth you of all that ye ask for but if ye count the favors of Allah, never will ye be able to number them."

Islam also recognizes that human desires are not limited. This is further attested by the Quran and Traditions that:

"Surely man is created greedy and impatient" (70:19)
"Fair-seeming to men is made the love of desires, of women and sons and hoarded treasures of gold and silver and well-bred horses and cattle and tilth: (3:13).

"And you love wealth with exceeding love" (89:20). "He thinks that his wealth will make him abide" (104:3). "If man is given a valley of gold, certainly, he wants the second and third one" (Sahih Hadiths)

Scarcity in Islam is, through and through, a *tabi'* phenomenon. Therefore, when scarcity exists, nature empowers people to make choices (*ikhtiyar*) as nothing is available for free anymore. Let's look at the problem of choice in economics and how they affect our lives.

Economists usually say that with scarcity, nothing can be obtained without costs. Hence, economics is a science or art of making choices dealing with the following questions:

- What goods and services people want and how much? This is the problem of the consumer.
- What is the most efficient method to produce goods and services that people want? This is the problem of the firm.
- How to reward factor inputs such as labor, land, and capital taking part in the production of goods and services that people want?
- How to reduce unemployment and inflation? This is the problem of the government.
- How to promote economic growth given the available supply of labor and capital resources? This is the problem of the market and government.

Making these difficult choices definitely requires knowledge. Making correct decisions based on knowledge defines what the study of economics is all about. The main focus of economic study is man himself. The knowledge he uses to make correct decisions is expected to help him find ways to overcome the problem he encountered in allocating scarce resources. The knowledge sought must give him a sense of certainty since any form of "knowledge" that is bound to create uncertainty and doubts would be of no use for him in making the right decision.

An Economic Problem arises from an Act of Choice (*Ikhtiyar*)

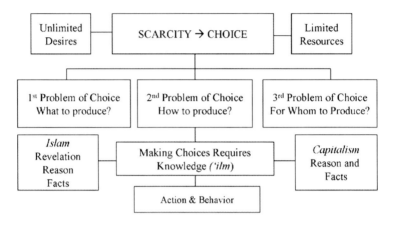

Figure 1.1 Islamic Economics

In mainstream economic textbooks, the term "economic principle" is often used to mean the fundamental law of economics, which is knowledge itself. In fact, these principles are the well-established economic theories that have passed through numerous tests. They have become economic laws that serve to guide the decision making of consumers, producers, capitalists, workers, investors, and government alike.

However, these economic laws (i.e., economic knowledge) are the product of the intellect (*'aql*) alone with the scientific method to dictate what truth is. Although Islam acknowledges the role of the intellect (*'aql*) and sense experience as a source of value and knowledge, ultimately revelation i.e., Divine guidance (*wahy*) is put above them both.

In this regard, revelation in Islam becomes the primary source of economic principles, with reason and experience playing the supportive role. The latter is popularly known as economic theory, while the former is embodied in the economic system. This means that fundamental laws and regulations governing resource allocation fall under the realm of divine guidance. These fundamental laws are manifested in the Islamic economic system.

In view of the positive attitude of the Quran towards scarcity and resource allocation, it must also be positive about wealth and property (*al-mal*). Early economist J.S. Mills sometimes defined economics as a study of wealth. That is, people make choices about what goods and services they want. People work to earn income and businesses are run to make profits. In layman's perspective, commodities, money, and profits constitute the wealth of the nation.

But one may now ask—is there a limit to wealth creation? How is wealth creation connected to man's objective in life, say achieving happiness? Does owning millions of dollars guarantee happiness? According to al-Ghazali, the famous eleventh century Islamic philosopher, man can attain ultimate happiness (*sa'ada haqiqiya*) by attaining excellences (*fada'il*) in many areas. One is through knowledge (*'ilm*).

By ultimate happiness, al-Ghazali does not mean gratification of desires for food and sex, possession of enormous wealth, widespread fame and influence. He does not agree with the general hedonistic view that the aim of human life is to enjoy the pleasure (*ladhdha*) and delight (*na'im*) of this world. It is worthy to note that it is not wealth that becomes unacceptable in al-Ghazali's theory of ethics. It is the love of wealth and acquisition for its own sake (*hubb al-mal*) that he disagrees with.

In Islam, wealth is not seen as the only means leading to happiness; beside knowledge (*'ilm*), al-Ghazali has placed wealth (*al-mal*) alongside influence, family, and noble birth (i.e., in a religious family) as one of the external goods (*al-fada'il al-kharijiyya*) leading to ultimate happiness (*sa'adat haqiqiya*).

To acquire faith through the acquisition of knowledge and building good character, one must possess health, strength, long life, and beauty (i.e., an attribute that creates a good impression on others). Wealth, according to al-Ghazali is not essential to happiness, but only useful to it. In other words, an individual who possesses ample wealth should be able to devote more time to knowledge (*'ilm*) and action (*amal*), for he is free from the care of the necessities of life.

In this sense, Islam enjoins wealth creation not for its own sake but as a means to attain peace and tranquility from knowledge (*'ilm*) and action (*'amal*). As such, the primordial Covenant (*al-mithaq*) requires him to acquire and dispose of wealth in accordance with the law of God. This law is none other than the economic system. It (i.e., the economic system) spells out the principles of motivation, ownership, decision making and the mechanisms for implementation that all economic system must address in resource allocation.

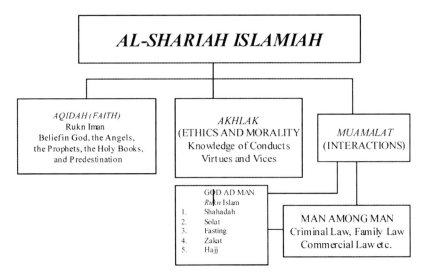

Figure 1.2 The *Shariah*

It means that in Islam, the question of right and wrong in resource allocation and the pursuit of economic stability and growth cannot be settled by a mere appeal reason and empirical observations. Man's indebtedness to God for creating him out of nothing is symbolized by his total submission and surrender to His Will (i.e., *al-Shariah Islamiyah*) by the way on which the economic system is built.

It follows that the meaning of man's economic existence in Islam is no longer related to scarcity and the problem of resource allocation alone. These are the byproducts of hypothetical guesswork without which economists will be left short-handed. As mentioned earlier, Islam does not deny scarcity and the subsequent problem of choice as fundamental characteristics in economic studies. However, it dismisses them as the sole purpose of man's economic existence.

The next question is, why does man in Islam submitted to the rules and regulations sanctioned by God? That is, why must he obey God in conducting economic activities? Why can't he resort to reason and facts in making resource allocation choices?

The answer lies in the conception of Islam as *al-din*. Islam in general means submission. Islam as *al-din* is also understood as a way of life. Interestingly, one of the meanings of *al-din* is indebtedness, i.e., man's indebtedness to his Creator. The term *din* is extracted from the root word *dyn*. It is this notion of indebtedness that gives deeper meaning to the reason for human economic existence in Islam.

But what is the story behind man's indebtedness to God? And what is he supposed to do under such a situation of indebtedness? When a reasonably good man owes someone money, he will not plan to default on the loan, but to repay it in full. The same applies to a true believer (*mukminum*), who will definitely pay his debt to God with a true sense of God-consciousness (*taqwa*).

According to al-Attas, in Islam, man is indebted to God, his Creator and Provider, for bringing him into existence and maintaining him in his existence. Man, who once did not exist, is given life and existence by God.

On this point, the Quran states, "Man, We did create from a quintessence of clay. Then We placed him as a drop of sperm in a place of rest, firmly fixed. Then We made the sperm into a clot of congealed blood; then out of that clot We made a lump; then We made out of that lump bones and clothed the bones with fresh; then We developed out of it another creature. So blessed be God, the Best to create." (Al-Mu'minun {23}:12-14).

When man is indebted to God for giving him life, in what way can he repay the debt? As God is in no dire need of anything since He is the Creator and Sustainer, it is quite difficult to gauge how man can give his life back to God. Does it mean that man has to commit suicide to pay off his debt?

In Islam, al-Attas says that paying or returning the debt to God means to give himself up in service, or *khidmah* to Him, to abase himself before Him, to consciously enslave himself to His Commands, Prohibitions, and Ordinances, and thus to live out the dictates of His Law.

It is clearly seen now that man's existence is explained by the debt he owes God and his subsequent enslavement to His law as a means of repayment. Man himself is the object of the debt. In fact, the Covenant (*al-mithaq*) that man sealed with God, when He says, "Am I not your Lord," (*alastuburabbikum*) and man's true self testifying, answered: "Yea!" We

9

do testify (*balashahidna*), requires man to manifest the Covenant (*al-mithaq*) by way of submitting his desires to His Will (i.e., the *Shariah*) in absolute true willingness.

The question now is how this meaning of indebtedness and the concept of *Al-Mithaq* becomes significant in explaining the meaning of human economic existence.

Recalling the four basic economic problems of mainstream economics, namely: resource allocation, distribution, economic stability, and growth, we see the issue is not only about what rules and techniques one can use to solve problems, but most importantly who determines these rules in the first place?

That is, to help solve the pressing problem of poverty, unemployment, inflation, environmental degradation, etc., one's belief must be based on a strong value system whose basis is divine. In this respect, the mainstream economics did not recognize the role of revelation in determining economic values. It identifies reason and sense experience as the determinant of right and wrong. Economists called these right and wrong "utility" and "disutility."

It can be seen now that Islamic economics remains the study of choice. Due to scarcity, man has to make choices, as he cannot have everything he desires. To make the correct choice, man must be driven by knowledge. There are two types of knowledge one can use in making economic choices. The first type is knowledge derived from the Quran and Tradition. This is Divine knowledge and is embodied in the economic system. The second type of knowledge is that derived from reason and sense experience, known as economic theory. In a sense, economic theory explains and predicts, but is only possible when an economic system is in place.

Islamic banking and finance is a specialization in Islamic economics. It deals with the problem of choice dealing with the demand and supply of capital as a factor of production. For example, in sourcing deposits, an Islamic bank cannot use interest (*riba*) to pay depositors. This is a Divine requirement, as Islam prohibits the payment and receipts of interest. However, by using reason and facts, one can further understand and measure demand and supply behavior of Muslim investors. The demand and supply determinants help explain the factors affecting behavior of depositors and fund users. These factors can be divinely inspired or simply mundane in nature. For example, *zuhd* (moderation) tendencies (i.e., divine) can increase the supply of capital but an increase in corporate earnings (i.e., mundane) can also increase the supply of capital.

Two
The Islamic Worldview

To possess a vision is crucial in determining our future place in this world. A vision tells us what we want to become and how to achieve it within a certain time frame. It helps us see in a more structured and systematic way, how to get things done, how to get ahead of others. Without a vision in life, we may get older, but not any wiser.

However, having a vision assumes that we possess a clear view about the meaning of our existence. It involves our knowledge about human values and attitudes, conscious or unconscious, reflected in a set of metaphysical beliefs or *Weltanschauung.*

A worldview deals with the ultimate questions or interpretations of the world we live in, such that a clear view about the philosophical, educational, political, economic, and moral character of our existence is well defined.

A man's understanding about his role in this world and his urge to fulfill his goals and missions must therefore be rooted to a *Weltanschauung* or worldview to give meaning to his existence.

But what actually is an Islamic worldview and what has it to do with Islamic financial markets? According to al-Attas, an Islamic worldview or *ru'yat al-Islam li al-wujud* is the vision of reality and truth that appears before our mind's eye, revealing what existence is all about. The worldview of Islam encompasses both *al-dunya* and *al-akhirah,* in which the *dunya* aspect must be related in a profound and inseparable way to the *akhirah* aspect, and in which the *akhirah* aspect has the ultimate and final significance. Such a worldview requires one to acquire knowledge about the concept of:

- *Din*
- God
- Man
- Universe
- Prophethood

Islamic Worldview

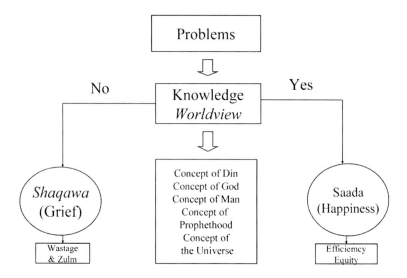

Figure 1.3 The Islamic Worldview

In fact, when one looks at the components of an Islamic worldview, it constitutes the pillars of Islam and Iman (faith). In this way, the Muslim people are obligated (*fard 'ain*) to acquire knowledge on these fundamentals, faith and religion. In fact, Muslims should see the Islamic worldview as a basic need, without which they will be in the state of utter loss and confusion. The Quran says, "By time, man is in loss, except those who believe and do good works and exhort one another to truth and to patience." (Al-Asr:1-3)

With an Islamic worldview, Islamic banks and financial institutions should be able to pursue transactions manifesting the Quranic conception of trading and commerce (*al-bay'*) as an alternative to *riba*. Using *al-bay'*,

Islamic banks should be ready to adopt new practices, such as risk and profit sharing with their customers. To conduct financing via *al-bai bithaman aji, murabahah, salam, istisna',ijarah, musharakah* and *mudarabah,* the element of risk-taking must be made evident in contractual obligations. These products will motivate people to be more creative and proactive, work harder and improve value-addition in production. They are also potent to help finance small and medium scale industries, particularly start-ups, turnarounds, or high-technology ventures.

But to do the above is beyond the scope of the banking business. The banking firms are not entrepreneurs. They only make interest-bearing loans and are very good at collecting debts too. They collect deposits and pay interests. And to put the depositors' money into direct production in the real sector is certainly not their cup of tea.

Conducting *al-bay'* in the banking business can be a tough assignment. Bank managers may get the boot if many *al-bay'* projects do not make the mark. Shareholders can be nervous to see their capital depleting as more projects are not moving well. Depositors may withdraw their money, knowing Islamic deposits receive no fixed returns and capital protection. An Islamic bank that uses *al-bay'* is inviting trouble. Should the Muslim people then abandon Islamic banking?

Islamic banking as a system does not only deal with the banking practitioners and shareholders, but equally important the government, academics, and banking customers themselves. As an alternative to *riba*-based banking, Muslims should take lessons from the experience of *hijrah* to see that Islamic banking is pursued with a sense of *taqwa* and purpose. The *hijrah* signifies Prophet Muhammad's (*pbuh*) emigration from Mecca to Medina.

For fourteen years, the Holy Prophet struggled to teach Islam to the Arabs in Mecca. In doing so, he was beaten and stoned. Attempts to kill him do not require mentioning. The Meccan people were strong in economics, finance, and military. But in the midst of plenty, the rich and powerful exploited the women, the poor, and the orphans. Their lives were driven by carnal pleasures and superstitions. Female infanticide is a deeply-rooted culture. Gambling, prostitution, drunkenness, black magic, and rampant use of false weights and measures in business is a way of life.

The central aim of the Quran is to establish a viable social order on earth that will be just and ethically based. The Quran is the guidance for mankind from God, Allah swt. This is the basis of the Prophetic teachings. The emphasis is monotheism (*tawhid*), i.e., belief in one God and to obey His commandment only. And Prophet Muhammad (*pbuh*) is the final Messenger of God.

The Prophet (*pbuh*) had succeeded in bringing some influential people into the folds of Islam, such as Abu Bakar, Umar al-Khattab, Hamzah, and Osman. But the Meccans were too strong. The campaign to physically eliminate the believers in Mecca increased with intensity. To remain in Mecca would prove suicidal for the Muslims. Many more will be killed. The future of Islam in Mecca is bleak. The Muslims must leave Mecca or face more tortures and deaths.

But leaving Mecca will mean leaving their properties and lands behind. They never know when they can return home again. The Arabs have great and intimate attachment to their lands. Leaving them behind is like losing their soul, their life and self-respect. But they were ordered by Prophet Muhammad (*pbuh*) to leave Mecca. So, they left the city in secret with virtually nothing except their faith in God and the Prophet.

The Hijrah also highlighted the spirit of love, compassion, and brotherhood shown by Muslims of Medina (*ansars*), who were willing to share their belongings with the Muslims from Mecca (*muhajirin*). The Hijrah, therefore, symbolizes the epitome of sacrifice and commitment of the early Muslims to Islam.

But equally important is to see the *Hijrah* as a strategy for setting up a power center in Medina, in the form of an Islamic government. It is in Medinah that many Quranic rules and regulations on civil life were revealed. Two examples are the categorical prohibition of *riba* and *zakat* obligations. The Quranic teaching, therefore, become the basis of the Muslims' life in Medina, leading them to harness considerable social, economic, and military power to defeat the Meccans, and eventually capturing the holy city of Mecca.

With the spirit of *Hijrah* in mind, Islamic banking should have moved forward with more substance and meaningful presence. With an Islamic worldview, man would no longer focus solely on the mundane, but pursue material gain with a view that his worldly existence will not last. It is the *akhirah* that matters more, but it does not mean one should become complacent and take it easy.

To hold an Islamic worldview will impress one's thinking that he or she is given by God the trust (*amanah*) to manage resources in the most efficient manner, and this includes capital as well. As such, making decisions and managing deposits and financing in the banking business constitute an act of worship (*ibadah*). In this manner, one can see the Islamic worldview puts the *al-dunya* and *al-akhirah* as two inseparable existences.

Three
Islamic Financial System

The Islamic financial system (IFS) in Malaysia runs parallel with its mainstream counterpart and claims *Shariah* legitimacy by virtue of contracts (*'aqd*) employed in financial transactions. To some extent, the system is well received. With untapped markets and potential product niche, Islamic financial markets in Malaysia can do better under strong government support.

But have current performances matched conventional operations? Are Islamic deposits attractive? Are people getting a fair deal from Islamic home purchase schemes and trade finance? Are the services excellent? Can Islamic funds outperform conventional funds? Answering these questions can be intimidating. Before doing so, an understanding about the meaning and objective of an Islamic financial system is necessary.

A financial system is usually defined as a set of rules and regulations governing and controlling the flow of funds from the surplus spending units (SSU) to the deficit spending unit (DSU). The household, business, and government sectors make up both the surplus spending and deficit spending unit. For example, households with excess income lend their money to households with negative savings.

In banking, the surplus spending unit deposits their funds with the banks, which in turn lend these funds to the deficit spending unit. Since any financial system deals with the nature or character of principles guiding the flow of funds from the surplus spending unit to the deficit spending unit, it is relatively simple now to explain the nature of the Islamic financial system (IFS).

In an Islamic financial system, guiding rules are derived from the Quran and Sunnah (i.e., sayings and actions of Prophet Muhammad swt). The *Shariah* spells out the Quranic teachings in three dimensions, namely *Aqidah* (faith and belief), *Akhlak* (ethics and morality), and *Muamalat* (transactions).

The role of reason (*'aql*) and sense experience too have been given higher order by the Quran, in that they help convey the truth that God desires mankind to acknowledge and obey. There are two types of guidelines one must observe in Islam, namely: 1) the legal guidelines, and 2) ethical guidelines. On the former, the Quran prohibits the taking and receipt of interest (*riba*) in financial dealings. (2:275). It also does condone wealth creation by means of investment in *al-bathil* transactions such as gambling (*maisir*)(2:219).

On the ethical side, the Quran enjoins trustworthiness (*amanah*) (2:282) and prohibits deceit (*khud'a*) and greed (*hirs*) in profit-taking. These commands and prohibitions by God are meant to generate harmony in economic activities such that justice prevails and, thus, man is able to obtain peace of mind.

Both legal and ethical dimensions of the *Shariah* are embodied into the rules and regulations governing the Islamic financial markets. These rules are:

1. Prohibition of *riba* (usury or interest).
2. Application of *al-bay'* (trade and commerce).
3. Avoidance of *gharar* (ambiguities).
4. Prohibition of *maysir* (gambling)
5. Prohibition in engaging production of prohibited commodities such as liquor, pork, and pornography.

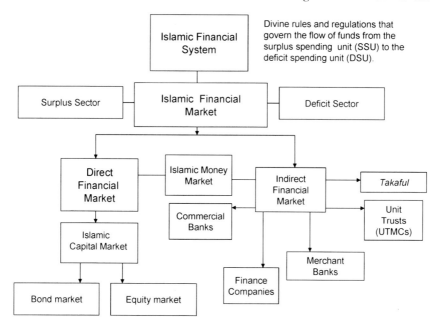

Figure 1.4 Islamic Financial System

When the divine rules and regulations are clearly spelled out, the flow of funds from the surplus spending to the deficit spending unit can be pursued in two ways: directly and indirectly. If the surplus spending unit wishes to purchase financial assets on its own, the direct financial market is the place to do so. In the direct financial market, investors purchase stocks, bonds, and short-term securities without intermediation. Investments in higher-risk securities such as stocks, and fixed income instruments such as bonds are made in the capital market. Securities with more liquidity such as treasury bills, negotiable certificates of deposit, and overnight funds are traded in the money market.

On the other hand, people who do not have time and skills to purchase financial assets on their own can do so using financial intermediaries such as banks, finance, unit trusts, and insurance companies.

Likewise, an Islamic financial market runs in similar fashion with conventional market. But it operates on the basis of rules derived from the Quran and Sunnah. For example, in the stock market, the Securities Commission has prepared guidelines on *Shariah* stock screening. About 80 percent of the stocks traded in the Kuala Lumpur Stock Exchange (KLSE) are *Shariah* compliant. And although not accepted globally, Malaysian Islamic bonds have a sizable 50 percent market share.

THE ECONOMY

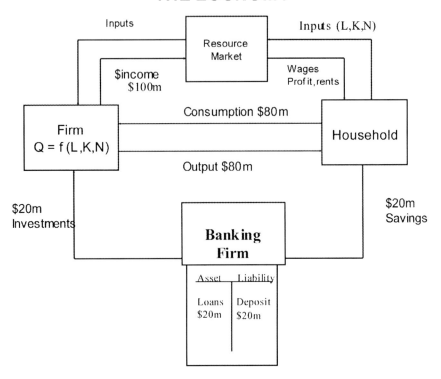

Figure 1.5 The Economy

Bay'al-'inah and *bay'al-dayn* contracts are widely used in the Islamic money market. These include the Khazanah bonds, Islamic accepted bills, and inter-bank money Islamic negotiable instruments (INI).

Takaful business is relatively new and commands about 5 percent market share. There is no window-based *takaful*. *Takaful* operations are run by four full-fledge *takaful* companies. They are Syarikat Takaful Malaysia, Takaful Nasional Malaysia, Mayban Takaful, and Takaful Ikhlas.

Undoubtedly, unit trust management companies (UTMC) are making inroads into Islamic financial markets. Issuance of units is made by the UTMC via the contract of *Wakalah*. As a *wakil* to unit holders, UTMCs charge nominal fees for the services rendered. There are more than thirteen Islamic funds in the market with about 5 percent market share. These funds are invested in *halal* financial assets as approved by regulatory bodies such as the Securities Commission and Bank Negara Malaysia. Some examples are *Shariah* Index, equity, and Islamic bond funds.

Islamic banking in Malaysia began operations in 1983 and is set to command a 20 percent market share by the year 2010. Currently, Islamic banking consists of two full-fledged Islamic banks and the Islamic banking system (IBS) banks. The IBS banks are previously known as the Islamic windows. They are governed by the Banking and Financial Institution Act (BAFIA) 1992, while the two full Islamic banks run under the Islamic Banking Act 1983.

As the Islamic financial system is based on the *Shariah*, it also means that the services rendered by the system, namely risk-sharing, liquidity and information must also be *Shariah*-driven. Investors and fund users should have a greater choice of products so that risks can be minimized. It is worthy to note that Islam enjoins risk-aversion and prohibits risk-avoiding behavior. In the latter, people demand fixed return as well as capital protection. This is *riba*. Risk-aversion is the willingness to take more risks with an expectation of earning higher returns. It runs along the principle of *al-ghorm bil ghonm*.

The Islamic financial system should also provide investors the opportunity to dispose of their financial assets at the lowest cost. Using the contract of *bay'al-dayn* with a discounting mechanism for this purpose is allowed (*halal*) in Malaysia, but not acceptable in the Middle Eastern countries.

Since the Islamic financial system runs on the principle of risk-taking, disclosure of information is critical. For example, when an Islamic bank draws *mudarabah* deposits, it must disclose all possible information about how these deposits are used. *Mudarabah* deposits are risky deposits. They are negotiable and banks cannot force depositors to comply with their (i.e., banks') policies, as the system is exposed to adverse selection and moral hazards if not properly monitored. In fact, Bank Negara Malaysia should put these *mudarabah* deposits under a trustee system similar to one found in the unit trusts business.

Four
Islamic Financial Markets:
Shari' and Tabi' Principles

In the early 1960s, Muslim economists were diligently writing about the Quranic prohibitions of *riba* and the need to establish Islamic banks as an alternative to the interest-bearing banking business. Today, the focus has moved into *takaful*, fund management and the capital market. With more than US$200 billion of Islamic funds available in global finance, attention on Islamic banking is no longer restricted to banking products, but how it is now connected to the economy-wide financial markets.

When one listens to discussions and lectures on Islamic banks, *takaful*, Islamic funds, and investment, it seems to gravitate to one issue, namely the *Shariah* guidelines. It deals with the permissible (*halal*) and prohibited (*haram*) as ordained by Allah swt. Islamic law of contracts (*fiqh muamalat*) has become indispensable, and *Shariah* scholars are sought after by many Islamic banks and fund managers.

However, Islamic financial markets do not deal with Divine rules alone, as business cannot run without making decent profits. The operational aspects of the Islamic markets should also be considered. But how? In what way are the *Shariah* aspects related to the mundane, namely the day-to-day running of the business? Is the mundane to be considered a secular and worldly affair, something *Shariah* advisors cannot intrude? If Islamic financial markets are propelled by *Shariah* values, what then is the role of reason and sense experience in financial transactions?

To make things simple, the study of Islamic financial markets can be divided into two aspects, namely the *Shari'* and *Tabi'*. In doing so, one can see the Islamic worldview in play where the *dunya* aspect is related in a profound and inseparable way to the *akhirah* aspect, and in which the *akhirah* aspect has the ultimate and final significance. This is the concept of Islamic worldview as expounded by Syed Naquib Al-Attas. The *dunya* aspect relates to the mundane, where man applies reason and experience to run their daily business, while the *akhirah* conveys the Divine rules that man must observe doing the same.

Since the *Shari'* principles are derived from the Quran and Sunnah, they are common in all aspects of financial transactions taking place, whether one deals with Islamic banks, mutual funds, investments, *takaful* and financial planning. This is where *Shariah* scholars are needed to help market players know and understand what is *halal* and *haram*. These *Shariah* principles are given by God and remain permanent. These are given below:

1. Prohibition of *riba.*
2. Application of *al-bay'* (trade and commerce).
3. Avoidance of *gharar* (ambiguities) in contractual agreements.
4. Prohibition of *maisir* (gambling).
5. Prohibition from conducting business involving prohibited commodities such as pork, liquor, illicit sex, and pornography.

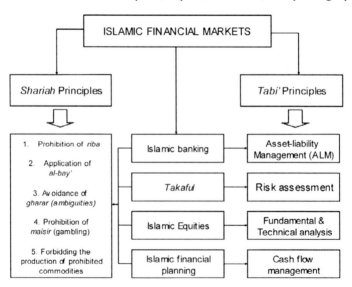

Figure 1.6 Islamic Financial Markets

But each of the above *Shariah* principles is unique in its own way when one looks at each particular market at a time. For example, the prohibition of *riba* is the cornerstone in the markets of deposits and funds in Islamic banking. However, when one deals with Islamic investments and derivatives, the gambling *(maisir)* and *gharar* issues seemed more urgent than *riba*. In *takaful, riba, gharar* and *maisir* factors are equally given importance, although the gambling factor is given more weight. In *Shariah* stock screening, more attention is given to the activities of issuing companies as relatively less given to the *gharar* factor. That is, first and foremost, the business must not be involved in the production of prohibited commodities.

But irrespective of the different emphasis and weights given to each of the *Shariah* principles, say on banking or takaful, one thing remains clear. That is, these principles are meant to uphold and promote justice (*'adalah*) and equity in business transactions. God has guaranteed that justice will prevail when man obeys His Commandments (*Shariah*). This is the *akhirah* aspects of the Islamic worldview. By adhering strongly to the *Shariah* principles, the *akhirah* aspect is well-guarded and truly observed by the contracting parties.

While the *Shariah* principles expounded the equitable nature of Islamic financial markets, other dimensions of market activities need not depend on explicit divine guidance. This is the *tabi'* aspect of financial market activities. It defines efficiency. *Tabi'* means natural. It is nature's way. *Tabi'* values are universal values. Once found, these values can be used by all people, irrespective of faiths and beliefs. Market players applied knowledge accumulated from reason and experience to understand how the market works and operates, which is a natural thing to do.

Thus, knowledge derived from non-divine sources cannot be downgraded as ungodly. In Islam, *'ainul yaqin* refers to the knowledge derived from sense perception, namely material (*jismani*) and facts (*haqiqi*) whereas *'ilm-ul-yakin* is based on reasoning (*'aql*) and human judgment (*khayali*). For example, to reduce cost per unit, the company should increase output. This is economies of scale. To increase sales, it should first conduct marketing research. To look for a credible partner, it should conduct due diligence and so on. The *tabi'* aspect of business cannot be ignored, even when it runs under an Islamic label. Muslims and non-Muslims alike are expected to obey the *tabi'* law. It has less to do with the faith (*aqidah*). Working against this law is only inviting disaster and chaos. Business is doomed to fail when the *tabi'* law is ignored.

As an example, to conduct an Islamic venture capital business, the *Shariah* principles are well known and readily given by the Quran. But the *tabi'* principles are different from that in banking. In Islamic venture capital, the *tabi'* aspects deal with 1) deal-making, 2) due diligence, and 3) market analysis. In banking, the *tabi'* aspects deal with 1) asset-liability management, 2) risk-management, and 3) marketing research. Likewise, in *takaful*, the *tabi'* aspects looks at 1) risk assessment, 2) promotion, and 3) fatality investigation. In equities, the fund managers conducted both fundamental and technical analysis to study what *halal* stocks to buy. They must know how to calculate the yield and when to exit the market. Defining what is *halal* and *haram* constitutes the *Shariah* aspects, but how and when to buy and sell is solely based on reason and facts. Man does not have to resort to the Quran or Sunnah to make economic forecast or execute stock purchases. The role of the intellect (*'aql*) is paramount here. This is what *tabi'* law stands for.

The concept of *tawakul* can be used to highlight the interlinking of *Shariah* and *tabi'* law. Investing in *Shariah*-approved stocks implies that firstly, one must know what constitutes the *halal* stocks. This is the *Shari'* aspect. Once the screening is done, the *tabi'* aspect is in play. To select a stock, one should consider its price-earning ratio, the return on investment, the earning per share. This is the company analysis. But company performance can be affected by macroeconomic variables such as inflation, unemployment, the gross domestic product, and exchange rates. This is where knowledge of the market and economy is crucial. This is *tabi'* law. The *Shariah* scholars know less about these things, as they have no expertise on modern economics and finance. Their main role is to define and execute the *Shariah* screening process and ensure that the *Shariah* stocks are always free from the prohibited elements. But sometimes the *tabi'* operations may implicate *riba* or gambling. For example, to avoid currency risk, a *Shariah*-approved company may indulge in currency trading as it tries to hedge against market volatilities. Promotion and marketing of mutual funds may be associated with unethical practices. Thus, some *tabi'* operations are purely free from *Shariah* rules, but some may not be. This is because the *Shariah* does not only deal with the legal aspects (*hukm*) of financial transactions but also the moral and ethical aspects (*akhlak*).

Five
'Iwad and lawful profits in Islam

There are more than US$200 billion Islamic funds in the global financial market today. For that reason, interest in Islamic finance has been overwhelming. In 1996, the New York Stock Exchange set up the Dow Jones *Shariah* Index. The Kuala Lumpur *Shariah* Index was introduced in 1998, while London and Jakarta have theirs too.

Islamic funds have also found their way to the banking sector. In fact, this is where it all began. Many Islamic banks were established to provide new avenues for mobilizing deposits and expanding finance. Malaysia is well known for its dual or parallel banking system, with Islamic banks running their business along with their conventional counterparts, while banks in Pakistan, Iran, and Sudan operate solely on a single Islamic banking system.

To some extent, companies engaging in the business of Islamic finance operate on the basis of profit maximization. This is to be pursued by observing the *Shariah* principles, one of which is the prohibition of interest or usury as *riba*. By doing so, profit maximization will be devoid of unethical practices, and puts Islamic banking business in the forefront of moral excellence.

Although the main trust of Islamic banking and finance has been the prohibition of interest, the application of trade and commerce (*al-bay'*) in financing activities has not received similar attention as had the interest (*riba*) factor. This has led many people to think that an Islamic bank is a banking firm that operates without interest, full stop.

Although this is true, it does not accurately depict what really an Islamic bank stands for. Instead, it would be more correct to say that Islamic banking business runs on the basis of commercial and trading principles (*al-bay'*) where profits made implicate value-addition (*kasb*) and risk-taking (*ghorm*) activities.

I need to make this point clear to prevent undue confusion. For example, when the polytheists in the city of Mecca say, "Trade is like *riba*..." and the Quran detested it by saying, "Allah allows trade (*al-bay'*) but prohibits *riba*," the former, i.e., *al-bay'* implies the existence of *'iwad*, or equal countervalue in the transaction. When the requirement of *'iwad* is fulfilled in trading (*al-bay'*), it brings along the sense of equity and justice into a business transaction, that rendered it superior to an interest-bearing system.

Interest is prohibited in Islam because it is seen as an unjustified means of profit and wealth creation, since the exchange of an equivalent for a higher non-equivalent does not require the creditor to hold market and systematic risks, as the loans are collateralized and secured by a third-party guarantee. The creditor provides practically no value-added services to the debtor. This is a common feature in most fixed-income instruments. In doing so, economic justice is at risk and the ensuing concentration of wealth in the hands of a few people can threaten social welfare and stability.

For this reason, the *Shariah* requires all legitimate exchange to contain *'iwad*-an equivalent countervalue. According to Ibn al-'Arabi (d. 543/1148), "Every increase, which is without *'iwad* or an equal quantervalue is *riba*." *'Iwad* is therefore the basic trait or *condition sine qua non* of a lawful (*halal*) sale. This is because a sale is necessarily an exchange of a value against an equivalent value.

What this means is that the price a consumer pays must be compensated with an equitable return that he enjoys from the purchase. When a trader sells at a price higher than the cost of inputs, the profit margin must be that which contains *'iwad*. As such, a theory of profit in Islam is therefore built on the principle of *'iwad*, and this is explained by the amount of effort and risk imputed in the sale.

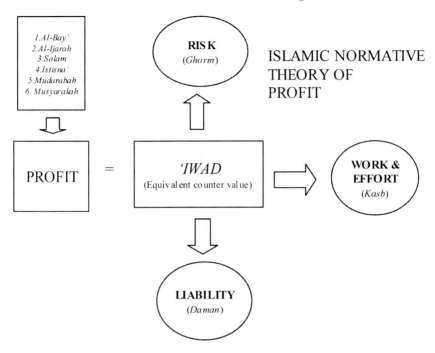

Figure 1.7 Islamic Theory of Profit

For example, Mr. Muhammad pays $1,000 for a Seiko watch. In other words, exchange of goods for money has taken place. The profit margin is created from the effort (*kasb*) rendered and risk taken (*ghorm*) by the trader. Thus, if cost of inputs is equal to $800, while the residual, i.e., $200 constitutes the profit margin, the exchange is said to contain *'iwad*. The surplus $200 constitutes the risk and effort components, while the $800 represents the cost of inputs. When the trader purchases the watch wholesale, he is risking his capital. He is also risking his effort, in case the sale is not made in the retail market.

In other words, in trading (*al-bay'*) an equivalent countervalue or *'iwad* shall consist of two main components, namely: 1) market risk (*ghorm*), and 2) work and effort, i.e., value addition (*kasb*). A third component, liability (*daman*) is also worth considering. In trading, the supplier provides guarantees on the goods sold. That is, the purchaser can return the goods if found defective. In this way, the trader deserves the profit, as the sale contains a warranty.

In the case of an interest-bearing loan, say $10,000 at 10 percent interest rate per annum, we are looking at an exchange of money worth $10,000 in year 1 for $11,000 in year 2.

The principal component, namely $10,000 constitutes the cost of inputs, while the extra $1,000 represents the profit or interest from the loan. The contractual surplus is free from risk-taking and value-added services discharged by the creditor. As the surplus does not contain *'iwad,* it is tantamount to *riba,* since by definition, *"Every increase, which is without 'iwad or an equal counter value is riba."*

It is therefore crucial to highlight the meaning of *al-bay'* and subsequently the concept of *'iwad,* when one wishes to understand issues concerning *Shariah* legitimacy in Islamic banking and finance. It would not be a good idea to jump into the *riba* issues without putting the *al-bay* and *'iwad* factor in their proper places, as it can cause great confusion if the one-sided approach, i.e., focusing on *riba* alone, is used to introduce the concept of Islamic banking and finance to the general public.

Six
Riba and Interest

The general position that interest is *riba* seems unchallenged today in view of the rapidly expanding Islamic banking services in Malaysia. Islamic facilities are available in most commercial merchant banks and finance companies. The inter-bank money market runs on *mudarabah* and *bay' al-'inah,* while Islamic private debt securities (IPDS) seemed to work fine under the *bay' al-dayn* (sale of debts) and *'inah* framework. Such potential development indicates that effort to integrate religion and business has seen some success.

Despite the good news, critical observers are still wondering on what basis interest (*riba*) is prohibited. Critical views come naturally when people's expectation turns sour. People are made to assume that interest is equal to *riba,* but they are not well informed what is behind the sanction— why interest is equivalent to *riba.*

So far, I am only referring to the Muslim community, some of whom are raising doubts about the labeling of interest as *riba.* Non-Muslims too will be curious why interest is prohibited, what the justification is for the prohibition of *riba,* and how rulings equating interest to *riba* were made.

The ethical factor is important because it (i.e., ethics) is the essence of Quranic teaching. Ethics is a study about morality and conduct. The Quranic ban on *riba* is made on the basis of justice and equity, both of which are important ethical precepts. Hence, it follows that any alternative to *riba* is expected to embrace these two elements of ethical principles. Islamic law must be based on solid ethical foundation. Otherwise, it is open to abuse and misrepresentation, one of which is the practice of legal device (*hilah*).

Riba in the pre-Islamic days was, in fact, an extremely oppressive business activity. A man is given a loan that is allowed to double and redouble if he fails to pay up. For example, if he obtained a $1,000 loan and fully paid the following month, he only pays the capital; he does not have to pay interest if he pays up on time.

But if he fails to pay up and asks for postponement to the next month, his new debt is $2,000. If he again cannot pay on time and ask for further deferment, the debt will increase to $4,000, and so on. Because of this process of doubling and redoubling (*adaf amuda'afan*) of the principal, the Quran refused to admit that *riba* as a kind of fair business transaction. Instead, the Quran permits commercial profits and encourages the spirit of cooperation (*ta'awun*) as opposed to that of profiteering.

Allah swt. says in the Quran, "O ye who believe, do not consume *riba* with continued redoubling and protect yourselves from God, perchance you may be blissful" (Al-Baqarah: 130). I don't intend to discuss whether modern interest is *riba,* but the need to be completely certain about our view about interest and *riba* is undoubtedly critical.

To observe the ethical dimension of Islamic banking is now in order. We can no longer use the classical excuse that interest is prohibited because it constitutes a fixed and contractual profit arising from a loan. This is because the profit from *al-bai-bithaman ajil* financing (BBA) and *al-ijarah* leasing is also a fixed and contractual sum.

It is also inaccurate to say that *riba* is solely prohibited because the amount is exorbitant. A look at the profit margin of *al-bai-bithaman ajil* (BBA) facilities shows that it is no better off. BBA seemed to cost more than conventional loans for some reasons.

Riba in the Quran

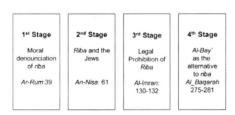

1st Stage	2nd Stage	3rd Stage	4th Stage
Moral denounciation of riba	Riba and the Jews	Legal Prohibition of Riba	Al-Bay' as the alternative to riba
Ar-Rum:39	An-Nisa: 61	Al-Imran: 130-132	Al_Baqarah 275-281

Figure 1.8 *Riba* in The Quran

It is a disappointment to see people beginning to have doubts about the legality of BBA and Islamic banks as the Islamic banking industry grew rapidly over time. In the worst scenario, people may find it unconvincing to say that interest is *riba*. This is because Islamic banking seems unable to free itself from the credit culture deeply rooted in conventional practices. And people can see easily see the resemblance, that the profit rate in BBA and the interest rate in loans are more or less equivalent. For this reason, it is critical to see that a theory of profit determination in BBA is clearly spelt out by the Shariah Supervisory Board of Bank Negara Malaysia.

When an Islamic bank earns profit equivalent to interest, people may start wondering that interest isn't bad after all. Although the contract (*'aqad*) of BBA is different from interest-bearing loans, its apparent resemblance to loan is a letdown. When this is true, the ethical dimension of Islamic banking was downplayed in favor of legalistic dictum.

It looks like the legal factor has overridden ethical considerations. Although the BBA contract is valid, its impact on justice and equity is questionable, given that it purely resembles conventional bank loans in almost all aspects. For example, the *al-bai-bithaman ajil* is a good case of relatively-risk free business with credit assessment and debt collections making up most of job routine. The risks on loans and *al-bai-bithaman ajil,* therefore, have no significant variance. Both deal with credit risk and demand collateral support, and legal actions on defaulters have been effective in recovering bad debts. When the contract favors only one party (i.e., the financiers), justice (*'adl*) is gone. Zealous Muslims who pay lip service attacking traditional banks on this ground should not embrace Islamic banks by sheer blind confirmation to faith (*taqlid*). Finally, BBA enhances Muslims to go into debts. It teaches them that to be debtor is good. It enhances the culture of borrowing and leverage that constitute the backbone of capitalism.

Seven
Riba, AI-Bay' and Risks (Ghorm)

Many may wonder why the application of *bai-bithaman-ajil* (BBA) is popular in Islamic banking today, especially in home financing. These deferred sale products have now embraced share financing, consumer financing, purchase of plant and equipment, etc.

The BBA model is doing well because Islamic banks can sell the *bai-bithaman-ajil* products to a third party for liquidity purposes, especially when the *Shariah* experts in this country see nothing seriously wrong with the *bay' al-dayn* (sale of debt) contract that emerges from the *bai-bithaman-ajil* sale. *Dayn al-bai-bithaman ajil* (i.e., debt arising from the BBA sale) is considered a tradable item, as it constitutes an object of trade (*mahallul 'aqdi*).

The main question is the impact of *murabahah* and *al-bai-bithaman ajil* transactions on the economy. Will BBA Intensive Islamic banks able to create new jobs, help set start-ups, increase productivity, sustain economic growth, maintain price level, and help reduce income disparities?

More people are asking whether present interest-free products deserve an Islamic label, since the only apparent attraction is the *halal* status. Otherwise, people using BBA purchase the same house and pay as much.

So, it is only rational to ask, "What is so bad about interest-bearing loans when the BBA schemes have no significant deviation from loans?" What is the underlying reason for the prohibition of interest, if the alternative (i.e., BBA) leaves more to be desired?

In the Quran, pre-Islamic Meccan commercial society says that "Trade (*al-bay'*) is like usury (*riba*)" and the Quran responded by saying that "... Allah hath permitted trade and forbidden *riba*..." (Al-Baqarah: 275).

But why is *riba* made unlawful while trade (*al-bay'*) is lawful? What is truly special about *al-bay'* that God has made it the alternative to *riba*? Does *al- bay'* in the Quran mean credit sale (i.e., BBA)? I will attempt to answer the above question by taking a closer look at the concept of *al-bay'* and see why it has become the Quranic alternative to *riba*.

In the Quran, *riba* is mentioned as the redoubling of the loan over time, *"O ye who believe, devour not in usury doubled and multiplied..."* (Al-Imran: 130). Such profit-making techniques are considered an unfair business practice because profits are created without mutual risk-taking.

In other words, there is an absence of risk-sharing between creditors and debtors. Of course, banks are exposed to default and interest rate risks but these too are borne by the debtors. That is, debtors are made to pay higher spread on loans.

In the interest-based debt financing system, the lender is guaranteed both the principal and interest returns. In government and corporate debt securities, lenders are promised a fixed return in coupons or a discount by the issuer.

Similarly, in the banking system, depositors are promised a guaranteed sum of principal and interest payments. Likewise, a bank charges interest with serious legal implications when the loan is defaulted.

Due to the absence of risk-taking, some say that the above approach is unfair as it disrupts the spirit of cooperation. Many bankers may laugh at this statement because there are always smiles and handshakes during loan contract signing ceremonies between them and the big corporations.

However, what about small businessman and those who aspire to expand operations but lack the credentials of giant corporations? Banks usually close their doors to these groups of businessmen. Taking them as business partners is taboo in banking. Equity financing must be avoided at all times. What we will see is more income disparity. That is why the Quran has warned, *"wealth must not circulate only among the rich ones among you"* (Sura 59: 7). To do so, Islam among others prohibits the taking and receipt of *riba*.

But what has that to do with trade and commerce (*al-bay*)? Certainly when the Quran puts *al-bay'* as the alternative to *riba*, it must be for a good reason. But what is the rationale for legitimizing *al-bay*? To appreciate the meaning of *al-bay'* one must understand the teachings of the Quran carefully. The main aim of the Quran is to establish a moral social order on earth. It requires mankind to work on the basis of cooperation (*ta'awun*) and brotherhood (*ukuwah*) with a sense of *taqwa* (God consciousness).

Economic activities should therefore be driven by these Quranic realities. *Al-bay'*, as opposed to *riba*, exemplifies these Quranic realities as profits generated from *al-bay'* are not risk-fee. Risk-taking and risk sharing are a manifestation of Islamic ethical principles, such as *'adl, taqwa, ta'wun,* and *ukuwah*. *Al-bay'* is therefore legitimate because it assumes risk-taking while profit from loans (i.e., *riba)* rejected the idea of risk sharing and risk-taking.

In the *Qawaid Fiqiah* (Islamic legal maxims), it is said that, *"Loss is burdened on those who have acquired profit" (al-ghurmu bil ghunmi)*. This means that man cannot expect to make profit without assuming loss or risk in his undertakings.

Al-bay' is a contract of sale, and no sale in Islam is free from risks. Profit from sale is an outcome of risk-taking, as the seller takes the risk to make sure that the market for the goods exists, that the price is right, and goods are in good condition. He will lose money if the goods are destroyed by natural calamities or if the market price dropped below cost. This is a legitimate way to make money. This type of risk is called *ghorm*. In economics, *ghorm* means price and market risks. In finance, it means systematic risks.

Profit from loans (i.e., *riba*) is created without risk-taking. Loans are collateralized. If the debtor fails to pay up, the bank holds the right to sell the collateral to recover the loan. In a sale contract, however, the seller will use his savings to purchase goods wholesale and sell them at retail price. But there is no guarantee that he can make money from the sale. There is nothing to back up this capital in case the business goes bust.

On the contrary, by putting money in interest-bearing deposits, people receive a predetermined profit plus a guaranteed principal amount, but minus the risk. Banks will, in turn, use these deposits to make loans and earn profit by charging interest.

The Quran uses *al-bay'* because the profit generated from it incorporates risk-taking, while the contractual profit from a loan (i.e., *riba*) is risk-free. *Al-bay'* and *riba* loans were two major forms of transactions widely used in pre-Islamic Mecca, but only *riba* was responsible for the economic unrest and perpetuation of the rich at the expense of the poor. As a remedy, the Quran enjoins man to invest his capital in *al-bay* related activities and not by way of *riba* loans.

One must not confuse what constitutes risk-free profit and predetermined profit. As an example, rental from *al-ijarah* (true leasing) is a predetermined amount but not free from risk (*ghorm*), hence it is allowed in Islam. Profit from *riba* is also a predetermined amount, but free from risk-taking. For these reason, *riba* is prohibited.

What one can see in the above is the ethical theory of *riba* in play. *Riba* is prohibited because it violates the principles of justice and equity. Justice will cease to exist when the contractual agreement puts the burden of risk only on one party. The contract of an interest-bearing loan is a good example.

But what about *al-bai-bithaman ajil* (BBA) and *murabahah*? Both products deal with sale of goods at a predetermined profit with no apparent risk-taking. Although both are *halal* by legal definitions, they are not worthy to imply the Quranic *al-bay*.

This is true because the *Shariah* advisors have yet to explain why profit derived from loans is prohibited, while profit from Islamic credit finance (BBA) is not. We knew well that credit price arising from BBA sale is higher than cash price. But very few are aware that the increment implicates time preference too. That is the margin is derived from waiting.

In *riba* economics, fixed interest is paid to a debtor to compensate him for postponing current spending. Does it mean that by using a contract that uses the term *"al-bay"* such as *al-bay' murabahah* or *al-bay'-bithaman ajil*, the fixed profit derived from positive time preference is now lawful?

No wonder the West today hails the current Islamic banking model as one model worthy to be exported worldwide, because unlike *mudarabah* and *musyarakah*, the credit sale model is not a threat to capitalism.

Eight
Islam and Time Value of Money

Despite the wide use of *bay' bithaman ajil* (BBA) financing in Islamic banking today, many may wonder why the credit price is always higher than the cash price, and, most important, how can one explain the Islamicity of profit earned from the BBA sale?

BBA contract is basically a sale (*bay'*) contract, while a bank loan is not. Any increase (i.e., profit) made from a sale is permissible (*halal*). For example, Mr. Ali purchases goods X at $500 wholesale, and sells them to Mr. Bruce at $550 retail. The $50 profit margin from the sale is *halal*.

Profit made from a loan (*qard*) in Islam is unlawful (*haram*) because it constitutes *riba*. *Riba* predominately originates from debt instruments like bank loans, as well as private and public interest-bearing bonds. The Islamic jurists (*fuqahas*) at the *Shariah* Supervisory Boards said that the Islamic alternatives to interest-bearing loans, namely *bay' bithaman ajil* (BBA) and *murabahah* are not based on debt contract, but rather on the contract of sale. It is therefore inaccurate to suspect the Islamicity of BBA from the amount of profit generated by BBA comparable to loans.

The *ulama'*, however, are rather silent about why BBA credit price is always higher than cash. They say that as long as the buyer is willing to pay the agreed price via bargaining and haggling (*musawammah*), *and* the sale is concluded with the offer and acceptance (*ijab* and *qabul*), then the contract is considered valid.

However, this explanation may have avoided important issues in modern economics and finance, namely time value of money and other related issues like opportunity cost, inflation, and credit risk. We now examine Islam's view on the concept of time preference.

Most people may say that time has an economic value. This is because all consumption and production activities take time. Time is a valuable economic resource.

By working one hour, a speaker today may earn a minimum of $100, while some may get as much as $5,000. By doing so, he has increased his self-worth and wealth, and if he chooses not to lecture and prefers leisure, he has lost the opportunity to increase his earning.

The same argument is applied in debt investments. When money is put to work over time, it increases in value. Place $10,000 in a fixed deposit today, and a year later it will increase to $11,000, given a 10 percent interest rate.

Time preference indicates the extent of a family's preference for current consumption over future consumption. The rationalization of interest as a price of credit began when people believed that present consumption was superior to future consumption. According to Bohm Bowerk, people prefer the present because the future is uncertain. They also think that present wants are more keenly felt than future wants.

Also, people think that the present goods possess a technical superiority over future goods. That is, the passage of time allows the use of more roundabout methods of production that are more productive.

Since current consumption brings more satisfaction than future ones, people who are asked to postpone current consumption (i.e., creditors) must be compensated for the benefits the pleasure foregone today.

Islam and Time Value of Money

Mujahid reported that 'Abd Allah b. 'Umar took some dirhams as a loan and paid back better dirhams. He said: O Abu 'Abd al-Rahman, these are better than the dirhams I loaned out to you. 'Abd Allah b. 'Umar replied: Yes I know, but I paid out of my own good will and pleasure".

On another occasion 'Ata b. Yasir reported Rafi' said:

"The Apostle of Allah (pbuh) took on credit a small camel. When camels of sadeqah arrived, and he asked me to pay back a like camel, I said: Apostle of Allah, the camels are all big and four years old. The Apostle of Allah (pbuh) said: Give from them. Virtuous are they who pay back their debts well".

(Muwatta Imam Malik)

Figure 1.9 Hadith on Time Value of Money

When people think that one dollar today is worth more than one dollar tomorrow, they become a true believer of positive time preference. Capitalism is based on the belief that people generally embrace positive time preference. The implication of positive time preference is the contractual payment and receipts of interest. Laws in financial transactions require debtors to pay interest on loans. In this manner, creditors who have forgone the pleasure of current consumption are guaranteed a contractual surplus on the loan as a compensation for postponing current consumption.

The problem lies when compensations for waiting are contractual in nature, coming out of a sense of belief that the future is uncertain. A contractual payment must be made to compensate for the utility loss from delayed consumption. This does not make sense when he in the first place is not certain of getting it himself.

For example, Mr. Ali invests his money in bonds to earn 10 percent interest a year. Can he get the same yield if he uses this money to run his own business? Certainly, he may get more or less than 10 percent. There is no free lunch. Business risk does not guarantee anything. But why this is not true for interest-bearing debt?

The fact that Islam forbids *riba* it does not mean it is against the concept of positive-time preference (PTP). Indeed, Islam does recognize PTF as evident in the sayings of Prophet Muhammad (*pbuh*). The Prophet (*pbuh*) said, "Virtuous are they who pay back their debts well."

The question now is why Islam enjoins people to pay their debts well. One thing for sure is gratitude. The debtor is thankful for the loan he gets. He knew the creditor has forgone his current consumption for the sake of helping him with the money. He also recognizes that the creditor has relinquished the opportunity to earn returns from loan given away. These returns are unknown, as they are subject to business risk. In this manner, one dollar today is seen as more valuable than one in the future. As a token of appreciation, the debtor pays more. But the incremental amount is not stated up front.

Thus, in Islam, recognizing PTP does not imply awarding a contractual increase on the principal loan. Any increase from an Islamic loan (*qard*) can only be stated on maturity and not up front as normally practiced in interest-bearing loan contract. The increment, which is voluntary, is set by the debtor. In contrast, the increment from *riba* loans is contractual and set by the creditor.

Nine
Money and the Law of Depreciation

Money serves many functions. It is a medium of exchange, a store of value, and a means of deferred payments. And many may agree that money is also a commodity, since money can earn interest. As a commodity, money can be rented out with contractual rentals income earned, known as interests.

Interest, often defined as the price of credit, is given away as an incentive to attract savings. Often, people receive interest as a reward for postponing their current consumption. Since the future is uncertain, people always think that spending a dollar today will always brings more satisfaction than spending tomorrow.

Therefore, as a reward for abstinence, interest is paid. This has been the rationale for the payment and receipt of interest today. However, when money is in abundance or when people feel that future spending creates more satisfaction than current spending, interest rates turn negative. Instead of receiving rewards, it will now cost those who lend. The Japanese economy is one good example. High liquidity sees real interest rates in the negative as the rate of inflation exceeded the nominal rate.

But this is a rather extreme case and is bound to happen when similar conditions persist. In general, interest rate is always positive. It is here we see how rich people can sit on their money and become richer. They don't have to do anything but wait for their bonds and fixed deposits to mature. Sitting on their money in this instance simply means that they do not take part in or assume the risk of production out of which sales are made and profits realized.

What this means is a simple fact that when interest rate is positive, money is the only thing that defies the law of depreciation. Lending money with interest means that they will receive more money in the future, and this time with certainty as the law guarantees the right of debtors to both principal and interest payments.

But all things in this world will undergo wear and tear. They lose value over time. This is a law in nature. In Islam, God is the only Being that cannot depreciate, as He is the Creator, and therefore all creation of His must depreciate. And keeping money from the natural process of depreciation is akin to treating it like God.

The Quran says, "Everything thereon is vanishing, there remaining only the Face of Your Lord, the Possessor of Majesty and Generosity." (55:26-27)

Submitting money to the law of depreciation is one of the essences of the Quranic ban on *riba*. Money must be allowed to depreciate, and this means that it must be open to both possibilities of appreciation and depreciation. Both will take place when money is channeled into trade and commerce (*al-bay'*). The Quranic prescription of *al-bay'* as an antithesis of *riba* therefore confirms the need to put money back into its natural place as God's creation.

When money is invested in trading and commercial activities (*al-bay'*), it can either appreciate or depreciate in value. When the venture is profitable, the investor gets back the capital plus profit. The value of the investable capital has appreciated. Likewise, when business incurs losses, capital depreciation is evident. Now, money obeys the law of depreciation. It no longer assumes the attributes of God.

The law of depreciation also works well on idle money. It will depreciate when the price level increases and people who hold idle money will now hold lower purchasing power. It is some sort of penalty on those who hold money for too long. Apart from inflation, idle money in Islam will depreciate as a result of *zakat* obligation.

In fact, *zakat* payments on wealth, including idle money, confirm the rule that money must obey the law of depreciation. This explains why Islamic people must not hoard money, since doing so will mean loss in purchasing power. Again, the *zakat* imposition on cash balances is a penalty on money hoarders.

Now, the question is, what is money? In the context of our present discussion, money is the currency in circulation plus demand deposit. This is known as M1. In Islam, M1 is subjected to *zakat*. Whoever holds idle cash or checkable deposits exceeding the *nisab* over a year, must pay *zakat* of 2.5 percent. This is one way how Islam helps discourage people to hold idle cash for an indefinite time, as doing so disallows those who needs the currency for transaction purposes.

A broader measurement of money M2 is M1 plus interest-bearing savings and fixed deposits. It is here we can see how rich people can sit on their money and yet are able to secure interest as a guaranteed return.

Here, when money is put into circulation the form of debt (part of M2), it defies the law of depreciation. What this means is simply that money now becomes the object of worship as the interest-based financial system guarantees that money in interest-bearing bank accounts can only move in one direction, that is to increase and appreciate in value.

My main point is to highlight the notion that first, when people hold cash, they will see the purchasing value of their cash holding to depreciate over time. Secondly, when money is put in circulation, and this time injected into trading and commercial activities, money too is subject to the law of depreciation, since there is a possibility that business may fail and owners of capital will see their investments vanishing.

But when money is put into circulation in the form interest-bearing instruments such as bank deposits, loans, and bonds, money has defied the law of depreciation, since interest guarantees capital appreciation. In making the payments and receipts of interest arising from debts as a lawful and civilized act, man has made money equal to God. This is tantamount to *shirik* (idolatry).

The Quran says, *"He is the God, other than Whom, there is none; He is the knower of the unseen and the seen, the Merciful and the Compassionate. He is the God other than Whom there is none, the Sovereign, the Holy, the One with peace and integrity, the Keeper of Faith, the Protector, the Mighty, the one Whose Will is Power, the Most Supreme."* (59:22-23)

In summary, it is true to say that when money earns interest, appreciation of money is guaranteed. Everything else depreciates except Allah swt.

When appreciation of money is guaranteed by virtue of the payment and receipts of interest, people seemed to have treated money like God.

Ten
Why *riba* is condemned in Islam

The debate whether interest is equivalent to *riba* is considered settled. It's taboo to go around messing the issue. The Muslim jurists (*fuqaha*) have made it crystal clear that interest is *riba*.

There is no doubt in Islam that *riba* is prohibited (*haram*). The prohibitions are clearly stated in the Quran (*Ar-Rum:29; Al-Imran: 130, Al-Baqarah: 274-80*). In fact, to the Muslim people, it is an act of disbelief (*kufr*) to say the contrary. Still, many would want to know the reasons behind its prohibition or in what way *riba* is equated to interest.

Literally, *riba* means "to increase, to grow, to rise, to swell." In the earlier days of the Prophetic Era, there was no legal prohibition of *riba*. The initial encounter with *riba* was the Quran's moral denunciation of the unethical commercial practices of Meccan society (ar-Rum:29).

It is therefore not surprising to see the earlier verses of the Quran (i.e., the Meccan surahs) contain a high level of condemnation of the profiteering commercial class. Later in Medinah, when Islam assumed political power, *riba* was legally prohibited (*Al-Imran: 130; Al-Baqarah: 274-280*).

The payment and receipt of interest as *riba* is essentially a credit-driven phenomenon. It deals with loans that command a contract of repayment plus a predetermined or fixed increase. It also involves exchanges of identical commodities of no equivalence. The former is known as *riba al-quran* or *riba nasiah* and the latter *riba al-hadith* or *riba fadl*.

The question now is, why is *riba nasiah* prohibited? *Nasiah* means "to postpone." Thus, *riba nasiah* arises when a loan payment is postponed to a later date, but with a penalty in the form of an increase over the principal loan. *Riba nasiah* is described in the Quran as a "continued redoubling" over capital. In this sense, *riba* has an exponential growth over time. This exponential growth is described in the *Muwatta* of *Imam Malik* as follows: *"In the pre-Islamic days, if a man owed another a debt, at the time of its maturity the creditor would ask the debtor: 'Will you pay up or will you increase?' If the latter paid up, the creditor received back the sum; otherwise the principal was increased on the stipulation of a further term."*

As an example, when a debtor cannot pay up a $5,000 loan in time, he must pay double to get a credit extension. In doing so, he now owes the creditor $10,000. If he further fails to settle the debt on time, further request for delay requires him to pay $20,000. Hence, the loan has doubled and quadrupled over some period of time, until he is unable to pay up. Eventually he sells himself to the creditor and becomes his slave.

To some extent, the same applies in modern-day financing, where a debtor nation has been constantly under enslavement to the creditor nation. Look at how the IMF and the World Bank impose trade and monetary polices on debt-ridden but resource-abundant Latin American countries. The end products were runaway inflation, gross unemployment, and political unrest.

This is one major reason why *riba* is condemned in Islam. On the legal prohibition of *riba*, the Quran says, *"O you who believe, do not consume riba with redoubling and protect yourself from God, perchance you may be blissful."* (Al-Imran: 130)

Hence, in the words of Fazlur Rahman of the University of Chicago, "*Riba* in the pre-Islamic days was a system whereby the principal sum was doubled and redoubled through a usurious process. Because of this process of doubling and redoubling the principal, the Quran refused to admit that *riba* was a fair business transaction. While permitting commercial profit, the Quran encourages the spirit of cooperation as opposed to that of profiteering."

It makes sense that the injustices created from *riba* have violated the essence of brotherhood (*ukuwah*) and cooperation (*ta'awun*) that Islam enjoins, but what has that to do with the interest rate?

When someone takes a bank loan, he must also pay interest. In fact, a bank's profit is the difference between interest on loans and interest on deposits. The bulk of banks' profit today comes from interest income.

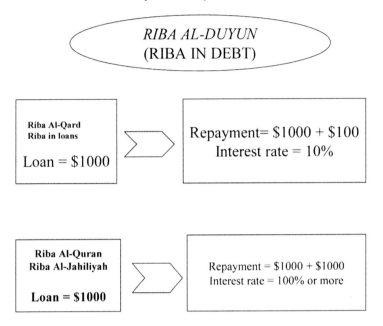

Figure 1.9 *Riba* in Loans

However, annual interest rates are lower than those depicted in the Quran—"redoubling," which is a 100 percent (doubled and redoubled) rate of interest and more. The base lending rate is about 7 percent and the ordinary borrower is normally pays 10 to 11 percent per annum.

So, if one obtains a three-year $10,000 loan at 10 percent flat per annum, the interest payment is only $3,000, i.e., a 30 percent increment over the principal loan; that is still less than a 100 percent increase.

Sometimes, though, the total cumulative payments (principal plus interest) can indeed be twice the original loan. For example, a person taking a 20-year $100,000 house loan and paying 10 percent annual flat per annum will end up paying more than $200,000 on maturity.

So now, the main issue is no longer the quantum of the increase. One should not look at the annual rate of interest alone, but what is most important is the cumulative increase over the total payment period. To that effect, the redoubling of the principal loan does take place in modern banking, although there are exceptions.

In fact, now the central issue is no longer the amount of increase, but the overall system of modern banking that cherishes the idea of contractual collateralized profit fixation in loans—which is no better than the *Jahiliyyah* practice. At least the latter imposes no collateral requirement on the principal loan. To that effect, *al-Bayhaqi* and *al-Sayuti* say, "Every loan from which a profit accrues is *riba*."

What, then, is the main reason behind the prohibition of *riba* or interest? Careful reflection of the following verse will help answer the question. God says, *"Allah has allowed trade and forbidden riba"* (al-Baqarah: 275). The Quran makes a clear distinction between *riba* and trade, which implies that fixed profit created from the loan (i.e., *riba*), is unlawful, while profit from trade is lawful. But what sets *riba* apart from trade? What are the religious principles that *riba* has violated but upheld by trade (*al-bay'*)?

Remember that Islam enjoins economic justice buttressed on the spirit of sharing. In business, it means a system of profit and loss sharing. *Riba* arising from loans does not deal with profit-loss sharing as it (i.e., loans) is based on the contract of debt. It defies the natural law of "no pain, no gain."

Relatively less consideration is given to the welfare of the borrower when he fails to maintain repayments. Since the loan is collateralized, it is not in the interest of banks to dwell into the factors responsible for the business failure. Through legal contracts, banks' profits are contractually fixed with no tendency of diminishing, as loans are well-screened from market risks.

Speaking of pre-fixed or predetermined profit, banking business is not about direct production, but seems to resemble leasing activities. A leasing business rents out assets with a pre-fixed rental, which represents a company's profit.

However, leasing also involves huge overhead expenditures (i.e., the rental assets), all of which are laden with market risks, which is not true in banking. An interest-based bank leases out or lends money for a predetermined profit rate, but does not encounter similar overhead expenditures met by a leasing company.

They are not confronted by market or business risks. Market risk is simply the uncertainty that an investment will earn its expected rate of return due to the nature of a firm's business. Interest income is therefore free from business risk as the bank knows with certainty about its future cash flow.

In this manner, banking business does not deal with real production. It is about making money when banks borrow (i.e., sells deposits) from the common man, and making loans to the able borrower (i.e., the rich).

Most borrowers are classified as rich, as they would easily fulfill the famous five Cs—credibility, character, capital, collateral, and capacity—required by banks for successful loan application.

Just imagine when the common man puts his money in the bank and is given about a 3-4 percent deposit rate, the money is then loaned out to the rich at 12 percent, from which they (i.e., the rich) make a hefty margin.

Likewise, banks approve 100 percent risk-free like real estate, but heavily scrutinize small businesses. Modern banking is nothing more than the art of making money with maximum safety at relatively zero market risk.

The total dismissal of market risks that enables banks to secure a contractual profit constitutes total negation of God's law that, "wealth must not circulate only among the rich ones among you" (Sura 59:7). Remember God's reminder to mankind, *"The wealth you invest in riba so that it should grow at the expense of other people's wealth, does not grow in the sight of God..."* (ar-Rum: 29).

People's wealth is taken away without any equivalent countervalue *('iwad)* given in return. That is, when a bank earns a 3 percent spread, one may ask in what way it deserves this 3 percent spread as profit. This is because, the bank does not take the risk of losing its capital as the loans are collateralized. It does not provide value to the borrowing party either.

That is, when a bank gives a business loan, it does not give financial advice on how to improve the bottom line. All it does is to see that borrower pays on time. It will send letters only to remind them about back payments. Threatening messages from lawyers will follow as borrowers struggle to pay up the outstanding arrears.

In view of the above, it is accurate to say that *riba* is prohibited because it constitutes wealth created at the expense of other people's wealth. Doing so is unjust (*zulm*). Muslim jurists, however, did not look at economic injustice as a basis of *riba* prohibition. In defining *riba*, they will always look at the fixed and contractual increment levied on a loan (*qard*) to justify the Quranic prohibition. As the ethical foundation of law is not given due attention, misrepresentation of Islamic law in the banking business is not hard to find. One good example is the practice of *bay' al-'inah* and the absence of equivalent countervalue (*'iwad*) in profit creation contracted via *al-bai-bithaman ajil* and *murabahah*.

Eleven
Trading and Partnership

The Islamic Banking Act 1983 defines Islamic banking as a banking business whose aims and operations do not involve any element that is not approved by the religion of Islam. Since Islam teaches mankind about faith (*Aqidah*), ethics and conduct (*Akhlak*) and also how man relate himself to God (*muamalat*) between man and God- (*i.e., the Rukn Islam*) and his fellow beings (*muamalat* among man), it implies that Islamic banking activities are not confined to Islamic commercial law (*fiqh muamalat*) alone.

Equally important is the role of ethics and morality (*akhlak*) in the banking business. For this reason, Islamic banking—as envisioned by early Muslim economists—is designed to impart a unique ethical dimension in the banking business, namely the spirit of sharing and cooperation.

These ethical attributes in banking will take the form of *mudarabah* and *musyarakah* relations between banks and their customers, although other contracts such as *salam, istisna', and al-ijarah* assume similar roles.

When the Quranic ban on *riba* was revealed in Medina (Surah ar-Rum: 30) and the subsequent alternative given, namely "trade" ("Allah permitted trade but prohibited *riba*" (al-baqarah: 275)), it does not imply that trade as mentioned in the Quran is only about buying and selling.

Although current deferred payment contracts (*al-bai-bithaman ajil*) have no explicit sign contravening *Shariah* rulings, its overuse in consumer and business financing today does not seem to highlight the special ethical message that Islam promotes, namely the spirit of sharing and cooperation (*ta'awun*).

In Islam, an individual's personal income (Y_p) consists of his salary or wages, profits from investments, and rents from properties. i.e., $Y_p =$ salary + dividends + rent. Before the personal income Y_p is spent, he is obligated to pay Islamic tax or the *zakat*. After *zakat* is paid to the relevant authorities, he can now spend what economists normally call disposable income, Y_d, on goods and services to fulfill his needs.

In Islam, consumer expenditure or consumption is known as *nafakah*, i.e., spending on food, clothing, and other essential daily needs for him and the family. If the disposable income is more than consumption, he can either invest the surplus or gave it away as charity *(sadeqah)* or both.

A nominal Muslim is therefore expected to spend his disposable income on *nafakah* (household spending or consumption), *sadeqah* (charity), and investment.

Talking about saving and investment, when the financial system is based on the interest (*riba*) system, people always assume that when one lends money, he must be rewarded with a fixed return. When an individual saves in bank deposits, he expects to get a guaranteed return on his savings.

When the Islamic banking business takes off, people still want the same carrots, knowing well that the system cannot do so as it amounts to *riba*. Now people are more aware that savings accounts in Islamic banking no longer deal with the contract of debt. Islamic deposits do not deal with contractual claim on the amount saved. The contracts of *al-wadiah* and *mudarabah* were placed as alternatives to the contract of debt in conventional deposits. They just don't promise depositors fixed income like conventional deposits always do.

The contract of *mudarabah* is used today to mobilize long-term deposits. Can such contracts attract savings to help increase investment and economic growth? An Islamic bank can attract more *mudarabah* deposits if it has a good track record on investments. For example, if the bank was able to give high dividends, the public will invest in *mudarabah* deposits as soon as they know about the good news. They will do so even though the *mudarabah* contract is more risky than fixed deposits.

They are aware they could lose money, but taking more risk with an expectation of higher returns will motivate them to invest in Islamic products. A similar situation is observed in the unit trust industry. People here are not expecting to earn fixed returns from their investment.

In other words, risk-taking investment is a virtuous act. In modern finance, it is called risk-aversion. People are willing to take more risk only with an expectation of earning much more. Risk-taking is not similar to risk-loving. The latter is about excessiveness, while the former is pure human nature. Risk-avoidance is worse, as it means enjoying fixed returns without taking risk. Islam considers risk-avoidance an immoral act, as it (i.e., risk avoidance) ignores the human side of investment, namely work and effort. It is immoral to earn money without work. The only people deserving to receive money without work are beggars and the destitute!

The point is, can Islamic banking offer competitive rates of return? Has the track record been impressive enough to reflect true label? Have they succeeded to convince institutional bodies and private companies to place their cash in Islamic deposits?

When the Quran says that "Allah permitted trade and prohibited *riba*," what it intends to promote is economic justice. This is the message behind the revelation. It implies that the Quran refused to accept the contract of interest-bearing loan as a fair business contract. The contract of trade (*al-bay'*) was forwarded as the alternative to loans.

Al-Bay' with Equivalent Countervalue (*'Iwad*)

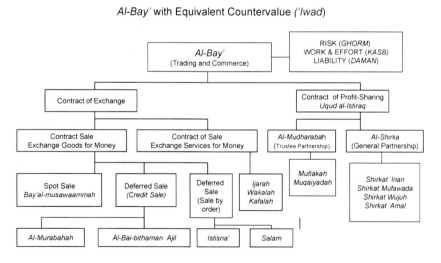

Figure 1.10 Trade and Commerce (*Al-Bay'*) in Islam

However, trading activities during the Prophetic Era were somewhat different from Islamic banking practices today. Prophet Muhammad (*pbuh*) obtained capital from Khadija. He purchased goods in Mecca and sold them in distant places at a higher price. Exchanges and payments were made on the spot. This was a common trading activity, where risks and danger of loss were commonplace.

In conducting trade and commercial activities (*al-bay'*), merchants traveled long distances. Deadly obstacles such as bad weather, robberies, and diseases were normal. In fact, the Quran recounts the life of the Quraish tribe, both nomadic and commercial: "For the covenants (of security and safeguard or safe conduct enjoyed) by the Quraish; their covenants (covering) journeys by winter and summer; let them adore the Lord of this House; Who provides them with food against hunger; and with security against fear of danger" (al-Quraysh: 1-4).

In view of the risks and effort put in trading, the profit earned by Prophet Muhammad (*pbuh*) is considered legitimate (*halal*). Goods were sold in cash and the profits realized distributed based on a contractual sharing ratio agreed earlier.

Current scenarios may not tell the same story. Banks served as financial intermediaries, while the Muhammad (*pbuh*) was not. Saidatina Khadija provided risk capital, and no bank will do the same. As we know, a banking firm borrows money from the surplus party and lends it to the deficit party.

Hence the application of trade (*al-bay'*) as an alternative to *riba* in Islamic banking industry should not be misconstrued as purely relaying on the literal meaning of trading (*al-bay'*). This is because the Quranic ban on *riba* is essentially about establishing justice (*'adl*) and justice is basically an ethical (*akhlak*) principle.

Taking profit from a *riba* loan is unjust (*zulm*), while making profit from trade is fair and just (*'adl*). This is because in trading (*al-bay'*), people expose themselves to the risk of losing their capital. There is no guarantee that sales are secured. It requires skills and talent to run the business. If the business fails, the trader's work and effort are not rewarded. For example, in the partnership between the Muhammad (*pbuh*) and Saidatina Khadija, the capital provider knew that no capital protection exists in *mudarabah*. Likewise, the nature of work the Muhammad (*pbuh*) undertook with

Khadija's capital, namely selling and buying, does not guarantee him any fixed salary.

Trading, (*al-bay'*) as we see today under *al-bai-bithaman ajil* (BBA) financing, has its own unique role in view of the high demand for credit, but it is not similar to the nature of business Prophet Muhammad (*pbuh*) ventured into. Instead, Islamic banking today has chosen the credit sale approach to trading (*al-bay'*). This credit sale model seems to have by-pass the role of risk-taking and value-addition as evident in the Quranic model of trade and commerce (*al-bay'*).

The partnership aspect of trading established between Muhammad (*pbuh*) and Khadija seems too problematic for banking application, according to the practitioners. How partnership can be turned in a viable financial product has remained an academic matter.

But as a Muslim, one should not give up hope. Sooner or later, the Islamic banking market will be saturated with the deferred payment installment schemes (BBA). It will create an urgency to fully observe the Quranic approach of *al-bay'* as exemplified by Prophet Muhammad's (*pbuh*) role model as trader. However, the application of *al-bay'* in Islamic banking can also see the application of contracts where risk-taking is evident such as *ijarah* (true leasing), *salam*, *istisna*, and *musyarakah*. The partnership model is one of the many models that an Islamic bank can adopt. It should not be misconstrued as the only model.

Twelve
Riba, Trade and Sadeqah

The Quranic ban on *riba* can be examined from three angles. First, the Quran provides an alternative to *riba*, namely trade and commerce (*al-bay'*) with the Quran saying, "while God has permitted trade and forbidden *riba*." Secondly, *riba* is condemned while charity *(sadeqah)* is enjoined. The Quran says, "God deprives *riba* of all blessing but blesses charity *(sadeqah)"* (2:276). Third, *riba* promotes injustices (*zulm*). In this context, the Quran says, "If you do not do so (that is, stop consuming *riba*), then be sure of being at war with God and His Messenger. But if you repent, you can have your principal. Neither should you commit injustice nor should you be subjected to it." (2:279)

People engaged in trading activities (*al-bay'*) put in a lot of hard work for their money. They also put their capital at risk. Profits arising from *al-bay'* are earned income. On the contrary, charities (*sadeqah*) are unearned income. Usually, the poor and disabled receive charities. They receive an income without providing an equivalent countervalue (*'iwad*). This is allowed in Islam because the giving and receipts of *sadeqah* is unilateral and does not constitute a trading (*al-bay'*) contract. Only in *al-bay'* that profit must contain an equivalent countervalue (*'iwad*).

But for people who have knowledge, skills, and opportunities, income creation must come through exchange, from work and effort. From these value-added activities, new wealth is created. In the absence of fraud (*tatfief*), true justice (*'adl*) will emerge in the market process. Justice will prevail because the creation of new wealth is made by way of competition and cooperation (*ta'awun*)—the foundation of *al-bay'*.

61

Deriving profit out of *riba* is an act of injustice, as the Quran says above. *Riba* is a price of credit. Based on the loan contract, the debtor is required by the law to pay interest with punitive implications if he fails to pay up the debt.

Islamic loans can also create an additional increase. Here, it is the debtor who sets the increase, not the creditor. Moreover, the increment is not contractually fixed, and declared only when the loan matures. If a debtor could not pay the loan due to, say, disability, the creditor is enjoined by the Quran to write off the debt. This is *sadeqah*.

The Quran says, "If the debtor is in difficulty, let him have respite or relief until it is easier, but if you forego out of charity, it is better for you if you realize." (2:280). This message may imply that firstly, an Islamic loan is a loan that requires no contractual return. In this manner, it is also charity (*sadeqah*). The charity is the interest given up. The Quran says again, "O believers, fear God and give up the *riba* that remains outstanding if you are believers." (2:278)

When a creditor no longer pursues payments and plans to write off the debt, he knows well that he has lost the opportunity to earn from the loss capital. He does not expect to earn any return from the loan. In this way, the loan is a charity (*sadeqah*). If the loan goes bad, he gave away the loan as charity. If the debtor pays the capital loan only, the creditor has forgone an opportunity to earn some returns. To do so is not easy, since there are not many people who are generous and compassionate. For this reason, an interest-free loan is also known as a benevolent loan (*qardhu hasan*).

In Islam, an Islamic loan is awarded via the contract of *qard or* most commonly called *qardhu hasan*. It is rather inaccurate to say that an Islamic loan is *al-bai-bithaman ajil* or *mudarabah*. *Qardhu hasan* is therefore a charity or *sadeqah*. It is a charity because, firstly, *qardhu hasan* does not require interest payments, and secondly, if the debtor cannot pay, the lender is enjoined to cancel the debt. Obviously both represent acts of benevolence.

However, on the borrowing side, it is also important to mention that it is an act of virtue to repay more than the principal amount, made as a token of appreciation. Doing so is a *sunnah*. Prophet Muhammad (s.a.w.) encouraged believers to pay more as long as no fixed increase was agreed upon earlier. The borrower can pay more if he can afford to so do.

It is worthy to note that in Islam, *sadeqah* can be broadly classified into two categories, namely compulsory *sadeqah* (*zakat mal* and *zakat fitr*) and optional *sadeqah*. *Qadhu hasan* is put under the second classification, which also includes *'ariyah, hibat, waqf,* etc. *Riba*, therefore, is different from *sadeqah* because in the former, the borrower will be legally obligated to pay interest as well as the principal loan.

In view of the nature of *qardhu hasan,* such Islamic loans may not find relevant applications in business or consumer financing. It is only useful in meeting personal needs where profits are not the dominating factor in determining lending decisions. That is why the Quran looks to trading and commerce (*al-bay'*), rather than *sadeqah* as an alternative to interest-bearing instruments such as bank loans, private debt securities, government bonds and other fixed income securities.

Thirteen
Risk-Sharing Financing

A proposal by the Federation of Malaysian Manufacturers (FMM) to set up a third board on the Kuala Lumpur Stock Exchange (KLSE) requires a serious look. The third board is meant to provide alternative financial access to manufacturers on downstream production and development of new products and processes at lower costs.

If approval is granted, retail and institutional investors can now take part in the venture capital industry. By doing so, the third board will ensure a continuous supply of venture capital funds in intensive technology investment to help propel Malaysia's competitive advantage in skilled intensive resource-based industry.

The proposal can provide a platform to encourage risk-participation financing in research and development and its subsequent commercialization. This point is implicit in FMM's recent memorandum for the annual dialogue with the finance minister on the 1996 national budget.

Among others, the manufacturing sector is reported to be losing its competitive strength in cheap, labor-intensive production. It is also facing acute shortages of skilled and technical manpower. The need to enhance research and development to forge greater innovation, efficiency, and competitiveness in Malaysia's manufacturing sector to satisfy today's global market is crucial.

The proposal for a third board in the KLSE is therefore a right step to help sustain the nation's rapid economic growth through investment in technical intensive and high value added manufacturing output.

It assumes that new firms must have their shares underwritten by merchant banks and venture capitalists. Although these institutions accept the risk of selling the stocks to investors at a lower price, the latter (i.e., venture capitalists) are at a worse position when the new firms fail to take off.

For these reasons, commercial banks are restricted by the banking law to engage risk-sharing financing in view of the safety and liquidity factors to avoid a bank run. In addition to that, commercial banks are not equipped with the relevant manpower to monitor business ventures. Risk management only concerns decisions to reduce default, interest, and forex risks.

But the same cannot apply to Islamic banking. The Islamic Banking Act (IBA) 1983 for example, allows Bank Islam Malaysia Berhad to run any form of business, as long as they are not contrary to the teachings of the *Shariah*. The *Shariah* enjoins businesses to participate in risk-sharing ventures as evident in the contract of *al-qirad* and *musharakah*.

What the Islamic Banking Act 1983 (IBA 1983) can do is to enlarge the scope of Islamic commercial banking. As the IBA allows Islamic banking to promote *musyarakah* and *mudarabah* investments, setting up a subsidiary company or an investment bank to underwrite stocks and securities using *Shariah* principles is no longer necessary.

Underwriting can be performed under one roof, as evident in some universal banks. It relieves these banks from high overhead costs incurred in setting a subsidiary company. At the same time, fee-based activities can be expanded when the bank takes an active role in the underwriting security business.

In fact, setting up Amanah Saham Bank Islam (ASBI) and Bank Islam Securities Sdn. Bhd. to cater for Islamic portfolio investment and fee-based activities was in contradiction to the true nature of Islamic banking.

As Islam requires production processes to achieve efficiency, using BAFIA banking framework (i.e., setting up subsidiaries) would mean losing many opportunities to reap economies of scale and scope arising from direct bank and commerce interlinks. But why does BIMB choose the conventional path?

It is indeed an irony to see how Islamic banks in Malaysia have not chosen to forgo and exploit such a rare privilege given by the government. In the United States, Congress is trying to repeal the 1938 Glass Steagall Act. The law categorically prohibits commercial banks from engaging in underwriting of securities and owning shares of companies. Since this legal constraint is absent in the IBA 1983, the FMM's proposal looks good for Islamic banks, as they can diversify their investments beyond credit finance.

As Islamic banks are permitted to pursue *mudarabah* and *musharakah* investment, they can hold shares of companies listed in the local bourses. The question now is, how is it possible to mobilize deposits into risky investments?

As the name indicates, *Mudarabah* Special Investment product has received approval by Bank Negara, and is now readily offered by many Islamic banks. In principle, the bank informs depositors what it will do with the money. If the investment turns out well, it means lucrative returns for banks and depositors. In a way, returns on these *mudarabah* deposits can outperform the market. Likewise, failed ventures will see customers losing their deposits.

The advantage about the system provides clear signal that investment in venture capital activities via the banking system is no longer reserved for a group of rich individuals, but is now available to the common man too. This point is in line with Quranic verse that says, "Wealth must not circulate only among the rich ones among you" (Sura 59:7). By conducting risk-sharing financing, equity-intensive Islamic banks can help narrow the income gap.

One advantage to propel the banking industry into risk-sharing activities is the ability to gain control over the participating firm. This is only possible when banks inject their own capital into the venture. In this manner, the bank would not dilute its capital with the investment deposits. The venture shall consist of three parties, namely the depositors, the bank, and the entrepreneur. The bank can also earn revenues from the management services rendered.

Fourteen
Al-Gharar and Risky Sales

The *Shariah*, in principle, recognizes risk and uncertainty dealing with the outcomes of investment and business decisions. This is because outcomes are unknown. Although people can predict the future, nobody knows what the future is like. It is thus believed that business is risky, since business outcomes are uncertain. Usually, the riskiness deals with the variation of outcome (i.e., probabilities of profits and losses), and not the terms and conditions of contract. This is an important point, as quite a number of writers tend to misjudge the Islamic view on risk and uncertainty.

Many writers on Islamic financing highlighted the principle of profit-loss sharing or risk sharing between banks and entrepreneurs as the viable alternative to debt financing. Mutual risk sharing can distribute the burden of loss to all parties equitably. It also helps reduce the concentration of loss to one party only, as evident in debt financing. As risk sharing tends to distribute business losses to all contracting parties, the spirit of brotherhood (*ukhuwah*) and cooperation (*ta'awun*) in business relationship can be realized.

But at the same time, the *Shariah* prohibits risk and uncertainty (*al-gharar*) in economic transactions. But are these two phenomena (i.e., about risks and uncertainties) contradictory in Islam? On one hand, there is a positive attitude towards risk and uncertainties, but on the other hand, it implied disapproval.

It is helpful to examine the *mudarabah* contract again. Islamic commercial law requires absolute certainty about the business partners and the terms of contractual obligations, such as the amount of capital invested, nature of project, termination, security, commitment, supervision, profit-loss sharing formula, settlement of disputes, etc.

In other words, perfect information is the rule such that none of the parties are exposed to duress (*ikroh*) and manipulation (*al-khilabah*). No elements of risk and uncertainty must exist in the terms and conditions of the contract, otherwise, the contract is deemed null and void (*bathil*).

However, risk and uncertainty are not disapproved of when it refers to business outcome as it constitutes a law in nature (*fitrah*)— "When there is profit, there is loss" *(al-ghorom bil ghonm)*. It is a way of life that business is associated with rewards, risk, and uncertainties. Hence, the essence of *mudarabah* investment is the risk and uncertainty about profit creation that nobody knows for sure, only God.

But risk and uncertainties cannot exist in contractual obligations. In the contract of sale (*al-bay'*), the objective of sale is the transfer of the ownership from the seller to the buyer. In other words, the objective of the contract, i.e., the transfer of property, must be executed with certainty. This means the seller must own the property before he can sell it.

But when trading (retailing, wholesale, distribution) constitutes the main activity of a *mudarabah* venture, the uncertain elements in *mudarabah* are those about business risk, i.e., uncertainty of income flows caused by the nature of business operation. If the industry is plagued with unstable prices, then the *mudarabah* project is highly risky (*ghorm*). But even if the nature of the business is highly risky, the terms and agreements in purchasing and sales must be free from uncertainties (*gharar*)

Gharar (Uncertainties in contractual agreements)

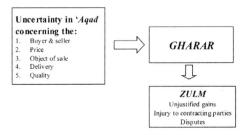

Figure 1.12 *Gharar*

The situation above does not hold in debt-financing contracts, especially in commercial loans, as there is no risk attached to the terms and outcome of the contract, except for the so-called credit and financial risk. The latter can be insured at a premium by trading interest futures and options. The former can be eliminated by not giving the loan or putting stringent collateral requirement.

Most people know how banks heavily scrutinize the loans on all fronts. On top of that, banks know in complete certainty how much profit can be made as these profits (i.e., accrued interest income) are clearly stipulated in the loan documents.

As an example, a three- year $10,000 loan at 10 percent flat annual interest would guarantee the bank an interest profit and fixed income of $3,000 over three years. This earning power is unfounded the ordinary non-banking business ventures. Ironically, the same practice is evident in Islamic banks using *murabahah and bai-bithaman-ajil* financing.

To conclude, it is safe to say that contractual agreements must not contain uncertainties about contractual obligations, i.e., obligations related to the object of sale, its price, etc.

As an illustration some of the popular examples of risky sales (*bay al-gharar*) in pre-Islamic transactions are given as follows. In *bay' al-hasat,* the vendor will say, "of these pieces of cloth or these sheep I will sell you those upon which falls this pebble thrown in the air, and the purchaser says, Yes. Hence, the exchange is executed on the basis of the offer and acceptance (*ijab and qabul*) in view of the distance the stone is thrown. Such sales are prohibited in Islam.

In *bay' al-mulamasah,* a sale is concluded by saying, "When you have touched this cloth, I have sold it to you." *Bay' al-muzabanah* is a contract to exchange harvested dry dates for a definite measure of fresh dates. In this case, the *gharar* elements are embodied in the number, weight, and measure of the dates, which are not known. In *bay' al-samak fi'l-ma,* the exchange involves the sale of fish in the water. In *bay' al-laban fi darul al-an'am,* it is a sale of milk in the udder of the animals. Sale of a fetus or *bay' al-haml* is prohibited. In *bay' wa salaf,* the buyer will say, "I shall take your goods for such and such if you lend me such and such."

According to Imam Malik, such a transaction is not permitted. This is based on the saying of the Prophet s.a.w., "prevent them (the people of Mecca) from making a selling and lending contract concurrently."

These sales are prohibited in Islam because they are contrary to the ethical teachings of the Quran and the essence of justice that the Quran seeks to enjoin in economic transactions.

Fifteen
Understanding Risk and Uncertainty in Islam: Gharar versus Ghorm

Using the terms "risk" and "uncertainty" as *gharar* to describe negative elements in Islamic commercial contracts has often led to confusion among many observers. For instance, sales such as *bay' al-muzabanah* and *bay' al-samak fi'l-ma* are banned in Islam because both contain *gharar*. Purchasing life insurance policy is prohibited in Islam because it is said to contain *gharar*.

In contractual agreement, *gharar* must be avoided, because when it exists, there is a risk that one of the contracting parties may lose out in the deal. What this means is that market agents must not allow ambiguities to exist when the contract is in play.

Islamic jurists (*fuqaha*) have made it clear that any contract is deemed null and void when *gharar* is found evident. When *gharar* in contractual obligations occurs, contracts can no longer be operative. The contract will become invalid and neither party shall receive protection from the legal system.

For example, when a person sells an asset he does not own, or does so when the asset is not yet in his possession, there is a possibility he may fail to make delivery. In this manner, the transfer of ownership rights cannot be executed as planned. *Gharar* of ownership is said to exist in this sale agreement.

When *gharar* exists in the contract, the buyer may lose out, since he has paid for the goods. This *gharar* must be avoided at all costs as it will create disputes. When people quarrel and fight unnecessarily, they will be distracted, according to Ibn Qayyim, from remembering God.

However, elsewhere, Islam enjoins market agents to take risks in their business engagements. In fact, the Islamic legal maxim such as "no reward without risk" (*al-ghorm bil ghonm*) is invoke to invite people to participate in ventures involving both risks and reward such as *al-bay', al-ijarah, salam, mudarabah,* and *musyarakah.*

Legitimate profit generated from commercial activities implicating elements of risk-taking is a virtue (*mahmudah*) in Islam. The term "no pain—no gain," again confirms a positive towards risk in business dealing.

More often than not, the term "risk and uncertainty" is used interchangeably to denote positive elements, as well as negative elements when one is dealing with business and the principles of contract, respectively. How one can then make a clear distinction between these two conceptions of risks, i.e., risks in contracts and risks in business outcome, is interesting to see.

To avoid confusion it is worthy to examine the nature of caravan trade before and after Islam in Mecca. The Quran has described this caravan trade in the following verse: "For the familiarity of the Quraish, their familiarity with the journeys by winter and summer, let them worship the Lord of this House, Who provides them with food against hunger, and with security against fear of danger" (Al-Quraish 1-4).

In essence, two types of commercial contracts can be observed in the caravan trade, namely *mudarabah* and *al-bay'*. In the former, the Meccans are known to wait for the arrival of the caravan with full expectations of profit as they have invested their money in the caravan trade via *mudarabah* or *al-qirad*. Indeed, this arrival of caravans is a big occasion in the city. It is a festive occasion and people are excited about the caravan they have invested in.

The caravan trade is by no means easy and smooth. The goods can be destroyed before reaching the markets. Sandstorms and sickness were most common. Highway robberies and accidents may just complicate the journey. These incidences are beyond one's control. They are risks that caravan trading cannot avoid. Such risk in *muamalat* is called *ghorm*. The legal maxim *al-ghorm bil ghonm* is directly related to this phenomenon of market risk.

Gharar is indeed different from *ghorm*, although the English translation of both has applied the same term interchangeably: risk and uncertainty. Now, *gharar* in the caravan trade can be observed when the *mudarib* buys and sells the articles of trade. As an example, he purchases commodity X in Mecca for say, $50 and later sells it for $100 in Syria. The sale contract normally involves the agents (buyer and seller), the object of sale, the price or consideration, and the offer and acceptance. It is here that *gharar* may or may not exist.

So the term "risky sale" at this point simply means the existence of *gharar* in the contract of sale (*al-bay'*). The main objective here is to avoid ambiguities in sale. *Gharar* or ambiguities about the buyer and seller, the object of sale and its price must be avoided. In fact, using the term "ambiguities" is more accurate than risks and uncertainties when one is dealing *gharar* in contractual agreement.

To make sure that profits created from the *mudarabah* venture are lawful, firstly *gharar* must be avoided between first, the *mudarib* as an agent-buyer and the seller in Mecca, and secondly, between the same *mudarib*-seller and a prospective buyer in Syria.

Secondly, both contracting parties in the *mudarabah* contract (i.e., the *mudarib* and *rabbulmal*) must recognize *ghorm*, i.e., risk and uncertainty in business outcome. That is, the *mudarabah* business guarantees no profit. This principle of *al ghorm bil ghonm* is fundamental in all *al-mudarabah* investments as well as *al-bay*, such as *al-bay' mutlak, al-ijarah, salam, istisna, etc.*

Based on the above, one can now distinguish *gharar* from *ghorm*. *Gharar* is destructive while *ghorm* is constructive. Profiting from *gharar* creates unjustified enrichment as it i.e., *gharar* leads to unfair and unethical dealings. On the contrary, profits created under the pretext of *ghorm* show the way to justice since these profits are not made by mere manipulation and deceit but via mutual aid and cooperation (*ta'awun*)

As mentioned earlier, contracts containing *gharar* are declared null and void. Sales involving nonexistent objects, or the non-stipulation of terms of payments are invalid on grounds of *gharar*. Sometimes *gharar* is called *khatar*, taken from the *mukhatara* sale.

GHORM VS GHARAR

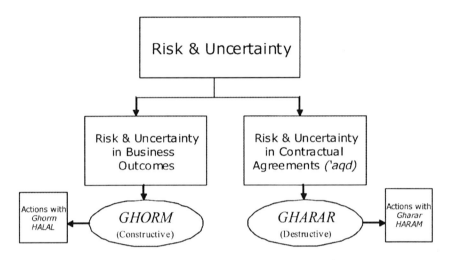

Figure 1.13 Differences between *Ghorm* and *Gharar*

Ghorm, however, is something that one must accept in business, as it constitutes a *tabi'* (natural) phenomenon. As mentioned earlier, the caravan trade is laden with *ghorm.* Highway robbery, devastating storms, the severe heat during the day and cold in the night, diseases and uncertain markets are some examples of *ghorm* in trade. As such, agents taking part in this venture will hold legitimate claims on any profit made, if any. The terms "risk" and "uncertainty" are therefore shorthanded to describe the difference between *gharar* and *ghorm.* In Islamic banking, this term should be used with care. That is:

1. Risks and uncertainties in contractual agreements (i.e., ambiguities) are called *gharar. Gharar* can be controlled in a sense that it can be deliberately introduced into the contract by either one of the parties.

2. Risks and uncertainties in business outcomes (i.e., systematic risks) are known as *ghorm. Ghorm* however cannot be eliminated because it is a law in nature (*hukm tabi'*). *No one is free from the vagaries of price volatilities arising from market movement.*

Sixteen
Islamic Investment Horizon

The development of Islamic banking and finance in Malaysia may reach greater heights when the system begins to embrace offshore banking services. However, the persistent use of credit-driven products such as *al-bai-bithaman ajil* and *al-murabahah* (sale with deferred payments), sale buyback (*bay' al-'inah*) and *bay' al-dayn* (sale of debt) is not to imply niche markets for Islamic banking. Convergence of Islamic and conventional system seems inevitable if less is done to reduce heavy dependence on Islamic credit-based finance. In trade financing, for example, fewer attempts are made to adopt partnership contracts or contracts based on the *salam* and *istisna'* models. Practitioners seemed more comfortable using *murabahah* letters of credit, *murabahah* trust receipts, *bay al-dayn* bankers' acceptances (AIB) and *kafalah* bank guarantees. Strangely, these facilities are drawn using conventional bank manuals. Creativity and innovation have taken a back seat since.

In the Islamic money market, one cannot fail to see how interest-bearing formulas are used to calculate the profit arising from Islamic instruments. Similar approaches were applied to government Islamic bonds (GII). In corporate finance, Islamic promissory notes and the zero coupon bonds are contracted using the *bay' al-'inah* and *bay' al-dayn* principles. In essence, contractual obligations of issuers and investors alike are still based on debt.

Why this phenomenon exists in Malaysia is a question one must address with sincerity (*ikhlas*). What may puzzle critical observers is the fact that Islamic banking in Malaysia does not seem to dramatically change the way banks and customers interact. It will take time, for sure, but at least this should be in the right direction.

Let us take one example in corporate finance where the objective function is to maximize the value of the firm. To do so, firstly the firm must find the best method to help it decide how to allocate scarce resources across competing uses. This is the investment decision; for example, should the company venture in property development or manufacturing?

Secondly, the firm should also find the best means to raise funds to finance the project it has decided to undertake i.e., the financing decision. Finally, the dividend decision; that is, upon making profits, the firm must decide how much to reinvest and how much to distribute as dividends to the shareholders.

In the financing decision, the firm may raise funds through borrowing or equity or both. How this is done depends a lot on the way the firm looks at the type of project chosen, tax advantages, and expected cost of bankruptcy. If the firm chooses debt financing, then the design and types of debt financing may involve a decision to borrow long-term or short-term at a fixed or floating rate. In other words, to make correct financing decisions, firms are expected to make use of the tools of corporate finance, such as present value, financial statement analysis, risk, and return.

Why a firm selects equity instead of debt in its financing decision is common knowledge in most finance textbooks. Firms lacking in captured markets or awarded contracts will raise equity funds. These companies will normally seek funds through joint ventures, if any. But most firms will choose debt-financing when they have successfully secured a contract, say a turn-key project.

Through contract financing, firms can earn higher margins. For example, an average housing project can earn an average of 30 percent gross margin. After paying the bank interest of 10 percent per annum, a project earns 20 percent net profit. Meaning that a contract worth $100 million will earn a whopping $20 million! Who is then too foolish to raise equity funds when a lucrative contract has secured a handsome profit? Doing so would benefit the shareholders, as opposed to his self-interest. As greed prevails, he will not want to share the profit with others.

Firms such as the above will seek Islamic trade financing facilities bearing financing costs similar to conventional instruments. Even if they are invited by Islamic banks to participate via joint venture it is likely to be turned down.

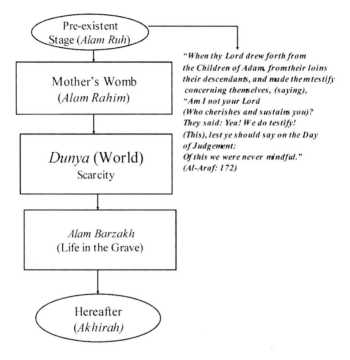

Figure 1.14 Islamic Time Horizon

However, the opposite is true when a firm with no contracts at hand tries to raise capital on the basis of partnership. This poses a great risk to the bank and most likely the application will be turned down. It is therefore not strange to see why so little *mudarabah* or *musyarakah* financing is conducted by Islamic banks today as they would stay away from projects with high exposure to market risks. It looks as if the demand and supply side do not match as both holds differing conception of risk and return.

Malaysian Islamic banking is based on the dual system. As customers are free to choose Islamic and conventional facilities, application of *mudarabah* and *musyarakah* in banking can be very difficult. This is because banks can only venture into *mudarabah* and *musyarakah* projects when depositors are comfortable with the structure of partnership they are about to enter.

The most important task is to convince Muslim individuals, companies, and institutions to place their deposits with the Islamic banks. They should be informed that profits cannot be made on money alone. Profit can only be realized when cash or money is converted into real capital with the production process exposed to market risks.

To encourage Muslims to participate in Islamic equities via the Islamic banking business, the spirit of sharing and cooperation must be intensified. How this is made possible is through education. Muslims must be informed that their investment time horizon should not be confined to this physical world only. In fact, one way is to gradually introduce the fact that in Islam, man's existence undergoes five distinct phases:

1) *'alam arwah* or *'alam dzar* where mankind first made his or her *Mithaq* or Covenant with God.
2) *'alam arham* or life in the mother's womb;
3) *'alam dunya* or life in this physical world;
4) *'alam barzakh* or life in the grave, and lastly;
5) *'alam akhirah* or life in the Hereafter.

Examining these stages of one's existence in greater detail is imperative. Its positive impact on investment behavior will help financial practitioners recognize better what's in the mindset of their Muslim clients and customers. For instance, when one looks at the *'alam dunya*, the Quran says that man has not been created in sport (23:15) but has a serious task. He is accountable for both his success and failure. But men are content to live their lives from day to day, from hour to hour: they are like cattle, indeed worse (7:19). Most people refuse to look beyond (*al-'aqiba*) and do not lay any store for the morrow as man do not want to attempt looking at long range moral goals of the human endeavor.

If left unguarded, Islamic banking may suffer from similar fate, as what seems to matter now is the legal judgment of Muslim jurists. When a product is deemed permissible (*halal*), the morality and ethical (*akhlak*) factor is no longer considered useful. Law and ethics cannot mix. Its impact on welfare, poverty eradication, and uplifting Islamic entrepreneurship is put aside, as what matters is the bottom line.

Economic justice is no longer relevant. Using legal devices (*hilah*) to justify permissibility has led bank directors and practitioners to adopt conventional products in most dimensions of Islamic banking operations, may they be pricing, collaterals obligation and legal documentations. It disregards what these can do to income distribution, economic stability, and growth of the nation.

Seventeen
Rational Investment Behavior

Islamic banking in Malaysia has one unique feature that sets it apart from the banking model of Iran and Pakistan. That is, the Malaysian model is based on a parallel system that allows conventional and interest-free banking to coexist, competing for deposits and finance. Since Malaysia is a multiracial and religious country, interest-free banking should be able to deal with situations where movements of funds no longer take place on the basis of reason and facts alone but also faith (*iman*).

Take note that in Islam, making a decision on the basis of faith does not mean rejecting reason. In economics, an individual is said to be rational when he can produce maximum output with minimum input. For example, as a producer, he tries to obtain level of profit by using inputs at the lowest cost. A rational producer is an efficient producer with decisions made based on costs and benefits alone. Maximization is achieved via cost minimization.

In the Islam faith, (*iman*) motivates people to produce goods and services in the most efficient manner. That is, faith will tell him that business conducted without considering costs and benefits are doomed to fail.

When the above notion of rationality is applied to deposit placement and financing, making choices (*ikhtiyar*) assumes that one adopts a value system. For Muslims, rational behavior would see that reason and divine values are not compartmentalized. For instance, even when the products are relatively more expensive, the choice of using them remains undeterred. This is because the choice is made on the basis of faith (*iman*), with pecuniary benefits coming secondary.

However, if this situation persists and less is done to see why Islamic products cost more, the divine values will incite a believer to investigate what actually went wrong; why are Islamic products more expensive than conventional? In this manner, a Muslim individual does not act on blind faith. He uses reason and factual evidence to see why the inconsistency has taken place. If he fails to do so, he may be a victim of a business dealing that uses Islam to make money.

The Quran holds man accountable in what he does and does not. If he puts his money with Islamic banks, he should see that it runs in the best possible manner. He should be able to detect why Islamic banks are giving more or less than their competitors. This is what we mean by Islamic rational behavior.

For non-Muslim customers, they can switch any way they want. In fact, they will gain most from the parallel banking system. They can look around and choose the products that benefited them most. Their value system is based mainly on the mundane. As rational investors, non-Muslim customers will make decision of the basis of market information. They will compare yields as well as risks.

The problem is what an Islamic bank should do when a rational decision of non-Muslim customers adversely affects profits. An example may help clarify the problem. It is well know that *al-bai-bithaman ajil* (BBA) products command more than 90 percent of financing in Islamic banking. BBA is a credit sale contract with payments made on fixed installments. Changes in market interest rates will not alter these payments.

Now, a rational non-Muslim customer will always compare the products that give him the most benefit. When he can enjoy more benefits from the Islamic products, such as higher *mudarabah* rates of return or lower BBA profit charges on BBA or *mudarabah* funds, he will opt for Islamic banking services. Likewise, if the rate on fixed deposits is higher than *mudarabah* deposits or when interest rates on loans are lower than BBA, a rational non-Muslim customer will naturally choose conventional banks. He therefore has the ability to substitute products that gave him the most pecuniary benefits.

The above case can help explain why the *al-bai-bithaman ajil* facility is popular choice among non-Muslim customers today. Due to future expectations of rising interest rates, taking interest-bearing loans for home financing may not be a rational thing to do. This is because borrowers will have to pay more when the base-lending rate increases, as it means a higher financial burden on them.

Such burden is absent in BBA financing, as the contract does not allow banks to adjust their profit rates, since doing so will alter the selling price, thus deeming the BBA contract invalid. In other words, as the interest rate increases, the demand for BBA will also increase, simply because the BBA profit rate remains the same. As the volume of BBA financing increases, Islamic banks are expected to make more profits.

What we see here is a situation where both parties seem to gain when interest rates are rising. Every dollar or ringgit of BBA financing must be supported by deposits. Without deposits, a bank has no funds to finance customer purchases. Deposit mobilization is therefore crucial to sustain financing activities. The point is, how would Islamic banks obtain deposits when interest rates are rising?

When the market interest rate rises, so would interest rates on deposits. Unfortunately, Islamic banks are not able to give higher returns on *mudarabah* deposits, because existing or non-maturing BBA profit rate is a constant. To grant higher returns to the *mudarabah* depositors with no vertical adjustment given to BBA rates would be senseless, as it will erode bank's earnings.

The effect on the supply of Islamic deposits is only obvious. Non-Muslim customers will choose to save and invest in interest-based deposits, because they can gain more from the rising fixed deposit rates. This may caused the supply of deposits in interest-bearing banks to increase, while the supply of deposits in Islamic banking to fall. This brings along a negative saving-investment gap.

In the event of greater demand for BBA financing, how would Islamic banks supply more BBA when the supply of deposits is declining? The point is, the parallel system was introduced to stimulate competition. Islamic banking must find ways to create new viable products as alternatives to BBA. They must also be mindful that customers whose loyalty is driven by faith are also rational and acquisitive.

To attract deposits, Islamic banks should offer products that are responsive to changes in market fundamentals, so that adjustment can be made to fit the requirements of sound business strategy. BBA intensive

Islamic banking should be toned down to make way for *istisna, salam, mudarabah,* and *musyarakah* options. These are niche areas that Islamic banks must build on to stay ahead of mainstream practices. Putting a clamp on BBA, Islamic bank should pave new ways to develop these niche products not found in conventional banks.

SECTION TWO

ISLAMIC BANKING PRODUCTS

One
Al-Bai-bithaman Ajil Financing

Very few people can afford to purchase a house on a cash basis. Many will buy it on credit, usually payable by installments. If Mr. Ibrahim purchases a notebook computer for $5,000 using a credit scheme, the loan contract will require him to pay back the bank an amount of $5,000 plus some interest. Economists say the interest paid is the price of credit. It is the opportunity cost forgone by the bank, which he compensates by paying interest.

Alternatives to interest-bearing installment schemes are also available. Based on the *murabahah* and *bai-bithamin-ajil (BBA)* or *bay' muajjal* contracts, Islamic installment schemes provide a direct line of credit sale.

What is the nature of *murabahah* and *bai-bitahman ajil products*? Are they a better alternative to interest-bearing loan and hire-purchase schemes? What makes them Islamic anyway? Before discussing further, it is important to know some distinctions between *murabahah* and BBA. This is because the main concern today is BBA financing.

First, let's look at *murabahah*. In principle, *murabahah* means mark-up sale. It is a sale contract in which the object of sale is sold at a price equivalent to the cost price and profit margin. If the cost price equals $500 and the profit margin equals $200, the *murabahah* price equals $700.

However, *murabahah* today has been associated with credit sale. This is not totally accurate. There are two types of *murabahah*, namely:

1. Cash murabahah i.e., a sale contract where the seller sells a commodity with a price equal to the cost price and a profit margin. The purchase is settled in cash.

2. Credit murabahah i.e., a credit sale with purchases settled by installment payments. The price is equal to cash murabahah prices but a premium is added over the profit margin to reflect time value of money. In Malaysia, short-term credit murabahah is simply called murabahah with payment payable lump sum. A long-term credit murabahah is known as al-al-bai-bithaman ajil (BBA). BBA is also known as bay'muajjal and murabahah in Pakistan and the Middle Eastern countries.

In a credit sale involving assets and properties, one will use the contract of BBA and not cash or credit *murabahah. Al-bai' bithaman ajil* (BBA) means sale with deferred payments, i.e., *Al-bai'* equals sale, *thaman* equals price, *Ajil* equals deferment. BBA is a sale. It is not a loan. But it a sale with deferred payment. It is not a spot sale. Still, it constitutes one form of trading and commerce. The Quran says, "Allah has allowed trade and commerce (*al-bay'*) but prohibits *riba*" (Al-Baqarah 275). Hence, profit from sale (*al-bay'*) is lawful, while profit from loan i.e., *riba*, is unlawful.

BBA is a type of sale where the buyer can pay by installment. Other types of sales, such as cash *murabahah,* require buyers to pay on the spot. For example, *bay' al-salam* requires buyers to pay on the spot, but they will get delivery in the future. Thus, *al-bay'* does not have to imply BBA alone, but also other lawful sales as well.

We will now see how BBA is applied in the banking business. Let's say Mr. Anas wishes to purchase a low-cost house at market price $60,000. How will an Islamic bank help Mr. Anas own the house?

In principle, the BBA sale deals with two parties only, namely the bank as the selling party and Mr. Anas as the buying party. But prior to the BBA sale, the bank must purchase the house from the vendor/developer. This purchase does not constitute a BBA sale.

But current practices today do not allow the above to take place. This is because a bank—whether Islamic or otherwise—can only provide financing facilities. It is not allowed to purchase and sell assets to earn money. In this way, banks cannot buy houses from the vendors. They only provide financing, i.e., make loans.

The same applies to Islamic banking. Civil transactions require the customer to purchase the property from the developer. The Islamic Banking Act (IBA) 1983 is a civil law and stays under the jurisdiction of civil court. It embraces some *Shariah* values but not enough to overrun existing banking laws to reflect genuine Islamic conception of sale (*al-bay'*).

To highlight the above, let's again see Mr. Anas. He will meet the developer/vendor and sign a sale and purchase agreement (S&P) after paying a 20 percent down payment, i.e., $12,000. In conventional practice, Mr. Anas will look for a bank that can lend him the remaining $48,000. Assume that Mybank approves the loan and pays the developer $48,000 on behalf of Mr. Anas. Thus, Mr. Anas gets a loan from Mybank, such that he can purchase the property from the developer on cash basis.

Mr. Anas will pledge the property as collateral via the charge or deeds of assignment on the $48,000 loan. Given interest rate at 4 percent flat over 20 years, Mr. Anas will pay the bank $38,400 more in interest. His monthly installment = ($48,000 + $38,400) / 240 = $360.

To sum up, conventional financing consists of the following contracts, namely:

1. Contract of loan between the bank and Mr. Anas
2. Deeds of Assignment/Charge.

The same procedure applies for Islamic banks. But things get complicated when civil transactions require Mr. Anas and the bank to stay mainstream. Even under Islamic transaction, Mr. Anas must purchase the property from the developer. He puts up RM12,000 as down payment to secure the Sale and Purchase Agreement (S & P) on his favor. In this manner, Mr. Anas becomes the beneficiary owner of the property.

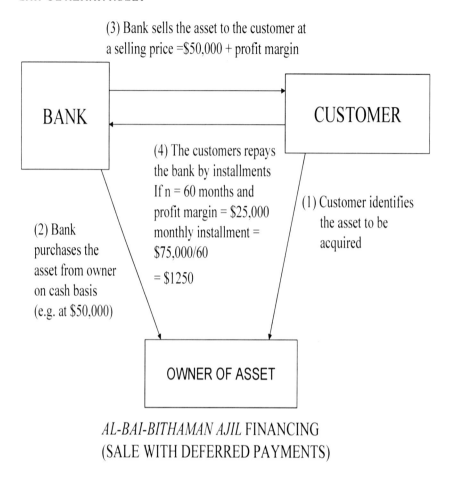

(3) Bank sells the asset to the customer at a selling price =$50,000 + profit margin

BANK

CUSTOMER

(4) The customers repays the bank by installments
If n = 60 months and profit margin = $25,000
monthly installment = $75,000/60
= $1250

(2) Bank purchases the asset from owner on cash basis (e.g. at $50,000)

(1) Customer identifies the asset to be acquired

OWNER OF ASSET

AL-BAI-BITHAMAN AJIL FINANCING
(SALE WITH DEFERRED PAYMENTS)

Figure 2.1 *Al-Bai-Bithaman Ajil* Financing

But how could Bank A sell the property to Mr. Anas via BBA contract when in the first place it does not own the asset? The Holy Prophet says, "do not sell what you don't own." Bank A must be careful not to violate the above *Shariah* injunction.

To do so, Bank A must purchase the property from Mr. Anas via the Property Purchase Agreement (PPA). The current practice indicates that the bank pays the customer $48,000, which it passes on to the developer.

Once the bank holds ownership via PPA, it then sells the property to Mr. Anas via the Property Sale Agreement (PSA). Here, the terms are as follows:

1. Seller (Bank A) and buyer (Mr. Anas)
2. Object of sale : Low-cost house
3. Price of object : Cost price ($48,000) + profit margin ($38,400) = $86,000

Installment payments = $86,000/240 = $380

Similar with conventional practice, the house will be placed as collateral via the Deeds of Assignment or Charge. It says that the bank holds the right of legal ownership of the property in the manner that it holds the right to sell it when Mr. Anas defaults the BBA facility.

To summarize, BBA sale consists of three contracts, namely:

1. Property Purchase Agreement (PPA): Bank buys property from customer.
2. Property Sale Agreement (PSA): Bank sells property to customer at BBA price.
3. Deeds of Assignment/Charge: Bank A holds property as collateral.

It seems that the above agreements were drawn to treat BBA as a loan rather than a sale (*al-bay'*). In a true BBA sale, the bank should purchase the house from the developer/vendor. Sale and Purchase agreement (S&P) should have taken place between the bank and developer. In this manner, the bank will hold risk of ownership (*ghorm*) and there holds the right to earn profits from the sale.

Since civil procedures require S&P agreement signed between customers and developers, Islamic banks are forced to introduce the Property Purchase Agreement (PPA) to secure ownership (*milkiyah*) before executing the Property Sale Agreement (PSA). If civil law allows Islamic banks to purchase the property from the developer, then the BBA sale shall consists of the following agreements:

1. Property Sale Agreement (PSA): Bank sells property to customer at BBA price.
2. Deeds of Assignment/Charge: Bank holds property as collateral.

Figure 2.1 helps illustrate BBA sale with S & P agreement taking place between the bank and the vendor. The BBA sale deals with Step 3 and Step 4 only. However, in real practise a contract of sale-buyback is readily evident as noted in PPA and PSA documents, where the costumer is required to purchase the asset that he has intially agreed to sell to the bank. This sale-buyback mechanism (i.e. PPA and PSA) in essence, constitutes a sale with condition.It seems that a *bay` al -`inah* mechanism is used in BBA since no purchase has taken place between the bank and the house developer. To avoid using *bay` al -`inah* in BBA financing, the bank should purchase the property directly from the developer.

Two
Al-Bai-Bithaman Ajil and the risk of ownership (daman milkiyah)

Al-Bai-thaman ajil may have received wide support among banking practitioners and *Shariah* advisors. Its dominating presence is quite worrying, as it is fast displacing the potentials of *mudarabah* and *musyarakah* financing. By using BBA, there is no need to introduce partnership product, because BBA has been able to give what customers wanted. There is no need to observe risk of ownership in *salam, istisna* and *ijarah*. Business application of *salam, istisna,* and *ijarah* will find no meanings. The whole idea of putting trading and commerce (*al-bay'*) as the alternative to *riba* will make no sense. The paralysis of the Quranic *al-bay'* is inevitable when BBA and its derivatives (i.e., *bay al-'inah*) are put in the forefront of the Islamic banking business.

The problem is, BBA has limited applications. It serves well when financing deals with asset purchases. But business today runs on many transactions. They need cash and working capital. Leasing can be a better option than purchasing, and some companies are more comfortable with a joint-ventures arrangement. When Islamic banks limit their products to BBA, they usually lag behind the competitors.

Furthermore, proponents of *mudarabah* and *musyakarah* banking today have constantly been labeled as naïve and unaware of actual banking operation or how things are run out there. They are also reminded to stop parroting the idea of risk-sharing or putting the risk-taking as the main basis of the *riba* prohibition.

93

At the recent conference on Islamic financial instruments organized by the Institute of Islamic Understanding of (*IKIM*), the same rhetoric was echoed by an international speaker, who seemed to be a staunch advocator of *al-murabahah* and BBA banking. The speaker looked more than convinced that the Quranic ban of *riba* is not about absence of risk-taking factors. Rather, the selling party must truly observe the ownership (*milkiah*) factor in sale (*al-bay'*). He must own the asset before selling it to the customers. Doing so will secure him a lawful profit.

At some point, it makes sense, since *al-bay*, namely trade and commerce, constitutes the Quranic alternative to *riba*. A contract of sale in Islamic law requires the seller to own the object of sale (*mahallul aqdi*) before executing the sale. The Prophet (saw) says: "Do not sell something that you do not own." What the speaker says is true. There is a link between ownership and market risk. When one owns an asset or property, the ownership risk will expose him to market volatilities. As a trader, the asset is therefore exposed to price or market risk.

The above *hadith* on ownership (*milkiyah*) actually conveys two main principles, namely: 1) transparency, and 2) risk-taking. First, when someone sells goods that he owns, the ambiguities (*gharar*) about delivery and ownership transfer should not exist. When the contract is transparent i.e., without *gharar,* disharmony and disputes between the contracting parties can be avoided.

Secondly, by requiring the seller to own what he sells, the main idea is the risk of ownership (*daman milkiyah*). Asset ownership is tied to risk-taking (*ghorm*) in a sense that holding an asset that one owns is risky as it may be destroyed or depleted in value. So, if one sells or rents out an asset that he owns legitimately, he holds the right to derive profits from the business.

In the case of a spot sale, the trader purchases goods from the wholesaler and stores the goods before any sale is made. This is where he is exposed to the risk of ownership. Failing to find buyers will see him holding piles of inventory with high overhead cost, as well as the risk of obsolesce. In the worst-case scenario, he may not be able to sell the goods at all. In this way, he will lose his capital investments. He may have spent $10,000 to buy the goods wholesale. Failure to sell them will mean losing the $10,000 capital. The trader is actually facing price or market risk (*ghorm*). Thus, it is clear now that ownership risk is connected to market risk.

In leasing (*al-ijarah*), the lessor is also liable to ownership risk such as maintenance and destruction of property. So, the rental income he receives must be a legitimate one. Similarly, in a deferred payment sale such as *al-murabahah* and BBA, the seller, namely the bank, is required to hold ownership before any asset sale is made. So the profit generated from *al-murabahah* and BBA is *halal* as the sale fulfills the requirement of ownership. By virtue of owning the asset, he is exposed to market risk (*ghorm*).

But when we look at money, the ownership argument has a limitation. Money serves many functions, including medium of exchange and a store of value. Let us suppose that Mr. Wahab, an engineer, receives $10,000 monthly. His salary is paid in cash, so he holds a legal claim on this money, which he puts in the bank.

In other words, Mr. Wahab, who owns the deposits, will receive $100 per year as interest, which according to the ownership argument, should also see $100 gain as permissible (*halal*). This is because Mr. Wahab has already fulfilled the ownership requirement. Even if he lends out the money, he will still hold a legal claim on the money. Similarly, if one adheres to this contradicting view, it also means that a bondholder who possesses a legal claim on the coupon will see *riba* becoming a lawful gain.

Actually, the ownership requirement must also be tied to the object of sale (*mahalul 'aqd*). In law of contracts, the object of sale must constitute property (*mal mutaqawwim*). Obviously, in Islamic law, money or currency is not *mal mutaqawwim*. In this way, it cannot be traded at a price. Thus, the ownership argument to signify Islamic legitimacy to profit cannot be applied to loans and bonds.

Another point to rebut this confusing view is *riba al-buyu'* or *riba* in sale involving the six tradable items, namely: gold, silver, dates, barley, oats, and salt. When someone exchanges 100 grams of gold for 120 grams of the same, *riba al-buyu'* or the additional 20 grams of gold, is created.

The contract is invalid since unjustified enrichment (*fadl mal bila 'iwad*) violates the Islamic concept of justice. But if we use the ownership argument, then the extra 20 grams is a lawful gain, since legitimacy now is made on the basis of ownership factor.

So, where does this ownership thing lead us? Well, back to saying that *riba* is legitimate gain. And this is truly wrong and blasphemous. It is clear now that the ownership factor alone cannot be made to explain the prohibition of interest in Islam. The speaker brought it up because he may be obsessed with *al-murabahah* and tries to find anything to prove his point.

In credit *murababah*, risk of ownership is fundamental. The same applies to spot sale (*bay' al muawadah*), forward sale (*salam* and *istisna'*), leasing (*ijarah*), trustee partnership (*al-qirad*), and general partnership (*musyarakah*). The Quran says that *al-bay'* is the alternative to *riba*. This is because the essence of *al-bay'* is mutual trade and cooperation (*ta'awun*) so that all economic agents taking part in the process of wealth creation are exposed to the risk of losing their assets. Unjustified enrichment is against the concept of *ta'awun* as *ta'awun* will not allow only one party risking their assets while the others do not.

Three
Reviving the Agriculture Sector – Bay' Salam Financing

Abdullah Badawi's concern on the decline of agriculture in Malaysia is both noble and realistic. Malaysia is way behind its neighbor in food production, buying rice from Thailand, Indonesia, and also the United States. Onions and flour are imported from India and Pakistan, and Malaysian beef is far more expensive than the Indian imports.

Making the manufacturing sector the engine of growth has made it hard to balance the need for self-sufficiency. Agricultural lands have been converted for industrial use. More mangrove swamps were reclaimed to make way for shopping malls, condominiums, and shop lots. And Malaysia has been buying fish from foreign fishermen who also invade its waters.

So what has gone wrong? Is Malaysia too small a country to achieve self-sufficiency in agriculture and food production? With more than 1.6 million acres of idle land in Malaysia, it's not size that matters. Can something be done to turn this land into productive uses? At least doing so can cut down the import bill. Converting these lands into agricultural use can be the answer.

Due to its fragmented nature, idle land may not be suitable for plantation crops such as oil palm, rubber, cocoa, and rice.But projects such as poultry, aquaculture, cattle rearing, and food commodities may provide good alternatives.

SAIFUL AZHAR ROSLY

The main problem is enforcement. There must be ways to convince landowners that reviving their lands is profitable, as the commercial value of food commodities is overwhelming. Refusal to take this challenge may require the government to start using the stick. But this is not a popular move. One remedy is to give farmers a financing scheme they can afford.

Financing of agriculture by the commercial banks today seems to tell the same story. In 1996, only 2 percent of total loans or RM4.5 billion was allocated to the agricultural sector. In Islamic banking, the figures are lower, with only RM152 million or only a 2.4 percent share of total financing.

Both banking systems have given undue attention to the property and construction sector, with the commercial and Islamic banks taking 17.2 percent and 18.4 percent of total financing respectively.

There are other avenues where the use of idle land can be pursued with more rigor. The role of Bank Pertanian Malaysia is vital and the RM600 million Fund for Food is a great opportunity to push for new land cultivation.

But these sources of financing often require collateral. This is problematic as most idle lands are Malay reserve lands. They hold multiple titles and make bad collaterals. What is needed now is a collateral-free financing.

In Islamic commercial law, the contract of *salam* provides even more goodies. *Salam* is both interest- and collateral-free. When traditional rural Malay farmers are looking for an interest-free financing, *salam* is the most suitable mode of financing for them.

In essence, *salam* is a prepayment sale, i.e., contract of sale with payments made today and goods delivered in the future. The buyer makes a sale order of a certain quantity of food commodity X, say onions, to be delivered by the seller in, say, six months. The price of the onions, known as the *salam price*, is set on the spot. Such an arrangement benefits both parties.

For example, the buyer can purchase the commodity at a discounted price. This is the *salam* price. If he buys it at the spot market six months later, he may have to pay more. Similarly, the seller receives early payments. He can use the money as working capital and to purchase agriculture machinery. In this way, he avoids interest-bearing loans.

Salam is not about commodity futures where delivery and payments are made in the future. *Salam* is a classical contract of sale that the Prophet (*pbuh*) fully supported, as it was able to aid farming in Medina, as farmers were paid in advance for their future produce. Unlike *al-bai-bithaman ajil* and *murabahah,* the *salam* contract does not invite juristic controversy. It is also free from the problem of legal tricks (*hilah*). But the problem now is how to apply *salam* in the banking business, since by nature it is not a contract of financing but rather a contract of sale.

We know well that a bank is a financial intermediary. It has no business to purchase and convert the commodities into final output. All it does is to provide financing. So how does one use *salam* as a mode of financing in the banking business?

The answer is not too difficult, but may require extra guts and risk-taking mindset to make it work successfully. This is because banks must be prepared to absorb loss arising from adverse price movement. And it cannot be applied in all cases of farming.

There are two models of *salam* financing. The first model deals with a plain *salam* contract taking place between a farmer and bank. Let's say Mr. Harun owns twenty acres of idle land in Perlis, suitable for mango farming. Current market price of *harum manis* mango is $6.00 per kilogram while wholesale price is $3.00 per kilogram. The mango trees will need three years to grow and mature.

The farm is estimated to produce about 100 tons of mangoes (100,000 kilograms). Mr. Harun needs capital to clear the land. Planting the trees and maintaining growth requires him to employ workers. Let's assume he needs at least $100,000 cash. An Islamic bank is currently offering a *salam* scheme.

As a company, the Islamic bank desires to make money from the *salam* scheme. But how? According to the *salam* contract, Mr. Harun is allowed to sell the mangoes, even though none is available now. But at what price? Certainly, it must be lower than the market price. Otherwise the bank has no incentive to buy the mangoes on *salam* basis. The bank and Mr. Harun can sit down and negotiate what price is most appropriate for both parties. For Mr. Harun, the *salam* price should also be lower than market price but not more than wholesale price. Otherwise the bank will not agree.

Suppose both parties set the *salam* price at $2.50 per kilogram. In this way, the bank will pay Mr. Harun $250,000 today in exchange for the ten tons of mangoes to be delivered in three years. From the *salam* price, it is easy to see how each party will earn profits from the *salam* transaction.

First, Mr. Harun should be able to earn $150,000 from his business. This is the value-addition factor. The cost of production is $100,000 while sales is $250,000. Mr. Harun is also happy because he has found a ready market, namely the bank. Although he gets less than wholesale price (i.e., $3.00 per kilogram), it does not bother him. He will have fewer headaches, since marketing is considered settled.

But the bank can even earn more if it goes the extra miles. It can either sell the mangoes wholesale or retail or both. Let's say the bank wishes to sell wholesale. Given the *salam* price at $2.20 per kilogram, he can sell the mangoes wholesale at $3.00 per kilogram and make $80,000 in profit (i.e., 80 cents x 100,000). In other words, the return on investment is $80,000/$250,000 = 32 percent or 10.6 percent per annum. But this is only the minimum.

The bank can also sell retail, but that can be a bit chaotic, as it will definitely involve marketing overheads. Worse still, the bank is not familiar with the trading business. Suppose the bank is able to supply the mangoes through its fruit chain venture companies (i.e., a company formed under a *musyarakah* venture) at the market price, the profit can be highly lucrative. In the above example, the margin is $280,000 (i.e., $2.80 x 100,000). If market overhead is $100,000, the bank can still earn a handsome $180,000 in profit. This is equivalent to ROI = 72 percent or 24 percent per annum

But the *salam* sale is not an easy one to do. There are risks involved. Usually, in *salam* both parties are exposed to the price risk. For example, the farmer may lose out if upon delivery the market price has gone up to, say $6.50 per kilogram. In this way, the *salam* price was a bit too low. Also, inflation may have cost him to pay more on overheads. This may trim down his profits. But once the *salam* price is set, there is no turning back. Mr. Harun cannot demand the bank to adjust the *salam* price upwards, as doing so will invalidate the *salam* contract.

Salam financing

Salam price < wholesale price < retail price

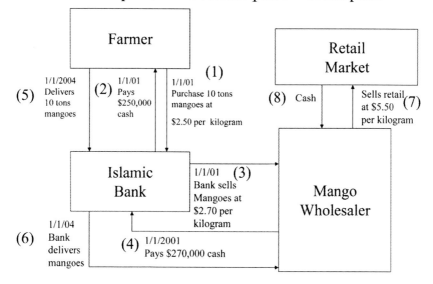

Figure 2.2 Salam Financing

Likewise, the bank is also exposed to market risk, i.e., risk arising from adverse price movement. If it fails to sell the mangoes at the right time and place, it may not be able to secure even the wholesale price. Marketing is a tedious job. It involves transport, storage, and inventory management. The bank must see that some kind of marketing infrastructure is in place before it is serious using *salam* as a mode of Islamic financing.

Finally, the bank can practice a refined version of *salam* if it chooses not to engage in real trading. This *salam* sale deals with one *salam* sale and a promise to buy and sell. Both must be independent. Otherwise, the *salam* is invalid. That is, *salam* sale cannot be executed based a contract to buy. This is to avoid the parties from conducting a conditional sale. In a sale with condition, the buyer must, say, sell goods X in order to buy goods Y. Such a contract is likely to harm one of the contracting parties.

The *salam* model is worth trying, given that the agriculture sector in Malaysia has been lagging behind. Although the decline can be attributed to marketing, subsidies, technology, and education, it is not wrong to say that conventional financing has not been friendly. Using interest-bearing loans with collateral has not been effective option.

It is important to know that the *'iwad* (i.e., equivalent countervalue) factor in *salam* financing is the price risk. Adverse market movement may see the bank unable to sell the produce at the targeted price. The producer makes money by sheer work and effort (*kasb*). He is also liable to damages incurred if the delivered produce does not conform to quality. This is the liability (*daman*) factor. The farmer may also lose out if market price increases above the *salam* price. In this manner, unlike *riba*, *salam* is a fair business transaction as both parties observe the requirement of *'iwad*.

Four
Islamic Hire-Purchase

An official quest for a floating rate financial instrument for the Islamic banking business was first echoed by Bank Negara in 1997, when Malaysia experienced a severe credit squeeze and a hike in interest rates. To some extent, Islamic banks were badly hit, as they cannot adjust the cost of financing to changes in interest rates. In the 1998 Bank Negara Annual Report, overdependence on *al-bai-bithaman ajil* (BBA) mode of financing was cited as the main culprit.

The contract of leasing (*al-ijarah)* seems to be the likely complement to BBA, if not as a substitute. The nature of *al-ijarah* allows flexibility in rental payments. This is made possible when both lessee and lessor renegotiate rental prices over time. This periodic adjustment can help Islamic banks make the appropriate response to unwarranted changes in cost of funds.

But it is the lack of legal infrastructure that puts a brake on the application of *al-ijarah* in banking. First, as stipulated by the Banking and Financial Institution Act 1992, a bank cannot directly operate a leasing business under one roof. It can do so by forming a subsidiary leasing company under the purview of the Company Act. Islamic banking divisions, too, are governed by BAFIA 1992, so the *al-ijarah* option is relatively closed here.

There are two main types of leasing. The one described in the above is a true or operational lease (*al-ijarah 'ain*). The second type of leasing, namely *al-ijarah 'amal* has less to do with the banking business, as it mainly deals with employer-employee relationship.

The main issue here concerns *al-ijarah 'ain* or operational/true lease. In true leasing, the ownership of an asset remains with the owner of the asset. To some extent, an Islamic bank that runs under the Islamic Banking Act 1983 is licensed to operate a true leasing business under one roof. The bank can enormously reap the advantages of true lease when some form of tax relief such as investment tax credits or an investment allowances are granted. Tax savings may also include deductions for depreciation of the leased property.

From the viewpoint of the lessee, operational lease allows him to enjoy full financing of the cost of capital goods. No down payments are required, as seen in other modes of financing such as loans. With relatively no pressure of margin requirement to meet part of the cost of leased equipment, it enables the lessee to retain his cash reserves to cater to other equally important business needs.

One more important advantage of operational lease to the lessee is the tax benefit. To a company, lease rentals as operating expenses are tax deductible. For Islamic banking, however, applying true lease will mean seeing the rental property appearing as a fixed asset on the balance sheet.

But soon, *al-ijarah 'ain* must deal with the demands of Hire-Purchase financing. According to the Hire-Purchase Act 1967, hire-purchase is a contract of lease with an option to purchase. This resembles the Islamic contract *of al-ijarah munthania bittamlek (AIMAT)* sometimes known as *al-ijara wa iqtina,* i.e., leasing ending with ownership. The Malaysian version is known as *al-ijarah thumma al-bay' (AITAB)* i.e., leasing ending with sale.

There are three main types *of al-ijarah munthania bittamlek* (AIMAT). First, AIMAT by way of gift (*hibah*), which means the transfer of legal title for no consideration or price. Second, AIMAT through transfer of title at the end of the lease for a token consideration or at a nominal price. Third, AIMAT through sale prior the end of the lease term for a price that is equivalent to the remaining *al-ijarah* installments. In some cases, AIMAT also means a gradual transfer of ownership resulting from a share-buyback arrangement between the lessee and the lessor.

One must not be misled to infer that the Islamic version of Hire-Purchase i.e., *al-ijarah munthania bittamlek* is equivalent to a financial or capital lease. Firstly, conventional hire-purchase is a mere term loan with an option to purchase. Hire-purchase in this sense does not see true or operational lease in action with a purchase option. In this sense, conventional hire-purchase is a loan, while *al-ijarah munthania bittamlek* is not. In *al-ijarah munthania bittamlek,* any attempt to make the lessor free from holding ownership risk is tantamount to making it an equal to conventional hire-purchase.

Secondly, *al-ijarah munthania bittamlek* is a true lease with a promise to sell. It does not entail two concurrent contracts of leasing (*ijarah*) and sale (*al-bay'*). The contract of sale is made separate from the contract of leasing. The former will be executed only when the lessor agree to do so when all rental payments are made.

What I am trying to say here is that any form of AIMAT designed under the purview of the conventional Hire-Purchase Act 1967 is bound to violate the true nature of Islamic Hire-Purchase. This is simply because an Islamic Hire-Purchase under the pretext of *al-ijarah munthania bittamlek* is a true lease plus the promise to sell. This is quite different from conventional hire-purchase, which is actually a financial lease with a purchase option.

The *Shariah* has made lease or rental income lawful by virtue of the ownership risk of the asset taken up by lessor. Hence, in Islamic commercial law, *ijarah* always implies true or operation lease. Whether an Islamic bank desires to use AITAB or AIMAT, the *ijarah* component must always be a true lease.

In a true lease, the lessor holds ownership, which means that he must pay for the insurance, tax and other owner-related expenses. The lessor is also required to bear cost of maintenance. Both risk and maintenance constitute the *'iwad* (i.e., equal countervalue) for a given sum of rental income.

The elements of *'iwad,* however, are not found in conventional hire-purchase. The bank does not hold ownership but claim the right of disposal (i.e., the right to sell the rental assets when the lessee fails to pay up) until lease payments are completed while the lessee pays maintenance expenses.

Finally, any future attempt to introduce a new version of Islamic Hire-Purchase instrument using the contract of AIMAT or AITAB must call for the amendment of the existing Hire-Purchase Act 1967 to accommodate the true lease features in all hire-purchase transactions. If that fails, a new independent Islamic Hire-Purchase Act must be formulated to downplay the problems pointed out in the above, failure of which will force Islamic banking to adopt the financial leasing model while at the same time using the Islamic label.

Five
Bay' al-'Inah Overdraft

Using *murabahah* and *bai-bithaman ajil* trade financing is applicable when it involves the sale and purchase of fixed assets. For example, when a contractor needs an additional crane to speed up his work, he can purchase the equipment from an Islamic bank at a credit price payable on installment basis. However, if he needs cash to pay for wages, salaries, advertising, utilities, and rental, it may be difficult to use the credit sale facilities, since these items are not tangible objects.

In conventional financing, the above expenses can be met when the entrepreneur is granted an overdraft facility by a commercial bank. An overdraft is an advance or loan granted under a current account, whereby the customer is authorized to draw on an account up to an approved limit. It is given out to finance working capital and short-term transactions. Interest on the overdraft is calculated using a simple interest formula, $I = PRT/100$, with P as the overdrawn balance at the end of each day, R as the rate quoted, and T as the number of days divided by 365.

The interest-free banking system today has made significant contributions to the development of Islamic overdraft facilities. They are marketed using different names such as *al-nakad, al-ujr, al-tamwill, bay' al-inah,* etc.

Let us now see how the Islamic overdraft works. Suppose Mr. Kasim needs $100,000 to meet his operating expenses. The contract requires him to sell an asset worth $100,000 to the bank. Mr. Kasim will then obtain the $100,000 cash, which will be credited to his *Al-wadiah* account. Next, when the first transaction expires, Mr. Kasim will purchase the asset from the bank at a higher price based on the *al-bai-bithaman ajil* contract, where he will pay the bank on an installment basis. At the end, we can easily see that Mr. Kasim gets what he wants, that is the cash, while the bank gets its principal plus the profit.

Apparently, there is a problem of repeatable sales, which is also found in *bay' al-inah* (sale of cash). *Bay' al-inah,* according to the *Maliki, Hanafi* and *Hanbali* school, is a void contract, while it is acceptable (*valid*) but discouraged (*makruh*) according to the *Shafie'* and *Zahiri* school. The latter says that both sales, i.e., sale of asset by Mr. Kasim to bank and sale of the same asset by the bank to Mr. Kasim, are both valid since they have dutifully observed all the principles of *'aqd* in the transaction. One cannot use intention or *niyah* as a reason to disqualify the contract.

Let us again see what is *bay' al-inah* and what the *niyah* factor has to do with it. The point is both parties want to get things done. The entrepreneur needs money to settle his bills, while the bank wants some form of guaranteed returns from his capital. In *bay' al-inah*, let's say Amir needs $25,000 cash. To get one, the bank will sell a "fictitious" object to Amir at a credit price of $30,000. Payment is made on an installment basis.

From the second sale, Amir will hold ownership again. He now sells the asset to the bank $25,000 on cash term. He therefore got the cash money he wanted while the bank earns $5,000 from the credit sale. The $5,000 is considered lawful as it is derived from sale and not loan.

But many are doubtful too. It seems that both parties are pretentious and have no commitment to the sale contract. The fact that both Amir and the bank have no intention of using the asset as any consumer does betrays one principle of contract in Islam, namely the objective of contract (*maudu'ul aqdi*).

Using *bay al-'inah* invites another problem. The overdraft facility charges users on the amount of drawdown made. The unused balance is free from any financial charges. But the number of drawdowns, say, per month made by users are not known. It varies according to business activities. Sometimes a customer withdraws ten times per month and pays back six times. At other times, he may withdraw five times but pay up more regularly. It is hard for banks to predict accurately the number of drawdowns and repayments. But this pattern poses no problem to conventional overdraft facilities, as the bank charges interest as the customers make their drawdowns. Unfortunately, using *al-bai-bithaman ajil* plus cash sale (i.e., *bay' al-'inah*) can be painful.

This is true since the BBA contract specifies a selling price i.e., the facilities granted. This price is also based on the number of times the customer makes withdrawals and repayments. For example, in the BBA facility, the customer has set a schedule target of fifteen withdrawals and twenty repayments per facility. Remember that the more repayments made, the less he pays interest. However, failure to observe the schedule will mean either paying more or less to the bank. If the targeted schedule of drawdowns and repayments creates a $25,000 Islamic overdraft facility, an unexpected change in the schedule may overshoot or undershoot it. In both ways, the selling price is altered and serves to invalidate the BBA sale.

It is quite clear now that the BBA Islamic overdraft facility can be inconvenient to use. No customer can provide a drawdown and repayment schedule and stick to it diligently. Business temperaments can change payment patterns. Using a system of rebate (*ibra'*) can help but the transaction cost can be quite demanding.

Six
Al-Ijarah Thumma Al-Bai' (AITAB) Car Financing

Purchasing a car on credit can be made possible via the hire-purchase contract. The rental paid (i.e., term charges) by the buying party runs on a debt agreement that implicates interest as *riba*. The Holy Quran says, "Allah has made trade or commerce (*al-bay'*) lawful but made *riba* unlawful" (Al-Baqarah: 275). Finding an alternative to the interest-bearing hire-purchase would mean resorting to the principle of *al-bay'*. One such commercial contract is *al-ijarah* (leasing).

However, the contract of conventional hire-purchase provides the lessee an option to purchase the leased property. An option contract provides the buyer the right to buy or not to buy. If he chooses to buy the car, the lessor must do so by selling him the car. This may imply that *al-ijarah* alone may not constitute the contract suitable to replace conventional hire-purchase.

Apparently, Islamic jurists (*fuqaha*) today have introduced an Islamic version of hire-purchase known as *al-ijarah thumma al-bay'* (AITAB) meaning leasing (*al-ijarah*) ending with sale (*al-bay'*). Does this imply that AITAB is a contract of lease with an option to purchase the asset?

In *fiqh*, *al-ijarah* means "to give something on rent." Literally, *al-ijarah* or *al-ajr* means substitute, compensation, recompense, indemnity, consideration, return or countervalue. *Al-ijarah* has two types of usufruct (*manfa'at*):

1. Usufruct of property or capital assets (*manfa'at al-'ayn*)
2. Usufruct of labor, employment, and service (*manfa'at al-'amal*)

Based on the above, *al-ijarah* is not only related to the leasing of property but also services, normally termed as employment. In *al-ijarah* of services, the employer is called *musta'jir* and the employee *'ajir*. The contract between the two parties involves the employment of the services of the *'ajir* based on an agreed pre-fixed wage or salary (*'ujrah*) given to him as reward for the services rendered in the transaction.

Thus, irrespective of whether the employer is making a loss or a windfall profit, he must pay the predetermined wages or salaries of his employees as specified in the *al-ijarah* contract. For example, in a corporation, under *ijarah 'amal,* the management receives salary. Likewise, a similar contract is used in government services.

In AITAB, the contract of *ijarah 'ain* is applied. The lessor is called *mu'jir,* while the lessee or hirer is known as *musta'jir* and the rent payable to the lessor is called *'ujrah. Al-ijarah* is not a sale, because in the latter, the ownership of property is transferred to the purchaser. In *al-ijarah,* the lessee has only the right to use the property but not the ownership of property.

Some basic rules of *al-ijarah* are as follows:

- *Al-ijarah* is valid only with consent of both parties to the contract. That is, to avoid *gharar,* the contracted usufruct or *manfaat* has to be absolutely ascertained.
- The usufruct must be lawful and must have a valuable use.
- All liabilities arising from ownership shall be borne by the lessor who owns the rental property.
- The rent, period, and purpose of the lease must be clearly specified.

In theory, the contract of *al-ijarah thumma al-bay'* shall consist of two different contracts, namely:

1) The contract of lease (*al-ijarah 'ain)*
2) The contract of sale (*al-bay')*

Al-ijarah and *al-bay'* are both categorized under the contract of exchange (*'uqud al-mubadalah*). The former relates to the exchange of usufruct for money, while the latter involves the exchange of goods for money. Actually, the contract of *al-ijarah thumma al-bay'* is not readily found classical book of *fiqh,* probably due to historical reasons as the need for such a contract does not exist.

Today, when high asset prices make it no longer possible to buy on a cash basis, most people resort to easy or installment payments. The need to create a new product that is *Shariah* consistent and able to provide people a cushion of comfort has given way to *al-ijarah thumma al-bay'.*

In AITAB, the contract of *al-ijarah* runs separately from the contract of *al-bay'.* Since both contracts are executed in succession, a new contract called *al-ijarah thumma al-bay'* (AITAB) can be used to describe the process of converting an *al-ijarah* contract into a sale contract. What is observed now is a new contract of leasing where the hirer will eventually own the rented property, which is also similar in concept to conventional hire purchase.

However, one must be careful what really constitutes the AITAB under *Shariah* rulings. This is because current AITAB runs under the Hire-Purchase Act 1967. In this way, it has to follow what the HP Act says. Accordingly, the HP Act says that in hire-purchase transactions, the lessee is given the option to buy the rental property before or on maturity. Further elements of AITAB under the Hire-Purchase Act 1967 are given below:

- The bank will purchase the asset from the car dealer.
- The bank as an owner of the asset will lease the asset to the customer according to the agreed upon terms and conditions, specifying market rental values and leasing period.
- The customer or hirer can return the goods at any time before the option to buy is exercised, and hence, terminate the agreement. The customer is not obliged to pay all the rentals.
- The customer or hirer elects to purchase the good when all the rentals specified in the agreement have been paid;
- The bank will receive the lease payments. The bank ensures that the option to purchase the car is made at a nominal value. The price of the car is equal to the total lease payments received by the bank during the leasing period.

- The transfer of ownership from the bank to the customer will take place at the end of the leasing period as soon as the customer exercises the option to purchase the car.

Based on the above, AITAB under the HP Act 1967 has put together the contract of sale together with the contract of leasing. The former is granted on the basis of the option clause. This, however, does not conform to the standard of the Accounting and Auditing Organization for Islamic Financial Institution (AAOIFI), according to which *Al-ijarah thumma al-bay' (AITAB)* or *al-ijarah munthahiya bittamleek* (AIMAT) is a contract of leasing with a promise (*wa'ad*) to sell. It must not be understood as a mixture or combination of the *al-ijarah* and *al-bay'* contracts. It is not a leasing contract with a condition to sell (*al-bay'*) Instead, the true AITAB shall consist of two separate contracts. It implicates two different contracts executed at two different stages. These stages are:

Stage 1: Executing the contract of true leasing (*al-ijarah 'ain*) with a promise to sell

Stage 2: Once lease period expires and the lessee completed all payments, the lessor will fulfill his promise by executing the contract of sale (*al-bay'*). That is, he will offer the asset for sale to the lessee.

Based on the above, it is clear by now that AITAB is a contract of leasing with a promise to sell the asset. The sale is made when the rental period expires and total payments are finally completed. The lessor will sell the asset at a nominal price once the last rental payment is made.

The AITAB product under the purview of HP ACT 1967 is also required to observe the interest-bearing mechanism. For example, if the customer wishes to discontinue the *al-ijarah* contract, he will be offered to buy the asset at a price equivalent to the difference between the total rental and the amount he has already paid as rent. For example, if the total rental is $30,000 and he terminated the lease after three years or has paid rental equivalent to ($500 x 36) or $21,000, the contract of AITAB requires him to purchase the asset for $9,000 (i.e., $30,000 – $21,000) less rebate (*ibra*).

Since AITAB has to operate within the Hire Purchase Act, it is necessary to understand some features of the Act. The Hire Purchase Act

1967 came into force on 11 April, 1968. Previous to this date, there was no specific legislation to control and regulate Hire Purchase in Malaysia, and Hire Purchase agreements came under the ambit of the ordinary laws of contract, and were covered by the Sale of Goods Ordinance 1957 as "agreement to sell."

However, it must be noted that the Hire Purchase Act 1967 remains a law governing an interest-bearing term loan granted by a bank to the borrower. In this way, AITAB assumes identical structure, as does conventional hire-purchase. The bank as lessor holds the right to sell the asset if the lessee defaults on payments. This is because the bank serves as a prospective owner of the rental property. One who buys a car, for example, should look closely at the legal papers. But ironically, the bank as an owner does not seem to fulfill its obligation as an owner of property, since it is the customers who are made to maintain the property and pay tax and insurance obligations.

The true model of AITAB can be a headache to many bankers. This is because:

1. It requires the bank as the true lessor to maintain the rental asset and fulfill other obligations as any car owner is supposed to do. In this manner, the bank must pay for insurance and road tax as well as car maintenance such as minor and major fine-tuning. This includes periodic change of engine and car parts such as timing belt, suspension, and exhaust pipe. This is done to observe the true leasing.
2. Customer cannot be forced to pay the remaining balance if he fails to pay rentals. He can inform the bank his intention to terminate the contract and not be liable to return the lessor any sum of money. This is done to conform to the concept of true leasing.
3. AITAB offers the customer a full-financing scheme. He does not have to put up a down payment as practiced by current AITAB under HP Act 1967.
4. Car maintenance rests on the bank as lessor. However, if the engine broke down due to negligence of customer, he shall be liable for the repair expenses.
5. Rental under true AITAB will be much higher than that under current AITAB model. The rental shall include cost of rental assets and cost of maintenance as mentioned above.

Prospective customers will be glad to use the true AITAB model. Although the rental can be relatively higher, customers will be less burdened with payments that lessor should be paying in first place. In the HP agreement, the bank claims to be a prospective owner. But why has it been able to transfer the obligation of maintenance to the customers while securing the legal rights of repossession and disposal?

Seven
Al-Ijarah and Leverage Leasing

One of the most-quoted characteristics of *riba* (interest) is the contractual increase on the principal loan. For a two-year $200,000 loan at 10 percent interest rate per annum, the loan agreement requires the debtor to pay the creditor a total sum of $240,000. Which means before the actual use of the loan takes place, the bank has already made a $40,000 profit, although in accrual term. In other words, although the loan is $200,000, the debt is much more, i.e., $240,000.

Since Islam prohibits *riba,* does the prohibition apply to property and labor, since a predetermined income in the form of rent, wages, and salaries is implicated? Is leasing a piece of land to a used car dealer for $5,000 a month considered *riba* since the rental is a prefixed sum? Is the signing of a contract that pays a new employee a predetermined monthly income of $2,000 considered *riba*? Of course not.

So what distinguishes "income from *riba*" from "income from leasing," as both constitute a contractual return in the form of interest, rent, and wages? What is the position of leasing in Islamic commercial law?

Firstly, leasing or *al-ijarah* is a commercial contract. It is neither a loan (*qard*) nor spot sale (*bay' al-mutlak*). *Riba* arises from loan (*riba al-qard*) and sales (*riba al-buyu'*). *Al-ijarah,* on the other hand, deals with the buying and selling of usufruct (*manfaat*) and not the rental property. Thus, by definition, *riba* and rent are mutually exclusive.

117

However, this cannot always be true when *riba* is defined as the rental on money. When money is treated as a commodity, it can become a rental property whereby interest is paid as rent.

Generally, leasing activities can be classified into two, namely true/operational lease and leverage/capital lease. In a true lease, the lessor who owns the property assumes the risk of ownership. He receives the pre-fixed rental income and retains the tax benefits associated with ownership, such as depreciation allowances.

True leasing however, is not practiced in banking, since the banking law does not allow banks to own assets and properties other than for the purposes of lending and borrowing. Thus, to do true leasing business, a bank must form a subsidiary company which is now governed by the Company's Act.

Banks can, however, operate leverage leasing. It is a three-party lease governed by the Hire-Purchase (HP) Act 1967. Under the HP Act, the bank grants an interest-bearing loan to customers. Although the term "hire" implies leasing, in actual practice, leverage leasing is simply a loan with interest obligation. For example, the customer applies a bank loan to pay for the goods he intended to purchase. He pays the rental over a period, which consists of the capital and interest components. Unlike plain loans, HP loans allow the customer to purchase the goods when the rental period expires. This is quite different from true lease, where no transfer of ownership takes place.

The Islamic alternative to conventional hire-purchase must therefore refer to the contract of *al-ijarah*. Let us see the nature of leasing in Islam and how it differs from conventional practices. In Islamic *fiqh, al-ijarah* means "to give something on rent," but *al-ijarah* is not only about leasing property, but also services, which we normally term as employment. Thus, the contract of *al-ijarah* can be used in two different situations, namely those involving services (*ijarah 'ain*) as well as asset and property (*ijarah 'amal*).

The main thrust of hire-purchase is the hire of asset and properties. In this sense, *al-ijarah 'ain* is most relevant here. But *ijarah 'ain* is true leasing and it does not deal with conventional financial leasing (i.e., hire-purchase) where 1) the payment and receipts of interest are taking place and 2) lessor does not have ownership of the asset.

The subject matter of *al-ijarah* in true leasing relates to the usufructs (*manfaah*) arising from rental property. In fact, these activities form a significant proportion of investments in Lembaga Tabung Haji, Baitulmal, and YPIEM. In Bank Islam (M) Bhd, *al-ijarah* encompasses about 10 percent of total assets. However these are not based on true leasing contract.

The contract of *al-ijarah* is not new in the leasing business. The lessor is called *mu'jir,* while the lessee is known as *musta'jir* and the rent payable to the lessor is called *'ujrah. Al-ijarah* does not involve sales of tangible object, but rather sales of intangible, namely the usufruct (*manfaah*). The lessee holds the right (*hak*) to use the property but not sell it. Some basic rules of *al-ijarah* are as follows:

- The subject of the lease must have a valuable use.
- All liabilities arising from ownership shall be borne by the lessor.
- The rent, period, and the purpose of the lease must be clearly specified.
- It is a risk-bearing contract, since the lessor holds ownership of property.

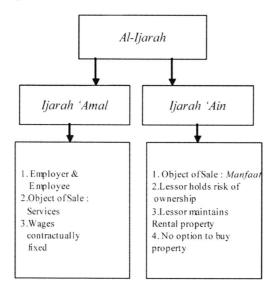

Figure 2.3 *Al-Ijarah*

The Islamic Banking Act 1983, in theory, allows Islamic banks to practice true leasing. In this way, banks can purchase heavy equipment and properties, which subsequently appear in the balance sheet as fixed assets. However, leasing in Islamic banking today has less to do with true leasing. Rather, it conforms to the conventional Hire-purchase Act 1967 but this time uses the profits instead of interest as term charges.

For example, a Proton Waja has a $70,000 price tag. After paying a 20 percent down payment, the customer applied for an *al-ijarah thuma al-bay'* (AITAB) facility. The bank purchases the car for $56,000 and leases it out to the customer. Monthly rental shall consist of the capital component and profit from the renting business. If the bank wants a 6 percent profit per annum, and a seven-year rental contract, then expected profit is $23,520. The rental shall be equal to $70,000 + $23,520 = $93,520, that is about $1,113.3 per month.

So why does profit created from true leasing is considered permissible (*halal*) while profit from leverage leasing prohibited (*haram*)? The answer is not a difficult one. All business dealings in Islam must observe the principle of *"al-ghorm bil ghonm"* meaning that there shall be no reward without risk-taking (*ghorm*). The same applies with the *al-ijarah* business. The risk element in *al-ijarah* consists of the following:

a. Market risk: the lessor must own the rental property. In this manner, the property is subject to price risk. The value of the property may drop, causing the owner capital depreciation.
b. Operational risk: the lessor must pay for maintenance cost, even though it may surpass the rental on some occasions.

Thus, even though the rental is fixed, there is no guarantee that the lessor receives capital protection and pays nothing more. The risk he is exposed to deserves him the fixed rental. Unlike *riba*, the fixed rental contains an equivalent countervalue (*'iwad*), namely the risk incurred by the lessor. Thus, by nature, *al-ijarah* is equal to true leasing. In this manner, the contract of *al-ijarah thumma al-bay'* (AITAB), requires the lessor (i.e., bank) to hold ownership of the rental during the leasing period. It must also provide provisions on maintenance that are both negotiable and mutually agreed by both parties.

Eight
How BBA home financing deals with interest rate volatilities

Bank Negara's recent move to curb bank lending on property is good news. The property bubble in neighboring Thailand is a good lesson to all, and Malaysia may be next. Bank Negara reported that banking system loans grew by nearly 28 percent to RM72 billion in 1995. More worrying is the loan growth to the property sector that rose from 26 percent in 1995 to 30 percent in 1996. The high demand for property is expected to increase the demand for manufactured products such as furniture and appliances, as well as electronic goods. But the loan to manufacturing grew only by 14 percent compared to nearly 30 percent in 1995.

Malaysia has been enjoying rapid growth for nearly a decade. During the boom times, risks are usually sidelined. Banks are willing to make loans simply because there is no indication of a slowdown. Loan defaults are no cause for concern. Firms are confident they can deliver the goods to fulfill loan obligations. It's like what Thailand's Pin Chakkapak, the Takeover King, said: "We have no defined structure. Touch and go, play it by ear, that has always been the way we operate."

The speculative nature of the Malaysian property market is not new by any standard. Indeed, there are many genuine buyers around, but existing policies to curb speculative purchases have no special mechanism to differentiate the speculators from the genuine buyers. Is there anything significant banks can do to prevent the onslaught of property bubbles in this country?

Bank Negara Malaysia may have done their part, but what have the commercial banks done to help make property prices in this country affordable to the local people? If one adheres to the law of supply and demand, it usually works in favor of the affluent foreign buyers and the local upper middle class people. But what about majority Malaysians who are desperately looking for simple a home to live in?

If Islamic banking is considered one way to help curb rampant property purchases, it's worthwhile to see how the system handles customer home purchases. The facility offered is based on a deferred sale contract known as *al-bai-bithaman ajil* (BBA). Instead of giving a loan, the bank theoretically purchases the house from the developer at market price (i.e., cost price) and sells it to the customer at a mark-up price.

The difference between the market price (i.e., cost price to the bank) and the mark-up price (selling price) constitutes the profit the bank makes over the installment period.

Here, profit earned from BBA is considered *halal* since it is based on a sale and purchase contract, rather than a loan. One unique feature of the BBA facility is the selling price itself, which is fixed throughout the duration of the tenure. Any change in price will make the contract null and void. The bank must make sure that the selling price remains unchanged till the contract expires.

And conventional bankers are able to do just the opposite. The selling price of a BBA facility is similar to the nominal value of a loan plus the total interest payment. But interest rates vary from time to time, as dictated by market forces. Any variation in the profit portion of the selling price will caused the selling price to change as well.

Interest rates on loans are adjustable to reflect changes in the cost of funds. But the same does not apply to BBA. The imputed profit rate must stay fixed even though cost of funds has changed. Therefore, when Islamic banks see higher interest rates on loans, there is nothing they can do to upgrade the BBA profit rate, as this will alter existing BBA price. Conventional banks can revise interest rates upward, and customers may have to pay more monthly. This is not possible in Islamic banking because by taking a similar move, it will increase the contractual selling price, thus violating the BBA contract as the principle of *'aqd* requires only one price in one sale.

The same argument holds in the case of default payments. In the past, there is no penalty on late payments simply because penalties will increase the selling price of the asset.

These two benefits of the BBA facility, namely: 1) fixed selling price, and 2) no penalty on late payments, have made the BBA facility a better alternative to loans, especially when market interest rates are rising. Customers who expect rising interest rates will opt for BBA to avoid paying more interest if they have taken a loan instead. The *Shariah* constraint imposed on the BBA, therefore, makes it a popular alternative in the event of rising interest rates, especially among non-Muslim customers.

Bank Negara's move to curb lending on housing purchases may reduce the demand for BBA and loan facilities, but only on houses costing more than $150,000. This credit rationing device is likely to generate better results, since banks now are only allowed to apportion a specified amount of loans to meet the demand for more expensive units, which normally are more exposed to speculative buying.

At this juncture, if the move tends to dampen the property market and the economy as a whole, the incoming recession may indeed hurt Islamic banking, since customers will opt to use loans rather than BBA. This is because interest rates are expected to fall during a recession and any further decline will mean lower adjusted monthly loan payments.

But the BBA facility cannot adjust the selling price downwards, as this may violate the sale agreement. Homebuyers will now see BBA as inferior to loans, as it is relatively more expensive. Subsequently, the demand for BBA is expected to fall more than the demand for loans.

Nine
Islamic Factoring

Whether the stock market is bearish or bullish will not change the fact that companies today are always on the move to improve cash flow. Cash is needed to purchase new equipment, expand business, increase working capital, and build up stocks and inventories. Without ample cash reserves, business resorted to bank loans. But to obtain a bank loan, the company must first command a good track record and ability to pay, which are hard to find.

One way to obtain cash without too much dependence on bank loans is factoring. The factoring business had an early start in the US in 1889, but is a relative newcomer in this country, having been introduced in 1981. Last year, total factoring volume was RM7.5 billion, up by 30 percent from RM3.3 billion in 1993. Today, there are more than 17 companies running the factoring business.

In essence, factoring is about selling or trading of debts involving three parties. These debts are the account receivables owned by the company. An account receivable is an amount due from a customer for goods and services sold on credit. It represents an investment of cash only when it is sold through factoring. Management of receivables is, therefore, crucial for business, as the receivables will become bad debts when guided by poor collection policy.

Before any Islamic input is given, let us take a look at a conventional operation. Company A purchases a cutting machine from Company B for

$100,000. The former was given a credit term of three months. In other words, Company B's accounts receivable has increased by $100,000.

But due to some unexpected investment opportunities, Company B needs $100,000 rather urgently, but most of its assets are stuck in the receivables. Through business factoring, Company B can sell the $100,000 receivable to a factoring company. Here, Company B becomes the client to the factoring company.

If the factoring involves both credit administration, such as administrating the sales ledger of the client, credit management and collection services, and financing, the cost of factoring will include a service charge. In addition, a discount charge is made on a day-to-day basis on the actual amount of funds used, based on the rate equivalent to that normally applied on unsecured overdraft facilities.

Thus, factoring as described above is a basic debt-financing activity involving the selling of receivables at an implicit rate of interest or discount rate. In Islamic financing, similar procedures are observed, except that now the contract is based on a sale and purchase of debt (*bay'al-dayn*). In a contract of *bay'al-dayn*, the object of trade (*mahallul 'aqdi*) is, therefore, the debt (*dayn*) evidenced by invoice. The process of Islamic factoring is given below:

1. Company A issues a purchase order to Company B, a client to the Factor Company.
2. Company B supplies goods to Company A on a credit term, say three months.
3. Company B sells the debt (account receivable) to the Factor Company.
4. Factor Company advances cash payments to Company B (say, 80 percent of total amount).
5. Factor Company sends factored invoice and notice of assignment to Company A.
6. Company A makes full payment to Factor Company at the end of the three-month credit term.
7. Factor Company releases the 20 percent balance to Company B after deducting service and other factoring charges.

The above procedures are adopted from the model of Amanah Factor Sdn Bhd, the first company to offer Islamic factoring in Malaysia. Simply, the model is about selling goods X valued at $100,000 to the factor company for $80,000. The debt (*dayn*) namely, the account receivable is considered an asset (*al-mal*) and thus, like any other object of trade, it can be traded at any price.

However, it is worthwhile to look at some of the inconsistencies arising from the use of *bay'al-dayn* in factoring. Looking at account receivable as an asset or property (*al-mal*) is also problematic, given the fact that Islamic accounting today is based on the cash rather than the accrual method. That is, profit is recognized only when cash is received. An asset, like land, can be sold for cash.

In the factoring model, an account receivable i.e., debt (*dayn*) is sold for cash less the discount rate. For example, the debt of $50,000 is sold for $42,000. Debt is exchanged for cash. This is what *bay' al-dayn* (sale of debt) is all about. In the above example, we are looking at sale of debt (*bay' al-dayn*) at a discount.

The question now is, what exactly is the rationale for discounting? Practitioners are rather silent on this point. Although there are benefits one can enjoy from factoring, pertinent issues such the *Shariah* legitimacy of *bay'al-dayn* should not be kept behind closed doors.

The contract of *hiwalah* can be useful the application of discounted *bay' al-dayn* in factoring. *Hiwalah* involves a transfer of debt (*dayn*) from the owner of receivables to the factoring company who will collect the payments from the debtor. But *hiwalah* does not permit any form of discounting. In what way a factor company runs without a discounting system is hard to see, since factoring is business and not charity.

Ten
Al–Rahn Islamic Pawn Broking

I slamic commercial contracts play an important role in Islamic finance, since they provide viable alternatives to interest-bearing instruments. These contracts can find ready applications and would not hinder the growth of corporate business in this country. Asset purchases can be made possible via *murabahah* and *al-bai-bithaman ajil* financing. For business expansion and start-ups, the *al-ijarah, mudarabah,* and *musyarakah* products have good potential.

But what if someone needs cash to pay debts or settle a down payment, buy shares, house renovation, or even to go on vacation? The above instruments may not help us get the cash we want. Currently, interest-bearing overdraft facilities, personal loans, and credit cards are available to fulfill customers' credit needs. Those who don't qualify may find comfort in pawnbroking. The desperate ones look for the loan sharks in town.

Despite the numerous credit alternatives available, one point is certain—that people don't like formalities and paperwork. Going to the bank for a small loan, say $1,000, may require them to surrender their personal documents. And choosing an illegal money lender can be outright risky and dangerous too. But what if you desperately need a quick $500? School opens next week and the kids at home need new books, uniforms, etc. Yes, most people would think of the local pawnshops.

A pawnbroking operation is relatively straightforward. The borrower simply needs to place a pledge or security for the amount of debt needed. For example, the pledged asset is a gold ring valued at $2,000.

The pawnbroker will lend the debtor $1,000 and charge a monthly interest of $2 for every $100 lent (2 percent monthly interest rate). The payment period usually takes six months. At the expiration date, the debtor is expected to pay $1,000 plus $120 interest ($20 x 6 months).

If the debtor fails to pay this sum, he can draw a new agreement for a new six-month extension at the same monthly interest rate on condition that he pays up the first six months' interest. In other words, if he plans to pay up in twelve months, he is paying 24 percent interest rate (i.e., $240/$1,000 = 24 percent) per annum. And this is much higher than the market rate.

Pawnbroking does not cater to payment by installments. The borrower must pay a lump sum of $1,000 plus interest within the specified period. Failure to pay will mean losing the collateral.

How does a conventional pawnbroker benefit from the deal other than the interest earned? Some say that customers are not financially sound and have little chance to redeem the pledge. Suppose the real value of the pledge is $1,500 but valued at $800. A pawnbroker may only lend $300. If the customer fails to pay up, his total loss is $1,500 - $336 = $1,164.

Apparently, conventional pawnbrokers make money through the high interest earned and the surplus gained from the ownership transfers. What then is Islam's alternative to interest-based pawnbroking? Islamic law offers a commercial contract known as *al-rahn*.

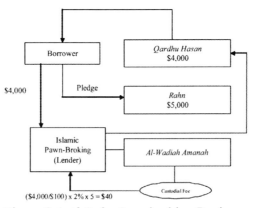

Figure 2.4 *Al-Rahn* Pawnbroking Business

It is presently in operation at Bank Rakyat Malaysia and some other non-bank firms in Kelantan and Terengganu. Currently, Bank Islam (M) Bhd, Bank Pertanian and EON Bank also provide similar facilities.

In the *Hedaya*, *rahn* literally signifies the detention of a thing (the pledge or security) on account of a claim that may be answered by means of that thing. In other words, in a *rahn* contract, we are simply looking at a collateralized debt without interest.

Given that interest (*riba*) is not implicated in the *rahn* pawnbroking business, how would a company running an Islamic pawn business (*murtahin*) make money? The answer is simple. Profits take the form of storage fees charged on the pledged property. There is a standard formula how these fees are determined. For example, in the case of a pledge valued at $1,000, the pledger (*rahin*) is required to pay a storage fee, say a percentage of the total value of the pledge.

According to Bank Rakyat, a pledge valued at less than $1,000 will cost the *rahin* (1,000/100) x 40 cents or $4 a month. Normally, only about half of the pledge value is given to the *rahin* as an interest-free loan. Thus, a $500 loan payable in six months will incur a storage cost of $4 x 6 = $24.

At the end of the term, the *rahin* will pay the *murtahin* $524. The *rahin* can ask for periodic loan extension, provided he pays an additional storage fee. On failure to pay the loan after a prolonged reminder, the operator holds the right to put the collateral on auction. The *rahn* company will claim loan plus storage fees due to them. The surplus therein will be returned back to the *rahin*.

In case he cannot be located, the proceeds will be forwarded to the *bait-ul-mal* from which the *rahin* is entitled to make future claims. Public response has been overwhelming, especially during the 1993 super-bull run.

In fact, *al-rahn* can be a better alternative to finance stock purchases, compared to credit cards and share-financing loans. At least the money an individual obtains via *al-rahn* is backed by productive assets.

Let us see how *ar-rahn* companies derive benefits from the pledge asset. That is, can the company use the asset to generate income? For example, if the collateral is a gold bracelet worth $10,000, can it be sold for investment purposes with the proceeds going to the company alone? This may be one way to compensate for the opportunity cost forgone by the company for the loan given.

However, according to the *Hedaya,* it is not lawful to take pledges for trusts such as deposits, loans, or *mudarabah* or partnership stock. The pawnee (*murtahin*) is not entitled to use the collateral (*rahn*), for his right is only in the possession of the pledge and not in its use. If the company uses the pledge for its own benefit without informing the debtor, and then incurs a loss, it takes full liability for the loss incurred.

Finally, modern commercialized *al-rahn* pawnbroking is an invention as it differs from the actual practice in early Islam. However, the good news is that the benefits seem to outweigh the costs, since the contract provides an opportunity for the common people to obtain small, collateralized interest-free loans.

To summarize, the Islamic pawnbroking business employs three contracts. When the operator lends out the money, it uses the contract of *qardhu hasan* i.e. benevolent loan or interest-free loan. To avoid loan defaults, it employs the contract of *al-rahn*. To earn profits, it will charge the borrower a custodial fee contracted under the principle of *wadiah amanah*

Eleven
Active and Passive BBA

Banking activities have revolved around receiving money from depositors and advancing them to customers as interest-bearing loans. But Islamic banking has changed things. Instead of making loans, the banks can now purchase and sell assets and commodities. This trading (*al-bay'*) model brings a brand new way for banks to make money the *halal* way.

The question now is how a banking business that uses trade (*al-bay'*) is able to stimulate economic growth. Currently, there are two full-fledged Islamic banks in Malaysia. Both operate under the Islamic Banking Act (IBA) 1983, that defines an Islamic bank as "any company which carries on Islamic banking business and holds a valid license." Further on, the IBA defines the nature of the Islamic banking business thusly:

> *"Islamic banking business means banking business whose aims and operations do not involve any element which is not approved by the religion of Islam."*

Earlier, the trust to develop banking activities according to *Shariah* values was given to Bank Islam Malaysia Berhad (BIMB) under the supervision of the Malaysian Central bank (BNM). The approach taken by BIMB and BNM is summarized as follows:

- a step-by-step approach to develop an Islamic banking system.
- a complement to conventional banking.

♦ for the first ten years, only one license is given out (i.e., BIMB) to develop and test out new instruments on a prudent basis.

The interest-free banking scheme (IFBS) also known as Islamic windows, was introduced in 1993 with twenty-one commercial banks, thirteen finance companies, and three merchant banks taking part in the scheme. The Islamic window system, however, was set up under BAFIA guidelines and not according to the rules of the IBA, as the latter deals with licensing requirements. Most of the IFBS bankers I met felt that this phenomenon is working in favor in BIMB, whose activities are not restricted by BAFIA.

BAFIA was introduced in 1989 to replace the Banking Act 1973 and Finance Company Act 1969. It restricts IFBSs from undertaking activities that BIMB is privileged to do under the Islamic Banking Act. According to BAFIA:

> *"Unless the minister on the recommendation of the bank otherwise prescribes, no licensed institution shall engage, whether on its own account or on a commission basis, and whether alone or with others, in wholesale or retail trade, including import and export trade." (Section 32.)*

Even though there are no clear guidelines on the sales and purchase of common stocks or even acquisition of companies via *mudarabah* ventures in IFBS, Bank Negara, on the recommendation of the finance minister, has allowed them to buy and sell assets under close *Shariah* supervision. Apparently, the *murabahah* and *al-bai-bithaman ajil* (BBA) deferred payment sale products are the only ones available in the market.

There is no doubt that deferred payment sale instruments will dominate Islamic financing, but their prolonged use is not good news to Islamic deposits, particularly *mudarabah* deposits. But if interest-free banks are now allowed to venture into merchandize trading, it will boost the growth of *mudarabah* deposits. It can buy wholesale and sell retail.

Although trading demands some storage and inventory costs, it is worth venturing into in view of the massive funds available in Islamic banks today. For example, IFBS can block purchase dozens of new houses and apartments at a discount prices. These homes can be sold later via BBA with renovation and interior accessories in one package.

Potential homebuyers need not worry about how to raise money for renovation and other essential needs such as fans, air conditioners, grills, kitchen cabinets, and even furniture. All these can be obtained in one home package via Islamic deferred sale instruments.

This is what I mean by active or value-added *bai-bithaman-ajil*. In fact, IFBS will no longer wait for customers to inform them of what type of houses they want. Instead, upon conducting a decent market study, they will hunt for new homes for the customers. This approach is expected to produce higher value-added activities that conventional banks normally cannot do.

The potential higher returns obtained therein, i.e., from the discounted purchase from manufacturers and extra revenues from upstream activities would mean a higher return for *mudarabah* depositors. It also helps stimulate new production and eventually economic growth. Meanwhile, venturing into active *murabahah* and *bai-bithaman-ajil* would be adequate to show that the new banking structure is cost-efficient.

Twelve
Salam and Istisna Financing

One of the principles of contract (*aqd*) in Islamic commercial law deals with the subject matter (*mahallul 'aqdi*). For example, in a contract of sale, the object must be in existence at the time of sale, and it must be in physical possession of the seller when the transaction takes place. Also, the seller must own the object prior to the sale. The object must be a property of value (*al-mal mutaqawwim*) and free from defects (*'ayb*).

The price of the object must be made known on the spot while the delivery of the goods sold must be certain i.e., it should not depend on chance. Islamic law requires these stringent conditions fulfilled to prevent undue ambiguities (*gharar*) in the transaction as it could create injustices (*zulm*), that often jeopardize human relations. It is therefore worthy to take a close look at object of sale (*mahallul 'aqdi*). Islamic law requires the object to have physical existence at the time of sale that can be quite difficult to observe today.

It is common practice that consumers pay a certain sum as a deposit prior to full payment. In the case of new housing, buyers normally wait at least two years before taking possession. This is because the goods are not yet produced and manufactured when the sale and purchase agreement is executed.

To protect public interest (*maslahah al-ammah*), has the Islamic commercial law failed to recognize that not all objects of sale must be delivered on the spot in a physical form? Certainly, the answer is a no, because both *salam* and *istisna* are exempted from this requirement. The permissibility of *salam* and *istisna'* in Islamic commercial law can make us realize that prevailing *bai-bithaman-ajil* contracts have been applied in a rather crude manner.

Basically, *salam* and *istisna'* are sale contracts whereby the seller undertakes to supply some specific goods to the buyer at a future date in exchange for an advance price fully or partially paid on the spot. In other words, the price is paid in cash (full or partial), while the supply of the goods is deferred to a future date.

In the case of *bay' bithaman ajil* financing, where payments are made by installments, the buyer will still be required to pay an advance payment (lump sum), after which he or she will take possession of the goods on the spot or wait until the goods are produced and delivered at a future date.

This is true in the case of home purchases under construction or even before construction begins. In this manner, the house will be delivered in the future with partial payments already made by way of down payments.

Hence, it seems that the *bay' bithaman ajil* contracts involving future delivery have violated the principle of *mahallul 'aqdi*, that "the subject matter must be in existence at the time of sale."

This is because the contract of *al-bay,* whether cash or deferred (*bay' bithaman ajil* or *bay 'murabahah*) assumes that the goods are delivered on the spot. We see many instances today where in *bay' bithaman ajil* transactions, not all goods have been delivered on the spot.

Using deferred sale contracts to include deferred delivery is therefore somewhat unjustified. Apparently, deferred delivery is only allowed in *salam-* and *istisna'*-based transactions, but deferred sale products such as *bay' bithaman ajil* tend to include deferred delivery as one of their prominent features. This may not be accurate, because in *salam* and *istisna,* the main feature is deferred delivery, while in *bai-biithaman ajil,* it is the deferred payment.

Istisna' Financing

Each party has the option to rescind the contract before it is implemented but binding once it has been constituted.
Once constituted, if the Al-Masnoo does not conform to specifications, the mustasni has the right to revoke the contract

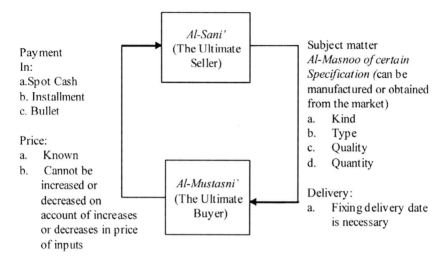

Payment In:
a. Spot Cash
b. Installment
c. Bullet

Price:
a. Known
b. Cannot be increased or decreased on account of increases or decreases in price of inputs

Al-Sani' (The Ultimate Seller)

Al-Mustasni' (The Ultimate Buyer)

Subject matter *Al-Masnoo of certain Specification (*can be manufactured or obtained from the market)
a. Kind
b. Type
c. Quality
d. Quantity

Delivery:
a. Fixing delivery date is necessary

Figure 2.5 *Istisna'*

Before I proceed further, it is necessary to explain the difference between *salam* and *istisna*. *Salam* usually involves agricultural products, while the subject of *istisna* is always a thing that needs manufacturing in which more attention is given to specifications of goods under order.

In *salam,* the price is paid in advance while in *istisna,* it may be paid in cash or by installment. This has a lot to do with the nature of agriculture production, when most activities took place in the planting stage. It is important to release all capital during this critical stage, after which less capital is required. In contrast, *istisna'* production, unlike *salam,* deals with production in stages all of which require capital injection. The time of delivery is an essential part of the sale of *salam,* while it is not necessary in *istisna'* that the time of delivery be fixed. Lastly, the contract of *salam,* once effected, cannot be canceled unilaterally, while the contract of *istisna'* can be canceled before the manufacturer begins work.

Because Islamic financing is predominantly an urban phenomenon involving *bay' bithaman-ajil-* and *murabahah*-based consumer and trade financing, the contract of *istisna'* can be more relevant than *salam*. But *salam* can also be applicable to manufacturing. It is not accurate to say that *salam* is specially made for agriculture alone.

Ironically today, *bay' bithaman ajil products* seem to take advantage of the twin benefits of deferred payment sale and deferred delivery, but are unable to allow the customer to exercise his right to cancel the order. The need to further study the nature of the *bay' bithaman ajil* contract and its application to the consumer, trade, and project financing is critical to protect customers from unwarranted hazards and difficulties.

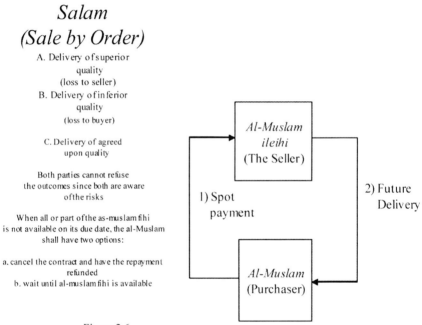

Salam (Sale by Order)

A. Delivery of superior quality (loss to seller)
B. Delivery of inferior quality (loss to buyer)

C. Delivery of agreed upon quality

Both parties cannot refuse the outcomes since both are aware of the risks

When all or part of the as-muslam fihi is not available on its due date, the al-Muslam shall have two options:

a. cancel the contract and have the repayment refunded
b. wait until al-muslam fihi is available

Al-Muslam ileihi (The Seller)

1) Spot payment

2) Future Delivery

Al-Muslam (Purchaser)

Figure 2.6

Thirteen
Musyarakah Mutanaqisah Home Financing

The Central Bank (BNM) has mentioned that Islamic banks were not able to perform well under a volatile interest rate environment. Although interest rates are going up, BBA contractual profit rates must remain the same. Changing the profit rate will change the sale price of existing BBA asset. The BBA contract becomes void when many prices are quoted in a single sale. BBA, by nature, does not allow profit rate adjustment to reflect changes in the cost of funds. Bank Negara has strongly recommended Islamic banks to look for a floating rate option.

Most analysts agree the incoming recession will stay longer than expected. This can mean more declines in interest rates and asset prices. So, would it be a good idea to use a floating BBA during an economic slowdown? The answer depends on how long we think the recession will last. If the recession stays on longer, then Islamic banks should forget about using floating rate BBA. They should know by now that doing so will only hurt their earnings again.

Floating rate BBA can only help Islamic banks when interest rates are rising. But once interest rates decline, fixed rate BBA is always a better choice, since it gives the bank a higher margin when other traditional banks have to trim theirs.

The point here is that a new problem will emerge, namely what type of BBA to offer—a fixed rate or a flexible rate BBA? The answer again depends on how well the research arm of Islamic banks feels about the future. If they see an early recovery, which means rising interest rates, then a floating rate BBA is a better option. One way to do away with the problem of choice in uncertainty is to apply the contract of partnership with declining ownership, also known as *musyarakah mutanaqisah*.

The *musyarakah mutanaqisah* partnership (MMP) was first used by the Islamic Youth Cooperatives (KBI) to help members buy a house without resorting to interest-bearing or even deferred-sale financing. However, the MMP is not geared for home financing alone. It is applicable to most banking and non-banking transactions involving assets, such as land, vehicles, factories, machinery, and office premises.

This is how it works. Figure 2.7 shows a simple MMP scheme when applied to a banking firm using *al-ijarah* as the income-generating engine. We assume that the bank wants diligent repayments, while the customer desires to finally own the house.

In a dual-banking structure, these repayments should reflect market movements, typically interest rates, so that the bank will not lose in case a violent movement of interest rates occurs.

Let us say the house is priced at $100,000. At 90 percent end-financing, MMP will see the formation of a partnership contract between the bank and customer. The bank will contribute $90,000 as capital while the customer contributes the remaining 10 percent i.e., $10,000.

However, in the MMP contract, the capital contribution ratio (CCP) is not fixed, as it can be adjusted based on negotiation and the nature of contractual relationship between the partnering agents.

For example, in the government's 100 percent financing housing scheme, CCP can be based on a ratio, say 1:99. Therefore, if the house costs $100,000, the initial capital contributed by the customer is only $1,000. This amount will not pose a great burden to public servants, who have rights to enjoy 100 percent financing.

The objective of MMP is to make profits from the investment, while the object of investment is the ownership of property, say a house. An *al-ijarah* contract will be applied as a mechanism to earn rental income.

As an example, the partnership will invest the $100,000 capital on a house, which is then rented to the customer. The monthly rental paid to the partnership shall be equivalent to the monthly payment that banks will receive on term financing.

As rentals are paid, it will be distributed as profits to the bank and customer using the contractual profit sharing ratio. The customer can use the profits to purchase shares from the bank. In this way, ownership claims by the customer increases over time, while the bank's ownership decreases.

To accelerate the share-purchasing process, a premium is added onto the true rental value of the property. This is to ensure that rental payments are able to reflect market value.

As an example, assuming identical cost of financing and maturities, traditional financing requires a customer to pay $800 monthly. But in MMP, rental is valued at $500. To make up the difference, the customer pays an additional $300 as a share purchase transaction. Total rental is therefore $800.

Soon after the first rental payment is made, the customer will secure $50 profit (that is, 10 percent x $500) from rental, plus $300 to buy a portion of shares that the bank holds. The customer now owns $10,000 + $350 = $10,350 as share capital after making the first payment ($800), while the bank holds a decreasing $89,650.

The capital contribution ratio now is at 10.3 : 89.6. This buy-back share process will help ensure the customer to hold 100 percent ownership of asset sold as the rental period expires. The *musharakah mutanaqisah* contract is terminated when total sale of shares is concluded. The way an Islamic bank responds to interest rate volatility will now depend on the periodic lease renewal agreement, usually made every two or three years. This practice is normal in the rental business.

(MMP) FOR HOME FINANCING USING *AL-IJARAH*
AS THE INCOME GENERATING ENGINE

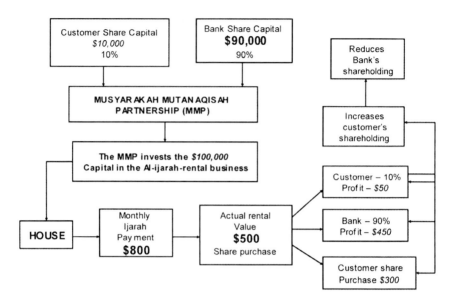

Figure 2.7 *Musharakah Mutanakisah*

If money is tight, the bank can direct the customer to increase the true rental value while keeping the added premium constant. The opposite is true when interest rates decline. This rental adjustment technique, although not thoroughly transparent from the *Shariah* viewpoint, requires more research in order to gain public acceptance.

There is one last point, though. To apply MMP in banking, one must identify who owns the asset? The bank or the customer? How does the asset appears in the bank's balance sheet? Theoretically, both should hold legal claim on the house. But what type of business entity the MMP should adopt? Will the Banking and Financial Institution Act 1989 (BAFIA) recognizes the partnership as a business entity? Finally, it is the partnership and not the bank alone that purchases the asset. The pricing of rentals and changes in premium payments for share buy-back requires meticulous care so that periodic adjustment to market movement in property and rental prices reflects a "win-win" deal.

SECTION THREE

ISLAMIC DEPOSITS
SOURCES OF FUNDS

One
Attractive Mudarabah deposits

The 38 percent national saving rate recorded for Malaysia promises sustainable economic growth as it moves ahead to address problems associated with the Asian economic crisis. Most of these savings are not voluntary but forced ones mustered by the Employees Provident Fund (EPF). Theoretically, without enough savings at hand, businesses and government are forced to borrow abroad, often with punitive costs.

Bank deposits constitute an important source of private savings. How much people save depends on many things, including the level of interest rates, income, and wealth. As the economy expands, the level of income will increase, and so does savings. Changes in interest rates can also affect savings. The recent 0.25 percent interest rate hike should see an increase in bank deposits.

Conventional bank deposits, particularly savings and fixed deposits, are in essence a loan given by depositors to the bank at a stipulated interest rate. For example, Arab Malaysian Bank offers 3.4 percent on a three-month deposit. The longer the maturity, the higher the rate of interest offered.

Deposit rates will also change when the Kuala Lumpur Inter-bank Offer (KLIBOR) rates go up or down. Normally, Bank Negara will enter the inter-bank market to secure the level of interest rates it desires. If it wishes to increase interest rates, the central bank will borrow heavily to reduce liquidity up to a level where the targeted rate of interest is reached.

It is well known today that the 0.25 percent interest rate hike will not raise the base lending rates (BLRs) of banks. What this means is a smaller margin for the banking business. Suppose the current rate on housing loans is 9 percent, while depositors get 4 percent. The bank easily makes a 5 percent or 5 sen profit from every RM1 loan it makes.

When the level of interest rates goes up by 0.25 percent, the margin will fall by the same amount, because banks are not allowed to raise the BLR. So this is not good news at all. Smaller margins can mean lower net worth and the price of banking stocks may fall.

Islamic banking should not be affected much in this case, since it cannot make any promise to pay a contractual rate of return on deposits. Islamic deposits are variable rate liabilities (VRL), meaning that the bank holds the right to reward or not to reward depositors. The contract of *al-wadiah yad dhamanah* or safe keeping with guarantee gives the right of profit distribution to the bank alone. So, even if conventional deposit rate increases, Islamic deposits need not do the same, as the prerogative to raise returns on *al-wadiah* deposits (*hibah*) rests on the bank alone.

The same is not true for Islamic fixed deposits, often known as the *al-mudarabah* investment deposits (AMID). Here, no guarantee is made on the safety of deposits and dividends, as this product assumes an equity character. AMID is risky, as the contract applied is based on a principle of profit-loss sharing. Profits are given away only when the investments are successful, while capital may depreciate or even diminish if the investment ends in losses.

Table 3.1 gives a reasonably good picture of what is on the offer. It is worthy to note that rates quoted by MayBank, Public Bank, Perwira Affin, and Arab Malaysian Bank are made on interest-bearing fixed deposits. The rate is set *ex ante*, i.e., on the day the deposits are made. On the contrary, rates quoted by Bank Islam (BIMB) are declared *ex post* meaning that they are announced the day the deposits mature.

Table 3.1 : Returns (percent) on fixed deposits as of early August 2000

Tenure (months)	Maybank	Public Bank	Perwira Affin	Arab Malaysian	BIMB
1	3.45	3.05	3.45	3.30	5.15
3	3.45	3.10	3.50	3.40	5.48
6	3.50	3.15	3.55	3.55	5.80
9	3.70	3.35	3.75	3.80	6.12
12	4.25	3.85	4.25	4.10	6.44

In general, rates on conventional fixed deposits are more or less at par, with Maybank giving the best. However, Bank Islam provides the highest, and we wonder why. It has significantly beaten Maybank on all fronts. Has Bank Islam done so well that it outperformed the largest bank in this country?

To measure bank performance information on modes of financing is also useful. But given the nature of Islamic banking today that puts heavy emphasis of *al-bai-bithaman ajil* financing, I can guess why BIMB's deposits had been somewhat bullish.

First, a low-interest rate regime may imply a relatively higher margin for BBA financing, since it can lock in profit, even when market rates are declining. When rates on conventional loans fell since mid-1998 as Bank Negara pursues a low interest rate policy, BIMB profit rate stayed relatively unchanged.

Note that if BIMB desires to lower profit rates on existing BBA, it will alter the selling price and thus invalidate the BBA sale. Retaining a relatively high profit rate while conventional banks are trimming down is therefore not a strategy but a consequence of high dependency on BBA financing.

The fact that BIMB's deposit rate exceeded the rest helped validate my thesis that in a low interest rate regime, the bank can indeed improve performance. Table 3.1 shows that BIMB was able to give more *hibah* since it was earning more from the BBA sales.

In other words, the profit margin on BBA financing is relatively higher as profit rate remains unchanged relative to interest rate, it must distribute the margin on the basis of the contractual profit sharing ratio. That makes the dividend payout higher than interest payout as the former is controlled by a profit sharing ratio set earlier.

The same is not applicable to *al-wadiah dhamanah* deposits, since here the bank is not bound to any contractual profit sharing ratio. So even if the margin remains high, the bank is not obligated to give higher *hibah*.

This can also mean that if conventional banks award low interest on deposits, an Islamic bank can also do the same by giving low *hibah* even if profits arising from financing activities are much higher. If this is true, it follows that the wider margin created from the investment of *al-wadiah* deposits in BBA sales will consequently increase the bank's net profits.

But such policy may not trigger people's interest to switch from Islamic to conventional deposits, unless the Islamic bank deliberately award higher *hibah*. Doing so should increase the size of Islamic deposits.

Two
Hibah and Demand Deposits

Usually, people place their money in a bank for two main purposes, namely transaction and investment. To fulfill transactional objective, Islamic banks offer *al-wadiah yad dhamanah* deposit (WAD), which means safe-keeping with guarantee. Using this product, depositors no longer act as creditors. Instead, they place deposits for protection.

Al-wadiah dhamanah means safe-keeping with guarantee. WAD depositors allow the bank to invest their money in return for deposit protection. But the bank has no legal obligation to pay depositors a fixed return, and may do so only on voluntary ground. In this manner, the bank holds prerogative on profit distribution policy in the form of gifts (*hibah*). As non-contractual monetary return, *hibah* is necessary to motivate people to place their savings in Islamic banks. Otherwise they will lose clients to banks that pay interest.

The point that I wish to raise today may sound trivial to depositors. This is because the amount put in bank deposits seems marginal, as most are used for transaction purposes. But be aware that summing them all, demand deposits or M1 form a large bulk of the nation's money supply.

It impacted macroeconomic variables such as national output, the price level, unemployment and exchange rates at the central bank's disposal. Hence, how banks formulate strategies to mobilize demand deposits is a national concern.

The *al-wadiah yad dhamanh* contract says that the bank will provide deposit protection and honor all withdrawals on call, provided that it is allowed to use deposits to generate earnings. Recall that the basic concept of banking involves borrowing public funds and lending out the same to make profit.

Interest is used to reward depositors, while borrowers must pay interest on loans. The difference between interest on loans and interest on deposits constitutes bank's profit. The same concept applies in interest-free banking, but now contracts applied are not based on interest-bearing debt contracts, but sale (*al-bay'*).

Given the nature of Islamic contracts in deposit taking, the need to reward depositors is a fundamental issue, since banks make money out of deposits. Giving *hibah* on *al-wadiah dhamanah* deposits is necessary because there is no free lunch in business. Refusing to distribute profits, although a permissible (*halal*) act under the *al-wadiah dhamanah* contract, will render Islamic banks recipients of subsidized funds.

On the other hand, an Islamic bank cannot promise to give depositors a fixed contractual income, as doing so runs against the principle *al-wadiah yad dhamanah* itself. If a bank wishes to give away *hibahs*, it must be done on free choice when they find it fitting to do so, especially when business is bullish. Making *hibah* compulsory on *al-wadiah dhamanah* deposits violates the basic principles of *al-wadiah dhamanah*.

But element of uncertainty in the system of *hibah* remains a setback in Islamic deposits mobilization, given that contractual interest income has been the norm in the market for deposits. Whatever the problem ahead, practitioners need something workable to play with. They are aware of the inconsistencies outlined above, but things must get moving. They know that some depositors may not take notice marginal changes in interest rate while others will refuse to save unless they know for certain how much the bank is willing to pay them.

Banks also felt that depositors should be rewarded, but how to do so is paradoxical when contracts are drawn along the *al-wadiah* principles. If the reward system is confusing, uncertainties will cause depositors to look for conventional alternatives.

Today, the solution has been rather evolutionary. When interest-free banking was spearheaded by Bank Islam Malaysia Berhad (BIMB), there was relatively less attention given to *hibah*. However, since the establishment of the interest-free banking system (IFBS), competition for deposits requires the IFBS and BIMB to acknowledge determinants of savings behavior.

Hibah, or gifts, are given out and calculated on the basis of bank performance. The point is, if the IFBS wish to give out *hibahs,* it must be based on some well-defined formulas and operational procedures that are *Shariah* compliant.

For example, when an interest-based bank offers 5.6 percent interest rate on a savings deposit, the rate is determined without leaving a single cent unaccounted for. The IFBS should, therefore, align methods of determining *hibahs* in the same profit-motivated spirit; being Islamic does not imply they should be less profit motivated.

In fact, when God assesses man's past actions during the Day of Judgment, it is done to the most minute detail. The Quran says, *"On that Day will men proceed in companies sorted out to show the Deeds that they have done. Then shall anyone who has done an atom's weight of good, see it and anyone who has done an atom's (Dharrah) weight of evil, shall see it"* (Al-Zalzalah: 6-8). Thus, Islamic banks cannot assume that Muslim depositors are less concerned what they can earn from WAD deposits, since a savings account is rarely seen as an investment product. In addition to that, non-Muslim depositors may be attracted to some aspects of *al-wadiah yad dhamanah,* but may be turned off when the deposits do not guarantee any returns.

Three
Quick return not possible for Mudarabah depositors

On a recent seminar in Kuala Lumpur, someone asked why Islamic banks find it hard to invest in *mudarabah* projects. One of the speakers, who himself was a banker, gave an honest answer. He said that many *mudarabah* depositors want a quick return, which is simply not possible.

As an example, if $100,000 were placed in the *mudarabah* account, investors want to know how much money they can make in one month, three months, etc. If Islamic banks cannot provide the similar offerings available in conventional banks, it may be too presumptuous to think that deposits can be mobilized through religion alone.

The speaker says that it is not possible to invest in *mudarabah* projects on a large scale because the profit cannot be realized within a short time, but in a year or more. The nature of the *mudarabah* contract may discourage people from investing in *mudarabah* deposits, as they are used to earn money via the fixed interest-bearing deposit.

For example, when a large sum of money is involved, especially on accounts held by state religious departments, they too want to know how much the Islamic bank can offer relative to time deposits. It is a rational thing to ask, since the opportunity cost of holding money today is the interest rate. So, in avoiding *riba,* would it be a wise decision to park millions of ringgit in the Islamic deposits, where uncertainties in earnings loomed all the time.

In its true form, investment in *mudarabah* deposits is risky, as there is no capital protection on safety and certainty on returns. This is because the deposits are mobilized under the profit-loss sharing system (PLS). These deposits are not fixed income instruments like time and certificates of deposit and private debt securities.

In view of the different philosophical base on which these instruments are structured, institutional depositors ought to be informed about the PLS system and how it can best serve their organizations.

But in business, the bottom line is profit. Islamic banks simply cannot afford to wait too long to see how PLS actually works in financing. Hence, it is imperative to reduce the uncertainty by using more *murabahah/bai-bithamin-ajil* instruments, as these products will generate regular and most importantly contractual cash flows collected from periodic installment payments.

Putting aside the supply-side problems, let us now look at the investment behavior of *mudarabah* depositors. Are they aware that investing in *mudarabah* deposits is risky? Does the principle of partnership make dollar sense to the banking business?

But why in the first place people invest? Undoubtedly, they do so to increase earning and wealth. But in Islam, wealth is not the end of things. Wealth or property (*al-mal*) is acquired as a means to seek a higher end— the Ultimate Happiness (*Sa'ada Haqiqiya*). I have discussed this concept of happiness in the earlier chapters. Imam al-Ghazali has clearly pointed out that to achieve ultimate happiness, man must achieve some excellences (*fada'il*) in this life, and this includes wealth.

But wealth must be acquired according to the will of God (i.e., the *Shariah*). Otherwise it will only serve to satisfy the animal needs (*nafs ammarah*) of man. But how much wealth is enough?

The answer is a straightforward one. Man (*insan*), when created by God, is given the intellect (*'aql*) so that he is free to differentiate the right from the wrong. In this manner, he is responsible over his own actions. In Islam, however, in the creation of wealth to sustain one's material well-being, is made on the basis of what is right (*wajib, halal, sunnat, mubah*) and wrong (*haram*) and these are provided for by the *Shariah*.

For example, God says: "O you who believe, eat not up your property among yourselves in vanities but let there be amongst you traffic and trade by mutual goodwill" (*An-Nisaa: 29*). In another verse, He says, "O you who believe! Stand firm for Allah as witness to fair dealing and let not the hatred of others to you makes you swerve from justice. Be just, that is next to piety and fear of Allah. For Allah is well acquainted with all that you do." (Al-Maidah: 8)

In a similar perspective, Ibn Qayyim *rahimullah* says that the basis of the *Shariah* is the wisdom and welfare of the people in this world, as well in the hereafter. This welfare lies in complete justice, mercy, well-being, and wisdom. Anything that departs from justice to oppression, from mercy to harshness, from welfare to misery, and from wisdom to folly, has nothing to do with the *Shariah*.

The prohibition of *riba* and the establishment of an Islamic financial system allow man to create wealth in the spirit of the *Shariah* stated above—that investment and profit generated must result from fair dealings and kindness.

But it does not mean that in seeking profits, a company must also fulfill the objectives of poverty eradication. Mutual goodwill (*ta'awun*) does not mean complacency and lack of competitiveness. Instead, mutual goodwill means that the conduct of business is free uncertainty (*gharar*) or earnings do not involve the game of chance (*maisir*).

This brings our discussion to a hadith of the Prophet (s.a.w.) that says, "Nine-tenths of God's bounties came from trade (*al-bay'*)." What Prophet Muhammad (s.a.w.) meant is that wealth creation arising from trading (*al-bay'*) activity is a risky venture. Unlike *riba*-bearing activities where risks and uncertainties of capital depreciation are transferred from the lending party to the borrower, trading (*al-bay'*) is exposed to market volatilities. The trader, whose capital is subject to the law of depreciation, will bear the uncertainty of making or losing money in the market. In this manner, trading is regarded as a fair business transaction.

In general, Islam admonishes man to create wealth through work and effort (*kasb*). But why? Based on the above *hadith,* the remaining one-tenth or 10 percent of God's bounties are derived from *sadeqah* i.e., "unearned income." *Sadeqah* is a gift reserved for the poor and needy only.

When *riba* is introduced as an incentive to save, it violates the law in nature. Investors and the richer folks receive "unearned income" in the form of interest. A $50,000 time deposit at 4 percent annual interest rate guarantees the rich people a $2,000 annual income without work and effort (*kasb*) in place. It is like charity given not to the poor, but the undeserving rich.

Now *mudarabah* depositors too want the same assurance. They want to ensure full protection of their money and insist on a guaranteed increase without them putting in work and effort. Since giving charity (*sadeqah*) to the poor constitutes unearned income, the rich now want to be treated like the poor and needy too, which is ridiculous. This behavior goes against the law in nature. But this is what the *riba* system has inflicted on society, such that the rich thrive on unearned income.

The irony is that Islamic banking has not been sensitive in addressing this problem. Instead, they feel it is necessary to declare upfront some rates of return (i.e., indicative rates) although this may not be fully guaranteed. They are forced to do so because of the fear of losing depositors, who may run away when they know that *mudarabah* deposits provide no guarantees to both capital and dividends.

Hence, to assure some rate of return comparable to interest rates, Islamic banking resorted to *murabahah/al-bai-bithaman ajil* products. Putting depositors' money into the risky *mudarabah* would mean uncertainties about profits and loss, even though it could mean a windfall if a project runs well. But uncertainties normally scare away depositors, since people are not used to doing business that runs on a risk-sharing principle. But through education, this problem can be overcome and remedies are not impossible to find.

Four
Al-Qardhu Hasan and Demand Deposits

Ever since the establishment of the interest-free banking system (IFBS) in 1989, it is not surprising to see how participating banks modeled their operations along Bank Islam Malaysia (BIMB). As a standard procedure, participating banks offer two main products, namely current and savings accounts. Islamic deposit uses the *al-wadiah yad dhamanah* contract to replace interest-bearing demand and savings deposits.

The *al-wadiah* instruments, as introduced by BIMB, use the *hibah* system as incentives to save. The *hibah,* meaning gift, is awarded to depositors since they have contractually allowed banks to use their money to finance bank operations.

According to the *Mejelle, hibah* is giving the ownership of property to another without an equivalent countervalue. In banking, the *hibah* takes the form in monetary return. It has nothing to do with the classical *hibah* where the donor does not want anything in return. The urgent need to compete with mainstream banks requires Islamic banking to introduce *hibah* as an incentive to save, hence replacing interest rates.

The nature of the *al-wadiah* contract does not warrant depositors to hold a legal claim over bank's profit. The *hibah* is given to make up for the opportunity cost of capital minus the legal obligation to do so. The amount is determined by the bank when the deposit reaches maturity. In this manner, depositors have no control over the distribution system under the *al-wadiah dhamanah* system.

One way to avoid public confusion on this issue is to use the *qardhu hasan* contract instead. It is presently applied in the Islamic Republic of Iran and worth considering. What it does is to maintain the lending-borrowing relationship between depositors and banks, but without implicating interest.

This is the essence of loan contract in Islam. *Qard* means loan, while *hasan* implies good or benevolent. A *qardhu hasan* loan, therefore, expresses the spirit of cooperation (*ta'awun*) and brotherhood (*ukuwah*) between debtors and creditors. But it does not mean an Islamic bank that employs the *qardhu hasan* product will enjoy using deposits are zero cost, thus making more profit than conventional banks. For example, interest rate on deposits is 4 percent, while interest on loans is 12 percent. Here, the bank makes a net profit of 8 percent.

Islamic loan vs Conventional Loan

Islamic Loan
Debt = Loan
Capital protection
No fixed and contractual return

Increment set by debtor and not mentioned on the contract
Increment given away by debtor as moral obligation
Increment is lawful (*halal*)

Conventional loan
Debt > Loan
Capital protection
Fixed and contractual return

Increment set by creditor and stipulated in the contract
Increment given away by debtor as legal obligation
Increment is unlawful (*haram*)

Figure 3.1 Differences between Islamic and Conventional Loan

An Islamic bank that pays no interest to depositors will charge *murabahah* or *bai-bithaman-ajil* facilities at 12 percent annual profit rate. Without a contractual cost of capital, net profit is 12 percent. It is here the issue of *hibah* becomes relevant to the *qardh hasan* contract, which is quite paradoxical in the case of *al-wadiah yad dhamanah*.

In fact, Prophet Muhammad s.a.w. has encouraged borrowers to pay more than the principal loan. The addition, however, are not contractually stated in the loan agreement. Narrated Jabir bin 'Abdullah: *"I went to the Prophet s. a. w. while he was in the mosque. After the Prophet s. a. w. told me to pray two Raka'at, he repaid me the debt he owed me and gave me an extra amount."*

On another occasion, the Prophet s.a.w. says, *"The best amongst you is he who repays his debts in the most handsome manner (al-Bukhari)."* The extra payment was not made contractually binding, but released according to the paying capacity of the borrowing party, and most important, his willingness to give more.

In essence, Islamic deposits should apply the *qard hasan* contract, since it has a Prophetic traditional linkage. The *qardhu hasan* contract is much easier to understand as it automatically allows borrowers to use the funds to fulfill their respective needs with guaranteed payments of the principal loan. The debtor may grant gift (*hibah*) when the debt matures, but the *hibah* cannot be mentioned in the loan contract. In a society that upholds *sadeqah* as a virtue and noble action, a debtor is expected to give the creditor a *hibah* for the following reasons:

1. The debtor is thankful for the loan given by the creditor.
2. The debtor is concern that inflation may cut real value of principal loan.
3. The debtor understands that the creditor suffers loss of opportunity to earn alternative income if monies are invested elsewhere.
4. The debtor is an individual with *iman* and *taqwa*.

One thing one must understand well is the difference between loan (*qard*) and debt (*dayn*) and how both make a difference in the Islamic system. If a one-year Islamic loan (*qardhu hasan*) amounts to $1,000, the debt arising from the loan is still $1,000. This, however, is not true in an interest-bearing loan. Given the same loan at 10 percent annual interest, the debt arising from this $1,000 loan is $1,100 (i.e., $1,000 + $100). In this sense, loan (i.e., $1,000) is less than debt ($1,100). The Islamic loan tells a different story, where loan is always equal to debt.

Five
Problems in Mobilizing SPTF Deposits

The production function of a banking firm does not only look at loans as output, but also deposits. Deposits are considered an input to the production of loans; i.e., to make more loans and more profits, banks must mobilize more deposits.

When a banking model looks at loans as the only output, the problem no longer deals with deposit mobilization but how to make loans to maximize the bank's earning. The model assumes deposits can easily be obtained at attractive rates of interest.

Today, however, banks are finding it somewhat harder to secure deposits, due to rapid growth of unit trusts and the fund management industry. In good times, investing money in the equity sector secures higher returns. As investors enjoy handsome dividends and capital gains, more surplus funds are now moving from bank deposits to the unit trust sector. To consider loan as an output is no longer tenable.

Table 3.2: Rate of Return on Islamic and Conventional Deposits

Al-Mudharabah Investment Account (AMIA) and fixed deposit (conventional FD) (as of August 1997)		Maybank (percent)		EON Finance (percent)		Bank Bumiputra (BBMB) (percent)		Bank Islam (BIMB) (percent)
Months	IFBS	Conventional FD	IFBS	Conventional FD	IFBS	Conventional FD	
1	6.03	7.30	7.1	7.7	6.03	7.5	4.63
3	6.18	7.40	7.2	7.7	6.07	7.5	4.92
6	6.33	7.50	7.5	7.8	6.10	7.5	5.21
9	6.48	7.50	7.9	7.8	6.12	7.5	5.50
12	6.64	7.50	8.3	7.8	6.18	7.5	5.79
15	6.82	7.50	8.8	7.8	6.21	7.5	6.08

Interest-free banking system (IFBS) is also not spared in the current competitive bid for deposits. Most SPTF banks and finance companies today have at least three basic deposit products on the offer, namely the *al-wadiah dhamanah* current account (AWCA), *al-wadiah yad dhamanah* savings account (AWASA), and the *al-mudharabah* Investment Account (AMIA).

The last one, namely AMIA, is worth examining, as they constitute the bulk of total deposits and are likely to shift from place to place seeking higher and more competitive rates. A casual look at Table 3.2 should give us some idea about Islamic deposits and their potential in the deposit market.

Returns on Islamic deposits are flexible in nature. These rates are quoted using the rates declared in the previous months. Thus, the rates are not fixed and contractual rates as offered by conventional deposits.

This is because the AMIA contract operates along profit-loss sharing principles, while fixed deposits are based on the contract of debt. In other words, AMIA is an equity product with no capital protection and legal claims. To make up for the risk taking, AMIA holders are expected to receive higher returns relative to that of fixed deposits. Interestingly, this does not seem to happen in SPTF deposits.

Table 3.2 shows that AMIA rates for Mayban and BBMB are much lower than interest-bearing fixed deposits. Given the fact that AMIAs are equities, it is interesting to examine why they have not been able to command higher dividends.

Al-Mudarabah Investment Account

1. No guarantee on deposits
2. No guarantee on returns
3. Flexible rate liability

Placement of deposits using the principle of
Al-Mudarabah (trustee partnership)

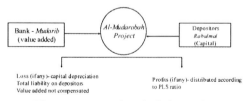

Figure 3.2 *Mudarabah* financing

A look at EON Finance casts a positive outlook. AMIA accounts of EON Finance yield the highest return. Dividend rates on shorter-term accounts such as the one-, three-, and six-month deposits are relatively lower, while rates were higher in the longer-term deposits. This indicates a larger portion of investments was long- and medium-term, such as home and car financing.

However, given Malaysia's multi-racial society, there is every reason to believe that non-Muslim customers in EON Finance may move their nine-, twelve-, and fifteen-month conventional fixed deposit accounts to the AMIA account with the same maturity.

Interest Bearing Fixed Deposits

1. Full guarantee on deposits
2. Full guarantee on returns
3. Fixed rate liability

Placement of deposits using the principle of
lending and borrowing (loans)

Figure 3.3 Interest-bearing deposit

This is because rates on these AMIAs are much higher than the conventional rates. But then, EON Finance may face difficulties in raising shorter-term AMIA deposits, as their dividend rates offered were lower as this may cause non-Muslim depositors to put their money in the short-term AMIA accounts.

A look at BIMB's performance is also interesting. The apparently wide gap between BIMB's dividend rates and the IFBS banks is quite strange. BIMB has begun operation about ten years earlier. But why were their rates much lower than the IFBS?

In general, there is a lack of coherence when one observes how rates of return on AMIA accounts were determined. At one point, SPTF managers need no longer worry about cost of funds in determining the rates of profits on financing, since the former is an *ex-post* entity, which means that IFBS dividends are distributed as residuals rather than a contractual claim. This may cause difficulties when depositors are looking for secured income, especially for budgeting purposes. Failure to raise enough deposits may require IFBS banks to source funds from the more expensive inter-bank money market.

Six
The Negotiable Islamic Debt Certificate (NIDC)

Islamic banks in Malaysia are heading for more difficult times if the level of interest rates keeps on rising. They must find new ways to make profits in view of the nature of the assets and liabilities they hold.

In fact, Islamic banks seem to have their own unique problem today. This problem is not about high non-performing financing (NPF/NPL) or the need for recapitalization. It deals with one peculiar characteristic of *al-bai-bithaman ajil* and *murabahah* products. That is, both constitute fixed rate assets (FRA).

At the same time, Islamic deposits can only promise a variable rate of return. In such a balance sheet, asset-liability management can be a pain in the neck.

As I have mentioned in the articles, banks' earnings are expected to fall when revenues remain the same despite increases in the cost of deposits. Islamic banks cannot raise the existing BBA rates, as doing so will change the contractual selling price. As the inter-bank rates (Klibor) go up, interest rates on loans and deposits will follow suit.

In a dual-banking system, Islamic banks cannot prevent customers to withdraw their deposits on call. The nature of *al-wadiah* deposits gives customers such right. So, when the level of deposits declines while financing remains long-term, an asset-liability mismatch problem is inevitable.

Banks must look for short-term funds to make up for the lost deposits. Doing so again is not cheap, especially when interest rates are rising. With a fixed rate BBA, the higher cost of funds will erode profits. Risk management is an option only open to conventional banks when they hedge in the interest rate futures for protection. Islamic banks are therefore fully exposed to interest rate risk; even though *riba* is not implicated in their business.

The problem can be overcome either by introducing a floating rate BBA or a fixed rate deposit. With floating asset financing, any change in market interest rates can be accommodated by the pricing model used by the bank.

By the end of the year, Bank Islam Malaysia Berhad (BIMB) is expected to offer a brand new floating rate asset financing. On the deposit side, last month, BIMB launched with a new deposit product with a fixed rate of return known as the Negotiable Islamic Debt Certificate (NIDC).

It is the Islamic version of the negotiable certificate of deposits (NCD) with some tweaking to claim *Shariah* legitimacy. The NIDC will help mobilize short-term deposits (less than twelve months) that guarantee a fixed rate of return. This can perhaps protect the bank from the pressure to increase rates of return in the short run and, therefore, enable it to maintain earnings in a high interest rate regime like ours today.

But first let us look at the conventional NCD. It is a debt instrument and pays the depositors a specified amount of interest during the term of the certificate. The NCD or CD is a debt certificate or security issued by the bank, which acts as the borrower. Let's say a one-year $10,000 CD pays 5 percent interest. At the end of the year, CD holders (i.e., the creditors) will get back $10,000 plus $500 interest.

NCD is non-*halal* since it pays the creditors a fixed contractual return, namely interest (*riba*). But NCDs are attractive because they can be traded in the secondary market. Companies with excess funds but only need them, say twice a year, will find this relatively liquid instrument useful. In 1996, NCDs issued accounted for 11.8 percent of total deposit.

Since Islam prohibits the taking and receipt of interest via debt instruments, it is rather hard to develop an Islam debt instrument bearing a fixed rate of returns. Doing so is tempting, since now an Islamic banks can mobilize funds at a fixed rate, thus able to shield themselves from interest rate risk.

The negotiable Islamic debt certificate (NIDC) is no longer based on debt, but on sale (*al-bay'*). This instrument in essence is made up of two separate processes, namely sale and deferred sale (*bay al-'inah*) plus debt trading. For example, Company A has $1 million as deposit placement. The company wants a fixed return, which the Islamic bank is willing to give, but only if the contract applied is permissible (*halal*).

To make the contract *Shariah* compliant, the bank must observe the following procedures:

➤ The bank sells an asset (Islamic bank share certificates) worth $1 million to Company A. So, the bank now secures a new $1 million deposit.
➤ Now, Company A sells back the asset to the Islamic bank at a deferred price. The deferred price is based on a profit rate of, say, 7.5 percent for a duration of six months, which equals to a profit margin of $37,500. So, the deferred sale price is equal to $1,037,500.
➤ The bank now will pay Company A through the issuance of a debt certificate or *shahdah al-dayn*, namely the NIDC, by virtue of the asset held by the bank.

The issuance of the NIDC to Company A is undertaken as evidence of the bank's debt with the depositing company. At the end of the six months, Company A can redeem the NIDC for $1,037,500. In other words, Company A purchases the NIDC for $1 million and sells it back at $1,037,500. Here, debt trading (*bay' al-dayn*) is actively applied. As an example, on maturity, Company A will sell the NICD for $1,037,500. However, if he wants the cash earlier than expected, he can sell the NICD in the secondary market at a discount. By way of *bay' al-dayn*, it is possible to liquidate the asset, since NICDs are considered property (*al-mal*) by *Shariah* Advisory Board of Bank Negara Malaysia.

SECTION FOUR

ISLAMIC PARTNERSHIP

One
Equity Financing for Islamic Business

Problems in applying *mudarabah* and *musyarakah* instruments in banking today seemed to disappear when Mahathir Muhammad urged banks to start taking risks and cease being camp followers. He said banks should not behave like moneylenders or chettiars. Given the need for high technology capital-intensive investments, finance is crucial and banks should lend support.

Mahathir knows that Malaysian banks do not take equities in business projects, much less in companies. One reason is the Banking and Financial Institutions Act, 1989 (BAFIA), which prohibits commercial banks from pursuing joint ventures (JV).

However, laws can be changed and Mahathir's positive remarks on the Japanese banking model may pave the way towards greater financial liberalization, making it easier for Malaysian banks to purchase common stocks via joint ventures. It is here the subject of venture capital is most relevant.

To pursue venture capital activities, stock ownership as a form of control and monitoring device is critical. Without stock ownership, it is useless to talk about partnership in projects that provide no guarantees to profits and capital protection.

Seemingly, the government is more aggressive than banks. The government seems to tell the bank what they should do. This is an irony because banks are private enterprises where motives are driven by profits alone.

They are expected be more creative, competitive and efficient, but why should they do so if the license given to them allows an easy way to profit? They can borrow at 5 percent and lend at 12 percent. The 7 percent margin is pure comfort. So why should they worry about generating profit from risky projects? Why should they provide equity funds to business that demands continuous painstaking monitoring while the routine debt collection is an easier way out?

Islamic banking is also not spared by Mahathir, at least indirectly. In fact, they should be the most embarrassed, given their privilege to purchase stocks as clearly outlined by the Islamic Banking Act (IBA) 1983.

The IBA practically defines what an Islamic bank can do, including buying and selling of shares and underwriting of securities. An Islamic bank practically sits in board meetings of companies it funds. It can make decisive moves to avoid mismanagement and provide assistance to help the company grow. This is how banks can play a positive role in economic growth and development.

A banking business that provides equity financing is a risky business. Most importantly, banks want to be prudent, as they are custodians of the borrowed money. Dr. Mahathir said that prudence is good, but bankers who want complete certainty in grossing profits but are not ready to take risks will become pure moneylenders.

They don't want to lend at lower interest rates and don't like to lend long-term either. So how do banks contribute to nation building? One viable option is equity financing.

In equity financing, banks need not venture into the seed stage, as it is highly risky. They should leave such activities to the venture capital companies or some government-funded agencies, such as the Malaysian Technology Development Corporation (MTDC).

Instead, banks should be more involved in second-stage or third-stage venture capital investment, such as business expansion financing and commercialization of new products. The financing of high-technology investment is also a good option for local banks, given the wide array of fiscal incentives and infrastructure support that government provides.

In Islamic banking, the *musyarakah* model is a viable option, since banks only hold a portion of a company's total stocks. An acceptable profit-sharing ratio (PLR) is negotiable to reflect respective capital contribution, but this is not an easy matter, because the non-capital component of the venture is equally important. The firm normally provides most of the value-added components in the venture, and this must be embodied in the PLR.

Conventional venture capital companies normally do not pay attention to the PLR factor. Instead, they are more concerned about ways to determine share ownership. This is because the main objective of a venture capitalist is to make capital gain when the firm goes public. It does not intend to stay long in the business.

Similarly, in banking, this is one way a *musyarakah* venture should end. Once the project is completed, banks can recover their capital and earnings to satisfy liquidity as well as profit targets set by the management.

Two
Islamic Venture Capital

Venture capitalists provide equity funds to small business, especially start-ups. At a later stage, they provide capital for a company that expects to go public within a year. Venture capitalists supported entrepreneurs with capital in exchange for an ownership stake of the business. Unlike banks and unit trust investors, venture capitalists work closely with entrepreneurs and investee companies. In this manner, the venture capital business elucidates the Islamic system of profit-loss sharing. It does not only inject risk capital, but venture capitalists also provide value addition, such as reviewing business plans, giving financial advice, and improving networking.

The essential element in Islamic venture capital is the profit-loss sharing system (PLS) than runs on the principle of *al-ghurm bil ghonm* (i.e., the entitlement to return is related to the exposure of risk). It can adopt the general partnership or *musyarakah* (i.e., *shirkatul alanan/amwal*) contract, but the task will not be an easy one. This is because *musyarakah* in general provides juristic rulings on explicit matters such as capital and work as well as rules on profit and loss distribution. Among others, the contract says that capital contributions can be made both in cash and in kind. It is a rule that contracting partners must contribute work in the venture. No capital protection is given; and losses caused by negligence must be borne by the guilty party. All *fuqaha* agree on these issues. In principle, the business must stay away from ventures involving Islamic prohibitions such as gambling, liquor, pork, etc.

One of the highlights of venture capital investments is the due diligence process conducted by the venture capitalists. It serves to investigate the characteristics of the entrepreneur who is seeking financing. Both the behavioral and mental traits of the entrepreneur will be assessed to measure his level of trustworthiness (*amanah*). Conducting the due diligence on the entrepreneur is therefore compulsory (*wajib*) to prevent undue moral hazards that may undermine the venture.

A venture capitalist usually makes profits through capital gains generated from sale of shares upon exiting either via public listing or by stock repurchase by the investee company. They are not interested in a venture on permanent basis. In this way, one must closely study the nature of the venture capital partnership and see whether it fits in the *musyarakah* framework.

The *musyarakah* contract stipulates profit distribution based of capital and work. But quantifying these inputs into ownership shares as required by venture capitalists can be a daunting task. This is because division of ownership in venture capital is not based on relative monetary investment of the two parties. Rather, determining percentage of ownership usually involves a number of uncertain investment outcomes, such as expected revenues, profit margin, and price-earning ratio, in order to obtain the current value of the company. Once the ownership share becomes contractual, profit distribution via share purchases and buyback will be executed on exit.

For example, based on a given amount of capital injection, say $1 million, a venture capitalist determines the percentage of ownership it holds in the venture. Let's assume that the valuation model stipulated 40 percent share ownership for the venture capitalist. Suppose the value of company upon exiting is $30 million; in this way, the venture capitalist will earn $12 million (i.e., 0.4 x $30m) revenue. From the sale of shares, it will make $11 million net profits over the investment period.

Most of the rules on *musyarakah* are *fiqh* i.e., they are derived from human understanding of the Quranic teachings about justice and equity. The *fuqaha* (Islamic jurists) use reason (*'aql*) when they exercise *ijtihad* (independent thinking) on pertinent issues involving welfare (*maslahah*) of the people. When exercising *Ijtihad,* they are guided by the Quran and will not make opinions based on whims and fancies.

The *fuqaha* must look into this issue on ownership determination as it (i.e., ownership shares) is a parameter bearing legal claims once profits are realized. The issue of *gharar* (ambiguities) is a cause for concern, since ownership is determined by estimated and projected variables such as:

1. Projected profit of venture
2. Price-Earning ratio (P/E)
3. Venture capital return (VCR)

To impute uncertain outcomes as the above in determining a contractual parameter such as ownership share invites *gharar*. *Gharar* must be avoided in Islamic law of contract (*'aqd*), otherwise the contract is deemed null and void. Currently, rules on *musyarakah* only define distribution by virtue of capital and work (i.e., value addition) contributions and not by percentage of ownership. Although it is logical for *musyarakah* to define distribution by way of ownership shares, it can be done by virtue of capital and work contribution alone.

Three
Can Islamic banks really practice Musyarakah?

The contract of loan in Islam (*qard*), may not find ready application in business, as it is not profit-driven. An Islamic loan (*qard*) is purely made on altruism since in Islam, a person is not expected to make money out of loans (*qard*). To this effect, it is a misnomer to say that an Islamic bank is in the business of giving loans to customers.

Since Islamic banks are not allowed to make profit by making loans to customers, what alternatives are available? Theoretically, Islamic banking can offer two categories of financial contracts. First, it deals with asset-based financing, such as *murabahah, salam, istisna', and al-ijarah.* Secondly, an Islamic bank can pursue business on the basis of partnership, such as *mudarabah* and *musyarakah.*

How useful these instruments are to the modern business world is interesting to see. In modern business, entrepreneurs obtain funds from a variety of sources, such as their own savings, family and friends, suppliers and trade credits, commercial banks, venture capital, public equity offerings, and many more.

Before money from these sources can be raised, it is important to know what the entrepreneur does with the money. Is it for business expansion, starting a new business venture, or simply to pay off debt? If he desires to start a business, he must first rely on his own savings or funds from friends and relatives. It will be futile to visit the bank for fresh loans, with no collateral and no interest-based banks would want to swallow the risks to finance a new business.

It is a big decision, as the risks involved can be enormous. Not only does he has to deal with problems pertaining to the human being, such as ethics and hard work, but also his ability to solve problems in the operational aspect of business, such as planning, forecasting, market research, sales, people management, product design, legal documentations, etc.

How would Islamic finance respond to the requirement of capital and risks associated with the new business? To answer this question, the *musyarakah* contract can be useful. It is useful to remember that *musyarakah* is not a financial contract meant for banking alone. In fact, it is meant for any ordinary financial transaction.

In Malaysia, the introduction of Islamic values in economic life has initially focused on the banking sector. It is thus natural that people always associate *musyarakah* and also *mudarabah* with banking.

In Islamic jurisprudence, the term *shirkah* is commonly used to denote *musyarakah*. *Shirkah* means "sharing." It can be classified into two, namely *shirkat-ul-milk* and *shirkah-ul-aqd*. *Shirkat-ul-milk* is a joint ownership by two or more persons in a particular property. This contract is not relevant to our present problems.

Musharakah Financing

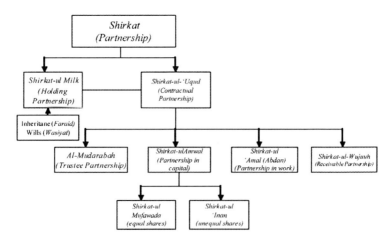

Figure 4.1 *Musharakah*

Shirkat-ul-aqd means a partnership affected by a mutual contract, which can be translated as a "joint commercial enterprise." Further classification of *shirkah-ul-aqd* into three categories will show its relevance to the requirement of setting up a new business.

The first category is *shirkat-ul-amwal*. In this financial contract, all partners invest some capital as well as expertise into the new business. Second, *shirkat-ul-'amal* involves only services rendered by partners. Finally, there is *shirkat-ul-wujuh,* where no capital input is required. Based on goodwill, the business purchases goods on credit and sell them cash.

The profit generated from the business of *shirkat* will be distributed among the partners at an agreed ratio or percentage. These business ventures require sophisticated marketing skills. Of the three types of *shirkat-ul-'aqd,* the first kind—namely *shirkat-ul-amwal*—is associated with *musyarakah* financing.

In fact, the term *musyarakah* is not readily found in books of *Fiqh.* It was casually used in Islamic banking literatures to imply *shirkat-ul-amwal,* as it deals with capital investment.

Leaving banking aside, let us look again at the role of *musyarakah/ shirkat-ul-amwal* in all business set up. In fact, all forms of modern business organization today are based on *musyarakah,* with the exception of sole proprietorship and a sleeping partnership.

In *musyarakah,* all partners are required to take an active role in running the business. Let's say Ligat Sdn Bhd is a *musyarakah* company. It manufactured product X with a ready market in India. Paid-up capital is $100,000 with the business is jointly owned by Aziz, Lim, Jamal, and Muthu, with a share capital of 50 percent, 10 percent, 5 percent and 35 percent respectively. They worked full time for the company on many things, such as product design, marketing, and promotion and finance.

What are the rules available in *musyarakah* on the distribution of profit? There is no single definite rule available, but here are some opinions of Muslim jurists.

According to Imam Shafi'i, each partner receives a profit exactly in the proportion of his investment. However, Imam Ahmad says the ratio of profit may differ from the ratio of investment if it is agreed between partners with their free consent. A middle view was adopted by Imam Abu

Hanifa that the ratio of profit may differ from the ratio of investment under normal conditions.

Despite the differences in opinion on profit distribution, the jurists are unanimous with regard to two principles. First, the distribution of profit cannot be determined in an absolute or lump sum amount. This is because there is no certainty of profit in the venture. In other words, in a financing contract in Islam only allows a predetermination of profit in ratios but not in the absolute sum.

Secondly, all jurists agree that each partner shall suffer loss exactly according to his capital investment. However, this does not imply that *musyarakah* is only confined to a limited liability company. If the loss exceeds the paid-up capital, the balance could be raised from the partners' personal assets. Further research should be done to clarify the legal implication of *musyarakah* financing on business profit and loss performance.

At this point, we assume that all capital for the new business is obtained from personal savings or assets of the owners. Capital injection from banks at this stage of business development is not needed. It becomes relevant when the company needs fresh capital for the purpose of business expansion. Suppose now the company wishes to expand production in India involving high overhead capital. Under a *musyarakah* arrangement, an Islamic bank can inject part of the capital.

The problem I want to highlight is the following: When an Islamic bank in Malaysia undertakes a *musyarakah* venture with Ligat Sdn Bhd, the problem of share-ownership is inevitable. In Malaysia, the United States, and most capitalist economies, a commercial bank is not allowed to buy over or undertake joint venture investments with a private company. This has something to do with the use of public funds for private benefit. There seems to be some conflict of interest. For this reason, the Anglo-Saxon banking system prohibits banking companies from engaging in joint ventures and underwriting of securities.

But does Bank Negara Malaysia allow an Islamic bank to conduct *musyarakah* via the Islamic Banking Act (IBA) 1983? Are they aware that *musyarakah* means practically linking banking to commerce? Indeed, if there is a clear reference in the Islamic Banking Act 1983 allowing such linking, it can revolutionize the banking industry in this country. When this happens, conventional banks will also ask for the same privilege.

We are not able to provide clear answers, but it is an irony that *musyarakah* financing have not been a popular choice among Islamic banks in Malaysia. The poor show of *musyarakah* in their balance sheet is appalling. When other countries are fast dismantling the wall delinking banking and commerce, Islamic banks in Malaysia are going in the opposite direction. They have been given such a rare privilege via IBA 1983, but unable to exploit the golden opportunity given to them.

Four
Mudarabah Financing and Human Capital

The application of trustee partnership (*mudarabah*) financing in the banking business has not received much attention as in fund management. In the Lembaga Tabung Haji (LTH) and Metrowangsa disputes, the latter serving as the *mudarib* (agent-entrepreneur) was entrusted to manage LTH's investments on a profit-sharing basis. Under the *mudarabah* system, the *mudarib* cannot declare upfront any contractual return on the investment, say 30 percent per annum. Likewise, the contract does not provide any form of capital protection.

The *mudarabah* contract is unique in the sense that it gives equal standing to human and money capital alike. The *mudarib*, the party who provides human capital (i.e., knowledge and skills) is not salaried. He will not receive the fat salaries normally awarded to general managers, even though he is holding similar obligations. He is also not furnished with a company car, exclusive golf club memberships, or other attractive bonuses. There is no disagreement among the school of fiqh (*mazhab*) on this matter.

The *mudarib*, however, according to Islamic jurists (*fuqaha*) can use some portions of the capital to pay for his subsistence needs, such as daily meals and traveling costs. In this manner, the *rabbul mal* will not be burdened with high overhead costs common in joint-stock companies. Hence, the objectives of the *mudarib* and *rabbul* will not clash, and agency problem can be kept to a minimum.

While modern finance only puts money capital as prerequisite to a business venture, *mudarabah* places human capital in equal footing. It put forth knowledge, skills, creative ideas, and experience as inputs. Here, human capital will not be paid on the basis of the contract of hire (*al-ijarah 'amal*), but profit sharing.

In this way, the *mudarib* is simply not a person who has no capital with which to start a business. Most importantly, he must have the knowledge and market skills and a proven track record in the business he intends to venture into. He must also have enough money to sustain his lifestyle and family commitment. In other words, the *mudarib* is financially stable and pursues *mudarabah* projects as a professional. He is not looking for fat salaries but the lucrative gains from profit-sharing contracts.

With the money-capital given to him, the *mudarib* will purchase commodities to be sold at a profit. The main feature of *mudarabah* is, therefore, trust *(amanah),* which means that the *rabbulmal* stands to lose his capital in the event of losses.

One may ask how *mudarabah* is different from modern partnership. The answer is simply that *mudarabah* is based on the partnership of capital and service. The *rabbulmal* contributes capital, while the *mudarib* contributes service. Unlike modern partnerships, no party in a *mudarabah* contract contributes both inputs.

In this sense, allocation of profits and losses between the *mudarib* and *rabbulmal* must be made with care to prevent *gharar* (uncertainty) in contractual obligations. In principle, *mudarabah* provides a system of distribution as follows:

- Profit distribution: the contract specifies a stated fraction or ratio, say 40 percent to *rabbulmal* and 60 percent to *mudarib*. The ratio is set on the basis of project risks, value-addition, and liabilities.
- Loss distribution due to market risks: absorbed by *rabbulmal*.
- Loss distribution due to negligence/moral hazard (*ghasib*): absorbed by *mudarib*.

On the loss distribution rule arising from market risks, it looks unfair to burden the *rabulmal* alone while the *mudarib* goes free. For example, if $50,000 is injected in the *mudarabah* business and sales only amounted to $20,000, the corresponding loss of $30,000 shall fall on the *rabbulmal*. Although the *mudarib* does not suffer direct financial losses, his real loss will be his opportunity cost he has forgone, that is the income he could have earned if he chose to work elsewhere. As a seasoned manager working for a big corporation, he could have easily earned $20,000 per month plus perks.

Islamic banking should consider the *mudarabah* financing model seriously if it desires to command a market niche. Unlike *al-bai-bithaman ajil* (BBA) and *al-ijarah thumma al-bay'* (AITAB), *mudarabah* financing is brand new. It allows the bank to inject fresh risk capital in to the *mudarabah* project only when it has identified the qualified *mudarib*. Rules of *mudarabah* protect the bank from moral hazard since firstly, fixed salary does not constitute *mudarabah* expenses. Secondly, as a form of unlimited liability partnership, the *mudarabah* contract will not prevent the *rabbulmal* from claiming the personal wealth of the *mudarib* (i.e., by due process of the law) if the losses arise from negligence.

Five
Mudarabah and Asymmetric Information

At least three factors can help explain why *mudarabah* is difficult to apply in the banking business. These are problems related to the guidelines in BAFIA 1989, double taxation, and legal disputes.

Mudarabah financing is also prone to the problem of information cost involving the financial structure of the banking firm. When information about the manager (*mudarib*) is known to the financier (*rabbulmal*), markets for *mudarabah* capital and *mudarabah* deposits are expected to operate more efficiently.

But how would it be possible for the financier to know that the *mudarib* is a trustworthy partner? How can he be certain that the *mudarib* uses the *mudarabah* capital according to the stipulated covenants? Can Islamic banking control the *mudarabah* operations?

It is true that information poses one major problem to the profit-loss sharing system (PLS) in the banking business. Financiers, namely the banks and depositors, possess little control over information, especially on fund utilization.

Financial intermediation is a natural consequence of asymmetric information, where one party in a transaction has more information than the other. In Islamic banking, the intermediary role is even more problematic, given the variety of new financial products available in the financial market. That is, people with differing tastes, preferences, and religious affiliation have many options open to them.

Generally, a firm has a number of options to raise capital. In the conventional market, it can use bank loans. On a broader scale, issuing stocks and bonds provides more liquidity, but only companies with high credentials can do so. When the Islamic options provide better prospects, the firms are expected to raise capital via *murabahah, al-bai-bithaman ajil,* and the *mudarabah-musyarakah* principles.

Product choice, however, depends on what is best for the fund users. When risk is low, the firm may want to use debt financing. Projects with higher risk profile will likely use equity. Often, when a firm approaches banks for funding, it is likely that the latter has less idea what the former has in mind. Hence, asymmetric information is a natural consequent of business and human relation. Due to asymmetric information, the following two problems are inevitable:

1) Adverse selection.
2) Moral hazards.

In *mudarabah* business, adverse selection is finding out of the true risk of the fund user (*mudarib*) before the *mudarabah* funding is injected into the business. It is here that due diligence is most important. It aims to assess risk and value added roles of the *mudarib*.

It requires the bank as *rabbulmal* to assess the firm's (i.e., *mudarib*) entrepreneurial visions and objectives. It must investigate the management team and the products and technology involved in the business. Business plans should be able to lay out the firm's market strategy, financial projections, and manufacturing processes.

As the *mudarabah* contract is new to banking, innovative techniques should be used to appraise project proposals that go beyond traditional risk and credit analysis. The due diligence process is not a banker's cup of tea. But getting new expertise to perform due diligence can steer a *mudarabah* venture successfully and help improve a bank's performance.

One danger is obvious when the bank resorts to using the profit-loss sharing ratio as the benchmarking criterion. For example, the bank may offer a prospective *mudarib* a profit- sharing ratio (PSR) of 20:80 (i.e., bank with 80 percent share) instead of a PSR of 60:40. The bank, in the final analysis, may have instead chosen a project run by a *mudarib* who turns out to be a fraud. The bad *mudarib* does not mind receiving a lower profit share (i.e., 20 percent), since he has plans to deceive the *rabbulmal* after all.

He is willing to accept the less favorable PSR, since he knows how to manipulate the partnership. What happens now is that adverse selection takes place when the bank displaces good *mudaribs* who find the PSR offered by bank too costly.

Of course, in *mudarabah,* the most important variable is the expected profit rate. In some cases, for example contract financing, the expected profit rate is known, and how much profit the bank wants to make depends predominantly on the negotiated PSR.

While adverse selection looks into the problem of displacing the good *mudaribs,* the risk of moral hazards is about monitoring a *mudarib* who unknowingly may have been wrongly selected. Hence the bank may have to deal with a *mudarib* who may not be using the *mudarabah* funds in the interest of the project, but for his own selfish interest.

Again, the monitoring cost will be substantial, and traditional banks may not be able to bear it. In conventional equity finance, the moral hazards are often seen in the principal-agent problem.

In *mudarabah* financing, the *rabbulmal* or shareholders own the firm's net worth, while the *mudarib* or the managers control the firm's assets. The moral hazard problem arises when the *mudarib* is motivated to maximize the firm's value as the owners do. Hence, to determine the proper utilization of the *mudarabah* fund by the *mudarib,* a detailed and costly monitoring system is an important factor to consider.

In view of the above problems, installing a support system is necessary to see the *mudarabah* mechanism effectively implemented. It is meaningless to arrive at complex models to generate a scheme of realistic profit-sharing ratios if the system is not transparent to cut down problems arising from asymmetric information. The future of *mudarabah* banking in this country will depend on the ability to produce such a support system.

Six
Mudarabah Investment Fund

The lack of interest in *mudarabah* and *musharakah* financing in the banking business can be attributed to many factors. One is quite obvious, that Islamic banks are worried that people will place their money elsewhere, since *mudarabah* deposits are risky. That is, a *mudarabah* placement does not provide fixed contractual return. It also does not offer capital protection. Likewise, losses incurred in *mudarabah* financing will not erode *al-wadiah* deposits, but shareholders' capital. Without enough deposits and capital, a bank cannot make BBA and AITAB financing, what more in equities.

As *mudarabah* cannot find ready application, the role of the interest-free banking system (IFBS) in promoting small and medium-scale industry (SMI), has been marginal. Although the IFBS may have other modes of financing on the line such as *murabahah* and *al-bai-bithamanjil*, they are not niche products. They cannot introduce radical changes to the banking business.

The equity model of banking through *mudarabah* and *musyarakah* has the potential to create dynamic changes in the banking industry. They should be given a chance to prove their worth in the market. It requires a serious commitment from the relevant authorities, namely the Ministry of Finance, Ministry of International Trade and Industry, and the newly formed Ministry of Entrepreneur Development to see successful run of the equity model.

One way is to set up a *Mudarabah* Investment Fund (MIF). Like many development funds offered by the government, such as the New Enterprise Fund (NEF), Bumiputra Industrial Fund (BIF), Principal Guarantee Scheme, etc., the *mudarabah* fund can be managed instead by the interest-free banking system under the guardianship of the Credit Guarantee Corporation (CGC).

In this case, certain policy adjustments are required in the CGC as it would now deal with equity capital rather than loans. The *Mudarabah* Investment Fund (MIF) will help secure the future success of the *mudarabah/ musyarakah* approach to banking in this country.

We would then be able to know whether the IFBS and Bank Islam (M) Bhd would indeed be willing to extract the benefits of the equity model, given the relatively reduced pressure in securing funds from depositors. If successful, more information can be obtained about the bank's profit performance and the economies of scale and scope generated from the *mudarabah/musyarakah* system.

My main concern here is about financing small and medium-scale industries. Although many entrepreneurs have attended development workshops to learn the skills of financial management, accounting, and marketing and to acquire numerous motivational tips to sharpen business acumen, the bottom line remains the same, i.e., capital.

Even though some say it is no longer capital but technology, I would still insist that the latter is only relevant to large capital-intensive export oriented companies. But capital is hard to find, especially for start-ups and entrepreneurs who have relatively less exposure to the vendor and umbrella system. They are required to present securities and collaterals that are impossible to find even though the business idea is genuine and has the potential to succeed. It is here equity capital finds its natural path.

The *Mudarabah* Investment Funds can now be used to try out the potentials of *mudarabah/musharakah* instruments in the interest-free banking system. If successful, the public can be assured that, if carefully monitored, the bank can generate more profits from the *mudarabah* system, which also means higher returns for depositors.

Then the question of fear and worry about investment in the *mudarabah* deposits becomes less stressful. Instead, more people are looking forward to invest in *mudarabah* deposits. The *Mudarabah* Investment Fund can only be set up after careful planning on manpower requirements on project or risk management are undertaken. The IBFS can either set up a subsidiary to execute project monitoring activities or hire consultants to do so.

This can be done with the cooperation of the CGC. The *Mudarabah* Investment Fund could be the only way SMIs can obtain capital from equity financing via the banking industry. Presently, equity finance is a privilege for companies listed on the KLSE. For expansion purposes, they can obtain funds from new share issues. So when big business flourishes thanks to equity participation, the small ones remain paralyzed as they are pushed to take loans bearing strict security requirements.

Small firms have to bear this unwarranted burden because the law does not recognize partnership as a separate legal entity and therefore inflicts unlimited liability of losses onto the individual entrepreneur. On the other hand, the corporations, as legal entities, would not be liable for liabilities more than their shareholdings.

Seven
Third party guarantee scheme for Mudarabah ventures

Early literature on Islamic banking is replete with ideas about applying profit-loss sharing principles in the banking business. Terms such as *mudarabah, al-qirad,* and *musyarakah* were used to explain the nature of Islamic banking as an alternative to interest-based lending.

Among the early writers were Abu Saud, Nejetullah Sidiqqi, and Muhammad Uzair, although other notable contribution by Naggar, Umar Chapra, and Zainuddin Ahmad are well-recognized.

These writings, in general, proposed at a conceptual level the application of profit-loss sharing (PLS) principles in the banking firm via *mudarabah* contracts. The PLS system is expected to produce an equitable business relationship where depositors, entrepreneurs, and financial intermediaries will collectively take part in risk-taking ventures.

At the theoretical level, some attempts have been made to analyze the economic implication of the PLS system. These include Mohsin Khan's mathematical approach to explain the advantage of PLS in the banking system liability management. Zubair Hasan spelt out how the profit rate in the PLS financial system is determined.

On bank asset management, the PLS system was argued to be anti-cyclical. But these models assumed the existence of a financial system that supports *mudarabah/ musharakah* banking, which has, however, oversimplified the real problems faced by bankers today. The Malaysian example is a good case to study.

The latest Bank Negara report indicated that in 1994, *mudarabah* constitutes only 0.04 percent of Bank Islam Malaysia Bhd's (BIMB) assets, while deferred sale activities commanded a handsome 90.5 percent. The question now is why Islamic banks are staying away from *mudarabah* and adopted credit sale activities, financing such as *murabahah* and *al-bai-bithaman ajil*.

There are three main factors why this is so, namely: 1) Islamic banking Act 1983/BAFIA 1989, 2) unfavorable system of taxation, and 3) legal disputes in Islamic banking contracts. Another problem is about capital protection of *mudarabah* investments. Does the *Shariah* allow *mudarabah* capital protection?

A guarantee scheme may not be relevant to *mudarabah* ventures, as the nature of the *mudarabah* contract does not require the *mudarib* to provide capital guarantees. This is because *mudarabah* is a profit-loss-sharing scheme. It is not a loan. Loans require collateral and guarantees. The need for a principal guarantee scheme (PGS) is only relevant when the loan is clean or unsecured.

In Malaysia, loan guarantee is granted by the Credit Guarantee Corp Malaysia Bhd (CGC) established in 1972 for loans given to small-scale enterprises (SSEs). Among others, the shareholders of the CGC are the commercial banks, finance companies, and the Central Bank.

Many guarantee schemes were provided by CGC, among which are the New Principal Guarantee Scheme (NPGS) introduced to replace the PGS, the Loan Fund for Hawkers and Petty Traders, and the Association Special Loan Scheme. Under the NPGS, since its introduction in February 1998, 3,146 loan applications amounting to RM530.1 million have been approved.

How does the NPGS work? Simply, the CGC will charge borrowing companies some commission on the guarantee cover. The bank concerned normally determines the interest rate on the loan based on its own terms and conditions.

For example, on a $100,000 unsecured loan given by ABbank to Gembira Sdn Bhd, the interest rate is 2 percent above ABbank's base lending rate (BLR). The guarantee cover of the same amount, say, 1 percent of the principal loan or $10,000. It is normal that borrowers have to pay higher commissions to CGC if payment periods are extended.

Can the principle of guarantee be applied to Islamic financing? The principle of *Al-Kafalah* is most suitable and currently applied in letters of guarantee. But given the present passive role of *mudarabah* financing, the need to set up an *Al-Kafalah* Islamic principal guarantee scheme (IPGS) is worth trying. This would motivate Islamic banks to give out more *mudarabah* funds to small and medium-scale enterprises.

There are two ways how this can be done. Firstly, the IPGS can be sponsored by the CGC itself. This requires BIMB, Islamic banking divisions, and the Central Bank to allocate special funds to guarantee *mudarabah* capital. In other words, CGC can open an Islamic window for Islam banking instruments, particularly for *mudarabah* and *musharakah* transactions.

In the second approach, a new company can be formed to complement CGC's activities. The company can be a subsidiary of CGC itself, or a separate entity altogether. For example, a company can be formed with BIMB, Islamic banking divisions, and Bank Negara Malaysia (BNM) playing the major role of shareholders.

The firm can be called *Mudarabah Guarantee Corp. Sdn Bhd* (MGC) or *Kafalah House*. The role of the MGC is crucial, given the risky nature of *mudarabah* activities that commercial banks have relatively less experience with. An overnight experiment in *mudarabah* without calculated preparatory work on risk analysis could be an uneventful venture. Hence, setting up the IPGS as a temporary measure is a necessity to help alleviate the stress faced by Islamic banks if they wish to conduct *mudarabah* financing.

However, the notion of giving a guarantee on *mudarabah* seemed to conflict with the philosophy of profit-loss sharing (*al-ghorm bil ghonm*). In fact, a legal opinion (*fatwa*) from *Dalla Albaraka* declared that giving a guarantee to the capital sum of *mudarabah* by the working agent (*mudarib*) is unlawful. However, if the guarantee is given by the government, then it is allowed. This is an opinion of the *fuqaha* in Jordan on the issuance of *muqarada* (also known as *mudarabah*) bond by the Jordanian government in 1997.

But all is not lost. The idea of guarantee on *mudarabah* capital does not involve loss due to market risk. It is merely made to protect investors (*rabbulmal*) from the negligence of *mudarib*. In this manner, the *rabbulmal* can demand surety or guarantee from the *mudarib* to return his capital if loss is caused by negligence. The guarantee can be acquired from a third party, government, or private entities. This is confirmed in a *Dalla Albaraka fatwa* about giving surety on *mudarabah* capital arising from the negligence (*ghasib*) of *mudarib*. The legal opinion (*fatwa*) read like this:

> Question: Is it permissible to ask the *mudarib* or entrepreneur for a sponsor or guarantee?

> Fatwa: Stipulating the condition for a sponsor or a guarantor from a *mudarib* is legally permissible as a surety against transgression or negligence (First *Albaraka* Seminar, *Fatwa* No 5).

In this manner, Islamic banks should not have given up hope to apply *mudarabah*. *Mudarabah* can certainly become a niche product when Muslim practitioners and Islamic banks' major shareholders put their will power and determination on trial. Otherwise, the business will soon end up converging with conventional practices, thus losing the Islamic identity.

Eight
Monitoring System in Mudarabah

The restriction of the Banking and Financial Institution Act 1989 (BAFIA) on share-holdings by commercial banks remains a paradox, given Bank Negara's drive to introduce interest-free banking facilities (IFBS) nationwide.

According to BAFIA, *"no licensed institution (commercial bank) shall acquire or hold any shares of, or otherwise have an interest in shares in any corporation" (section 66).* Of course, there are exceptions especially in the share purchases of approved public listed companies up to 15 percent of bank's paid-up capital."

But this is too restrictive, as it hampers the bank's ability to do joint-ventures (JV) in the small and medium-scale industry. It also discounts venture capital investments by banks.

The introduction of the dual-banking system clearly indicates that the future of Islamic banking in Malaysia today no longer rests on Bank Islam Malaysia Berhad (BIMB) alone but also the interest-free banking system. The latter should also be given the same opportunity to exploit shareholding rights. However, some may ask a simple question—what has shareholding to do with interest-free banking?

The answer to the above question requires one to understand the concept of *mudarabah* and *musharakah*. If an interest-free bank buys shares of a listed company, the bank as an investor (*rabb-ul-mal*) is playing a role of a capitalist-cum-sleeping partner unless it owns substantial shares to gain control.

The latter would help reduce the agency problem arising from asymmetric information while the former would require some form of disclosure regulation to inform the public about the financial health of the firm.

Thus, the role of the firm as a *mudarib,* the agent providing management and operation expertise, is expected to be less prone to moral hazards and adverse selection inherent in most firms seeking external finance.

However, the above scenario only explains how the *Shariah* via the *mudarabah* and *musharakah* products, allows interest-free banks to participate in profit and risk-sharing activities of well-established companies. This is a good policy insofar as short-run profits are concerned, but should not be pursued as the ultimate *mudarabah* strategy, since it would tend to favor the rich over the lesser known entrepreneurs.

The Quran has clearly said that *"wealth must not circulate only among the rich ones among you"* (Al-Baqarah: 188). This also implies that Islamic banks should also pay attention to the capital needs of smaller firms, so that they too can enjoy a decent share of the nation's wealth.

The Malaysian legal system allows the formation of holding companies that indirectly utilize bank deposits at a relatively subsidized rate to pursue their profit-maximizing activities. For example, major owners of a commercial bank can form a holding company. This allows the holding company to acquire a significant portion of the bank's share capital. Thus, the bank becomes a subsidiary to the holding companies.

Now, if the company wishes to establish more subsidiaries, i.e., expand operations, and requires more capital to do so, by virtue of its direct link and therefore influence on the bank, it can obtain loans at the base lending rate.

What happens here is simply the following. Depositors will earn the normal rate of return (3 percent per annum) while the holding company makes much more since it has access to cheap loans. In the long run, banks and holding company owners get richer while depositors, the general public, practically gain no benefit from the activity.

The above scenario shows that there are always ways commercial banks can bypass BAFIA's restriction on shareholding. Who are the losers? Certainly, these are not the banks but the ordinary people, namely the depositors. The future of small companies is threatened when banks find comfort making loans to the big holding companies.

Thus, the need to place the interest-free banking system (IFBS) under the governance of Islamic Banking Act 1983 (IBA) is critical. This is because the direct participation of interest-free banks in commerce via equity investment is expected to generate higher earnings, that in turn will increase returns on Islamic deposits.

For example, depositors who wish to assume higher risks in view of higher returns may invest in the special *mudarabah* account. This is only possible when the bank has substantial control of the firm. In view of the need for close monitoring, the monitoring competence and risk management must be pursued with rigor.

Setting up a monitoring agency to detect financial distress in the enterprises and taking proactive measures to restructure or reorganize distressed companies should be the next step towards making *mudarabah* or *musharakah* a viable investment tool in interest-free banking. This will help nurture trust and confidence, thus reducing transaction costs and promoting healthy coordination as entrusted in the *mudarabah* contract between banks and non-bank companies.

Nine
Human Risk in Mudarabah Business

Al-mudarabah has constantly become a controversial instrument of Islamic finance today since it is, in its original mode, not made for real production. In essence, classical *mudarabah* is concerned with merchandise trade, and does not involve the production process in the modern sense. In *mudarabah,* the provider of capital (*rabbulmal*) invites a second party (*mudarib*) to embark in a trading mission on a profit-sharing basis. With the money-capital given to the *mudarib,* he will purchase articles of trade to be sold later at a profit. That is, the business vehicle of *mudarabah* is *al-murabahah* (mark-up cash sale).

Mudarabah, in essence, is not partnership of capital. It is a partnership of capital and human knowledge and skills. The main feature of *mudarabah* is, therefore, trust *(amanah),* which means the *rabbulmal* stands to lose his capital in the event of closure. For example, if a sum of $50,000 is injected in the *mudarabah* business, but sales only amount to $20,000, the loss amounting to $30,000 shall fall on the *rabbulmal*. The loss to the *mudarib* will be his opportunity cost, that is, money he can earn if he chooses to work elsewhere, say as a salaried worker.

The *mudarib,* however, is not an entrepreneur in the modern sense. The latter is responsible for making day-to-day decisions on how the best combination of factor inputs can be found to produce the profit-maximizing output. This mode of production is relatively absent in the pre-Islamic era, where goods are usually produced by artisans and craftsman and then directly sold at the bazaar.

SAIFUL AZHAR ROSLY

Islamic economists, however, have tried to interpret the relevance of *mudarabah* for modern application involving industrial capital and eventually ended up thinking that the banking firms as financiers should act as *rabbulmal*.

But can *mudarabah* be applied in banking when manufacturing, rather than trading, becomes the main line of business today? In this context, the *mudarib* will hire workers, and rent factories, and purchase machinery. Process of production such as these will not only end at the assembly line but right at our doorsteps. So, it involves marketing as well. This entrepreneurial skill is not the feature one finds in classical *mudarabah* where in the latter, a considerable effort is spent on long-distance caravan travel.

But can trust factors (*amanah*) become central in a *mudarabah* business where market risks are high and real losses can be disastrous? One can easily find in *mudarabah* literature that risks of losses due to negligence are liabilities the *mudarib* must bear. But losses arising from market risks fall only on the *rabbulmal*.

In a modern setup, this will not happen easily since entrepreneurial skills require the *mudarib* to exercise a considerable amount of freedom to execute business decisions. So, applying *mudarabah muqaiyyadah* (restrictive *mudarabah*) may not work entirely since this may distort creative and visionary approach to business. But giving too much freedom to the *mudarib* may lead him to make mistakes that can adversely affect sales and profits.

Should Islamic jurists presiding over *mudarabah* disputes make the *mudarib* liable for the losses caused by erroneous business strategies? Certainly under these circumstances, the *mudarib* is not in a position to provide capital guarantee. This will go against the *mudarabah* principle that says no capital protection except under the purview of negligence.

But can we say that incorrect business policy (i.e., unsystematic risk) is an act of negligence? This problem calls the need to investigate to what extent people are willing to become *rabbulmals* if no legal sound opinion on unsystematic risks is available.

In modern finance, unsystematic risks can be diversified if not eliminated completely. But systematic or market risks cannot be eliminated. So, any losses made here belong to the *rabbulmal*.

As expressed by Sarakhsi in his *Kitab al-Mabsut*, "in principle the *mudarabah* capital belongs to the owner, and as soon as the agent takes custody of the capital, he becomes a *wakil* (an authorized representative) in it. If the contract becomes improper (*fasid*), the worker gets wages equivalent to his labor expended in the business transaction. If the agent acts contrary to the instructions of the capital owner, he becomes a usurper (*ghasib*) and therefore responsible for the capital."

But what is the opinion of Islamic jurists (*fuqaha*) on unsystematic risk, since it has no clear definition under Sharaksi's observation above? Can the *mudarib* be penalized for his error as he tries hard to make profits? Does this error amount to *ghasib*? How will the *fuqaha* distinguish losses arising from negligence and those from unsystematic risks?

These are problems that Islamic economists must try to study with full conviction, as the remedy does not only fall on the Islamic fund providers such as Islamic banks, unit trusts, and the *Baitulmals* alone. A model on Islamic risk management must be in place before anyone tries to experiment *mudarabah* in an economy like Malaysia where the production function and customs are quite different from that found in the early Islamic history.

SECTION FIVE

MACROECONOMIC ISSUES

One
Idle-Balances in Islamic banking

Banking performance depends, among other things, on the products sold. A bank can also improve performance by reducing overheads and paying low interest to depositors. Since profit is the difference between total revenues and costs, a sound asset-liability management policy is vital in determining a bank's long-run growth.

The same applies to Islamic banking today. It must explore untapped markets with niche products. To gain the respect, Islamic banks should look for a competitive advantage somewhere. But how?

Investment in equities such as *musyarakah* is one option, although the risk factor may not allow banks to do so. This is because Islamic banks are acting more like creditors than a business and trading partner. They cannot afford to assume risks that may prove detrimental to depositors and shareholders.

Al-bai-bithaman ajil (BBA) has been widely used in both retail and business financing involving landed properties, cars, machinery, and working capital. BBA is claimed a better alternative to equity because it is relatively safer. It is also able to meet liquidity needs via securitization and seem able to conform to the principles of profitability, safety and liquidity in banking.

Up to May 1996, total deposits in Islamic banking amounted to RM2,031.2 million while total financing settled at RM1,366.7 million.

213

There seems to be a gap of RM664.5 million not fully used by Islamic banks. In contrast, in March 1996, traditional commercial banks were able to mobilize RM174.586 billion of deposits but not enough to finance RM185.235 billion of loans and advances made to borrowers.

This negative saving-investment gap seems to show that Malaysians are spending more and saving less. This is not healthy, as low domestic savings invites more borrowing, especially from foreign sources. The point is, why a negative gap for conventional banking while Islamic banks saw a positive gap? Why so much idle balances in Islamic banks? Why the high liquidity?

Partly, this is because Islamic banks have relatively no new products on the shelf. Currently, the prospect of *musyarakah* and *mudarabah* investment is not good unless Bank Negara directed all Islamic banks to apply partnership contracts in financing. At present, *mudarabah* investment of Islamic banks only serves to fulfill statutory liquidity requirements via investment in government Islamic Investments (GII).

Islamic banks can also help improve the structure of the current BBA product. For example, it can do away with the general security deposits not found in conventional banks. It can also look for better alternatives to existing methods of profit determination.

For example, *al-ijarah thumma al-bay'* (AITAB) auto financing runs on Rule 78. This rule tends to favor the bank when borrowers opt for early settlement. The payment system remains to show a pyramid pattern with most profits collected during the early period of repayment. Although banks will give rebates (*ibra*), the amount given is far less than the expected savings from early repayment.

God says in the Quran that, "Those who believe and work righteousness, no burden do We place on any soul, but that which it can bear..." *(al-A'raf: 42)*. But God also says that, "do men think that they will be left alone on saying, 'We believe,' and that they will not be tested." *(Al-Ankabut: 1)*

In other words, God is Most Just (*Al-'Adlu*). When man is given a job, whether he is a janitor, bus driver, teacher, or banker, the job is a test from the Creator. To pass the test, he should do his job in the best possible manner. Failing to do so is ingratitude. When done deliberately, he is disregarding God's bounties. The responsibility and trust (*amanah*) put on shareholders and managers of an Islamic bank are indeed enormous.

Islamic banks must find ways to close the gap. Failing to do so can mean many things. First, Islamic banks are less likely to help stabilized the economy. The huge cash balances will stifle investments, and markets cannot be cleared. Accumulating inventories will see fewer people with jobs. Secondly, holding huge idle balances is akin to hoarding (*ihtikar*). Business cannot expand because there are not enough operating funds to play with. Although Islamic banks may have the cash, it could not be released without the appropriate financial products. For example, manufacturing and agriculture financing can use loans, but not BBA. They need profit-sharing products and new products such as *musyarakah*, *al-qirad*, *salam* and *istisna'*.

But Islamic banks cannot supply these niche products. They seemed trapped in the BBA mindset. Third, BBA may work in retail banking as most deal with asset purchases. It has no potency in development financing. In this manner, Islamic banking operations are limited to retail business involving asset purchases such as homes, cars, electrical appliances, and some machinery.

To depend on BBA alone is bad policy, as the banks cannot make a meaningful breakthrough in manufacturing and agriculture. Cash balances will accumulate. A bank with a high cash/asset ratio is always a troubled one and an Islamic bank with one is not any different. In 2002 and 2003, the financing-deposit (FD) ratio has increased from 68.9 percent to 80.7 percent. This good sign of asset utilization seems to show that Islamic banking is doing well. Bank Negara Malaysia reported that the drop in the FD ratio is largely due to rapid increase in financing compared with deposits in the same period.

One likely reason for the rapid increase in financing is the higher demand for BBA home financing given that prospective home buyers believed that cost of funds is on the rise. BBA as a fixed rate asset is a better choice since it protects customers from paying higher instalments as interest rate rises.

Two
Islamic Universal Banking

In 1995, Islamic banking was reported to command only 1.7 percent and 1.9 percent of total deposits and financing in the banking industry. Now the market share has risen to about 10 percent. Given more than a decade (twelve years) of operation, Malaysian Islamic banking practitioners could have done a better job, only if they take note of the theoretical foundations of the system.

In theory, an Islamic bank operates to make profits and it must do so to promote economic justice. The term "trading and commerce" (*al- bay'*) in the Quran refers to a type of business dealing that invites cooperation and mutual help. It leads to economic justice, since no one gets hurt in the process. Through the spirit of sharing and cooperation, as embodied in any commercial endeavor, business transactions run on fair prices. In this way, an equitable distribution of income can be realized such that wealth according to the Quran, "does not circulate among the rich among you." (59:7)

The question now is, can the pursuit of economic justice via the Islamic banking industry help increase the size of deposits and financing to, say, 5 percent by the year 2000 and 20 percent by 2010? What are the necessary strategies needed to propel Islamic banking towards that end? Banking practitioners can lend some answers but let me try to propose one option.

This has something to do with reducing overhead costs in the banking business. Doing so can also help reduce prices of *al-bai-bithaman ajil* products. Cheaper financing can lead to higher demand for BBA funds and increase the volume of Islamic financing.

Likewise, to increase financing, bankers need more deposits. This is only possible when Islamic deposits provide better rates of return than conventional deposits. But this approach requires an Islamic bank to diversify its assets by reducing BBA financing. A good mix of equity, leasing, and credit sale activities is a workable option.

The main idea now is to conduct these financing facilities under one roof, say by bank A. If a customer wishes to renew or purchase an insurance policy, he can do so in bank A; or if he wants to purchase stocks, he does not have to waste his time seeing a broker elsewhere, since bank A can handle stock transactions as well. Companies that hold accounts with bank A and plan to go public do not have to look for underwriters, since bank A can also underwrite securities. What we see here is a simple model where bank A does not have to form new subsidiaries to undertake these "non-banking" activities. It can save operations costs and help reduce the cost of banking services and the price of financial products.

I am referring to the simple textbook concept of scale economies. A firm is said to benefit from economies of scale when cost per unit falls as output increases. BAFIA 1992 does not allow banks to be engaged in leasing, insurance, stocks and underwriting transactions under one roof. Hence, to skip banking laws, attempts to venture into new "non-banking" activities can only be made by forming subsidiaries.

These subsidiaries are no longer governed by banking laws. However, if bank A plans to form a subsidiary, or many subsidiaries, the cost of doing so is not cheap. New CEOs, managers, and officers must be appointed, which adds more pressure on manpower shortages. More costs such as rentals of office premises and maintenance must be met, putting pressure on capital.

However, when these "non-banking" operations are carried out by one bank alone, unnecessary costs can be avoided. It can reduce the cost of banking operations. Banks can run more efficiently when they are allowed to take on "non-banking" activities under one roof.

In banking, cost reduction from economies of scale refers to the non-financial aspects of banking operations, namely the non-interest costs and non-profit costs in the conventional and interest-free banks respectively. These costs include the physical cost of operations, sometimes known as the resource costs involving personnel, fixed overhead, and buildings. How these costs are translated into cost of financing, namely interest rate or profit rate, can easily be observed in the following equations.

1. Contractual interest rate = base lending rate (BLR) + risk premium (spread)
2. Contractual profit rate = base profit rate (BPR) + risk premium (spread)
3. Base lending rate (BLR) or Base profit rate (BPF) = cost of deposits + operating cost + bank's profit margin.

If a bank embarks on the "non-banking" activities under one roof, it can reduce cost of operation (eq. 3). This, in turn, lowers interest rates on loans or profit rates on BBA and *murabahah* products.

In Japan and Germany, banks are allowed to do all of the above, hence the name "Universal banking." They are allowed to purchase stocks of publicly listed corporations as well as those over the counter. In Germany, a bank provides insurance as well as stock-broking services. But in Malaysia, the Banking and Financial Institution Act 1992 limits commercial banks from doing the same. However, they are allowed to do so by forming subsidiaries.

Interestingly enough, the only full-fledged Islamic bank in Malaysia, namely Bank Islam Malaysia Berhad (BIMB) is free from BAFIA 1989, since BIMB runs under the Islamic Banking Act 1983. The Act says that an Islamic bank is, *"any company which carries on the Islamic banking business and hold a valid license."* Further on, the Act defines the nature of Islamic banking business as *"a banking business whose aims and operations do not involve any element which is not approved by the religion of Islam."*

If I am not wrong, business relating to insurance services (*takaful*), leasing (*ijarah*), stock-broking (*wakalah*), unit trusts (*wakalah-mudarabah*), underwriting (*al-bay'*) and equity (*musyarakah*) are approved by the religion of Islam. So why are they not pursued under one roof by BIMB?

Economies of scale can only be realized as size increases, which means portfolio diversification. What seems to happen today is the opposite. BIMB promotes credit sale products. When the Islamic Banking Act literally allows BIMB to offer multiple services under one roof, it opted to do so by opening subsidiaries, namely Takaful Sdn. Bhd. (insurance), Amanah

Saham Bank Islam (unit trusts), Bank Islam Brokerage (stock- broking), Bank Islam Consumer Financing (trading) and Bank Islam Research and Training (BIRT).

What we see in the above is an Islamic banking operation that seems to run under BAFIA control. The losers are not the bank managers, since they are salaried personnel, but customers. If BAFIA 1992 put a wall between banking and commerce, why didn't they (i.e., Islamic banks) pursue universal banking when such wall does not exists in the IBA 1983.

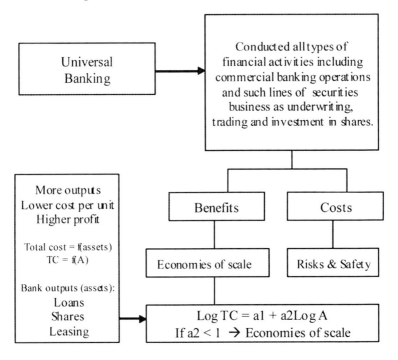

Figure 5.1 Universal Banking

Three
Islamic and Foreign Banking in Malaysia

Foreign banking activity in Malaysia has been on the decline. The share of foreign banks in total loans and advances was around 69 percent in 1970, which declined to 26 percent in 1993. Foreign banks have been complaining about the discriminatory nature of the various policy measures of Bank Negara Malaysia.

In 1959, there were eighteen foreign banks out of a total of twenty-six commercial banks. These 18 banks, mostly dominated by British and Chinese overseas banks, operated 99 branch offices out of the total 111 branch offices. The network of branch offices of foreign banks was concentrated in the large population centers and their main concern was financing of international and domestic trade and the provision of working capital to large firms.

Such predominance of foreign presence in the commercial banking industry gave a sense of urgency to the government. Using two policy measures, namely licensing and requirement for prior permission to open new branches, the dominance of foreign banks was reduced. Between 1959 and 1973, new banking licenses were awarded to nine domestic banks and eight foreign banks. But there was only a net increase of three foreign banks due to the closing down of six of them. At the end of 1973, there were seventeen domestic banks and nineteen foreign banks, compared to eight and sixteen respectively at the end of 1958.

In the post-1973 period, no new foreign banks were given licenses. At the end of 1983, there were sixteen foreign banks, compared with nineteen foreign banks at the end of 1973. There is no change in the number of foreign banks since 1983. Furthermore, Bank Negara has prohibited the establishment of new domestic banks in the country, as Malaysia is already believed to be "over-banked."

To avoid possible limitation on the development of contacts with the outside world, two types of foreign banking representations have been allowed, namely the establishment of representative offices of foreign banks and allowing foreign banks to buy shares of merchant banks. It is not surprising to see that all the twelve merchant banks in Malaysia are joint ventures between substantial Malaysian and foreign interests. For example, at the end of September 1988, of the total paid-up capital amount of RM306.5 million, 75 percent and 25 percent were subscribed by Malaysians and foreign interests respectively. Furthermore, the launching of Labuan as an offshore international financial center on October 1, 1990, gave foreign banks access to both Malaysian and Asia-Pacific markets.

In the management of assets and liabilities, foreign banks dominated the domestic market in terms of deposits, loans, banker's acceptances and Malaysia securities in the 1970s, but their dominance started to decline after 1975. In 1983, their share of deposits reached a level of 25 percent of the total deposits of the banking sector.

In the wave of globalization and financial liberalization today, further decline in foreign banking activities in Malaysia is unlikely. The recent announcement by Bank Negara safely indicates a bright future for foreign banking in this country. How they would dominate the banking business depends on the ability of domestic banks to compete in the marketplace.

The relative absence of controls on the base lending rate (BLR) and interest on deposits would see how domestic banks survive in the midst of the aggressive moves of foreign banks to capture new markets. Bear in mind that foreign banks are simply exportables, meaning that they are not given protection by any quarters and therefore expected to be efficient and highly competitive. They have operated elsewhere around the globe and understand well what to do in the event of crisis.

It is also worthy to note that their present involvement with the merchant banking industry would intensify financial engineering activities in commercial banking. For example, the half-billion ringgit syndicated

Islamic revolving underwritten notes for PKNS were arranged by local Arab-Malaysian Merchant Bank Berhad. Bank Islam Malaysia Berhad could have done the same given that underwriting activity does not contradict the Islamic Banking Act 1983.

With more experience in merchant banking and financial engineering, foreign banks can play a significant role to boost interest-free banking (IFBS). No doubt the demand for credit-based products (i.e., BBA) is increasing, thanks to the booming economy, but what cushion can IFBS provide under an economic downturn? Financial engineering is crucial to stimulate diversification with niche products created under the *al-ijarah, istisna, salam, mudarabah* and *musyarakah* principles.

One interesting observation is certainly the *Shariah* standard adopted by foreign Islamic banks. As they are mostly Arab banks such as Dalla Barakah, Kuwait Finance House (KFH) and Rajhi bank, it shall be exciting to see the contracts applicable to trade finance, credit card, and personal financing. *Bay' al-'inah* and discounted *bay' al-dayn* instruments are banned in the Middle Eastern Islamic banks. Likewise, non-Arab foreign banks such an HSBC and Citibank, well-known for their participation in Islamic banking, may want to comply with Middle East standards, given they have substantial business there.

Four
Bank Run and Islamic Banking

With the closure of seventy-four banks and finance companies in Indonesia and Thailand, what lies ahead for Malaysian banks remains a mystery, despite Daim Zainuddin's assurance that the banking system is solid. The good news is that bank panic and bank runs are relatively absent in Malaysia. Generally, the Malaysian banking system is believed to be in good health. Look at Maybank. Despite falling banking stocks, Maybank reported an impressive RM1.4 billion in group profit last year.

As depositors, the Malaysian people should remember that no matter how profitable a bank is, there is no guarantee it can honor withdrawals under a bank run. But people couldn't care less to find out. Coupled with a buoyant economy and good earnings, they think their money is safe with the banks. They can withdraw on demand any time they want.

Banks normally apply the law of large numbers to help predict withdrawals. According to the law of large numbers, if individual withdrawal decisions are independent and the number of depositors is large, the bank is capable of knowing how many loans it can make and yet still be able to honor withdrawals by depositors.

This is true in a situation where individuals carry on their normal everyday life as if the same thing is taking place every day for the next hundred years. However, in the case of an economic crisis, individual decisions are no longer independent. The herd mentality prevails over reason, and man tends to behave foolishly, often ignoring sound economic fundamentals. If the same predicament hits the banking sector, particularly the market for deposits, a bank panic will be the last thing banks and depositors want to see.

What is a bank panic? A bank panic occurs when the failure of one bank to honor its deposits leads the general public to fear that other banks will be unable to honor their deposits.

When this occurs, individuals will try to withdraw their deposits before the bank collapses, and in doing so, put the bank under great pressure and even jeopardize its ability to honor the massive withdrawals.

Before going further, it is worthy to explain something about the bank-depositor relationship. In conventional banking, when Mr. Mansur puts $10,000 in a savings deposit, he is in fact giving the bank a $10,000 loan. As a debtor, the bank promises to return the principal and a fixed return of, say, 6 percent per annum. In this case, Mr. Mansur holds a legal claim on 1) the principal loan of $10,000 and 2) the interest income of $600 per annum.

The bank will then use the $10,000 to make loans. For example, it will lend the money to a businessman, Mr. Ali, and charges him 12 percent interest rate per annum. The bank now has a legal claim on the 1) $10,000 loan, and 2) $1,200 interest income. Upon his failure to pay the loan, the bank can take legal action against Mr. Ali.

What we see in the above is the bank's ability to make $600 ($1,200 – $600) from a $10,000 deposit. Suppose Mr. Ali has a problem keeping up payments and eventually defaults on the loan. He may be declared a bankrupt, but the bank has not recovered the full loan. How does the bank pay Mr. Mansur when it has less than $10,000 on hold?

As another example, a bank gave $800 million loans to finance properties and shares purchases. Then both the property and share market tumbled by 40 percent. Asset value declined from $800 million to $480 million.

Here the bank will become insolvent, because its total liability i.e., deposits ($800 million) exceeds the value of its assets which is now at $480 million. Even if the bank sold all its assets, it may not be able to pay all those to whom it owed money. In the worst case scenario, bank's capital is not adequate to pay off deposits. It is this type of problem that eventually causes depositors to panic, resulting in a bank run.

In the Malaysian interest-free banks (IFBs), deposits are made on the contract of safe custody (*al-wadiah dhamanah*) rather than loan. The bank guarantees full deposit withdrawals on demand. In this way, depositors hold legal claim on the deposit only. Since Islamic banks don't pay interest, they have less pressure to pay a predetermined rate of return as conventional banks always do.

However, it does not mean that IFBs are not sensitive to saving incentives. The non-contractual returns i.e., *hibah* are distributed to depositors on the basis of projected earnings. With more earnings, depositors will get more *hibah*. And when the bank is not doing well, it can forgo *hibah* distribution but keep deposits intact as depositors hold a legal claim on them.

In fixed deposits, Islamic banks applied the *mudarabah* contract. Here, the bank has no legal obligation to pay the full capital and returns since *mudarabah* is a contract of profit-loss sharing. So, if Islamic deposits run on *wadiah* and *mudarabah* principles, is an Islamic bank free from the danger of a bank run? The answer depends on how much bank financing is exposed to default risks.

If the size of *wadiah dhamanah* deposits is much bigger than *mudarabah* deposits, then the prospect of a bank run is inevitable, as *wadiah* depositors hold a legal claim on deposits. However, if the opposite is true, a bank run in an Islamic bank is highly unlikely. Bank panics may not take place, since people know the principles of partnership.

Five
Islamic Banking and the Education System

According to the Bank Negara Annual Report 1996, the Islamic banking sector has showed encouraging progress over the last three years, with more players, increasing deposits, wider financing base and a broader array of products. Among the interest-free banking system, Arab-Malaysian Merchant Bank emerged as best performer. There seems to be no turning back now as the society is beginning to accept Islamic banking as a viable alternative to mainstream banking.

However, Islamic banking's market size is still small. In 1996, Islamic banking deposits and financing accounted for only 2 percent and 2.2 percent respectively of the total deposits and loans of the banking system, and the share of the Islamic banking divisions were even smaller, 1 percent and 1.3 percent respectively. In 2003, Islamic banking market share has shown commendable growth. The share of Islamic banking asset and deposits increased to 10.4 percent and 10.3 percent respectively.

To increase market share, education is the next step. People must know the new system. They provide deposits and they too ask for loans. Failure to inform them how the two systems differ would make it tough for Islamic banking to go up another level.

But education must begin in school. No doubt that some aspects of Islamic banking is part of the school curriculum today, especially in subjects like economics and commerce, but it should also be introduced into subjects like Religion of Islam (*Agama Islam*) at the high school level. Teachers should be given decent training on the subject to ensure that they can deliver this knowledge to students effectively.

Incidentally, I had the opportunity to conduct a workshop on Islamic economics for school headmasters organized by Institute Aminuddin Baki. Among others, the institute serves to train school administrators on the arts of management, such as finance and human resource development.

Most of the participants taught economics and commerce at the high school level. On Islamic banking, they have invited people from the Islamic banks to brief students about the new system and products. Since Islamic banking is relatively new, the education process has not been an easy one. Many are still confused about the Islamic banking business.

For example, how could one differentiate an interest-free instrument from an interest-based instrument? Let's say, if a man wants to purchase a house and engages an Islamic bank for help. What would he learn then?

Islamic banks will say that the Islamic instrument is based on a cost-plus or a deferred payment concept. They will go on to explain the nature of Islamic deposits or the nature of returns depositors will receive.

My own approach to the above is also a simple one. What needs to be said in the beginning is the type of contract involved in the transaction. For example, in a conventional bank, deposits and loans are based on the contract of loan with fixed payment, namely interest.

Thus, when someone deposited $1,000, he is actually lending his money to the bank at a specific interest rate, say 5 percent. The bank will then use this borrowed money to make loans. For example, the bank make a loan to a customer, say at 10 percent interest per annum. Bank's profit is the difference between the interest revenue made on loans and interest cost paid to depositors.

However, in Islamic banking, deposits are not mobilized on the contract of loan. Rather, deposits are mobilized via the contract of safe-custody with guarantee as *al-wadiah yad dhamanah.* Here, the bank is no longer a debtor but custodian instead.

Since the bank uses the money for investment, depositors may receive some returns called *hibah. Hibah* is not interest (*riba*), since it is not a contractual sum. Since *wadiah* is not a contract of debt, return given to depositors is considered lawful. The bank is however not obligated to give *hibah* while the depositors hold no legal claim on the same either. The bank will only guarantee the principle deposit.

On the financing side, an individual who plans to buy, say, a house can apply for a conventional loan facility. When the customer took up this loan, he establishes a debtor-creditor relationship with the bank. The loan facility is based on a debt contract that charges the debtor interest.

In the Islamic banking business, the contract is based on a buy and sell concept. Now, instead of acting as a creditor, the bank becomes a seller. By doing so, the bank buys the house from the developer at cost or market price and sells it to the customer at a mark-up price. The bank charges a higher price, since payment is made by installments. The customer is not a debtor as the transaction is based on a sale contract.

Thus, bank profit is generated from a buy-and-sell contract rather than a debt contract. The profit made is therefore legitimate (*halal*) since the transaction is based on trading, i.e., buy and sell. Allah (swt) says in the Quran, "Allah permits trade (*al-bay'*) but prohibits *riba.*" (Al-Baqarah: 275)

Apart from the deferred payment contract (*al-bai-bithaman ajil/ murabahah*), Islamic banking has also utilize non-debt instruments such as *mudarabah, musyarakah,* and *al-ijarah, salam* and *istisna'. Mudarabah* and *musyarakah* is a partnership contract, while *al-ijarah* is a leasing contract. Actually, the whole range of Islamic financial products is based on risk-taking principles. This is a great departure from interest-bearing products where almost all (i.e., personal loans, housing loans, auto loans, trust receipt, bankers' acceptances, and overdraft) run on a contract of loan. Lastly, most Islamic banking assets are fixed-rate, while the deposits are variable-rate liabilities. However, assets can bear some flexible rate character when more is put into *mudarabah, musyarakah,* and *al-ijarah* activities. This is important to secure some stability arising from asset-liability mismatches.

To further put Islamic banking into mainstream financial markets, the education system must allow Islamic economics and banking education to begin early in schools. The Ministry of Education can do so by forming a national taskforce to secure Islamic economics and banking a respectable place in the school and university curriculum. This task force should be able to give credible recommendations to the government about nature of

Islamic economics and banking to be imparted at different phases of the education process.

Currently, there is a trend among private colleges and university colleges to offer diplomas on Islamic banking. This is only rational given that the Islamic banking industry is growing fast and with good job opportunities for graduating students. However, the Ministry of Education should take notice that these programs are using the Islamic label. The implication can be a headache to the colleges given that teaching staffs must acquire formal education in the field of Islamic economics, banking and finance.

The National Accrediation Board (LAN) is put to a task in the above. To receive accreditation, the colleges and universities concerned are expected to provide convincing teaching and research infrastructure so that students actually got what they want. There is a need to sent teachers and lectures to take certified courses on Islamic economics, banking and finance. They should also be encouraged to pursue their post-graduate degrees on Islamic economics, banking and finance as these will enrich research and development on this new discipline.

Meanwhile, one should also receive partial recognition on Islamic banking and finance expertis by way of attending any of the following programs:

1. Seminars, workshop and conferences on Islamic banking and finance
2. Certified short-courses of Islamic banking and finance
3. Certified on-line courses on Islamic banking and finance

Students who write thesis and dissertations on the above subjects will also stand out as resource person and therefore able to claim some level of authority on the subject he or she researched on. Finally, to help stimulate the Islamic banking business, university leadership must motivate the academic community to establish contacts with the industry, thus putting a fertile ground for hands on approach to the teaching of Islamic banking and finance.These contacts should not be limited to the Shariah scholars alone but also academics with legal, economics and finance background.

Six

Moral Hazard and Adverse Selection during an Economic Recession

The decline of the ringgit has made Malaysia reconsider its massive import dependent investment in infrastructure. To further pursue investments in mega-projects can worsen the current account deficit, putting more pressure on local currency—the ringgit. Infrastructure projects demand lumpy capital. Companies will raise capital via bank loans and bond issuance. If they don't hedge against volatility, further ringgit depreciation would deem the project non-viable. As the production sector is import dependent, further slide of the ringgit puts pressure on import bills, thus slashing corporate earnings. Firms relying heavily on debts to sustain production may not be able to meet loan obligations; bankruptcies are inevitable.

The 5 percent projected growth next year would mean stronger investment spending, but at a slower rate. To ride on the lower ringgit, the focus is export. More loans will be injected into the productive sectors, especially the labor-intensive and resource-based export industry. Money supply (M1) grew moderately by 6.4 percent at the end of October 1998, compared with 7.5 percent at the end of September 1998.

The question now is, are banks going to make new loans under increasing market uncertainty? With rising interest rates and no sign of stock market recovery, loans can be hard to find. In the absence of profit-loss sharing (PLS) investments in Islamic banks, will the supply of *al-bai bithaman ajil* (BBA) suffer a decline too?

Assuming that banks have ample deposits to finance business spending, making loans or BBA would now require banks to persistently protect their business from moral hazards and adverse selection problems that can get worse at the nation slips deeper into the financial crisis.

The problem of moral hazards and adverse selection occurs when lenders and borrowers do not have complete information about each other's intention in the business deal; which is largely due to asymmetric information. Lenders are exposed to adverse selection as borrowers with bad credit risks are those likely to seek loans. At the same time, lenders will face the problem of moral hazards when they run the risk of the borrowers engaging in activities undesirable to the lender's business objective.

For example, rising interest rates in Malaysia could mean lower investment spending. Firms with risky investment projects are willing to pay the highest interest rates, while good firms with good credit ratings are not willing to borrow. To prevent adverse selection and consequently defaults, banks make fewer loans, cutting down investments. A big slowdown in lending reduces business activity.

Looking at the declining stock market, banks will also try to protect themselves from the consequences of adverse selection and moral hazards. They will cut down lending. For example, as the share market declines, the net worth of companies falls as share prices reflect business net worth. When a company's net worth declines in this manner, lenders have less protection. Without credible collateral, losses arising from bad loans can force banks to make fewer loans. This lowers investments; economic recession is inevitable.

In the same manner, when the net worth of companies declines, prospective debtors will venture into risky investments. They have less to lose if the investment fails. Thus, when the stock market suffers a sharp decline, such as the one in Malaysia, the problem of moral hazard is expected to increase. It gives banks little choice but to stop making loans. Again, a decline in lending reduces investment spending.

Banks that fail to protect themselves from moral hazards and adverse selection will find it difficult to get away with bad loans, and many may close down. When banks are out of business, like those in Thailand and Indonesia, the amount of financial intermediation will fall. It reduces the supply of borrowed funds. With fewer loans available, investment and output will fall. With factories cutting production, unemployment increases. With lower earnings, consumption expenditures are likely to contract. The impact on the GDP is obvious.

In Islam, the occurrence of adverse selection and moral hazard is mainly due to the violation of trust or *amanah*. On this point, the Quran says:

> "O ye who believe! When ye deal with each other, in transactions involving future obligations in a fixed period of time, put them in writing. Let a scribe write down faithfully as between the parties: let not the scribes refuse to write: as God has taught him, so let him write. Let him who incurs the liability dictate, but let him fear his Lord, and not diminish ought of what he owes" (Al-Baqarah: 282-283).

In the last verse, "… and not diminish ought of what he (debtor) owes" may imply that a debtor must find all possible ways to pay up his debt. The point here is that during economic decline, the desire and urge to default is greater as firms are not able to make profits to pay loans plus interest. Profits are not contractual earnings but rather residuals. However, loans and interest are contractual payments to the banks. If loans alone are contractual, it may pose less pressure to the firm to pay up. But when interest income is made a legal claim, it puts debtors under severe pressure. It tempted people to exploit uncertainties. For this reason, adverse selection and moral hazards are always on the rise during an economic recession. An economy that runs on debt and *riba* will not be free from the problem of adverse selection and moral hazards. But running on equity too does not guarantee the opposite. Whether one practices debt or equity, the fundamental principle of trustworthiness (*amanah*) is the lifeline of business.

Seven
Leveraged Dependent Economy

As expected, the stock and currency crisis has finally put the local banking sector under public scrutiny. Massive losses in the stock market would cause many to default on loan payments. Manufacturing companies that failed to hedge against currency volatility will find it hard to sustain production with increasingly more expensive import components and raw materials.

With lower sales and earnings, it is becoming hard for these companies to keep up the monthly bank installment. Those who fail to pay up will file for bankruptcy. With rising interest rates and tighter credit conditions, small and medium industries will be severely affected unless drastic measures are taken to help them.

The question is, who is likely to default under an economic slowdown? The revision of growth rates from 6 percent to 4.5 percent implies that the level of consumption, investment, spending, and exports will fall. The problem now is what will happen to creditors and debtors? A simple illustration will help clear this issue.

When the economy is monetized, i.e., we use fiat money as currency, using credit to finance consumer and business spending has become a norm. The price of credit is the interest rate. Now the question is, who gave the loan and can it be paid back?

When one speaks about loans, we normally turn to the banking sector, the middleman that helps facilitate the flow of funds from the creditor to the debtors. For example, when Mr. Yahya put his $10,000 savings in Cyberbank, the relationship between Yahya and Cyberbank is that of a creditor-debtor; i.e., Yahya lends Cyberbank the sum of $10,000. But what motivates Yahya to place his money with Cyberbank? What makes him want to lend his money out?

Most probably, the incentive is interest rates. As the interest rate increases, savings will increase too. In conventional banking, the debt contract between Yahya and Cyberbank stipulates that Yahya's legal claims on the $10,000 deposits plus $500 interest income, assuming interest on deposit is 5 percent.

In Islamic banking, however, the contract between Yahya and Cyberbank SPTF is not based on debt, but a contract of safer custody with guarantee (*al-wadiahDhamanah*). Here, Yahya's legal claim is only on the $10,000 deposits.

Now, with Yahya's deposits, Cyberbank lends the money to Ibrahim, an entrepreneur, at 15 percent interest rate. Again the relationship between Yahya and Cyberbank is creditor-debtor. Here, Cyberbank has a legal claim on the principal loan $10,000, as well as the interest income of $1,500.

As a middleman, Cyberbank certainly has to incur operating expenses such as salary and rental payments, office supplies, and other equipment such as computers, as well as security and advertising. In economics, these expenses are known as resource costs, most of which are taken from the bank's equity capital and reserves.

The question now is what if Ibrahim defaulted on the loan and Cyberbank can only recover 60 percent of the debt? Now Cyberbank has only $6,000 in assets, while Yahya wants his $10,000 deposit, due to some urgent calls. It is here that the bank's capital is of utmost importance.

If Cyberbank owns $5,000 share capital (i.e., Cyberbank's owners invested $5,000 to set up the bank), then Yahya will get his deposit without trouble. The loss of $4,000 will be absorbed by the bank's capital, leaving the bank with only $1,000 capital.

What if Cyberbank has only $2,000 share capital instead of $5,000? Now Cyberbank will find it hard to pay Yahya, since it has only $8,000 in hand ($6,000 asset + $2,000 share capital). Here, Cyberbank will be declared insolvent since its liabilities (deposit + capital) are more than its assets. Yahya panics and news about Cyberbank bad loans are everywhere.

If Cyberbank has 100,000 depositors, it will undergo a bank run as people no longer have confidence in Cyberbank's ability to guarantee deposits and interest payments. When people fear that claims cannot be met and banks begin to close their doors, we will gradually lose faith in what banks can do with our money. The consequences are severe. When people panic and rush to make withdrawals, the good banks are also affected. They too would find it hard to meet sudden payments, causing them to close as well.

When many banks fail, small and medium industries will find it difficult to obtain loans to sustain production. Investment will fall. This will cause them to reduce output, thus forcing cutbacks in employment. As unemployment increases, people have less money to spend. Sales of consumer goods will fall.

With low sales, retail supermarkets and small outlets may find it difficult to make loan payments. Let's say before the crisis, the margin of retail business is 20 percent while cost of credit is 12 percent. Now the margin falls to 10 percent while interest has increased to 15 percent. The only way out now is to default on their loans, causing more banks to fail.

Similarly, those who invest in the stock market using borrowed capital will stand to suffer from the present crisis. When the market is bullish and credit is cheap, share financing is good business for many banks.

For instance, Mr. Lai expects to make an average 50 percent margin in the stock market and has been able to do so for the past three years. With only a 10 percent interest rate to pay on a $100,000 share-financing loan, it's a good deal. He can net a 40 percent gain with, say, only $1,000 to pay monthly. But when the market went south, his assets put as collateral depreciate, to $30,000. The value of the loan exceeds the value of the collateral.

When Mr. Lai defaults on his loans, Cyberbank will have to absorb the losses. If Cyberbank's equity capital is small and unable to absorb the losses, it too will become bankrupt, just like Mr. Lai.

In Islam, wealth creation can only be generated through trade and commerce or *al-bay'*. The Quran says, "Allah permits trade and commerce but prohibits *riba*" (Al-Baqarah: 278). Making profits from lending and borrowing activities are therefore prohibited as this could lead to economic disasters described above.

God says in the Quran, "O ye who believe! Eat not up your property among yourselves in vanities: but let there be amongst you trade by mutual good will." (An-Nisaa: 29)

Islam, however, does not discourage people from making loans. In fact, giving loans is an act of worship. An Islamic loan has no stipulated or pre-fixed contractual rate of return. If it does, it is *riba.* In Islam, the repayment of a loan (*qard*) is obligatory. The Prophet (*pbuh*) is reported to have said, "Every loan must be paid..." Also the Prophet (*pbuh*) is reported to have said: "The best of people are those who discharge or pay their debts in the best manner." The Prophet (*pbuh*) also says that "delay in the payment of debt on the part of the rich man is injustice."

Since an Islamic loan does not promise a contractual and pre-fixed rate of return, it may not be a viable financing instrument in business today. As an alternative, *al-bay'* is given, which includes *mudarabah* (trustee partnership), *musyarakah* (general partnership), and *al-ijarah* (leasing). If businesses are conducted on the basis of risk-taking and profit-loss sharing, the number of bankruptcies and bank failures is expected to be lower.

Table 5.1 Hypothetical Asset-Liability

TABLE 1: HYPOTHETICAL BANK ASSET-LIABILITY STRUCTURE (ASSUME SRR = 10 percent)	
Asset	Liability
Statutory Reserves $10 m Loans $90 m **NPL $15 m** Note: Bank can survive given enough capital to pay off NPL.	Deposits $100 million **Capital $20 million**
Statutory Reserves $10 m Loans $90 m **NPL $50 m** **Capital $20 million** Note: Bank closing down. Share capital not able to pay off NPL.	

Eight
Gap Management

The use of credit sale instruments, *al-bai-bithaman ajil* in particular, took a forward leap when five Islamic banking system (IBS) banks agreed to participate in the share financing scheme made for Abrar Unit Trust. The scheme is a simple one, i.e., the banks will purchase shares issued by the unit trust company. These shares are then sold again to investors at a higher price, with payments made by installments.

Investors as unit holders will obtain yearly dividends, say 12 percent. The bank charges a profit margin of, say, 10 percent annually. Banks as intermediaries stand to gain and, of course, the unit trust management will find ready market. The use of *bai-bithaman-ajil* has now embraced a new market, namely share financing. Together with consumer and trade financing, future *bai-bithaman-ajil* investments in Islamic banking are expected to increase. How would this affect bank's performance?

The Bank Negara Annual Report 1995 says that prices are expected to remain under pressure, and tight monetary policy indicates the pressure on interest rates is on. When interest rates are on the rise, banks normally resort to positive-fund gap policy. Here a larger portion of investments is placed in variable return assets (VRA) and a smaller portion in variable return liability (VRL).

So, when interest rates indeed go up, the bank earns more from loans. Deposits will cost less and therefore banks make positive earnings. However, Islamic banking in this country may not be able to do the same because they are caught in the credit sale debacle. Irrespective of inflation or recession, application of *al-bai-bithaman ajil* and *murabahah* investments will remain a dominant one.

The portion of fixed return assets (FRA) will remain high while the variable rate deposits (VRL), namely *al-wadiah dhamanah* and *mudarabah* accounts, will remain large, since an Islamic bank is not allowed to give guarantees on earnings. For example, the *murabahah*/BBA products are essentially fixed return asset (FRA). That is, despite changes in the inter-bank offer rate and the subsequent change in base lending rate (BLR), BBA profit rates are simply not adjustable.

Because liabilities of Islamic banks are based on a variable rate, the banks in fact (consciously or unconsciously) adopt a Negative Fund Gap Strategy. Here, the portion of variable rate assets to total assets (VRA/TA) is smaller than the ratio of variable rate liability to total liability (VRL/TL).

Under the conventional model, the above strategy is applicable when interest rates are expected to fall. A decline in interest rates will not reduce interest earnings on loans as much as the reduction on cost of funds. Therefore net interest earnings will increase.

Islamic Asset-Liability Management

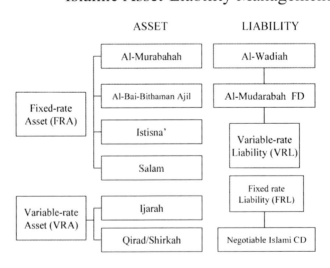

Figure 5.2 Islamic fixed and variable assets and liabilities

However, in Malaysia today, interest rates are rising. To be competitive, rising interest rates may require Islamic banks to revise their *hibah* upwards.

Cost of funds will then increase. At the same time, the bank cannot adjust existing profit rate upwards because the contract of *murabahah*/BBA does not allow that to happen. Hence, profits are expected to fall.

In view of the above, overdependence on credit sale instruments should be put to a stop. Putting *mudarabah* and *musyarakah* facilities as well as *salam, istisna'* and *al-ijarah* into Islamic banks' product line must be taken seriously.

Nine
Al-Bai-Bithaman Ajil and the Business Cycle

Bank Negara's recent move to curb property financing is something Malaysians should take note of. The property-bubble has burst in neighboring Thailand. Malaysia may be next. Bank Negara's report shows that banking system loans grew by nearly 20 percent to RM72 billion last year. More worrying is the loan growth in the property sector that has risen from 26 percent in 1995 to 30 percent in 1996. Such high demand for property is expected to increase the demand for other related products, such as home furniture and appliances, but the loan to manufacturing grew at only 14 percent, compared to nearly 30 percent in 1995.

Malaysia has been enjoying rapid growth for nearly a decade. The point is, in boom time, risks are usually ignored. Banks are willing to make loans simply because there is less indication of a slowdown. Firms are confident they can deliver the goods to fulfill their debt obligations. It's like what Thailand's Pin Chakkapak takeover King said, *"We have no defined structure. Touch and go, play it by ear, that has always been the way we operate."*

The speculative nature of the Malaysian property market is not a new phenomenon today. Indeed, there are many genuine buyers around, and policies to curb housing purchases have no special mechanism to differentiate the speculators from the real buyers. Is there anything the commercial banking system can do to help prevent the possibility of an acute property-bubble in this country?

The central bankers have done their part, but what have the commercial bankers done to help make property prices in this country affordable to local Malaysians? If we adhere to the law of supply and demand, certainly this will work in favor of affluent foreign buyers and the local upper middle class, but what about the majority of Malaysians who are desperately looking for low- and medium-cost houses today?

If Islamic banking is considered one way to help curb rampant property purchases, it's worthwhile to see how the system handles customers' demand for home financing. The facility offered is based on a deferred sale contract known as *al-bai-bithaman ajil* (BBA). Instead of giving a loan, the bank now buys the house from the developer at market price and sells it to the customer at a mark-up price. The difference between the market price (cost price) and the mark-up price (selling price) is the profit the bank makes over the installment period. The profit is *halal* since the contract is based of a sale and purchase agreement rather than a loan.

One unique feature of the BBA facility is the selling price itself. The selling price is fixed; thus, any change in it will make the contract null and void. So the bank must make sure that the selling price remains unchanged till the last payment is made. The selling price of the BBA facility is similar to the nominal value of a loan plus the total interest payments.

Interest rates or conventional bank profits vary from time to time as dictated by the market, but cannot hold for the BBA, as any variation in the profit portion of the selling price will cause the selling price itself to change, thus violating the BBA contract. Therefore, when Islamic bankers see higher interest rates on loans, there is nothing they can do to upgrade the price of existing BBA facility.

Conventional bankers can revise interest rates upwards and customers may have to pay more monthly, but this is not possible in Islamic banking. Upward revision of the profit rate is not possible, as doing so changes the BBA selling price. The same argument holds in the case of default payments. In the past, there is no penalty on late payments simply because penalties will increase the selling price of the asset sold.

There are two apparent benefits of the BBA product; namely:

1) fixed selling price and
2) no penalty on late payments.

This has made BBA a better alternative to loans, especially when interest rates are rising. Customers who expect rising interest rates will opt for BBA to avoid paying more interest if they have taken a loan instead. The *Shari'ah* constraint imposed on the BBA, therefore, makes it a popular alternative in the event of rising interest rates.

Bank Negara's move to curb lending on housing purchases may reduce the demand for BBA and loan facilities, but only on houses above $150,000. This credit rationing device is likely to generate better results, since banks now are only allowed to portion a specified amount of loans to meet the demand for more expensive units which, normally, are more exposed to speculative buying.

At this juncture, if the move tends to dampen the property market and the economy as a whole, the incoming recession may indeed hurt Islamic banking, since customers will opt to use loans rather than BBA. This is simply because interest rates normally fall during a recession, and any further decline will mean lower adjusted monthly loan payments.

Since the BBA facility cannot adjust the selling price downward, as this will violate the sale agreement, home buyers will now see BBA as inferior to loans, as it has become relatively more expensive. The demand for BBA is expected to fall more than the demand for loans.

Overall, there is less indication that Islamic banking can survive the recession unless it ventures into manufacturing, therefore increasing investment, aggregate demand and income. The question is, can manufacturing activity in this country be driven by BBA financing? Certainly, we have seen that BBA financing today is widely used in the construction sector. Would Islamic banking be able to make a breakthrough in manufacturing?

Ten
Islamic Banking and Interest Rate Volatility

A lthough the Malaysian government has refrained from using interest rates to prop up the ringgit, interest rates remain high to reflect tighter monetary policy. The threat of imported inflation and the urgent need to cut money supply growth has pushed up the three-month KLIBOR to 8.25 percent in mid-October 1995.

As the Base Lending Rate (BLR) is pegged to KLIBOR, BLRs of major banks have also risen to about 10 percent. For example, BBMB has increased its BLR to 10 percent while Maybank is up to 9.75 percent. Ban Hin Lee Bank, BSN Commercial, RHB Bank, and Hong Leong Bank all have set their BLRs at 10.10 percent. The question now is, how will this scenario affect the performance of interest-free banks?

If we think that interest rates can further go up, it is possible that customers would opt using *Al-Bai Bithaman Ajil* (BBA) facilities, since SPTF banks are not allowed to raise the selling price in existing contracts. Doing the opposite will violate the third principle of *al-bay'*. It says that a contractual price cannot be altered at all cost. The law of contract says there must be only one price in one sale. A sale with two or more prices is not a valid sale.

When an Islamic bank sees conventional banks raising interest rates on loans, there is nothing much it can do to stop customers coming, since now loans are relatively more expensive.

Although it is ideal to increase BBA financing, it would be relatively difficult to do, because Islamic banks need more deposits. As existing BBA financing has locked in a specific profit margin, Islamic banks will find it tough to compete with conventional deposits that offer higher interest rates. To give more *hibah* would cut earning, since the locked-in BBA financing is unable to generate more revenues.

In the final analysis, Islamic banks will find themselves on the losing side. To secure more deposits, they have to resort to the inter-bank money market, where the cost of funds is even higher than *hibah* rates.

However, if one feels that the three-month KLIBOR will ease down, Islamic banks may see more trouble. This time, the bad news is excess liquidity. As more people expect interest rates to fall, the demand for BBA financing may drop. Now it can be more expensive to use BBA. This is because existing loans can now charge lower interest rates that existing BBA cannot do.

For example, if a BBA annual profit rate is 12 percent, a drop in KLIBOR cannot allow Islamic banks to revise the rate downwards, as this will induce changes in the contractual selling price. Suppose at 10.5 percent profit rate per annum, an asset costing $150,000 will command a selling price of $428,882 at a monthly installment of $1,416 with a 25-year maturity.

If the bank plans to reduce profit rate to 9.5 percent to keep up with the competition, the monthly installment will fall to $1,310, which translates into a lower selling price of $393,162. Changes in contractual price such as this will invalidate the BBA contract.

Just as the currency crisis opens new opportunities for export expansion, BBA financing can attract more Islamic deposits, under a declining interest rate regime. In fact, most analysts forecast a lower KLIBOR next year. If the public feels the same, they will see conventional banks cutting loan rates, which also mean lower deposit rates.

In the case of Islamic banks, inability to cut profit rates will make it possible for them to increase return on Islamic deposits. To some extent, non-Muslim depositors will find Islamic deposits more attractive. Placing their money in the Islamic deposits shifts some deposits away from conventional products.

What we see in the above is the following: a lower demand for BBA but higher supply of Islamic deposits. Such a mismatch can destabilize Islamic banking operations. It leads to excess liquidity, as the BBA-dependent Islamic banks have less option in financing. One cannot blame the non-Muslim market. The bottom line is money. They look for competitiveness. The dual-banking system also cannot be held responsible. At both ends, non-Muslim customers gain from interest rate volatility, while Muslim customers secure much less.

It is therefore timely to see Islamic banks consolidate to put things straight. For one thing, people want to see equitable relation between banks and customers, and between Muslim and non-Muslim customers. For example, during rising interest rates, non-Muslim customers will use BBA financing, but may place their savings in conventional deposits. By doing so, they have benefited in both worlds, namely, cheaper credit and higher returns on deposits. Muslim customers, on the other hand, don't have much choice but only to look. Islamic banks will be stuck with less deposit. To acquire funds at higher costs would cut down earnings.

On the contrary, when interest rates are declining, non-Muslim customers will use loans instead of BBA as the cost of borrowing now is lower. But since Islamic banks are able to pay higher *hibah* and dividends (i.e., since existing BBAs have locked in a relatively higher profit rate), the supply for Islamic deposits by non-Muslim customers will go up.

Again, Muslim customers can do nothing but only look. Islamic banks will see non-Muslim customers shifting some deposits from conventional accounts to Islamic accounts. However, this cannot be translated into more BBA financing, since the demand for BBA has dropped, thus cutting earnings arising from excess liquidity.

The remedy points to diversification. Islamic banks should pursue financing with floating rate options such as *al-ijarah, mudarabah,* and *musyarakah*. Malaysia's dual banking system and its unique multi-racial society has shown the need to rethink how Islamic banking should operate to remain competitive and successful. As the economy slides into a recession, it would not hurt to introduce some change since the demand for financing is expected to slow down.

Staying relentlessly with the same product line may not be a good strategy, as time has shown that nothing can last forever. What we would like to see is a model where all market agents, Muslims, non-Muslims, and bankers alike will gain from the Islamic banking system, whether or not interest rates are rising or falling.

Eleven
Islamic Banking and Economic Development

The launching of the Bank Islam Unit Trust (ASBI) by Anwar Ibrahim has paved a new era for Islamic banking in Malaysia. Presently, *mudarabah* investment account holders at Bank Islam (M) Bhd (BIMB) obtained, on average, 5 percent annually. Investing with ASBI can mean getting more returns, but this also means taking more risk. Ten million units at RM1 each were sold out in two days. The good public response is expected to increase the number of Islamic funds in the unit trust industry.

Apart from the religious factor, some other elements may explain why people are keen to invest in Islamic funds. For example, Islamic funds help people put their money in less speculative investments as it provides a safer and less risky investment. But religion can prove to be a potent force that pulled people into Islamic funds. It implies that government's effort to instill Islamic consciousness among the Muslim people is bearing fruit.

Whatever the reasons given, more people are now spending money on long-term non-speculative investment. This is exactly what Islam desires people to do. But by no means has the *Shariah* prohibited speculative investment. As long as the elements of *riba, gharar, jahala, maisir,* and *tatfief* are not implicated, speculative investment constitutes a permissible act.

253

Islam enjoins man not only to create wealth but to spend it as well. The Quran says, *"Those who spend their wealth night and day secretly or openly, they shall have no fear, nor shall they come to grief."* Investment is a noble act in Islam, as it increases stocks of capital, which helps stimulate future production of real goods and services. It is thus useful to see what Islam has to say about wealth creation.

Wealth can be created in both product and financial markets. To ensure that economic justice is pursued with rigor in wealth creation, two laws or principles are in order.

The first fundamental law is that no one shall get more or less than what is proportionate to his input, either in terms of capital or in terms of labor. The Quran states, "Woe betide those who take more than they give *(wailin li'l mutaffifin)" (Sura 83:1)*. Again, *"Do not curtail or diminish what is due to other people" (Suras 11:85; 26:183)*. Further, *"Do not consume wealth of other people by wrongful means" (Sura 2:188; Sura 3:292)*.

The second law states, *"Wealth must not circulate only among the rich ones among you" (Sura 59:7)*. Economic justice therefore implies that wealth creation must not be monopolized by the few rich. In this way, the establishment of unit trusts serves to promote welfare, as it opens new opportunities for the average man to participate in the capital market. On this matter, Islamic banks deserve praise, but more is better. Doing so does not necessarily mean providing them access to the capital market via ASBI scheme alone. It also means providing direct finance to small and medium-scale industry. Unlike conventional banks, Islamic banks have extra flexibility to inject funds into the SMIs since it can invest in equities via *mudarabah, musyarakah, salam,* and *istisna'* financing.

Mudarabah and *musyarakah* instruments run on profit-sharing principle (PLS). This means SMIs are not required to place collaterals over the capital injection. For example, under the *musyarakah* framework, banks provide equity funds into the project and take an active role in the management of the project as well; which means they no longer act as debt collectors.

Experience in Pakistan has shown that an equity approach in banking does not work too well. Banks are not ready to manage equity-based projects simply because they are not familiar with the project financing. The high exposure to market risk chased deposits away and deprived banks of funds. There is no apparent mechanism the bank can use to deter the business partner from abusing the contract. This explains why Islamic banks around the world have opted to use *murabahah* and *al-bai-bithaman ajil* contracts in their business.

In both contracts, Islamic banks sell goods to customers on credit payable on installment basis. These banks no longer make loans, but purchase the goods people want to buy with the loan. Profit is the difference between the cash and the credit price. *Murabahah* and BBAs made up more than 90 percent of BIMB's assets. The same applies to the Islamic windows. It is a good achievement but not a good enough to induce innovative and high value-added production. The future of Malaysia's economic development depends on technology; and businesses lacking in it will see more trouble ahead.

A shift from trading-based activities to equity participation is imperative to take Islamic banking into a new frontier. But substantial structural change must take place, as this is what Islamic banking should become—an agent of change. Anwar Ibrahim says that Islamic banking must no longer be content with its own brand of financial instruments but do what it can do to eradicate poverty. It requires new strategies to create new jobs on the line. It must open wider opportunities to help increase wealth creation.

Most loans awarded to the SMIs in this country are assisted by the Credit Guarantee Corp. (CGC). It helps small borrowers to obtain credit facilities from the commercial banks at reasonable costs. The number of loans granted under the CGC schemes has increased substantially, from 148,526 at the end of 1986 to 185,516 at the end of June 1993. In 1993, the total lending under the scheme amounted to RM312 million. It only secured 28 percent of total bank lending to the private sector. How Islamic banks can help increase the share of funds allocated to SMIs depends on many factors.

The first is the attitude of bank managers towards risk. The main reason behind the prohibition of *riba* in Islam is the violation of the first fundamental principle stated above. Interest is a fixed profit set in the loan contract, and debtors are required to place collateral to protect the loan against default. The *Shariah* does not want people to step on each other's heads. The loan contract imposes severe stress on debtors as total market risks are put on them alone. This helps explain why conventional banks are hesitant to make loans to the SMIs without securities guaranteed by the CGC.

Capitalist banking requires the optimal management of assets according to principles of profitability, safety, and liquidity, under which loans extended to small and medium-scale industries are considered highly risky, unsafe, and therefore not viable. This is because the SMIs are highly fragmented and characterized by a lack of product differentiation and integrated production process, as well as insufficient skilled manpower and appropriate technology (IMP 1983). They are also devoid of having sophisticated technical, financial, and management expertise.

An Islamic attitude towards risk in Islamic banking should pave the way towards more equity-based financing in SMIs. An Islamic legal maxim fully enjoins this thinking, stating that "liability and risk must be proportional to its benefits, and the benefits must be proportional to its liability and risk" (*an-ni'mah bi-qadril-niqmah, wan niqmah bil-wadri-ni'mah*).

The ethical factor, too, will play an important role in determining the future course of Islamic banking in this country. It is the moral obligation of Islamic banks to see that SMIs get the proper treatment, given their role in Malaysia's industrial growth, especially in reducing the dependence on imports. This is one way Islamic and conventional banks can help people see that they have indeed embraced the caring society philosophy.

However, ethical elements alone may not be adequate without ample legal support. At present, interest payments are considered an expense item, and therefore eligible for tax deduction. As the same does not apply to dividends (i.e., when Islamic banks participate in *mudarabah* and *musyarakah*), companies would choose debt financing over equity. To see that both conventional and Islamic banks run on a competitive basis, the same incentives must be given to both.

Twelve
Islamic Banking and Economic Stability

Some problems of *murabahah/bai-bithaman-ajil* (BBA) products have been discussed in light of the creeping inflation surrounding us today. Interest-free banks that carry too many BBA assets will find their asset value depleted over time. This is true as they cannot sell goods at different prices under one contract. Failure to maintain the real value of the BBAs can mean diminishing profit.

In the final analysis, *mudarabah* depositors will absorb the erosion of profits. They will receive lower dividends. On the contrary, inflation is not the major concern in *mudarabah* ventures. This is because in *mudarabah*, profits are not contractually predetermined but realized in accordance to economic conditions.

Since during inflation, price levels increase, sales and profits of *mudarabah* ventures are expected to increase also. On the liability side, these inflationary conditions will translate into higher returns for *mudarabah* depositors, but a point of caution is in order. The above argument does not say that the successful *mudarabah* venture requires more inflation. Instead, *mudarabah* and *musyarakah* ventures in banking can play a significant role to help central bank control inflation.

Is this possible? During a boom period, the economy observes a relatively high level of trading and production activities. With higher expected returns from potential investment projects, high levels of investment spending eventually follow. Money supply increases as loans expand to meet business demands.

Input shortages and, eventually, inflation normally accompany boom periods. We all know that inflation is basically a phenomenon in which society experiences a fall in purchasing power. On the demand side, it is partly due to a higher level of deposit creation in the banking system, due to a higher level of lending.

This is a rational thing to do in the profit-maximizing banking business. As a result, we see more money chasing fewer goods. When the industry competes for existing resources to satisfy demand, cost of production will go up. Unless something dramatic is done to stimulate the supply side, inflation will continue to eat into our hard-earned cash. This has something to do with the nature of loans given by conventional banks.

In general, two types of loans make up the bulk of funds supplied by the interest banking industry, namely production and consumption loans. Production loans are normally injected into industry, while lending to consumers helps stimulate the demand for houses, automobiles, home appliances, etc. On the other hand, too much money creation due to more lending during an economic boom can produce more inflation.

In fighting inflation, the role of *mudarabah/musyarakah* banking ventures can best be observed if one appreciates the cautious approach to investment. *Mudarabah*-based interest-free banks will make sure that the approved projects are able to garner inputs effectively without hurting cost efficiency.

For example, projects that require cheap labor and imported machinery would face potential rejection, as Malaysia has no comparative advantage on these factor endowments. Hence, intelligent selection of equity projects will help ease pressure on the resource market.

This cautious approach to investment will help reduce the rate of increase in the money supply during inflation. This is highly unlikely in conventional lending, as bankers will not put these factors high in their agenda. Existing financing of industry via the *murabahah/bai-bithaman-ajil* instruments, too, is expected to exert inflationary pressure on resources. This is because deferred sale activities are less sensitive to the general from the deal.

Hence, the purchase of special capital equipment via *murabahah/bai-bithaman-ajil* will take place even if the price is exceedingly high. As more deferred sale contracts are concluded, money supply will increase to meet new sales and purchases. Here, the bank is not so concerned with how much the fund user will make from the *murabahah* deal, or what the sale will do to the overall price level. Unfortunately, apart from the *halal* element, the impact of deferred sales transactions on the economy has no significant difference from loans.

However, there is some advantage in the *murabahah/bai-bithaman-ajil* (BBA) instruments, as they can help put a check on speculative activities. A control on speculative investment activities is needed to help reduce inflation caused by excessive money creation. The *mudarabah* scheme is a potential remedy when applied to real property, such as land and residential assets.

Once purchase of assets is tied to the BBA scheme, speculative buying can be reduced, since the price of assets bought under a BBA contract does not reflect present current market price, but the expected future market price of the asset, namely the credit BBA price. Hence, person who buys a $200,000 two-story house at Bandar Sri Damansara at $400,000 BBA price will not sell the house a month later on a speculative deal unless someone wants to buy it at more than $400,000, which is highly unlikely.

Once such a framework is set up, demand for money tends to be smaller due to a slowdown in speculative purchases. The impact of the Islamic banking system in reducing the rate of expansion of money supply during an economic boom can therefore be observed by replacing consumption loans with *murabahah/bay' bithaman ajil* credit sales, which can ensure genuine purchases of consumer goods.

Coming back to *mudarabah/musharakah* ventures in banking, when business risk is borne by the respective investing parties, we can say that the cautious approach to investment can help ease stress on resources. This is not possible when industries are financed by *murabahah/bai-bithaman-ajil* instruments, as they are not structured to venture into risk-taking and project monitoring activities.

Thirteen
Islam Banking and the SRR

$\mathbf{B}$ank Negara Malaysia increases the statutory reserve requirement (SRR) by one percent from 11.5 percent to 12.5 percent. A higher SRR would mean banks now have fewer reserves to make loans; this can cut down the money supply. The rationale to increase the SRR is inflation control.

Inflation happens when too much money is chasing too few goods. In the Malaysian context, inflation is mostly demand-driven, fueled by too much money creation via the deposit multiplier. Prices go up, including prices of labor and capital. In an open economy like ours, the higher interest rates can attract "hot money" that often triggers demand-pull inflation. It makes exports more expensive and reduces Malaysia's competitiveness in global trade.

Policymakers may be more worried about interest rate differentials between Malaysia and the rest of the world as excess liquidity caused by influx of "hot money" is an outcome of arbitrage. With more deposits at hand, banks are willing to make new loans as business are looking good.

But the increase in SRR may not reduce money supply when banks convert their bond holding into cash to make fresh loans. Policymakers knew well the pro-cyclical behavior of commercial banks. Earlier they have taken the necessary steps to reduce bank lending and private consumption. Minimum payment on credit cards was raised to 15 percent from 10 percent of the monthly balance. Interest rates were raised by fifty basis points to 6.5 percent. Real property gains tax went up by 5 percent to 10 percent and a maximum margin of financing of 60 percent was imposed for non-owner-occupied properties. Hence by increasing the SRR, some targeted growth rate of money supply can be achieved. It can help strengthen the ringgit and reduce the current trade deficit a little bit.

But some may ask how the change in SRR would affect reserves of Islamic banks. If a higher SRR would reduce loans and deposit creation, how could the same happen in the Islamic banks. Let's not forget most Islamic financial instruments are based on credit contracts. So, how would products based on debt contracts differ from those based on credit when changes in SRR are made?

Actually the difference is only minimal when a large portion of a bank's asset is invested in credit products such as *murabahah* and *al-bai-bithaman ajil* contracts. The impact of SRR may be similar under both debt and credit contracts.

For example, an increase in SRR may reduce the ability of banks to make new loans. Similarly, an increase in SRR may not allow interest-free banks to sell new goods and services based on the *murabahah* and *al-bai-bithaman ajil* contracts. Either way, no new checks will be written on the borrower and buyer. There is now no new deposit created in the banking system. Money creation will be reduced no matter what banking system is used, debt or credit-based.

Things may be a little different if a large portion of investments is injected in equity-intensive products using the *mudarabah* and *musyarakah* as a mode of financing. This is because equity investment is not a trading activity. The latter is about buying goods at a lower price and selling them at a higher price.

It is relatively easier to do so once buyers are readily available. The amount of profit to be made is a known variable. Likewise, interest earning from loans are prefixed in the lending agreement. Hence, both returns on loan and deferred sale have similar features although the contracts on which they operate do not.

With regards to equity instruments, the decision to reduce equity transactions due to higher SRR is not as evident in trading contracts. This is because successful equity projects often produce higher profit margins than trading or debt instruments. Hence, the bank may try to mobilize new sources of funds to ensure that sufficient amounts of equity projects are pursued. It will stimulate the supply-side, which increases the level of output and consequently the price level.

This is a possibility, because unlike the demand-driven *murabahah* and *al-bai-bithaman ajil* instruments, equity investments are directly involved in real production and the provision of value-added goods. A higher SRR may be relevant to credit-based products but it may do harm to equity investments, if any. It may be able to reduce demand pull inflation but may also dampen the supply-side driven by *mudarabah* and *musyarakah* investments.

Fourteen
Islamic loans and inflation risk : Using the Islamic Dinar

The Department of Statistics (DOS) released Malaysia's Consumer Price Index (CPI) for January 1998, which saw a 5.2 percent increase in the price level compared to 0.9 percent for the same month last year. Among others this confirmed the economic recession recorded in 1997 will spill over in 1998.

A fall in the producer price index (PPI) in 1998 accompanied by easy monetary policy normally means too much money chasing too few goods. That explains well the 5.2 percent inflation in January 1998. According to DOS, most increases in the price level were found in food (9.0 percent) followed by beverages and tobacco (10.6 percent), while falling prices were evident clothing and footwear (1.3 percent) and transport and communication (0.3 percent).

A rise in the CPI will usually bring a chilling sign that our living standard may soon deteriorate. Without a proportionate wage increase, our purchasing power is expected to fall. Economists at CUEPECS and MTUC therefore are always on guard to ensure that proper policy decisions are made to protect the interests of workers nationwide if the CPI rises abnormally.

The same applies to the banking business. Interest rates on loans are set to capture increases in the price level. This is to prevent the bank from unexpected losses due to a decline in the real value of loans made to borrowers. Textbook economics always says that lenders normally lose from inflation while borrowers set to gain more. This explains why banks imputed the inflation premium on loans to protect themselves from the risk of inflation.

For example, given cost of funds of 7 percent and expected rate of inflation in 1999 is 6 percent, the interest rate on a risk-free loan is 7 percent + 6 percent = 13 percent. But this may not be enough if actual inflation is 8 percent. In this case the bank stands to lose since it should have charged customers at 15 percent rather than 13 percent. So, interest rate forecasting is crucial in the banking business.

In the Islamic banking business, the difference between expected and actual inflation too plays a significant role in determining its performance. If the forecasting model is a weak one, the bank may stand to lose when the actual inflation exceeds real inflation. This is because the bank cannot make up for the error by adjusting the selling price upwards, as this may make the *al-bai-bithaman ajil* sale invalid. As a remedy, the bank should use less *al-bai-bithaman ajil* since a disappointing BBA performance will always mean less *hibahs* and dividends given to Islamic deposits.

Since creditors always lose, while borrowers gain from inflation, in what way can the creditors be compensated for the loss in purchasing power? For example, Harun lends Faris a sum of $3000, which is equivalent to 100 packs of rice at $30 each. When he is paid $3,000 two years later, the price of rice has risen to $40 per pack, which means now he can buy 74.5 packs of rice. It shows that his money two years ago is worth more than it is today. How can Harun be compensated for this loss?

In conventional economics, interest is used to compensate creditors for the erosion of purchasing power due to inflation. As shown earlier, an inflation premium is added to the cost of funds. But can the same apply in Islamic loans?

The answer lies in the nature of loans in Islam. Interest-bearing loans are replaced by credit sale instruments such as *al-bai-bithaman ajil, al-murabahah, bay'al-inah* and *al-naqad.* The only Islamic loans available— known as *qardhu hasan*—are given on a non-commercial basis, a facility only accessible to banks' staffs and workers.

To protect the welfare of creditors, the need to impute inflation premium on loans is necessary in Islam but it can only be done on *ex-post* basis. What this means is best described by the following narrative in the

Muwatta of Imam Malik. Mujahid reported that `Abd Allah b. `Umar took some dirhams as loans and paid back better dirhams. He said: "O Abu `Abd al-Rahman, these are better than the dirhams I loaned out to you." `Abd Allah b. `Umar replied: "Yes, I know, but I paid out of my own good will and pleasure."

In another occasion `Ata b. Yasir reported Abu Rafi' said: "The Apostle of Allah (*pbuh*) took on credit a small camel. When camels of sadeqah arrived, and he asked me to pay back a like camel, I said: 'Apostle of Allah, the camels are all big and four years old.' The Apostle of Allah (*pbuh*) said: 'Give from them. Virtuous are they who pay back their debts well.'"

It is quite clear in the above that paying more reflects one's ethical superiority. An intelligent borrower will not be ignorant about inflation and the risk a lender faces when he gives his money away. As lending is not profit motivated, his willingness to lend his money is a sacrifice no ordinary businessman will do. So, in an Islamic loan, any compensation given out is a matter of one's virtuous personality, but a legal injunction it is not. Which means that *ex-ente* fixed compensation i.e., interest is not expected from the borrowing party.

So, can an Islamic loan that imputes an *ex-post* compensation act as a viable alternative to conventional lending? The answer is both yes and no. If the loan is made on business dealing, it can only succeed if a strong moral and ethical relation exists among businessman so that business here must be conducted on the basis of mutual aid (*ta'awun*) and not cutthroat competition. Otherwise, lenders will only stand to lose either from default or erosion in purchasing power.

Another narration from the *Muwatta* of Imam Malik helps explain the real nature of loan in Islam. Malik reported that it reached him that a man came to `Abd Allah b. Umar and said: "I gave a loan to a person and fixed a better repayment." `Abd Allah b. `Umar said: "This is *riba*." He said: "O Abu `Abd Rahman, why do you give such a verdict?" `Abd Allah b. Umar said: "Loan is of three kinds: 1) A loan given to earn Divine goodwill, 2) loan given to obtain a friend's goodwill and pleasure, and 3) loans of valid goods for forbidden goods. This last one is *riba*." The man said: "What do you command me now, O `Abd Allah b. `Umar?" He said: "I think it is proper that you tear the document. If the man brings you goods the same as you gave him, take them; if he brings them of worse quality and you take them, you will reap good reward; if he out of his own will and pleasure, brings things of better quality than he took from you, he will be repaying your gratitude and the time that allowed him for so long will fetch you its reward."

To apply the above principles of Islamic loans for business application demands the debtor to command a high level of ethical and moral conscience (*akhlak*). Otherwise, one can apply the Islamic dinar to combat inflation risk in Islamic loans. This is explained in the following.

Suppose Bank A gave Harun a $150,000 loan facility payable in 3 years lump sum. The main point is to ensure that the bank does not suffer from inflation risk when the loan matures. To do so, loan contract must be contracted in Islamic dinar while payments are made in fiat currency. As an example, it is assumed that one Islamic dinar (i.e. about 3.4 gram of gold) = $100. Thus the value of the loan in Islamic dinar is 1,500 dinar. Since the contract of loan is based on dinar, an exchange between gold and gold has taken place involving an exchange of equivalence for equivalence (*al-mithlin bil mithlun*). Although it involves deferment and time value, no surplus from the loan amount can be created. Otherwise, the dinar contract will implicate *riba*.

On maturity, the issue on inflation risk can be overcome. If the inflation rate is up by say 5 percent so does the price of gold. In this case, although on maturity the debtor pays the bank 1,500 dinar, it however will cost him more in nominal amount. Since the current price of gold is $105, he must spend $157,000 to buy 1,500 dinar. Upon receiving the 1,500 dinar, the bank can sell it for $157,000. Although in nomimal amount of the Islamic dinar is higher, the purchasing power of $157,000 remains the same. The Islamic dinar can thus be used by Islamic banks to hedge their loan facilities against inflation without resorting to service fees and other methods to justify an increase against inflation risk.

The above example is only applicable to loans payable lump sum. If the mode of payment is made by installments, a system of rebate (*ibra'*) can be applied. The same applies for a BBA facility where the bank may put an inflation premium on top of the cost price. By using the Islamic dinar, there is no need to impose the premium, thus relieving customers from unnecessary additional payments.

Fifteen
Can Bank mergers benefit man on the street?

ABN ABRO view on Malaysian bank mergers is an eye opener and a challenge. Yet much more need mentioning, as the mergers mean a lot more than just lost jobs. The merger can reduce costs and strengthen capital base, but the bottom line remains blurred—how it impacted the man on the street.

People with fixed income normally rely on interest earned from savings usually in bank deposits. In Islamic banking, it translates into earnings derived from *hibah* and *mudarabah* dividends. Since it is unsafe to stack all savings into equities, namely unit trusts and stocks, bank deposits remain a source of safe and secure earning to most people.

We know well in economics that wages or salary, profits, rental, and interest make up what economists call personal income. Interest income remains an important source of earnings, which also includes interest arising from deposits.

The same applies to *hibah* and dividends from Islamic deposits. To pensioners, for example, low deposit rates normally mean lower earnings, and hence a decline in the quality of life. The low interest rate regime we see now will mean lower earnings from interests, *hibah* and *mudarabah* dividends, thus lowering personal income, household spending, and aggregate demand. At the end, pursuing a low interest rate regime can potentially reduce national income.

But this adversity can be neutralized if the supply of loans increases due to rising demand. However, if the bank uses a higher discount rate in making project appraisal by attaching higher risk premium, a low interest rate regime can hardly affect economic growth in a positive way. This is because many projects no longer become viable since discounting future cash flows using high discount rate will mean lower valuations of projects under application.

Likewise, how bank mergers can help stimulate economic recovery remains a mystery to many. But economists have studied this phenomenon with some interesting conclusions at hand. One model, known as the structure-conduct performance model, studies the impact of market structure on performance. A market structure looks at the number of firms in the market and the condition of entry.

For example, the merger will see small number of large banks with no prospect of giving new domestic bank licenses. Conduct in a market is determined by the market structure and takes the form of how decisions about prices, advertisement, etc. are made by the bank. The outcome is market performance, normally measured by profitability. And profitability is simply the difference between revenues from interest on loans and costs from interest paid on deposits.

Empirical evidence has shown that a negative relationship exists between interest rates on deposits and bank concentration. That is, the higher the bank concentration (small number of large banks), the lower the interest paid on deposits. Studies by Berger and Hannan (1989), Jackson (1992) and Molyneux and Forbes (1993) confirmed this negative relationship.

What this actually means to us is the fact that a small concentration of large banks will not be beneficial to depositors who may earn less from their savings. Monopolistic tendencies may increase profitability, but only at the expense of depositors. The high profit did not come from higher interest revenues, but only through lower interest costs.

Certainly we hope Islamic banks will not fall into this trap. If so, it is true that Islamic banks today are no different from conventional banks. It is hoped that this move for mergers will help Islamic banks find new ways towards making Islamic banking the pride of Muslims in this country.

However, the structure-conduct-performance (SCP) model is not without flaws. It is challenged by the efficient market (EM) model that says some firms can earn supernormal profits because they are more efficient than others. Efficiency is related to market share.

So it is not concentration one should relate with profit, but market share. When the SCP model advocates reducing monopoly, the EM model wants the market to be left alone. However, this may not hold true for the Malaysian case because some banks that command small market shares were made anchor banks. To what extent they can achieve efficiency remains to be seen.

Sixteen
Social Obligations of Islamic Banks

Doing business in Islam always means asking whether the firm must put aside some of its profits to fulfill social obligations. This social obligation seems to be the icon to anything that claims an Islamic label. The question is, must an Islamic firm be torn between its profit and social objectives? Does a conflict exist between private and social interest in the Islamic banking business?

By social obligation, we mean the inherent duty a firm must observe to promote the general welfare not within the scope of its business agenda. But does such an obligation exist in Islam? People seem to confuse this issue when they see companies making charities and donations to the sick, poor, and needy. Some money must be set aside to somewhat purify these companies by virtue of the charities given away.

There is no doubt that an Islamic firm, say an Islamic bank, must fulfill some social obligations. Certainly the payment of Zakat is one good example. But can this go beyond Zakat obligations, say giving Qardu Hasan loans to poor and the start-up companies or financing low-cost houses. These two activities serve to help two social groups, namely new companies with no security and the homeless poor.

We can see that the above are not profit-making ventures, but only those that serve a higher-end obligation which is moral in nature. But must Islamic banks do these things? Does an Islamic label require the bank to put up with these non-commercial objectives?

The answer, however, rests on our understanding about rules and regulations governing the operations of an Islamic bank. Without this understanding, we might end up trying to rationalize all conventional banking culture but using the Islamic label.

First, we must not try to debate how an Islamic bank can fulfill the twin goals of efficiency and equity. Or how a bank can maximize profits but at the same time play in the same level field. In an imperfectly competitive market like ours, it is just impossible to achieve this. To some extent, what one earns is a loss to the other. Efficiency is self-centered, while equity has a more altruistic flavor. Both cannot co-exist, yet people are trying to find out how a firm can do both.

The culture of capitalism saw firms making charities to make up their social shortcoming. That is, until detected by the authorities, they can pursue a monopoly way of doing business, repress workers or practice coercion to cut competition, all of which can adversely affect the welfare of consumers and the common public.

To put social obligation in its proper place, we must be able to see that an Islamic firm has two main objectives. The first is not about profit-making or profit maximization. That takes second place. Profit maximization, i.e., to produce goods at minimum cost, is a constructive phenomenon, rather than a destructive one.

In *Shariah*, the legal value (*hukum*) of making business profits is permissible (*mubah*). However, profits can only be made on the basis of *Shariah* guidance. That is, businesses must not involve themselves with the prohibitions. Therefore, it is forbidden (*haram*) to take and receive *riba,* to cheat or lie in order to secure a business agreement. It is *haram* to allow *gharar* (ambiguities) in business transactions.

The question now is what compels the Islamic bank to observe the rule of profit maximization constrained by *Shariah* rulings. One answer has to do with the first or primary objective of the firm. This objective can help secure the social protection the public often demands from the business community.

The primary objective of an Islamic firm, a banking or a non-banking one, is to uphold and observe the Covenant (*Al-Mithaq*) that it once made with the Creator. This has taken place in the primordial stage of life in Islam. The Quran relates four main events taking place in this primordial stage. First, man is created from clay, dust and mud (*tin, turab*) which God molded with His own Hand and when it formed, breathed His Spirit into it (Surah 94:4). The second event narrated the conversation between man and God, in which man bore witness that God is the Creator, the Nourisher. This is the day of *Al-Mithaq*. (Al-'Araf: 172)

By making this covenant, man confirms his indebtedness to God and pays this debt, i.e., his life to God, by submitting his desire and wants to His Will, the *Shariah*. The primordial stage also tells the story of Adam, who was appointed by God as His Vicegerent on earth but heavily protested by the arrogant Satan. The last event saw man's willingness to accept the trust (*amana*) which the heaven, the earth and mountains refused. (Surah 33:72)

Certainly, the primordial stage is the unseen (*ghayb*), which is only known through revealed knowledge. But it contains the basic ingredients to incite man to pursue the maximum. Which means that making profits defines the minimum, while man can gain more from business by making profit, as defined by the *Shariah*. Doing so, he will see that cutthroat competition is severely curtailed. It can help reduce pure monopoly and coercion, prevent food adulteration, reduce pollution, and make our environment a healthy place to live. Certainly these are social responsibilities that firms must not try to ignore.

Lastly, an Islamic bank could also fulfill its social responsibility by becoming an efficient bank in running its business. Efficiency means using the least to produce the maximum. When a bank is efficient, customers should be able to enjoy less expensive banking services. Social obligations also include efforts to reduce income disparities. Islamic banks can help reduce income disparities by increasing the application of equity products and profit-loss sharing products such as *mudarabah* and *musyarakah.* Unfortunately, *al-bai-bithaman ajil* (BBA) products have been the popular choice today. Although technically, a BBA product is *halal,* its positive income distribution effect is negligible as the impact of BBA and interest-bearing loans on economic stability and welfare is the same.

Seventeen
Interest rate hike: Impact on Islamic banking

The twenty-five basis points interest rate hike, according to most analysts, will make no significant impact on the stock market. Theoretically, when interest rates go up, funds will move into the fixed income market. Some may go to fixed deposits while others to the bond market.

Usually, the higher interest rate means higher cost of capital. With no significant increase in revenues, profits will decline. This can mean many things; for example, firms lose value. Some investors may want to get out and invest in deposits and bonds instead.

But this may not happen in the Malaysian case, as the hike has not been abrupt. People build expectations as the news has been around for quite some time. The question now is why the hike? Is the economy heating up? Economic theory gives some good insights, especially when Bank Negara's thinking has always been Keynesian. The low interest rates regime, pursued since mid-1998, no doubt has stimulated spending a little by putting the economy back on track, but at the expense of private savings.

Low interest rates mean less incentive to save. More seriously, people may bypass savings in local banks by way of capital flight. The elderly and pensioners are also hurt as interest income gets depleted by the day. Learning from the Japanese experience is a good thing. Low interest rate regime does not pay when at the same time people don't feel secure about their future. Even if the interest rate is low, the Japanese will not spend much. So economic theory proves futile this time. Does the same apply to Bank Negara?

It all depends. We basically don't know what lies in the future. The best we can do is to predict. Making guesses in the name of science often makes people confident what the future can bring. More often than not, making predictions remains an option when uncertainty rules. Nobody's perfect.

The point is, there must be a problem; otherwise, why the need for such a hike? Are our banks too complacent with high interest margins earned since 1998? Is Bank Negara targeting interest-sensitive sectors, and which one and why? Certainly, it has less to do with our depressed stock market. There may be inflationary pressure, but why only 0.25 percent? Perhaps online capital and money market investments may have drained out private savings into foreign hands. Which one is true?

A gradual hike may work well for the U.S. economy, since the technology sector provides most of the increment in productivity, thus dampening a slowdown. But does the same hold for Malaysia?

The impact of the hike on Islamic banking is also worth a look. Certainly for the past two years, the low interest rate regime has benefited Islamic banking business a lot. Why? Almost all Islamic deposits are variable-rate liabilities. Meaning that the bank can change the rates of return, since they are not contractual in nature.

On the contrary, most assets are fixed rate. *Al-murabahah* and *al-bai-bithaman ajil* (BBA) are fixed rate assets since the profit rate is locked in for good. Determining the selling price requires the bank to set only one profit rate, which is based on current cost of funds. Once market interest rate declines, the selling price stays put. An Islamic bank cannot adjust the profit rate downwards (i.e., to follow market movement) since it will change the selling price announced earlier. Doing otherwise will make the BBA contract void.

So who benefits and who gains when the interest rate is falling? Conventional customers will see lower installment payments, as interest rates are flexible downwards. Floating rates are good for customers and not too good for the bank (it depends how much fixed rate asset the bank holds, especially from hire-purchase) but it is quite the opposite in Islamic banking. Customers pay the same installment while depositors get less. So, profit margin widens.

But without a floating rate BBA, Islamic banks will soon be in the red again, because people who buy a house today at a relatively low profit rate will be paying the same installment, even though the market rate moves upward as the bank cannot adjust the rate upwards. With the old but low profit rate locked in, profit margins on existing BBAs will fall. Unless the bank gives low *hibah* and dividends, existing depositors will move to conventional deposits looking for better returns. Operating in a dual-banking set up does not warrant any affirmative action.

So is Islamic banking stock a good buy today? Well, it depends how one forecasts the direction of interest rate. If rates are steadily increasing, and my assumptions are not wrong, buying one in a short run is certainly not a wise move. So where do we go from here? It seems that Islamic banks will do well when interest rates are falling, while the opposite is true when interest rates go uphill. In the long run, it will balance up to break even. Perhaps for long-term investments, buying one isn't bad after all. But who is thinking long-term these days?

Eighteen
Can Malaysian Islamic banks go international?

Amirsham Abdul Aziz, the CEO of Maybank, recently called on Islamic banks in Malaysia to go international, in view of the need to further improve efficiency. By going international, Malaysian Islamic banks are expected to find new ways to fund international projects. They can also pull more deposits using existing Islamic deposit products.

But on the local front, apparently Islamic banks have somewhat slacked behind conventional banks. The loan-to-deposit ratio for Islamic banking divisions (IBDs) and full-fledged Islamic banks (Bank Islam Malaysia Barhad & Bank Muamalat) was only 54.3 percent, against 87.1 percent for conventional banking operations. Liquidity is a problem Islamic banks can no longer ignore.

It is also worthy to note that more can be done locally before one goes international. For example, the contract of *Salam* is not yet fully exploited. The agricultural sector is in need of capital to stay alive if not competitive with neighboring countries. *Salam* is a forward sale contract where the bank pays farmers up front, prior to delivery.

Other contracts which are taboo to Islamic financing today are *al-qirad* (trustee partnership) and *Shirkatul amwal* (general partnership). The problems of asymmetrical information, namely moral hazards and adverse selections, may explain why Islamic banks are not willing to go all out to apply these profit loss sharing (PLS) contracts. Using the contracts of *qirad* and *shirkatul amwal* can help the growth of start-up companies. With the control acquired, Islamic banking can steer these companies into adopting Islamic management and marketing policies.

The opportunities to go international are worth mentioning here. In 1998, the gross domestic product (GDP) of Muslim countries as a group accounted for 5 percent of the world's total. Its foreign reserves accounted for 7.8 percent of the world's total. Thus, the purchasing power of Muslim countries cannot be undermined.

It is also noted that the average GDP of Muslim countries is much higher than the average GDP of developing countries, with 56.5 percent against 37.3 percent respectively. Muslim countries are also heavily in debt. As of the end of 1997, the total external debt of Muslim countries amounted to US$712 billion, or 31 percent of all developing nations. For the least-developed Muslim countries, the ratio is as high as 81 percent.

It will be a great achievement if Malaysian Islamic banking can play a significant role in fulfilling the demand for funds in these countries. With Islamic funds in Malaysia accounting for more than 10 percent of global Islamic funds, the move to go international is quite inviting.

Table 5. 2: Some Development Indicators for Muslim Countries

Development Indicators	Percentages
1. GDP of Muslim countries to the world's total	5 percent
2. Foreign reserves to world's total	7.8 percent
3. Total debt of Muslim countries to developing countries	31 percent

Source: The Star, February 21, 2001

However, a point of caution is in order. A considerable amount of Islamic banking products are not in tune with global flavor, particularly countries in the Middle Eeast. This is true when one looks at the wide application of *bay' al-'inah* and *bay al-dayn*, both of which are not acceptable to the Maliki, Hanbali, and Hanafi schools of thought (*mahzabs*).

These two contracts have given birth to many products, such those as listed below:

1. Personal financing and Overdrafts (*Bay' al-'inah*)
2. Negotiable Islamic Certificates of Deposit (NICD) (*Bay' al-'inah & bay' al-dayn*)
3. Islamic Accepted Bills (*Bay' al-Dayn*)
4. Islamic bonds (*bay' al-inah & bay al-dayn*)

Given the above scenario, it will be quite premature to go international with such a high handicap. Without these products, Malaysian Islamic banks will have less ammunition to compete with international conventional banks in Muslim countries. They can sell the usual *murabahah-* and *al-bai-bithaman ajil-*based products for home and vehicle purchases and trade finance. But these are already available in Muslim countries. Other than that, they will be quite impotent to do anything meaningful.

Nineteen
Labuan Off-shore International Islamic Financial Market

Recent developments in Labuan Offshore IFFM saw the issuance of the world's first US$100 million offshore Islamic bond by Kumpulan Guthrie Pte. A memorandum of understanding between Kumpulan Guthrie and the dealer-arranger Bank Islam (Labuan) Ltd. was signed on 22 November, 2000, witnessed by Labuan Offshore Financial Service Authority (LOFSA) Chairman Zeti Akhtar Aziz.

According to reports, the bond, with a five-year tenure will be issued in the first quarter of year 2001. The proceeds were used to finance the development of Kumpulan Guthrie's oil palm plantations in Sumatra, Indonesia.

Islamic finance has thus benefited from the wide array of services offered by Labuan International Offshore Financial Center (IOFC). Labuan IOFC has its own legal framework with integrated offshore financial services. It offers both conventional and Islamic financial instruments, mostly in the non-ringgit currencies. As it deals mostly with non-residents, no exchange control has taken place there.

Table 5.3 Labuan International Offshore Financial Center

	1991	2003
Banks	5	52
Insurance and insurance-related	1	101
Leasing	0	35
Fund Managers	0	25
Trading/non-trading	27	2,391
Trust companies	8	18
Legal/Audit firms	9	35
Total	50	2,657

Source: Bank Negara Report 1991 & 2003

As an integrated IOFC, financial activities include investment holding, investment banking, insurance, trust business, mutual funds, unit trusts and fund management, leasing, factoring, and Islamic financing.

As of December 2003, there were more than 2,657 companies in Labuan IOFC. More details are given in Table 5.3 above. It is worth noting that these firms provide both conventional and Islamic financial and non-financial services.

Labuan IIFM forms one integral part of LOFSA. Labuan IIFM is the Islamic wing of Labuan LOFSA. It strives to stimulate cooperation among Muslim countries in the area of banking and finance. The players include governments, financial institutions, and corporations, while a wide range of *Shariah*-compatible instruments are readily available.

In the area of Islamic finance, the capital and money markets seemed to dominate media headlines. The Guthrie Offshore Islamic bond is a capital market instrument. It has applied the *bay'al-'inah* and *bay'al-dayn* contracts, which is also commonly practiced in Malaysian inshore Islamic bond market.

In view of the unpopular status of *bay'al-'inah* and *bay al-dayn* among Middle Eastern investors, the Malaysian government has successfully issued the Global *Sukuk Ijarah* in 2002. This Islamic bond is relatively free from *bay'al-'inah* and *bay al-dayn*. It has received strong institutional support both in Malaysia as well as the Middle East. Only time will tell how the Globak *Sukuk* will performe under private issues. This is because the *Sukuk* is principle a government guaranteed bond.

Labuan LOFSA has also set up the Labuan Offshore Islamic Money Market involving three main parties, namely LOFSA, the Islamic Development Bank and the Bahrain Monetary Agency. It constitutes a cooperation among Muslim countries in the field of Islamic finance. The first meeting on 7 December, 1999 was held in Bahrain, followed by several others in Labuan, Jeddah, Brunei, and Iran.

Here the main concern is the problem of liquidity (*al-suyulah*). Islamic facilities for liquidity management are a critical element in making investment decisions. Prospective investors will not be interested in purchasing Islamic papers if secondary trading is thin.

More important, excess funds must not be left idle in a traditional interest-bearing money market. The Labuan Islamic Money Market will ensure that these funds will find their way into proper channels that are *Shariah* compliant.

The main participants of the Labuan Islamic Money Market consist of Malaysia and foreign banks in Labuan, as well as Islamic banks from Muslim countries. On the mode of financing, Islamic finance via asset securitization will be offered by the surplus financial institution to the deficit ones.

As the term "securitization" normally implies the application of *al-ᶜinah*, the Labuan offshore money market has now introduced *al-ᶜinah* in international finance. The procedure is similar to the Guthrie case, but the assets used in the *'inah* sale are not fixed assets but securities. The *ᶜinah* sale can either originate from the surplus or deficit sector. For example, Bank A has a US$200 million asset that it will securitize, from which a money market instrument is issued to raise short-term funds.

The asset will be sold to the surplus bank in return for cash payments. The surplus bank will sell the same asset to the deficit bank at a mark-up price. The difference constitutes the return on the investment by the surplus bank. The *Shariah* advisors considered the contract lawful since the *'inah* sale is in essence a contract of sale and not a loan.

Although there are disagreements on the issue of *bay' al-'inah*, it is vital that parties from both the Malaysian and the Middle Eastern sides discuss the matter and see what can be done to make the Labuan Offshore IFFM an important centre for global Islamic funds. By doing so, idle Islamic global funds can find ready investments. In this way the Muslim Ummah can gradually see that Islamic banking and finance is making a positive move in the field of economic growth and development.

Twenty

To use or not to use Al-Bai-bithaman Ajil

Sales from the House Ownership Campaign launched late last year were reported to have grossed about RM3.5 billion. Although this is short of the RM5 billion targets, it looks like property demand is still going strong. This demand however is driven by easy credit. And how consumers can pay up is another issue matter policymakers must not undermine.

In the house ownership campaign, some observers may wonder how many sales were taken up by Islamic banks. Does it really matter to consumers which bank suits their tastes—interest-bearing or Islamic? Are they aware what to gain or lose from in making these choices?

Consumers are quite in the dark how, for example, changes in interest rates, income, and economic growth can impact their interest-free purchases and hence, economic welfare. Although this role should be taken up by the Bank Negara via education, it has yet to inform the public in what manner Islamic financing, *al-bai-bithman ajil* in particular, can best serve their interest.

So far, Bank Negara in its 1997 annual report was able to highlight problems encountered *by al-bai-bithaman ajil*-intensive Islamic banks in a volatile economic environment. The observation was, however, made on the banking side only, while impacts on consumer welfare were not given any mention. As Islam desires to protect public interest (*maslahah al-ammah*) consumer welfare should receive equal treatment.

It is thus important to further examine home financing schemes offered by Islamic banks. The only mode of financing available today is the fixed rate *al-bai-bithman ajil* (BBA) sales. As an alternative to conventional loans, many would agree that BBA is similar to the interest-based financing. Worst still, its fixed-rate mechanism has introduced an element of uncertainty into consumption behavior. Let me explain how.

When information is freely available to consumers, buying decisions may no longer be based on current events alone. Equally important is the role of expectations; namely, in what way future events can affect current behavior. Since nobody but God knows what lies ahead, man can only make guesses or form his own expectations what the future is like. It is here that forecasting and projections become crucial in determining our failure and success in economic undertakings. For example, people may postpone buying home property now if they expect the property market may slip down further in the future. Doing so allows them to save more or even purchase a better house later. So current prices are not the only factor governing consumer spending today.

Fixed rate BBA, in fact, has made the expectation factor a crucial element in determining whether Islamic banking customers will—in the final juncture—emerge as either winners or losers. I will cite an example below, and this has a lot to do with our current economic problem.

The Home Ownership Campaign attracts consumers in three ways, namely: 1) property offered at discount prices 2) lower price of credit, namely interest rates, and in some cases 3) full financing. When the fixed-rate BBA comes into play, a new dimension of choice behavior will emerge. This concerns the choice or option to seek financing using loans or the BBA.

Now that the interest rate in Malaysia is low, there are two possibilities how it will move in the near future. It can either fall further or go up. If people feel that interest rate has already bottomed out, then the next thing is to see it rising. To many investors, this is the time to sell bonds and purchase stocks instead. But if we are confident that interest rates will fall some more, then it is good idea to buy bonds today. Fixed income investors can make hefty capital gains when the rates indeed fall.

Similarly, rational consumers who are looking for the best home financing package in the market will try to see what lies ahead if they intend to use BBA product. If they feel that interest rates will drop further, then using a fixed-rate BBA will severely affect their savings relative to those using floating-rate loans. To some extent, the demand for BBA will fall. This is a cause for concern for Islamic banks, who now have to work harder to find new customers. If they are unlucky, Islamic banks will end up with new BBA customers who are bad paymasters; which means those who fail to obtain loans will eventually qualify to use BBA financing. This is a typical problem of adverse selection, which, in the final analysis, inflicts losses on Islamic banks.

However, if more people are inclined to believe that interest rates will go up, a fixed rate BBA is good for consumers but unfortunately bad for Islamic banks. Again, this requires Islamic banks to reduce the BBA dependency and perhaps introduce a new product that can help eliminate losses arising from interest rate volatility.

In 2003, Bank Negara Malaysia has produced a document to explain the Islamic Variable Rate Mechanism (IVRM) as an alternative to the exisiting fixed BBA system. The IVRM uses a system of rebate (*ibra'*) to protect Islamic banks from losing money when interest rate rises. Since there are indications that interest rate may soon increase, Islamic banks will protect themselves by setting a BBA price based on a higher profit margin. What this means is the new flexible BBA profit margin is deliberately imputed higher than current cost of funds.

For example, let's assume that banks expected cost of funds to increase by 2 percent over the financing period. Given current base lending rate (BLR) plus profit rate of 10 percent per annum, the bank will set a ceiling rate of 12 percent. Based on the 12 percent profit rate, the customer pays an equal monthly instalment of RM1,000 over the agreed period. If market rate rises to 11% per annum, the customer pays only RM700 which means he receives a rebate (*ibra'*) of RM300. The rebate system serves to produce an effective profit rate (ceiling profit rate less rebate) to reflect the fluactuating market interest rate. It will help the bank provides higher rates of returns on Islamic deposits under rising marker rate. Doing so, reduces the possibility of deposit migration to conventional banks. Finally, at maturity any differences between the selling price and total repayments plus the monthly rebates, would be rebated. For example, if selling price amounted to RM250,000 while repayments RM230,000, the rebate on the RM20,000 unearned profit is given to the customer.

By virtue of the implementation of the Islamic Variable Rate Mechanism (IVRM), Bank Negara Malaysia has made it compulsory on Islamic banks to give rebates (*ibra'*) in the event of early settlement or redemption or termination of contract. However, the IVRM may have come too late to protect customers who took BBA financing when interest rate is on the decline. Malaysia pursued a low interest rate policy from 1999 to the present (i.e. 2004) as one way to stimulate the economy. For example, if the customer pays a total RM250,000 on 12 percent profit rate, should the bank gave the customer a cash rebate when the market rate actually dropped to 11 percent with a BBA price amounting to RM230,000? The rebate system should have been implemented soon after Bank Negara commented on the demise state of Islamic banking in its 1997 annual report. In this way banking customers could be protected from paying heavily on using a fixed rate BBA product under a decling interest rate environment.

Twenty-One
Bank Lending and Default Loans

With regional financial markets still in turmoil, the banking sector gets more blame over piling bad loans. Although, the region posts average investment to GDP ratios above 40 percent, the resultant growth rates of 8 to 9 percent do not seem to show that investment activities are efficient enough. The low marginal efficiency of capital (MEC) hints that investments end up in the less productive sectors, such as property and share markets.

Now that the good times are over, reforming the banking sector will be a tough job. Banks failing to recover loans will cease to operate, while defaulters face bankruptcy. To reform the banking sector, among other things, one must study how banks actually approve loans.

But let us take a look at some basic economics how a banking firm determines the contractual loan rate it charges debtors. A bank's contractual loan rate is equal to the cost of deposits (r_d), operating costs (c), profit margin (p) and a risk premium. If we take away the risk premium, we get the targeted interest rate (r_t), which is also known as the prime or base-lending rate (BLR). The BLR is the interest rate charged to a bank's best customers, consisting of the interest rate on deposits (r_d), operating cost (c), and a profit margin (p).

Based on the above, $r_t = r_d + c + p$. Let's say that bank pays depositors 7 percent and incurs 1 percent in operating cost and a 2 percent profit margin. The targeted interest rate is therefore 10 percent.

Now, the bank receives a $180,000 loan application from Mr. Chen. After full assessment of his credit ratings, the bank felt that Mr. Chen has a 20 percent default risk ($p_d = 0.2$). This also implies that the probability of Mr. Chen making full payment is 80 percent (p_f). Given this information, the question now is how much should the bank charge Mr. Chen for the $180,000 loan? Or what is the contractual loan interest rate (r_c)?

The contractual loan interest rate is an interest rate set in the loan contract. Given that Mr. Chen is a risky borrower, the bank may not want to charge him the prime rate. Certainly now, the contractual loan rate is expected to be higher than the prime rate or BLR.

To obtain the contractual loan rate, the bank must first determine how much profits it desires to make from the loan. Meaning that the expected rate of return (r_e) must be computed to find (r_c). Since the bank's targeted rate of return (r_t) is equal to the BLR, it also means that expected rate of return (r_e) must be equal to the targeted rate of return (r_t).

Now given Mr. Chen's 20 percent probability of default, which is assumed to cause the bank a 10 percent loss (r_d), the expected rate of return (r_e) and contractual interest rate are given below:

Computing the Contractual interest rate (r$_c$) on a Risky loan

- $r_e = (p_f \times r_c) + (p_d \times r_d)$
- $r_e = (0.8 \times r_c) + (0.2 \times -0.1)$
- $r_t = r_d + c + p$
- Since $r_t = 10$ percent or 0.1
- $0.1 = 0.8r_c - 0.02$
- $r_c = (0.1 + 0.02)/0.8 = 0.15$ or 15 percent; $r_c > r_t$

We can see in the above illustration that the contractual loan interest rate ($r_c = 15$ percent) is higher that the targeted rate of return ($r_t = 10$ percent). This is simply because Mr. Chen is a risky borrower and thus was charged 5 percent higher than the bank's best customer(s) who by definition have no credit or default risk at all. In other words, for risky borrowers, the contractual loan rate is set above the targeted rate. Likewise, the lower the default risk, the lower is the contractual loan rate relative to the targeted rate. For example, if the probability of making full payment is 95 percent, the contractual loan rate is 1 percent above the BLR or targeted rate of return.

It should also worthy to note that in the example, where Mr. Chen has a 20 percent default risk, the extra 5 percent risk premium he has to pay is equal to the expected loss the bank would incur if Mr. Chen indeed defaulted on the loan. This 5 percent risk premium is also equal to the contractual loan interest rate (r_t) x the probability of defaulting the loan (p_d). What this means is a simple fact that risk must be paid up front.

Although theoretically banks should apply the above method to obtain the contractual loan rate for each individual borrower, it seems that banking firms today tend to treat all customers alike. For example, in housing loans, the contractual interest rate = BLR + 1.2 percent. The amount of loan given out is less than the mortgage value and customers, irrespective of their goodwill, are charged the same risk premium.

It seems, there is less transparency in discerning good borrowers from bad borrowers except from collateral provided. Good and genuine customers who often make full repayment pay 1.2 percent risk premium while risky customers who use the loan to speculate also pay 1.2 percent. These funds are further utilized to hike up property and stock prices both of which contribute less to gross domestic product (GDP) as relatively less value added is created.

In a broader scope, there are many potential entrepreneurs out there whose technical skills and a marketing niche can help stimulate value-added production. However, lack of collateral prevented access to bank loans. Even in Islamic banking, efforts must be made to assess funds application more equitably by practicing the due diligence process. Customers must not only be rated by material factors alone, namely collateral, but also by their personal goodwill, namely their moral conduct (*akhlak*). It calls for creative thinking to assess the *akhlak* factor in funds application.

Twenty-Two
Islam and the Cooperatives

They are many reasons why Islamic banks are not eager to venture into equity investments. One factor is market risk that banks have no control over. Another is the legal constraint in BAFIA 1989 that does not allow banks to participate in equity ownership of companies.

Both factors explain why Islamic banks are more keen to conduct trading business such as *murabahah* and *al-bai-bithaman ajil.* But trading activities in general generate less value added, compared to real production. The question now is whether trading-based Islamic banks can help promote economic growth and improve income distribution. For example, personal income of depositors will increase as they receive higher returns from deposits. This is the distribution effect of the banking business. Likewise, lower cost of capital will increase the demand for bank funds and therefore investments; and subsequently increase economic growth.

The answer depends on how depositors perceive their respective roles as a bank's clients. Normally, banks and clients have little in common, for each strives for different ends. It often creates uncertainties and doubts about each other's intentions. Consequently, to maximize shareholders' wealth, bank management pursues asset-liability management strategies, sticking fast to the principles of profitability, safety, and liquidity; that often runs counter what the public desires. For this reason, more people are looking at alternative forms of investment such as unit trusts and the cooperatives.

It is worthy to see now what a cooperative can offer the investing public. This is in response to a recent statement made by Anwar Ibrahim at the second meeting of the International Cooperative Alliance Regional Assembly for Asia and the Pacific in Kuala Lumpur. He said that, "Cooperatives have emerged as an important instrument for socio-economic transformation. They also serve as a mechanism for income distribution." He added that "Current social and economic trends are more in favor of corporations and conglomerates and the concentration of wealth and economic power among a handful of individuals, and although in theory the public could participate in the ownership of these corporations through the purchase of stocks and participation of mutual funds, they have influence in the direction of these companies."

Anwar says that in cooperatives every member has a say in the affairs of their cooperatives that is not seen in modern-day corporations. The concept of cooperatives, therefore, seems to contain more goodness than the present day Islamic banking. Using the one-man one-vote system, the cooperatives have given man his true position in a business enterprise.

In present-day corporations, the voting power of the public depends on their share of ownership, i.e., the more shares owned, the more influential and powerful the shareholder becomes in controlling the direction of the company. Money becomes the measuring rod of control, while man and the intellect take a backseat.

Cooperatives allow the individual to exercise his true expression of freedom in a business enterprise. With the one-man one-vote system, the Cooperative Act 1993 has empowered the individual member to determine who is elected as the directors of the cooperative, no matter how small the size of his investment. The directors may then appoint a team to manage the business of the cooperatives, all of which reflect the decisive role of the general membership.

One unique character of cooperatives is the common goals shared by members who are also capital providers. These objectives are expected to be manifested in the business activities run by the management team. Obviously these are relatively absent in Islamic banking today, where the bulk of "capital" is sourced from deposits, while shareholders' equity often remain a small portion of total liabilities. *Mudarabah* depositors investors have no say how the management operates the Islamic banking business.

In other words, a bank's customers have no legal means to outdo management if they find pricing and the product offered to them had failed to protect their interest. Worse still, the retail shareholders cannot do anything to steer directors' interest towards goals bearing strong long-term growth, say investment in manufacturing via profit-sharing.

A cooperative governed by the Cooperative Act 1993 can invest in almost all assets including equities and merchandises. It can conduct *al-ijarah, salam, istisna'* and *musyarakah* i.e., products Islamic banks have stayed away from. The only negative point is that cooperatives can only mobilize deposits from the members and not the general public. In this way, market penetration may be an obstacle. Bank Kerjasama Raayat has done it but strangely, why is BBA still the popular choice? Are the members not informed about Islamic commercial law and how the bank can best exploit it to help intensify their investments using profit-sharing financing schemes?

Twenty-Three
Don't sideline Islamic Banking

Bank mergers as an organic and natural process of business expansion and consolidation should benefit both banks and customers, especially in cost-cutting measures. Bigger asset size can lower operations cost and consequently raise profits. This is scale economy. Mergers will also see multiple uses of a single product, such that cost of product design and marketing is lowered. This is economy of scope. Both should bring about greater efficiency in using scarce capital resources. In the long run, the bank's performance can improve significantly.

But cost reduction is not the only objective of bank mergers. Others include the desire to maximize shareholder wealth, to minimize risk, to increase management prestige, to achieve growth-rate target, and to enter new markets. The government wants the mergers to produce powerful banks that can withstand the onslaught of globalization.

To what extent Malaysia's banking mergers can achieve the above objectives is yet to be seen, especially in scale and scope economies. For this to happen, a competitive market must free itself from external interference. But government support must be present, especially to amend the banking laws in order to make way for a new banking structure.

Failure to do so will defeat the purpose of mergers. One cannot ignore the fact that the new bank will now have to deal with multiple products under one roof. Without a meaningful amendment of the Banking and Financial Institution Act, it will simply be impossible for the anchor banks to reap the benefits arising from economies of scale and scope. We certainly

301

do not want to see small numbers of big and powerful banks that operate when average cost is declining. That is, a big bank must be efficient, or else it will turn out to be a monopoly.

The impact of the merger on Islamic banking is rather interesting to see. The mergers will divide the banking industry into three parts. First, the six local anchor banks will continue their Islamic window banking business. Secondly, the foreign banks too will operate their Islamic windows as usual. Finally, we see three full-fledged Islamic banks, namely Bank Islam Malaysia Berhad, Bank Bumiputra Muamalat, and Bank Rakyat. Bank Rakyat says that its future new savings and financing products will be all Islamic.

One interesting factor would be the size of Islamic assets held by each anchor bank. This may be small in size if an anchor bank takes in those banks with minimal Islamic participation. It is not uncommon to see quite a number of banks raising Islamic deposits but only to invest the proceeds in the money market. Full stop. It is done only to comply with Bank Negara directive. Deposits normally cost these banks, say, 4 percent *hibah* rate, but they can make 1 percent margin if these deposits are put into the interbank money market at 5 percent. Relatively less is done to offer basic facilities like Islamic home, car, and trade financing.

That is why, when selecting an anchor bank, its performance in Islamic banking must at be given due recognition. If an anchor bank has less experience in Islamic banking, it may jeopardize the application of Islamic principles in the new and bigger banking business to come.

Two banks have shown considerable commitment in Islamic banking, namely Arab Malaysian and Rashid Hussain Bank. Unfortunately, as we all know, both are not front liners. Selecting Maybank and Perwira Affin has been a right choice, as both have shown stronger performance, but relatively less is heard about Multi-Purpose and Southern Bank.

Public Bank, to some extent, is not dormant but showing good progress. But there are a number of smaller banks that have been active in the Islamic banking activities, such as Ban Hin Lee Bank, Pacific Bank, Eon Finance, and Bank Simpanan Nasional. Bank of Commerce, which took over Bank Bumiputra Malaysia Bhd, is also less known in the Islamic banking business. Bumiputra Commerce should now see the need to take in Islamic banking practitioners from the acquired banks. Certainly it cannot be taken from Bank Bumiputra, as its Islamic banking division will turn full-fledged Islamic bank under the name Bank Muamalat.

The question now is how an anchor bank that has less contact with Islamic banking operations pays for the goodwill and expertise they are about to enjoy from the acquired banks that were more active in Islamic banking business.

Certainly now, we need to discuss the determinants of value. Valuation of the prospective banks must include a premium in recognizing the extra value acquired from banks with strong Islamic goodwill.

There are quite a number of valuation techniques for bank mergers, among which are: 1) book value comparisons, 2) price-earning comparisons; and 3) earning comparisons.

For Islamic banking purposes, a good technique should revalue assets and liabilities of the acquired bank on the basis of product niche. Apart from making valuation on the basis of market prices in the case of bonds and securities, loans can be revalued to reflect both credit and interest rate risk. In the Islamic sense, even if the Islamic banking division is entitled to the above-mentioned premium, valuation must also recognize potential defaults and risks arising from the credit sale, such as BBA.

A system of weights attached to Islamic assets and liabilities should be introduced to capture this goodwill while valuation procedure must seek to eliminate potential risks of default and drop in earnings from market volatility. Once a system of weights is in play, the resulting value of liability will be subtracted from the revalued assets to give an adjusted equity value. This can be used as a realistic market value of the acquired bank. Soon after, we can see that banks that have contributed strongly to Islamic banking will be handsomely compensated.

Lastly, the onslaught of foreign banks with Islamic banking products must not be taken lightly. The new players include Standard Chartered, Citibank, Hong Kong and Shanghai Bank (HSBC), and Overseas Chinese Banking Corporation (OCBC).They may come in a big when the time is right. Competition at this juncture implies efficiency that new anchor banks must pursue with vigor. But efficiency cannot be met by only giving focus to acquisition of traditional banking assets and liabilities. The merger should have included acquisition of non-banking business such as insurance, fund management, and stock brokerage. Only then can one see a universal banking making way to increase bank's performance via economies of scale and scope.

Twenty-Four
Margin financing

Achieving sustainable economic growth is not easy, since as human beings, we are often forgetful. In times of prosperity, we tend to spend too much, thinking less about things to come until it is too late. But when recession hits us hard and spending is crucial to stimulate economic activities, too often we find ourselves without enough resources, especially money. Resorting to borrowing has been the remedy, even if this means living beyond our means.

The Asian crisis explains too well what borrowing and leverage have done to us. It pulls debtors and lenders into financial turmoil. Islam, in a sense, does not encourage people to borrow, especially when modern life today places a high value on the material aspects of life and its wealth-seeking ways. But borrowing to purchase capital goods or seeking borrowed funds to, say, purchase stocks is not the way one should strive to earn a living in Islam. There are many instances in historical Islam where the act of borrowing and lending for business is not encouraged at all.

It is related in the *Muwatta* of Imam Malik from Zaid bin Aslam who reported from his father that Abd Allah and Ubaid allah, who were both sons of Umar al-Khattab, went to Iraq for *jihad*. On their return, they met the Governor of Basrah Abu Musa Ash'ari. He welcomed them, glorified them, and said: "Oh that I could do you some good or profit, I would do it." He said again: "Why not, there is some property I intend to send to the Commander of the Faithful (that is Umar al-Khattab). Here I shall give you a loan of the amount. Buy goods of Iraq. Sell them at Medina, Give the principal to the Commander of the Faithful and you take the profit." They say: "We agree."

When the two arrived, they sold the goods and obtained profit and took the principal property to Umar al-Khattab, who asked: "Was such loan given to each man in the army?" They said: "No." The Commander of the Faithful said: "Then he must have given the amount to you knowing you to be the sons of the Commander of the Faithful. Pay the principal as well as the profit." Abd Allah was silent, but Ubaid Allah said: "O Commander of the Faithful, you should have acted thus, for if the goods had been damaged or lost, we should have paid the penalty." He said: "Pay." Abd Allah was still silent but Ubaid Allah repeated the statement.

Meanwhile, one of the Companions of Umar (Abd al-Rahman b. Auf) spoke out and said: "O Commander of the Faithful (*Amirulmukminin*), it would be better if you do *mudarabat*." Then Umar took the principal and half the profit, and Abd Allah and Ubaid Allajh took the remaining half of the profit.

It is clear in the above tradition that Umar al-Khattab had chosen *mudarabah* arrangement over loans. Since the business of buying goods in Basrah and selling them in Medina can bring lucrative earnings if the danger of caravan trade is minimal, it is rather unfair to allow his two sons and the Muslim army to protect and caravan, although this was not done on purpose. Also, Umar al-Khattab was not happy with the loan, since it was not given to the rest of the soldiers.

In doing business, Muslims must stay away from debt, as it brings many problems. When capital is in short supply, using *mudarabah* and *musyarakah* is one option. The business of Islamic unit trust is one example where Muslim customers should not be encouraged to borrow in order to invest in Islamic funds. If Islamic funds are invested in new share issues, it can indeed contribute to economic growth, since the proceeds will be used to buy capital goods.

However, the unit trust industry can do less to stimulate economic growth when all it does is buying and selling stocks already in circulation. The purchase of old stocks, as we know, does not add up to economic growth. All it does is help create the "wealth effect" which is good in the shorter term, but turns into inflationary pressure when too much money coming from the paper wealth ended up chasing too few goods.

In the open market, there should be ways to provide brokers the necessary funds for margin trading. By now, banks may be hesitant to lend, for fear of another round of financial crisis. Does Islam allow margin trading? The *Shariah* certainly prohibits margin trading when an interest-bearing loan is implicated. But if margin trading is driven by some profit-sharing arrangements between banks, securities companies, and investors, will it be allowed by the *Shariah* advisors?

In this sense, the Securities Commission should not only try to introduce Islamic values in stock trading by virtue of identifying *shariah*-linked counters or producing the KLCI *Shariah* Index, it can further do justice by giving ways to make margin financing *Shariah* compliant.

But what is margin financing? Margin financing or buying on margin is a transaction in which an investor uses a loan to purchase shares using the latter as collateral. Suppose Ali has $10,000 to invest and plans to purchase Telekom shares at $20 each. Doing so implies that he can buy 500 shares. Normally, his broker can help him to buy more shares by giving him a loan that the broker gets from a bank. If the loan is $10,000, Ali can purchase an additional 500 shares. So a share collateral worth $20,000 supports a $10,000 loan. If the Telekom share rises to $25, Ali will make a handsome $5,000 profit.

But if the price drops to, say, $10 then Ali loses $10,000 and this can mean many things. He can wait for Telekom shares to go up and keep on paying his loan. Or he can simply realize the losses and pay the broker the difference. In the worst case scenario, Ali will not pay up, and leaves the broker in debt. Again, one can see that using loan can be disastrous to both parties. It is thus important that an investor abstain from borrowing and uses his own money to buy the shares.

Twenty-Five
Declining interest rate : Impacts of Islamic banking performance

Low interest rates can be good for business. In the early 1990s, when the American economy dipped into a recession, keeping interest rates low helped the economy recovered. It beefed up the stock market, increased personal wealth, and stimulated spending and production. But the same failed to take place in Japan. Since the bubble burst in 1989, the recession in the Japanese economy seems never-ending. The Japanese stock market fell from 39,916 on the Nikkei Index in December 1989 to 14,309 in August 1992. The net worth of Japanese households fell by US$14 trillion (RM53.2 trillion). This includes a 63 percent fall in stocks, 33 percent and 85 percent fall in urban residential commercial land respectively, and 55 percent losses in foreign assets when evaluated in yen.

But why have low interest rates not worked so well for Japan? One reason is that Japan is an export-dependent country. Unlike the United States, Japan's domestic demand is relatively weak, as Japanese economic power lies in its exports; it could not lift the economy like the American domestic economy was able to. When an economy is export dependent, its performance will depend a lot on external factors. Weak global demand will mean weak exports and a fall in income. An economic downturn follows. This is what happened to Malaysia during the 1983-1986 recession.

Now that the Malaysian economy is poised for recovery, a low interest rate regime is already in play. Just like the Japanese economy, Malaysia is export dependent. It has trade surpluses with the US but deficits with

Japan. What it means here is that the surplus pays for the deficit. Again this means that the Malaysian economy is widely exposed to the performance of the global economies. A recession in the US will impact Malaysia the same way. It will not have enough reserves to pay for imports, and may have to do away with the currency peg.

But will a low interest rate regime do the work here in Malaysia? Will Malaysia, too, become like Japan, unable to pull itself out from stagnation? Textbook economics tells us that a fall in interest rates means a fall in the cost of credit, which is expected to increase household and business borrowings. This will increase consumption and investment and therefore should see increases in the GDP. But can the same theory applies to the Malaysian economy?

Remember that the Keynesian prescription can do the trick in an economy with strong domestic demand like the U.S. It does not work too well for an export-oriented country like Japan, though. In 1989, deposit rates went as low as 0.34 percent, but still the Japanese stock and property markets have not recovered since.

Low interest rates will mean less income for depositors. A three-month fixed deposit will only give around 3.75 percent. And with the BLR at about 7.25 percent, it looks like Malaysian banking institutions are still not efficient enough, as operating costs claimed nearly 4 percent of total borrowing cost. What this says it that even at low interest rates, nominal rates remain non-competitive, which will be less useful to the common people. As so much personal wealth was destroyed when the local bourse took a 60 percent plunge in 1997, what more bad news than declining deposit rates.

It is interesting to see now the impact of declining interest rates on Islamic banking profits. Since some portion of Islamic bank deposits are contracted on the *mudarabah* principle, higher bank's profit can mean more returns on the *mudarabah* deposits. In 2003, *mudarabah* deposits commanded 61.5 percent of total deposits. Demand and savings deposits however are contracted on the *wadiah dhamanah* principle. Banks hold no legal obligation to distribute profits under this arrangement. However, it has been customary (*'urf*) among the Islamic banks to give some portion of the profits as gifts (*hibah*). Doing is inevitably and strategically sound to prevent deposits moving into conventional banks.

When a customer contracted a fixed BBA financing under a declining interest rate environment, Islamic banking can be heading for a good time. A fixed BBA system says that a fixed profit rate is locked into the selling price during the financing period. This locked-in property is unique in BBA financing since BBA is contracted not on the profit rate but the selling price. Once the selling price of BBA is agreed upon by the buyer and seller, it will stay unchanged irrespective of changes in the market rates. Doing otherwise will deemed the contract invalid (*bathil*).

Theoretically, when an Islamic bank contracted a 15 year BBA sale based on a 9.5 percent profit rate, say in 1999, a customer pays $1,049 monthly instalment. But as market rates declined to 8.5 percent, the customer pays the same amount but a new BBA customer pays only say, $950 on the similar facility. In this manner, the Islamic bank earns higher finance income from the first customer compared with the second customer while paying similar returns under declining market rates. In otherwords, the profit margin derived from the first BBA is higher than the second one. In principle, the extra margin should be put into a reserve account the bank might find handy when market rates go up again. Otherwise, the bank should give higher dividends on *mudarabah* deposits The same should hold for *wadiah dhamanah* deposits.

The higher finance income earned from fixed rate BBA financing contracted during the high interest rate environment of 1997-1998, may have benefited Islamic banks when interest rates declined in the following years. Islamic banks recorded an increase in pre-tax profit from RM355.3 million in 1999 to RM534.5 million in 2000. In 2001, pre-tax profit rose by 69.9 percent amounting to RM905.9 million. The higher profitability recorded was largely due to the increase in total finance income of RM2.9 billion. In 2002, pre-tax profit increase by 12.3 percent to RM948 million.

Table 5.3 : Islamic banking pre-tax profit 1999-2003

Year	Pre-tax Profit (RMmillion)	Financing	Deposit	Financing-Deposit Ratio (percent)
1997	153	10,800	9,900	108.6
1998	148	10,900	16,400	66.6
1999	355	13,723	24,700	56.6
2000	534	20,891	35,900	58.2
2001	906	28,201	47,100	59.9
2002	948	36,718	53,306	68.8
2003	977	48,615	60,200	80.7.

Source : Bank Negara Annual Report; various issues

Table 5.3 shows that Islamic banks experienced declining profits during 1997-1998 financial crisis. It was partly due to the lower profit rate contracted on BBA financing prior to the crisis. However as interest rate declined beginning 1998, profits has somewhat increased dramatically. It is highly likely that a large portion of the increase is derived from higher financing income attributed from the fixed BBA financing contracted in 1998 and 1999.

Finally, declining interest rates may also see a drop in BBA financing when customers begin to notice that BBA monthly payments are not reduced to reflect declining cost of funds. Many may have opted for conventional loans. Any drop in BBA financing will trigger higher idle-balances since Islamic banks have relatively no new products to offer. The financing-deposit ratios from 1999 to 2002 were still on the low side although interest rate is falling. To what extent this is caused by low demand for BBA financing is an interesting topic for further research.

Twenty-Six
Hybrid products for Islamic finance

Developing Islamic financial instruments can both be a challenging and frustrating affair. Practitioners often pursue the adaptive approach. One example is *al-murabahah* and *al-bai-bithaman ajil (BBA)*. They retain the main features of the loan contract and blend it with some buy and sell features that the *Shariah* permits. Another example is *al-ijarah thuma al-Bay'*. It is a hybrid product drawn along the lines of the Hire-Purchase Act 1967.

A further application of hybrid products in financing is personal financing. In the Bank Rakyat model, the BBA will first be applied followed by *al-bay' mutlakah* i.e., a spot sale based on a fixed price. Other variant, say the Bank Islam model the BBA is preceded by *bay' mutlakah*. The two *bay' al-'inah* models are not found in classic Islamic commercial law (*fiqh muamalat*) contracts, as both constitute a form of legal device (*hiyal*).

Hiyal or *Tahayyul* is defined as Abu Ishaq al-Shatibi as follows: "When a *mukallaf* (believer) uses certain means in order to escape an obligation or to make some forbidden thing permissible for him, this use of means which causes an obligatory thing to become apparently non-obligatory and forbidden thing apparently to become permissible, this is called *hila* or *tahayyul*."

Al-Shatibi explained *tahayyul* in the following example. Somebody wishes to sell 20 dirhams in cash for 30 dirhams on credit. Here we are dealing with the unequal exchange of commodity money, namely gold. Because of the prohibition of *riba*, this transaction is not allowed. But by using *hilah,* he will be able to evade this prohibition. What he will do now is to purchase a piece of cloth for 20 dirhams and sell it for 30 dirhams on credit. By doing this, he has transferred the value of selling dirhams (which is prohibited) to the act of selling the cloth (which is permissible).

On the liability side, some degree of hybrid application has also been attempted. For example, *Al-wadiah* savings will automatically become *mudarabah* investments when some levels of savings are attained. Another is the negotiable Islamic certificate of deposits. This hybrid product uses three contracts, namely spot sale *(al-bay' mutlaqah)*, deferred payment sale (BBA), and sale of debt *(bay al dayn)*.

The first two contracts are also known as *bay'al 'inah,* while the third involves selling debts at a discount. What we can see in the above are attempts to enrich Islamic banking activities with hybrid products that strive to adopt conventional modes of financing.

The adaptive models seem to be the easy way out for most people. *Al-rahn* financing, for example, allows a better understanding of how the adaptive models work in a non-banking scenario. Originally, *al-rahn* was non-commercial in nature, but the widespread practice of interest-bearing pawnbroking business suggested an Islamic alternative.

In the business of *al-rahn* today, two contracts are applied in succession, namely *qardhu hasan* and *al-wadiah amaanah.* Customers must pay some service charges for the custodial service rendered by the *al-rahn* operator. In fact, it is a misnomer to call Islamic pawnbroking *al-rahn,* since the latter constitutes a contract of pledge *(al-rahn)* while Islamic pawnbroking encompasses beyond *al-rahn.* That is, it also includes *qardu hasan* and *wadiah amanah.*

But this has been the business aspect of modern *al-rahn.* The contract of loan *(qard hasan)* therefore, even though interest free, has zero default risk since it is supported by a collateral, namely the pledged asset under the *al-rahn* contract. *Al-rahn* pawnbroking business, however, is not *hilah.* It serves well the welfare of Muslims in a real way compared with products using *bay' al inah.*

In the capital market, hybrid contracts have taken shape using both *bay' al-'inah* and *bay' al-dayn* in Islamic bond issues. On this matter, I have no more say, since both the *Shariah* Board of Bank Negara and the Securities Commission made no objection to their use. But when one blindly agrees that the Malaysian view is lawful without a *caveat,* it is not wrong to say that one's sense of justice (*'adalah*) in promoting Islam in the financial markets is no better than capitalism itself.

The design of hybrid products normally intends to capture the benefits or advantages of debt and equity instruments. In the Islamic sphere, this must include two more classical instruments, namely *al-bay'* (spot sale) and *al-ijarah* (true lease). Some form of hybrids, such as sale and leaseback and lease and buyback have been developed recently, but we do hope to see all these products have passed the test of *'iwad*. In the *'iwad* litmus test, profit created from all hybrid products is expected to contain two main things, namely, 1) ownership risk (*ghorm*) and 2) valued-addition (*kasb*)

One worry about Islamic financial engineering is inputting conditions on contractual obligations. For example, in *ijarah wa iqtina* or *ijarah thumma al-bay'*, the principle of conventional hire-purchase is adopted. Here the lessee is given the option to purchase the asset. In AAOIFI, the lessee does not own the option to buy. Instead, the contract stipulates that the lessor will promise to sell the asset to the lessee once the leasing period expires.

The Islamic insurance also shows how concepts and contracts are assembled to bring out a new product called *takaful*. *Takaful* is not a contract. The same applies for *tabaru'*. But both constitute the basis of Islamic insurance. The contract of *mudarabah* is also applied but does not concern the purchase of *takaful* policy. Again, consolidation of contracts in the takaful industry requires more transparency. Otherwise *gharar* (uncertainties) may make a *takaful* contract invalid.

As mentioned earlier, no matter what Islamic hybrid products one wishes to create for the banking business, profit created therein must contain three essential elements:

- risk-taking (*ghorm*)
- value added (*ikhtiyar*)
- liability (*daman*)

The three elements in the above constitutes *'iwad*. *'Iwad* is originally intended to address fair business dealings in trading of commodities *(al-bay')*. It demands that any increase in equity or debt capital must contain *'iwad*.

Twenty-Seven
Islamic Banking Division (IBD) vs. Bank Islam Malaysia Bhd

I am not trying to imply anything spurious here, but truly we have to look at all this in a positive way. Bank Islam Malaysia Bhd (BIMB) was set ten years earlier than the Islamic Banking Divisions (IBDs) so the "big brother" figure that BIMB holds may contain some truth.

However, some may not agree that the older one is the wiser. For more than ten years, BIMB went on to strike the balance between religion and the mundane in the banking business without the benefit of competition.

Now as the IBDs are taking the bigger slice of the cake coupled with the emergence of Bank Muamalat Bumiputra Malaysia (BMBM), BIMB may find it relatively hard to seek comfort in religion alone to survive in this uncertain business of Islamic banking.

BIMB was formed under the governance of the Islamic Banking Act (IBA) 1983 and I have hinted a couple of times that it can save costs by going universal. It can do so by adopting the universal banking mode. BIMB can actually do without much legal hassle since the model does not work against IBA 1983.

Unlike IBDs, whose operations are still controlled by the Banking and Financial Institutions Act 1992 (BAFIA), BIMB can offer multiple products such as trading, leasing, *takaful*, fund management, underwriting, and investments in stocks.

By going universal, operational costs can reduced. Profits will go up as these facilities are offered under one roof. Setting up subsidiaries to do the same job should be costly, with economies of scale unrealized.

However, to some extent, BIMB has indeed offered a variety of facilities that commercial banks are not allowed to. Bank Negara's Annual Report puts BIMB as a commercial bank, but it is allowed to buy and sell assets and properties via *al-bai-bithaman ajil* (BBA) and *al-ijarah thumma al-bay'* (AITAB).

BIMB has also performed a merchant banking role such as arranging the issuance of KLIA Islamic bonds. By going universal, which BIMB has actually taken up piecemeal, cost savings should mean cheaper facilities from which consumers can readily benefit. This may attract more deposits and increase the bank's ability to financing trading activities.

But now, a holding company called BIMB Holdings was instead formed to control all Islamic financing business that BIMB once oversaw. The prospect of seeing *takaful,* fund management, research and training, securities and leasing business done under one roof has finally gone down the drain. However, giving up hope is not the way out in Islam. Hopefully, Bank Muamalat Bumiputra (BMBM) will take full advantage of the privileges given by IBA 1983. Although the big brother may find adopting the Anglo-Saxon model more comforting, it is better late that never for BMBM to enjoy the merits of the universal banking model. It should pursue this model of banking.

The recession seems the best time to do so, when cost cutting and downsizing is critical for survival. Since all subsidiaries of Bank Bumiputra are likely to merge with Bank of Commerce, the logistic now favors BMBM, which can avoid the painstaking process of adopting BIMB Holdings model.

Forming new subsidiaries to handle the so-called non-banking business like leasing, fund management, insurance, stock brokerage, etc. will require new capital to purchase operating assets such as office supplies, computer and security systems, company cars, etc. This may contradict the essence of mergers and acquisitions that BBMB and Bank of Commerce have both undertaken.

Restructuring the Islamic banking business here along the universal banking model follows the natural path. However, the same must also apply to the Islamic banking divisions (IBDs). They should push Bank Negara

Malaysia to allow them to diversify along the universal bank model when the same privilege is handed to BIMB and also BMBM.

The potential of strong growth is real for the IBDs, given that they have all that it takes to leapfrog via scale economies. However, this means more work for the bank's owners and also the people running it, but the rewards will be high too. Studies on universal banking in Germany, Switzerland, and Japan indicate that this is the path Islamic banks should take, given that the Islamic banking law (IBA 1983) is not against the practice.

Twenty-Eight
Predicting Bankruptcy

Regional financial turmoil and the credit crunch in Malaysia today will see more poor corporate earnings leading to loan defaults and bankruptcies. This is the essence of an interest-based economy in which financing is made on the basis of contractual or legal claims on the principal loan and interest payments by the financier. Businesses using loans, especially short-term foreign loans, will find it hard to pay up as the ringgit further depreciates. These loans are raised in the international capital market and through bank lending and inter-company borrowing.

According to Bank Negara, Malaysia's short-term debt accounted for only 30 percent, rather than 56 percent, as quoted by the Bank for International Settlements. Unlike South Korea, Malaysia's reliance on multinational investments (MNIs) has put less pressure on the country to seek loans to finance its industrialization.

Whatever the figures on Malaysia's short-term debt actually are, the main worry is the impact of business failures on Malaysians. News about retrenchment in the financial services market, such as those in Singapore involving remisiers, dealers, central buyers and analysts, is a good example. In our import-dependent production sector, lower sales and earnings due to China's new competitive edge are expected to cause more firms to cut production and work shifts. The effect of the regional financial turmoil is beginning to hit this country.

As recession in most East Asian countries is inevitable, more companies will close down largely due to their problems with debt.

Basically, business failures and bankruptcy occur when the company is not able to meet maturing financial obligations. When financial difficulties begin to bite the company, they will affect the price-earning ratio, ratings, and effective interest rates.

Therefore, as the ringgit is still under heavy pressure with no possible rapid stock market recovery in sight, it is perhaps useful to find out to what extent Malaysian companies will fail to brace for the recession. The Altman's "Z-score" is often used as a comprehensive quantitative indicator to predict business failure.

The impact of the weakening ringgit and stock market on company's performance is best observed in its debt to equity ratio. In the Altman's Z-score model (*see illustration*), the debt to equity ratio = (market value of common and preferred stock/local liabilities). Since the lower the Z-score the higher the probability of failure, a fall in any of the above ratios will result in a lower Z-score.

Looking at the debt to equity ratio, a fall in the ringgit will cause companies heavily dependent on foreign debt to assume higher total liabilities. For example, if MAS bought new airplanes in 1996 worth US$300 million by issuing bonds in the United States during which the exchange rate was US$1 = RM2.5, the value of the loan is (300 million x 2.5) or RM750 million. Now as the ringgit falls to RM4.5 to the U.S. dollar, MAS' new debt is (300 million x 4.5) or RM1.35 billion.

The collapse of the stock market has also reduced the net worth of companies. In the Altman's Z-score model, common and preferred stocks represent net worth. In Malaysia, the CPI has fallen by more than 60 percent since July 1996.

So, if the company holds $200 million in common and preferred shares, now the value is only $80 million ($200 x 0.4). It is apparently clear now that the ratio of stocks to total liabilities has become smaller, thus reducing the Z-score. The probability of bankruptcy is now higher.

By now, it is clear that highly leveraged companies will be the likely victims of financial turmoil. If companies have relied more on equity equaling to $200 + $650 million = $850 million and less debt, (say, $100 million), a 60 percent fall in the CPI will reduce equity to $510 million.

In the Z-score, the debt to equity component is therefore equal to $510/100 x 0.6 = 3.06. However, if the company is highly leveraged, the debt to equity component = ($80 million/ $1.35 billion) x 0.6 = 0.038, which could reduce the total size of the Z-score. What we see here is that companies that rely too much on debt finance would be likely to fail when the economy runs into a global financial crisis.

Similarly, if Islamic financing in this country tends to overly use Islamic private debt securities (IPDS) to finance business and infrastructure projects, the likelihood of companies becoming bankrupt for failing to pay maturing IPDS is inevitable. This is because IPDS are not equity instruments by definition. Issuers are legally required to pay the capital loan, failure of which will put them in insolvency.

For long-term stability, Muslim practitioners should think about issuing *musyarakah* and *mudarabah* certificates instead. Even if equities may sometimes cost more than debt, the long-term stability of an equity-based financial system is a proven case.

Table 5.4 Altman "Z-Score"

Altman "Z-score" = [(working capital/total assets) x 1.2] + [(retained earnings/total assets) x 1.4] + [(operating income/total assets)] x 3.3] + [market value of common and preferred stock/ total liabilities) x 0.6] + [sales/total assets) x 0.009]	
Score	**Probability of Failure**
1.80 or less	Very high
1.81 - 2.99	Not sure
3.00 or greater	Unlikely

Twenty-Nine
Impact of Inflation on Credit Sale Instruments

As the national election is now over, Malaysians will see how the winning parties are committed to their promises. It is also time to see the hard realities of our economic problems; namely, the appreciating yen against the ringgit. On top of that, the ringgit is fast appreciating against the dollar. These are expected to produce dramatic changes in the price level, trade deficits, and external debts.

As the dollar puts pressure on the Asian economies, there is no point to talking about zero inflation now. Mahathir Muhammad may be not wrong after all, as some stability in the foreign exchange market was assumed then, but now with the apparent "benign neglect" of the dollar by the Federal Reserve, Malaysia's competitive advantage on cheap labor may be short-lived. It may be timely for Bank Negara to tighten credit. It can help push up the ringgit, thus cutting down imports.

Remember, it's the imported inflation people are worried about. With major export-based industries and infrastructure investments tightly dependent on imported tools and machinery, a stronger yen would mean Malaysia paying pay more for the same goods it used to buy from Japan. If corporations insist on their multimillion profit, consumers must pay for the expensive imports.

The recent increase in the BLR (base-lending rate) of major commercial banks and finance companies has somewhat verified my observation above.

It is also a major signal of Bank Negara's tight money policy as investment and consumption need more control to help fan down inflation.

During the past eleven years, inflation has not been the concern of policymakers. Malaysian planners are more worried about foreign investment and the necessary deepening of infrastructure to help boost the export industry. Paradoxically, inflation was maintained at an average rate of 4 percent, but, given the current foreign exchange crisis, how long can Malaysia's inflation rate stay that low?

The upcoming meeting of the Group of Seven industrial countries (G7) will show whether they can pressure the U.S. to take some drastic measure to prop up the dollar. Other than that, it is futile to talk about price stability in this country. Rather, attention should now be focused on the question of who will lose and gain from inflation?

Under inflation, we knew well that debtors will win and creditors will lose. The same holds for Islamic banking today. As most assets are invested in *murabahah* and *al-bai-bithaman ajil* activities, they will see the adverse effect of inflation on profits.

Let me explain how this is possible. As a promoter of equity-based Islamic banking, this is my honest criticism about credit-based Islamic banks.

As we have noticed, the *murabahah/bai-bithaman-ajil* products are based on a deferred-payment contract, which means that the bank sells the asset to the customer at a pre-fixed credit price payable on an installment basis over a period of time.

1.BBA is a fixed rate asset
2. Contract price = selling price
3. In determining the selling price, the bank sets the profit margin rate per annum, say 10%
4. Cost price (CP) = $100,000
5. Financing period = 10 years
6. Total profit margin (TPM) = (0.1 x $100,000) x 10 = $100,000
7. Selling price = CP + TPM= $100,000 + $100,000 = $200,000
8. Selling price cannot change throughout financing period
9. BBA contract will become invalid if selling price is changed to accormodate changes in market interest rate
10. Profit rate = cost of deposit + overhead cost + inflation premium + default risk premium (spread)

Figure 5.1 BBA Financing

For example, the bank buys a house for $100,000 and sells it to the customer for $200,000 payable in twenty years. So, the bank makes a profit of $100,000 in the transaction. Would the real value of the $100,000 profit remain unchanged when the inflation rate goes up from 4 percent to 10 percent? Certainly not. Would the bank sits still only to see the house appreciate to, say, $400,000 when the payments mature?

Now, how does the bank arrive at the credit price in the first place? Of course, they will assume a certain rate of profit plus some rate of inflation. It's no surprise to see how the base lending rate is closely related to the deferred sale's pre-fixed rate of profit.

The main idea is the following: Under severe inflationary pressure, can Islamic banks revise their profit rate upwards similar to the recent upward revision of the BLR? Can Islamic banks impose a condition to the *murabahah/bai-bithaman-ajil* contracts that they will revise the credit price accordingly with the changing rate of inflation?

For example, if the rate of inflation is 3 percent, the BBA price is $200,000, but if the rate increases to 8 percent, the bank will sell the house for \$300,000, and so on. Of course, this is a rational thing to do on new BBA contracts, but it virtually violates the *Shariah* when a new price is imputed onto existing contracts.

But why not? It is simply because the flexible price policy produces ambiguities (*gharar*) in the price element, as many prices will be set under a single contract at different rates of inflation. If the bank went on to change the prices, not for profit but to maintain the real value of the asset.

With creeping inflation, the real value of funds extended on the deferred sale will fall and banks will see the gradual depletion of the real value of *murabahah/bai-bithaman-ajil* assets over time. What we will see now is the gloomy future for deferred payment instruments (BBA) if the economy is severely hit by inflation. With the depleting real value of BBA assets, can Islamic banks now comply with the demands of *mudarabah* depositors who are sensitive to inflationary expectations?

Certainly, depositors want a higher return when they know well that the price level was not what it used to be. In the final analysis, should Islamic banks scale down their profit in view of the need to offer higher returns to *mudarabah* depositors?

Currently, conventional banks can resort to various measures to reduce the risk of interest rate movements due to inflation. They can buy an interest rate options contract, undertake factoring, etc. These instruments are not available in Islamic banking today. Perhaps the *mudarabah* Cagamas scheme can lend some help. Cagamas usually buys BBA and loan receivables at steep discounts, and this may not be a good option unless banks are in real trouble looking for deposits.

Finally, the idea of indexing the contract to maintain some stable standard of deferred payment system is interesting but laden with spurious juristic interpretation. The Islamic dinar is one way out. For example, BBA contracts will be based on dinar but monetary payments in ringgit. When the inflation rate increases, so does the price of gold and vice-versa. Each installment payment is contracted in dinar but paid in ringgit. For example, each installment is worth 3 dinar and equivalent to \$500. Under inflationary pressure, the customer still pays 3 dinar but now the ringit amount is higher, say \$600. Under deflationary condition, the 3 dinar may be worth \$400. Thus, the dinar system is able to balance out the discrepancies arising from price volatilities without resorting to manipulate the BBA contract.

Thirty
Capital requirement for Islamic banking

The push for cluster-based industrial development outlined in the Industrial Master Plan Two (IMP2) calls for a serious look at industrial financing, especially R & D activities and technology acquisition. The cluster concept implies the presence of all components for the successful design, manufacture, and distribution of any one product within the country. This concept is a great step away from the assembly-based manufacturing.

Our new phase of industrialization is now promoting industries with higher levels of technology, local content, and value-added. This means the imminent need for labor-saving, skills-intensive, and capital-intensive techniques in the manufacturing sector. But they are not easy to find.

In industrial financing, it not only means increasing lending to the manufacturing sector but also widening the coverage of industrial financing to include activities involving research and development, which also include industrial manpower development. What this actually means is the increasing role of the banking industry in profit-sharing and risk-taking investments such as venture capital.

Speaking of risky investments, the role of Islamic banking cannot be discounted. In fact, they are tailor-made to do just that, theoretically speaking, but in practice, we see today a different ball game. Many banks prefer to invest their assets in the *murabahah* and *al-bai-bithaman ajil* financing. The recent launch of KFH Ijarah House Sdn Bhd. showed that trading-oriented Islamic financing has remained a popular choice. But why was equity financing put in the back seat?

The problem is obvious. Failure to perform well may cost bankers their jobs. In assessing a bank's performance, the ROA i.e., return on assets (net income after taxes divided by total assets) is usually used to measure managerial efficiency. It shows how bank management was able to convert assets into earnings. For example a ROA of 1.3 percent means RM1 of bank's asset can generate RM1.3 in earnings. The higher the ROA the better, but profitability objective must also consider safety.

At the same time, banks must see that depositors are able to withdraw on call. More important is the returns to bank shareholders, namely the return on equity or ROE. It measures the net benefit stockholders received from risk capital, namely share capital.

The question is how much concern Islamic bank shareholders gave to the philosophy and objectives of Islamic banking. Are they only concerned about the ROE? As rational investors, ROE is top agenda, but is that all? Let's say all they care about is the ROE.

To ensure a high ROE, bank managers must also make sure that the ROA is high. This is because the ROA and ROE are both related. However, to increase ROA, the bank must either diversify or reduce the cost of operations, in which the latter is most unlikely. So, diversification may be good thing to do, but such strategy may be very risky and shareholders may not agree.

In the case of Islamic banking, can we say that the directors are reluctant to let the management pursue with rigor more investments in *mudarabah* and *musyarakah*? For example, in 1995, *al-bai-bithaman ajil* and *al-murabahah* financing in Bank Islam Malaysia Berhad (BIMB) amounted to RM1.3 billion, compared to only RM29 million in *mudarabah* and *musyarakah*. Such a digression from risk-taking investment is puzzling enough, knowing that these are the people who seem to champion the Islamic banking movement and the Islamic religion itself. When asked about Islamic banking, the first thing that comes from their mouth is the profit-sharing principle. But nowhere is profit sharing found except the *mudarabah* deposits. Why must they use the PLS system as their selling point when they only do BBA, *bay' al-'inah* and *bay' al-dayn*?

In the true spirit of Islam, shareholders are expected to contribute more capital to see that investments in *mudarabah* and *musyarakah* are taken in more rigor. They should not put capital risk onto the *mudarabah* depositors alone. Doing so forces bank managers to conduct *al-bai-thaman ajil* and *murabahah* alone, since these are safe and less risky assets.

My point is, capital requirement for Islamic banking should not be higher than the conventional ones if the former uses profit-loss sharing (PLS) deposit. *Wadiah* deposits are less demanding than interest-bearing deposits in the sense that they (i.e., *wadiah* deposits) are given only capital protection.

By definition, capital requirement is the equity of shareholders or simply the bank's capital. Capital requirement = capital/assets. For example, capital requirement of 1 percent means that for every $100 of loan is supported by $1 of capital. But this is too low. Banks are therefore required to maintain a minimum 10 percent capital adequacy ratio. It serves as a buffer against bank insolvency when losses on loans and other securities occur. When all other forms of defense are exhausted, such as selling loans and other securities, banks must use the capital of shareholders to absorb losses from bad debts, poor securities investment, crime, and mismanagement. Only when the shareholders' capital is exhausted will the bank have to close down.

Since some banking products have greater default risk than others, it is critical to see that bank's capital requirement is based on some risk-adjusted ratios. If this is not done, the capital requirement may not be enough to absorb losses arising from loan defaults. For example, cash and treasury bills have zero percent weight, while loans and bonds hold 100 and 50 percent weights respectively. Usually, when risk-weighted assets are applied, the capital requirement is usually higher. In 2003, the Islamic banking system recorded a strong risk-weighted capital ratio (RWCR) of 13.1 percent and core capital ratio of 11.4 percent

Based on the above, it may not be accurate to retain the *mudarabah* or *musyarakah* framework as a basis of bank and depositor relationship. In the context of *mudarabah* investment account, the bank now is no longer the *mudarib* since it also owns capital. Likewise, bank managers cannot be called *mudarib* because they are in essence the bank's employees where wages and salaries are paid on the basis of *ijarah* contract. Hence, a *musyarakah* investment account sounds more meaningful as it now adds more weight to the role of bank's shareholders in risk taking.

In other words, a financial product that runs on a partnership contract shall consist of three parties, namely: 1) the PLS depositors, 2) the bank, and 3) fund users-cum-entrepreneurs. This *musyarakah* contract will see the bank risking its own capital in the venture. In this manner, bank's capital requirement should be lowered since the operation does not implicate credit or BBA sales. However, when a *mudarabah* contract is instead applied, higher capital adequacy is necessary to guarantee capital protection against negligence.

Likewise, when PLS deposits are used to finance *salam* and *istisna'* projects, the capital requirement should be lower. This is because losses from the *salam* and *istisna'* transactions are absorbed by either one of the contracting parties. But the same does not apply to *wadiah* deposits. Here, the capital requirement should be higher, as the bank guarantees deposits.

Thirty-One
Banking on Productivity

B ank Negara's annual report released in 1995 may help widen the scope of Islamic banking in Malaysia. With a growth rate of 8.7 percent in 1994 and a current forecast of 8.5 percent, productivity will be the main focus of investment.

In 1994 the economy was largely investment-driven most of which heavily depends on imports. Unless productivity improves, the expected revenue generated from these import-intensive investments, which accounted for more than 85 percent of total merchandise imports, may not be the answer to Malaysia's widening RM8.2 billion in overall balance.

To improve national productivity, the role of the banking industry is vital. The governor said some commercial banks should merge to gain the benefits of economies of scale and scope. Diversification of a bank's portfolio into fee-based income activities apparently shows that commercial banks today are not relying on traditional interest income alone.

With the manufacturing sector playing a dominant role in the country's economic growth with a 14 percent increase in 1994 the need to accelerate the growth of venture capital companies is found to be urgent. Apparently, more banks are setting up venture capital company subsidiaries. They are expected to streamline financing into high productivity technology-based sectors. It can help reduce Malaysia's future dependence on imports.

What is the role of Islamic banking in the above? As an alternative to an interest-based banking system, Islamic banks are expected to be more receptive to the changing demand of economic growth. The system offers two main instruments; namely, *mudarabah* and *musharakah* that can potentially improve productivity in the manufacturing sector. The contract of *salam* and *istisna* (sale by advance payment) can play similar roles.

But these instruments are not offered by commercial banks. Some restrictions in the Banking and Financial Institution Act (BAFIA) 1989 explain why. As more banks realized that traditional lending is no longer a niche, a direct link to the manufacturing is possible via venture capital subsidiaries.

In principle, venture capital is synonymous with *mudarabah/ musharakah* financing. With these new developments in the banking industry, it would be timely that Islamic banks look into the potentials of the *mudarabah* and *musharakah* system. It is better late than never. I think they are aware of the problem at hand and possibly looking for ways to reduce their obsession with *murabahah* and *bai-bithaman-ajil* financing.

As an academic, I have always been critical about Islamic banking's overdependence on credit-based products, whose potential to induce productivity growth is doubtful as Islamic banks remain a debt-collecting agency. Public complaints are no longer an isolated issue as these instruments are more expensive than loans, even though they are religiously sanctioned as *halal*. In 1994, more than 90 percent of BIMB assets were injected into these trading-based instruments, which in essence is credit financing. So, what is the future of the *mudarabah* and *musharakah* in Islamic banking? Certainly bleak since BBA is fast replacing the potentials of the PLS system. PLS product has no chance to take off, simply because deferred payment financing (BBA) is an easier application and control is even better.

Earlier works on Islamic banking, especially in the Indian subcontinent, have emphasized the role of *mudarabah* contract as the main pipeline of operation. The contract is based on the profit-loss sharing principle.

However, the writers have misjudged the legal and structural aspects of the modern banking industry. They have also underrated contracts such as *al-ijarah, salam,* and *istisna* as alternatives to interest-bearing loans.

Most of these writers are university teachers having relatively less exposure to practical banking operations. They can speak about basic characteristics of the *mudarabah* contract but have less contact with modern banking structure and regulations. They were able to produce theoretical arguments in favor of *mudarabah*, that profit-loss sharing principles can stimulate economic growth, stabilize the economy, and reduce income inequality.

But these are not the main concern of Islamic banks today. At the end of the day, the bottom line is still profits. They must meet monthly deposit and financing targets. To keep default low, funds are only given to people with collateral and guarantors. They must see that customers do not miss payments. They do so by threatening bankruptcies. But these are things we also see in interest-bearing banks.

Islamic banks have yet to understand the spirit of Islamic banking. People running the banks do it probably because it is their job, their bread and butter. Academicians, likewise, suffer from the same dilemma. As long as they get their papers published in journals, it is a job well done.

But the objective of Islam in the field of Islamic banking is to produce a viable alternative to the interest-bearing system under the banner of *al-bay'* (trading and commerce). Using al-*bay'*, profits are created via mutual trade and cooperation. People no longer become debtors, and banks will not behave like debt collectors. Banks look for entrepreneurial talents. They are excited over new technological breakthroughs because they want to be part of them. They take risks in the business. This is what mutual trade is all about in Islamic banking. It oozes out productivity and creativity.

SECTION SIX

LEGAL ASPECTS OF ISLAMIC BANKING

One
Addressing the varied legal opinions on Islamic banking

Seeking legal opinion on matters involving Islamic banking and finance can be tricky, not because there are not enough experts around, but more because of the lack of standards. Opinions vary with different personalities, from the *Shariah* scholars to the various schools of fiqh (*mazhab*).

In Malaysia, for instance, the membership of *Shariah* panels of Bank Negara Malaysia and the Securities Commission consist of scholars and practitioners who hold fast to the Shafie school of *fiqh* (*mahzab*). They make legal opinions supposedly on Iman Shafie's strict principles, but apparently giving green lights to products that conform to conventional tastes. One good example is approving the practice of *bay' al-inah* and *bai' al-dayn* in Islamic banking, capital and money markets.

Bay' al-inah and *bay' al-dayn* products are essentially credit-driven. When these two contracts are allowed to flourish without control, Islamic banking ends in a similar fate with conventional players in a crisis situation. In fact, these instruments are expected to perform far worse as there is no floating rate option. So our worry is only common sense.

If the *Shariah* advisors have performed *ijtihad* (independent thinking) and issued a legal opinion (*fatwa*) that al-'inah sale and discounted *bay' al-dayn* with a third party is permissible (*halal*), it also means that other view representing other school of *fiqh* should be given the opportunity to challenge these *fatwas*. An Islamic financial system loaded with *al-'inah* sale and *bay' al-dayn* can be a liability to the Muslim *ummah* in the long run. The *maslahah* of the *ummah* can fall under threat if less is done to explain the true picture. I am a firm believer that an Islamic banking system based on *al-'inah* sale and *bay' al-dayn* will finally converge with conventional practices in all respect. When this happens, great tragedy has inflicted the Muslim *ummah*.

For example, over-borrowing and over-lending is one root cause of the Asian economic crisis. If the interest-bearing system is blamed for this over-borrowing and over-lending behavior, then *'inah* and *dayn* sale can produce the same thing. In this way, what is so exceptional about the Islamic system if they end up replicating conventional practices? What is so unique about the Islamic system if it cannot keep away from trouble caused by overlending and borrowing?

Shariah scholars in the Middle Eastern countries too have their own system of making legal opinions. The Organization of Islamic Countries (OIC) *Fiqh* Academy in Mecca is well known for consistent views on many modern Islamic commercial financial transactions. Among others, these include the ban on *bay' al-inah* and *bay' al-dayn*.

The point is that a large numbers of Malaysian *Shariah* advisors graduated from the Middle Eastern universities such as the al-Azhar University in Cairo, Egypt and Medina University. So why are views from these institutions not heard in Malaysia? To find a viable solution to the problem, one must to take a look at the possibility of enlarging the membership of the *Shariah* panels.

Firstly, they must include *Shariah* people who are experienced in making *fatwas*. *Fatwas* are made through *ijtihad,* and *ijtihad* requires a great amount of research and thinking. *Ijtihad* can only be done when no answers can be found in the Quran, Sunnah, and Ijma.

So the problem at hand must be a critical one when performing *ijtihad*. Normally, the *muftis* are responsible for making *fatwas,* since they are officially appointed by the government to produce legal opinions that serve as a basis for solving problems. *Muftis,* therefore, must be research-oriented.

Secondly, members who do not hold a *mufti* post must have or hold formal education in the field of *Usul Fiqh* and *Muamalat* or Islamic commercial law.

It will be a mistake to invite people who may have strong knowledge of, say, Islamic family and criminal law, *dakwah, usuludin* or the Arabic language (*lugatul arabi*) but not an expert on Islamic jurisprudence (*Usul Fiqh*) and Islamic law of transactions (*Fiqh Muamalat*). Thus, qualified *Shariah* people should be given a role in the *Shariah* Board of Bank Negara and the Securities Commission so that any legal opinion made is based on solid research with comparative *fiqh* approaches.

Lastly, Islamic banking practitioners who do not possess the above qualifications should be allowed to participate but only in the capacity of advisors or consultants. Their role is to make *Shariah* members understand the problem at hand i.e., the economic and financial concepts so that the *ijtihad* can be exercised with objectivity and accuracy.

Two

The Role of Fatwa in the Islamic Financial System

Islamic financial engineering demands more than the know-how to understand the principles and applications of conventional hybrid instruments. It is tempting to adopt and modify them to demonstrate that Islam has all the solutions to the problems of modern finance.

Normally, theory takes precedence over practice. So the need to know the principles behind a ruling or opinion on Islamic financial instruments is fundamental. This knowledge cannot be put in cold storage since it involves the making of legal opinions (*fatwa*).

For example, the *Shariah* Advisory Council (SAC) of the Securities Commission has established that the mechanism of the futures contract as permissible (*hala*). Supposedly, the *fatwa* was issued via *ijtihad* as the futures market is a modern phenomenon not readily found in classical contracts.

It is crucial to see the public having access to these *fatwas* to understand how they are made, as the livelihood and welfare of the Muslim *Ummah* are at stake. The *Shariah* serves to protect wealth and property (*al-mal*). If futures contract is deemed *halal*, it means that the *Shariah* advisors are pretty sure that using financial derivatives will not destroy wealth of human beings. But we have seen how the derivatives markets have wrecked nations. Hedge funds use derivatives to make money. How they ruined the Asian economies in 1997 is common knowledge. The same applies to the *fatwas* or sometimes called resolutions approving *bay' al-'inah* and discounted *bay' al-dayn*. It promotes financing and investments that demand contractual returns and capital protection.

The disagreements among the *fuqaha* on the above rulings are serious since they involve the fundamental (*nass/usul*) and not the branches (*furuq*) of religious obligations. As an example, the *fuqaha* will not disagree on the number of daily prayers (*solat*) that a believer (*mukallaf*) must perform, but they can disagree how the rituals may differ. In Malaysia, during *solat*, one puts both hands on the stomach while in Africa Muslims put the hands down.

Thus, when a *fatwa* is issued, it must not deal with problem of *nass* and *usul* but only the *furuq i.e.,* branches of the law. It is thus important to further examine the nature of *fatwa,* such as what is a *fatwa* and who can make *fatwas*?

According to D.C. Macdonald, a *fatwa* is a formal legal opinion given by a *mufti* or canon lawyer of standing, in answer to a question submitted to him either by a judge or by a private individual. A *mufti*, says Joseph Schacht , is a specialist on law who can give an authoritative opinion on points of doctrine and his considered legal opinion is called *fatwa*.

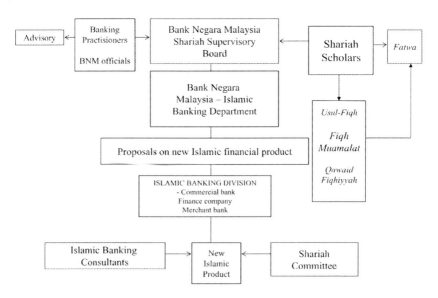

Figure 6.1 *Shariah* Board Supervision

In Malaysia, one well-known *fatwa* on Islamic transaction (*muamalat*) was issued in 1974 by the National *Fatwa* Council (NFC). It involves a ban on conventional life insurance since it is said to contain the three prohibitive elements of *riba, gharar* (uncertainties), and *maisir* (gambling) The *fatwa* led to the formation of *takaful* business in Malaysia. However, *takaful* business is presently using conventional insurers to reinsure itself. So is the practice of *retakul* permissible in Islam?

Certainly this problem requires *muftis* and Islamic *Shariah* scholars of the National *Fatwa* Council (NFC) to make the necessary judgment. As we can see, the *fatwas* made by the NFC are documented and gazetted, making it available for public use. This means that it invites transparency. *Fatwas* are therefore open to juristic refutation as it is made to withstand refutations. In this manner, the scientific method is not new in the Islamic methodology.

Because a *fatwa* is made to withstand refutations, it, (the *fatwa,*) according to Ibn Qaiyyim, cannot be issued unless the person really understands the Quran, its *nasikh* and *mansukh* and their rules, *ta'wil* and the reason on the occasion of revelation (*asbab al-nuzul*). Among others, he must understand the Hadiths as deeply as he understands the Quran and know the Arabic language and the situation of the society where the *fatwa* is to be made. A *fatwa* may change according to time, place, situation, objective for making the *fatwa* and the type of problem for which the fatwa is invoked.

It is therefore crucial to see that some uniformity and standards are set to ensure that all legal opinions on *muamalat*, especially those involving the financial system, are made with full disclosure. This means that the committee members of any *fatwa* council must be well-qualified and brave to put their arguments and findings public. One good example is the National *Fatwa* Council. It was formed during the Conference of Malay Rulers on 1 July, 1969 and serves to coordinate the activities and administration of Islamic religion in Malaysia.

Rule 11 of the Council gives the structure of membership or the composition of its committee members. First, the chairman is appointed among the committee members. The Council also appoints the *Muftis* from the eleven states. Non-*Muftis* include five Islamic *Shariah* scholars and a Muslim representative from legal service.

Based on the above structure, we can have full confidence that any *fatwa* made by the committee is well-researched and performed with high-level of *akhlak* and discipline. This is important, so that we can obtain sufficient information on what lies behind the *fatwas* or in what way agreement and refutation has or can be pursued.

Three
A Need for Shariah-trained economists

The supply of banking practitioners with *Shariah* training remains one big challenge to Islamic banking industry today. Banking practitioners may have attended many seminars and workshops on Islamic banking but they are not trained to deal with *Shariah*-related problems in the banking business. Doing some requires an intimate knowledge of the *Shariah*. There is no shortcut but to pursue formal education in Arabic, *usul-fiqh, fiqh muamalat* etc. is mandatory.

Many banks turned to people with *Shariah* degrees for advice, but their understanding of economic principles and how banks operate is suspect. *Shariah* experts have categorically approved new financial instruments with less idea how that would impact bank's earnings, consumer welfare. economic stability and income disparity.

Future introduction of Islamic values into financial activities will see the potential opening of Islamic windows in the insurance and securities industry. Should the supply of *Shariah*-trained economists be given low priority, speedy development of Islamic banking this country may not come sooner.

For example, the introduction of *bai-bithaman-ajil* products has attracted many customers who want to hedge against interest rate risk as the price of the BBA asset will not change when the market rates go up. Certainly, under such an arrangement, customers will gain at the expense of bank's profits. The *bai-bithaman-ajil* products will, in the final analysis, reveal some structural weakness of Islamic banks.

What I want to say is the simple fact that universities and colleges can no longer ignore the potential Islamic financial markets as an engine of growth. Putting religious sentiments aside, people should accept this phenomenon as a healthy development that may help generate greater efficiency in financial transaction.

When the interest-bearing banking system is put to test, consumers can have more options where to put their hard-earned savings. How well depositors can respond to this new development in banking would again depend whether the Islamic instruments on the offer have a competitive edge.

This may, in turn, depend on the people who make policy, research and planning. When Islamic banks fail to produce a blueprint to furnish the R&D department with well-trained graduates and professionals with formal *Shariah* training, it is likely that problems are attended *ad hoc* and solutions sought piecemeal.

For example, it has been about twenty years since *bai-bithaman-ajil* products were first launched. But Islamic banks are still wondering whether an amendment to the Hire-Purchase Act 1964 is forthcoming to make way of true leasing (*al-ijarah*) over financial leasing. The *bai-bithaman-ajil* contract is also found to be losing ground to conventional term loans since the profit rate is not adjustable.

These problems can be attended with more rigor when banks open their doors to *Shariah*-trained economics graduates. It would be too presumptuous to think that one or two conventionally-trained personnel who may have attended some workshops and short courses on Islamic banking can deal with pressing juristic issues and controversies?

Speaking about the role of *Shariah*-trained economists, one must not think they could only handle *Shariah*-based problems alone. For example, at the International Islamic University, economics students are required to take courses in finance, management, accountancy, information technology, Arabic, law, Islamic economics, and banking. Economic theory and quantitative subjects like mathematics, econometric, and forecasting are standard. Adding to the curriculum additional *Shariah*-based courses like Islamic jurisprudence (*usul-fiqh*) and transactions in Islamic law (*fiqh muamalat*) would make the IIUM graduates unique and special.

The lack of interest in partnership (*mudarabah* and *musyarakah*) financing is one main drawbacks of Islamic banking policy. Apparently, banks could see less what *mudarabah* and *musyarakah* can offer. Instead they focus what *mudarabah is bad at*. The fear of losing deposits is one main reason why *mudarabah* financing is marginalized. But a *Shariah*-trained economist may have a different perspective about *mudarabah*. He will see that depositors are given ample information about *mudarabah* investment. For example, the role of trustees and disclosure of *mudarabah* projects to investors. So, *mudarabah* infrastructure must be available before it is put to use. Thus, using a *Shariah* scholar alone to deal with financial instruments and infrastructure may do injustice to his profession, as he may not be aware how these affect factors determining a bank's performance, like market size, return to assets, economic growth, and globalization.

Four
Legal disputes in the Islamic banking business

When Muslim economists first introduced the profit-loss sharing *mudarabah* model to banking, little did they think about its legal implications for a community like Malaysia. In theory, they assumed an Islamic state to be a homogeneous society within which resides the benevolent, ethical Islamic man. The modern corporation, secular banking laws and global finance were not among the issues highlighted. Attention was primarily focused on the evils of usury as *riba*, rules of determining profit-sharing ratios, as if Islamic banks are destined to enjoy ultimate success guaranteed by God Almighty.

But what if the business suffers losses? Who will assume full responsibility? A look at the *Mejelle* will give some ideas for further thought. On the loss of *mudarabah* property, the *Mejelle* says, "If the quantity of the *mudarabah* property is lost, in the first place it is taken from the profit. It is not set against the capital. If it exceeds the amount of the profit and is set against the capital, the *mudarib* is not responsible for it. In every case of damage or loss, it falls on the owner of capital."

If that is the case, who will participate in *mudarabah* if all risks and losses are put on the *rabb-ul-mal*? Is Islamic law against rik capital or does it discriminate against people who have worked hard for money and investments—the *rabb-ul-mal*? Could this be the reason why Islamic banks today are hesitant to mobilize a larger portion of their assets in *mudarabah*-based projects?

Although *mudarabah* remains unpopular in the Islamic banking circle, I still believe that it will become a powerful financial product once the legal problems pertaining to commerce-bank interlinks, disputes and taxation are attended to.

On risks, profits, and losses in business, Islam has made it clear that justice is established once the Commandment of God is obeyed. The Quran declares: "We send our messengers and revealed the Book through them so as to establish justice among the people." (*al-Hadid: 25*)

Basically, losses can be attributed to two factors, namely due to the negligence of the *mudarib* and market risks. On the former, the *Mejelle*—a codified Islamic law of the Hanafi school of thought says: "If the owner of the capital says 'Do not go to such a place with the partnership property' or 'Do not sell property on credit' and after the *mudarib* has been forbidden, he acts contrary to it, and goes to that place with the partnership property, if the partnership property is destroyed, or if he has sold the property on credit, and the money of the partnership is lost, he is responsible."

As I have shown earlier, *mudarabah mutlaqah* or absolute *mudarabah* seems to put more pressure on the *rabb-ul-mal,* as he has less control over determining or restricting activities pertaining to business ventures, time, location, and market setting.

As a remedy, Islamic commercial law allows contracting parties to put conditions onto *mudarabah* or *mudarabah muqaidah* agreement. This is done to see the *mudarib* is restricted by the contract to confine business activities within specific limits determined by the *rabb-ul-mal.* If the *mudarib* fails to comply with the restrictions and consequently ends up losing, he will be fully responsible for the losses. But how could the *mudarib* compensate the *rabb-ul-mal* when he has no capital share in the business? Is a *mudarabah* company a limited or unlimited legal entity?

To what extent Islamic banks should use *mudarabah mutlaqah* and *muqaidah* depends on how one looks at the banks' balance sheet. On the asset side, Islamic banks are expected to use *mudarabah muqaidah.* This is because an Islamic bank does not give away credit as conventional banks do. In debt financing, the bank has no control how the loan is spent by the debtor's business. Certainly this is not a problem since in the lending contract, the bank has legally fixed a contractual claim on the principal loan, namely the interest rate.

However, once an Islamic bank extends *mudarabah* funds to a business, a partnership is then formed, but now the claim on capital and net profit by the bank is not longer fixed. As I have said earlier, *mudarabah* is based on a profit-loss sharing principle. This implies that no fixed claim by either partner will be declared in the contract. The *mudarib* cannot demand a monthly salary and other perks often enjoyed by any normal business manager as he is not an employee of the company.

Likewise, the *rabb-ul-mal* is not expected to demand his capital or expects a contractual profit as he is not a lender but a partner who cannot eliminate the risks associated with his business. The next question is, to whom should the *mudarabah* partners turn to for protection in case of a dispute, may it be about fraud, profit distribution or contract termination?

According to the *Shafi'* school of thought, the *Minhaj At Talibin* says on profit-sharing: "In the case of a dispute to the share of profits stipulated for by the managing partner, both parties should take an oath, and the court then awards the managing partner a reasonable remuneration for his trouble."

The question now is, who should settle disputes involving Islamic financial transactions? In Malaysia, can we allow the civil laws to judge Islamic affairs such as marriage, divorce, and inheritance? Surely not, as the *Shariah* court is readily available to deal with the Islamic family law.

However, the Islamic banking Act 1983 and Takaful Act 1986 do not constitute an Islamic law as defined by the Federal Constitution. Although they are based on Islamic principles, these law falls under the jurisdiction of the civil courts. Disputes are presided by civil court judges who may not be familiar with Islamic jurisprudence (*usul fiqh*) and the Islamic law of contracts (*fiqh muamalat*).

The above discussion on *mudarabah* and how civil judges will make judgment on *muamalat* cases are made to bring about awareness that banks' customers deserve a fair trial. One thing they should know well is that judges will make decisions on what is written in the legal papers of the facility given. In this manner, they must read through the lines carefully and know what is actually offered, paid, and delivered, i.e., whether they have entered into loan contract or a BBA sale. They must be aware what action the bank will take if they defaulted on the facility or make early payments. Likewise, they should be able to known what to do if the bank fails to deliver the goods on time.

To highlight the above, it is interesting to look at three civil cases involving disputes between an Islamic bank and its customers. These are discussed as follows:

1. **Bank Islam Malaysia v. Adnan b. Omar** (Kuala Lumpur High Court Suit No. S3-22-101-91 unreported). This case involves a *bay' al-'inah* transaction although it was called *bai-bithaman ajil.* The defendant (i.e., Adnan b. Omar) was granted a facility amounting to RM583,000. He, however, has defaulted on his payments. In the *bay' al-'inah sale*, the defendant sold a piece of land to the plaintiff for RM125,000 which the plaintiff simultaneously resold the land for RM583,000, payable by the defendant in 180 monthly installments. The defendant charged the land to the plaintiff as a security for the debt. In the above case, the judge was in favor of the plaintiff. The judge in her judgment says that the defendant knew with full knowledge that the facility was to implement a loan and the repayment is made inclusive of the profit margin. The judge agrees with the plaintiff that the amount of advance was RM583,000 and not RM125,000. In this way, the defendant cannot dispute the amount. He is required to settle the full amount and not the amount he actually received i.e., RM125,000. But later on appeal, the judge ordered Bank Islam to give the defendant the rebate (*ibra*).

2. Dato' Haji Nik Mahmud vs. Bank Islam Malaysia

This case is about Dato' Haji Nik Mahmud who has defaulted on a BBA facility but took a legal action against Bank Islam for not complying to the Kelantan Malay Reservation Enactment. The BBA facility was given to the plaintiff to develop a piece of land that he owns. The facility is actually a *bay al-'inah* sale but named as *al-bai-bithaman ajil* (BBA). To develop the land (i.e., in the state of Kelantan), the plaintiff needs a sum of RM520,000. To do so, the plaintiff sells the land using the property sale agreement for RM520,000 and immediately resold by the defendant via property sale agreement for RM629,200. The defendant contested that the property (Kelantan Malay Reserve land), cannot be handed to Bank Islam, as it is not a Malay. Upon further investigation, the judge found that no transfer of title has taken place between the plaintiff and defendant and the proprietorship still remains with the plaintiff. In this way, the case brought up by the plaintiff does not hold. This case has clearly shown that what has taken place is in fact a plain collateralized loan given by the bank to the plaintiff as no actual transfer of ownership was evident in the BBA facility.

3. Tinta Press Sdn. Bhd vs. Bank Islam Malaysia Bhd

In the above case, the Bank Islam Malaysia brought a legal action against Tinta Press for defaulting on its rental obligation. The bank intends to recover possession of the equipment and to recover arrears of rent. The defendant says that the facility was a loan, but the Bank Islam denies it, as it does not give out *qardu hasan* loan. The Supreme Court says that the facility was in fact based on a lessor-lessee relation. Bank Islam as the lessor is the legal owner the equipment, while the defendant only has the right to use it. The court is in favor of Bank Islam Malaysia. The judge makes no reference to the contract of *ijarah*, i.e., leasing.

The above three cases seemed to put customers in a tight jacket. In the first case, the customer does not understand the concept of BBA and how it affects settlement of debt outstanding balance. He thought all along that the contracted price under BBA is equal to the cost price of BBA asset sold. In the second case, the customer thought the facility is based on a buy and sell concept. But it did not as no transfer of ownership is evident since the land is put under charge to the bank. In the third case, the customer has failed to understand the contract he has entered with the bank. He taught it was a loan, but the contract is actually based on leasing.

As Islamic banking and finance in Malaysia is gaining more ground, legal cases may also involve disputes dealing with *takaful* and Islamic private debt securities. Thus, the proper authorities should see that the civil courts are able to preside these prospective cases. It can expose civil lawyers and judges to Islamic law or even resolve the cases through arbitration involving people well acquainted with Islamic law of contracts (*fiqh muaalat*).

SECTION SEVEN

ISLAMIC EQUITIES

One
The Islamic Capital Market

A recent capital market conference Daim Zainuddin says that the time for coddling and protection of local players has passed. The upcoming Anwar Ibrahim's New York road show will affirm Malaysia's commitment to becoming capital market center in Asia. Major reforms introduced in June 1997 will make it painless for global players to invest in Malaysia's massive infrastructure and privatization projects.

But one may ask why so much talk about the capital market? Are the local banks unable to supply loans and capital needed for economic development? Based on rapid economic growth over the years, a RM550 billion capital investment is required to realize national economic growth target in 2000. The private sector is expected to mobilize about RM380 billion from this amount, out of which RM152 billion has to be raised through the capital market. In 1994, net private funds raised were about RM15.3 billion, and further deregulation may help boost these figures higher. In 2003, both private and public sector raised RM54.03 billion from debt and equity issuances.

Before discussing further, it is worthy to examine the capital market more closely. What does it do and how does it differ from the market for loans and deposits in the banking business? And how does the Islamic capital market fit in?

In essence, a financial system guides the flow of funds from the surplus sector to the deficit sector. In a market economy, the flow of funds is governed by market forces. To invest directly in the financial market implies doing so without using the middleman, i.e., the financial intermediaries. It can done directly via the money and capital market.

The money market deals with short-term investment in treasury bills, banker acceptances, etc., while the capital market caters for longer-term investment. In 2003, total money market transactions amounted to RM 15.3 billion. Capital market instruments are subject to greater price fluctuation. As investment in the capital market prone to market risk and volatilities, people looking for safer investments may do so via financial intermediaries like the commercial banks, finance companies, merchant banks, unit trusts, insurance companies, etc. Financial intermediaries help reduce exposure to risk, but it also comes with higher transaction costs.

To appreciate the Islamic conception of the capital market, it is worthy to look at the financial instruments available in the conventional market. Essentially, the demand and supply of funds in the capital market runs on the basis of debt and equity contracts. In the debt market, issuing companies sell interest-bearing bonds. Creditors are paid fixed income plus capital protection. In equity contracts, investors' exposure to market risks means that with no guarantees on earning and capital protection are in place. But the income and capital gains can be lucrative when money are put in well-researched stocks.

In the bond market, loans are given out directly by the lender to the borrower without the use of financial intermediaries. In Malaysia, the government sector issues the Malaysian Government Securities (MGS) to pay for expenditures. In 1994, net funds raised were RM1.6 billion In 2003, gross proceeds from MGS issuances were RM41.3 billion. In the same year the size of the Government Investment Issues (GII) has gradually expanded to RM1.7 billion to meet the increasing demand for Islamic capital market instruments.

Private sector borrowing via the bond market is made using private-debt security (PDS) instruments. They have a fixed life with some liquidity features, since they can be traded in the secondary market. With variations on tenure and maturities, PDS includes the zero-coupon, long-term coupon bonds, or fixed- or floating-rate bonds that operate under similar underlying debt principles. In 1997, investment in PDS amounted to about RM8.3 billion. In 2003, PDS issuances increased to RM170.2 billion and accounted for 53.3 per cent of total bonds outstanding.

In Islam debt finance, one cannot treat profit as legal claims, as it implicates interest as *riba*. More seriously, debts cannot be traded for capital gains. In Malaysia, the Islamic version of coupon and zero-coupon bonds are classified under Islamic private debt securities (IPDS) issues. In 1994, these Islamic notes amounted to about RM330 million with Petronas Dagangan Sdn. Bhd contributing RM300 million, while the remainders were issued through Cagamas *Mudarabah* bonds. The first issue of an Islamic debt was made in 1990 for Shell MDS Sdn Bhd involving a *bai bithaman-ajil* transaction worth RM24 million. In 2002, total funds raised via Islamic bonds amounted to RM13.8 billion.

Setting aside the juristic debates on the permissibility of IPDS at a discount and other related issues, it is critical to see further expansion of IPDS market. It can help mop up excess liquidity in Islamic banking. This liquidity problem is not new. For example, as of 30th June 1997, Islamic financing assets amounted to only RM2.5 billion as against Islamic liabilities of RM5.2 billion. The need to create new capital market instruments is therefore critical.

But the fundamental problem in Islamic debt financing remains unresolved. Money deposited with the Islamic banks channeled to the big corporations. No doubt, this can help mop up the excess cash in Islamic banks, but what about the smaller companies that certainly cannot compete with the big players?

When too much focus is given to IPDS, the future *mudarabah-musharakah* financing will be in limbo again as more Islamic debt instruments are displacing potential Islamic equity financing. Islamic banks will buy IPDS when not enough instruments are available to get rid of idle cash. But this means the supply of IPDS must continue to rise to fill up the holes. But displacing potential equity financing with IPDS may not be the best solution in the long run as Islamic bank's portfolio will be bloated again with debt instruments.

Two
Islamic Stock Market Index

The bullish run at Wall Street in 1995 saw the birth of the Dow Jones Islamic Market. The index serves to guide global Islamic investors to spend their money in the New York stock market. It shows that global Islamic funds are no longer marginal. Islamic fund managers are eagerly looking for *Shariah*-approved stocks to satisfy their clients' Islamic tastes and preferences.

Malaysia, too, launched its first public Islamic Index, known as the KLCI *Shariah* Index or (KLCI SI). However, this is not the first Malaysian Islamic stock index, as the Rashid Hussin Bhd Islamic Index (RHB Islamic Index) was launched much earlier in 1996.

But what can an Islamic Index actually do to help investors? It can help us assess the performance of companies that run along *Shariah* guidelines. An index is a pure number, such that the Islamic Stock Index is always expressed in numbers. So are other indexes such as the consumer price index (CPI) or the producer production index (PPI). I will discuss some of the basic features of an Islamic stock index and how it can be further adjusted to reveal the true Islamic color.

Whether the investments are made directly or through the middleman, the stock index remains the barometer of market performance. For example, if the index increases from, say, 115 to 120 points, the market goes up by 5 points. Normally, a stock index can be computed where samples, namely the selected stocks, are assigned weights to reflect the corresponding investment opportunities at any moment.

For example, the Dow Jones Islamic index is a price-weighted index, while the KLCI SI and Rashid Hussin Islamic indexes are value-weighted. Table 7.1 shows how a value-weighted Islamic index is constructed.

Once the index is constructed, the need for revision often rises when, say, the size of the sample or number of stocks is reduced or increased. But this is only a technical matter. However, the need to do so is a *Shariah* requirement, especially when the changes are made to reflect greater participation of new *Shariah*-approved companies or the need to exclude companies that may have lost their *Shariah* status due to, say, merger and acquisition exercises involving *Shariah* non-compliant companies.

Lastly, construction of an Islamic stock index should also address the capital structure factor. For example, a highly leveraged *Shariah*-compliant company should be given a lower Islamic weighting compared to one with lower leverage.

Table 7.1 A Hypothetical Islamic Stock Index

CONSTRUCTING A VALUE-WEIGHTED ISLAMIC STOCK INDEX				
Shariah-Compliant Company	Total Shares outstanding on both dates	Based period market price April 19th 2004	Recent period market price April 24th 2004	Percentage price charge
JEBAK (oil palm plantation)	60,000	$30	$45	+50 percent
ANGKAT (construction)	20,000	$25	$80	+220 percent
MINANG (iron & steel)	90,000	$65	$85	+31 percent
TOTALS	170,000	$120	$210	

VALUE-WEIGHTED ISLAMIC STOCK INDEX
(Islamic content defined on the basis of Activity / Production Approach only)

(April 19, 2004 market value/ April 24, 2004 market value) + 100
([60,000 x 30] + [90,000 x 65] / [60,000 x 45] + [20,000 x 80] + [90,000 x 85])
($11,950,000 / $8,150,000 x 100 = 146.63
*Interpretation: The three stocks increased by 46.63 percent from their base date April 19 on average.

Leverage is measured by the debt-equity ratio. Although a *Shariah*-compliant company does not implicate the prohibitive activities, it may have sourced some capital from interest-bearing bond issues and bank loans.

The future of an Islamic stock index will therefore depend on the greater participation of Islamic bond issues and bank equity financing so that the capital structure has zero interest-bearing debt content. As such, companies looking for capital should be given incentives to use equity rather than interest-bearing bonds. This can be done by treating dividend payouts as a tax-deductible expense.

My conviction to see more application of *mudarabah* and *musyarakah* financing in the banking sector is also to see that the debt-equity ratio of *Shariah* complaint companies be reduced to zero. Certainly this is not possible for the Dow Jones Islamic Market Index but something achievable in this country.

Three
Ethics and the Stock Market

A lan Greenspan's remarks on the state of US stock prices may have stunned the world market. The KLSE Composite Index plummeted 33.62 points while the Emas shed 8.88 points. The Dow Jones was down almost 2.5 percent. His dark warning on overpriced stocks has led dealers and investors to believe that interest rates will go up as the Feds can no longer ignore the link between the stock market and the U.S. economy.

What actually happened is a simple matter of textbook economics. When irrational exuberance rules the market, it may be hard to sustain the low inflation and economic recovery the U.S. has enjoyed recently. Higher stock prices and further escalation of asset values has put Japan under unexpected and prolonged contraction, a trap that the U.S. doesn't want to fall into.

For the Federal Reserve, a market correction can be introduced by raising interest rates, which market players believe Greenspan will certainly do. In the open-market operations, the Fed can do so by selling securities. Higher interest rates can do two things.

First, investment in fixed deposits and other debt instruments becomes more attractive. Investors may sell their stocks to invest in deposits instead. Secondly, raising interest rates depresses the present value of assets. In other words, the value of, say, firm A will fall. This is because higher interest rates usually imply higher cost of running business and this means lower corporate earnings.

Normally the price of stocks is positively related to the value of the firm. A fall in the value of firm A is expected to cause its stock price to fall. Nervous investors will dispose of their stocks. That explains the worldwide market plunge.

What is interesting about Greenspan's statement concerning market excesses and irrational exuberance is potency of ethics and morality is determining the health of the economy. When people fail to control their lust, and trade their soul for more money and wealth, it is the purpose of the law to see that such desires are guarded. The market is not a structure whose behavior can be predicted with full accuracy. For example, add any acid to an alkali—one is sure to see water and oxygen coming out. But the same does not apply to people.

The market is people, i.e., consumers and producers, whose unpredictable behavior is the reason why complicated theories and forecasting models are built. In Islam, one of the purposes of law is to protect the public interest *(maslahah al-ammah),* namely religion *(deen)*, life *(nasl)*, intellect *('aql)*, family *(nasl)*, and wealth *(mal)*. On the last *maslahah*, that is the protection of wealth *(mal),* the state is made responsible by the *Shariah* to protect the wealth of the nation from destruction arising, say, from escalating inflation, budget deficits, trade imbalances, and prolonged unemployment or overcapacity. For example, madness in the stock market means unwarranted volatilities. It can mean two things, namely healthy financial market or simply a potential market fallout.

Market volatility can be either caused by economic fundamentals, say, an oil embargo, or simply conspiracies involving, say, insider trading. According to Ibn Taimiyyah, the thirteenth century Islamic jurist, "Rise and fall in prices are not always due to an injustice *(zulm)* by certain individuals. Sometimes, the reason for it is deficiency in production or decline in imports of the good in demand. This scarcity or abundance may not be caused by the action of any individual; it may be due to a cause not involving any injustices or sometimes, it may have a cause that involves injustice..."

Ibn Taimiyyah's observation explains the inherent role of government intervention. Market failure cannot be ascribed to wrong planning or unexpected natural events alone. Man himself is the root of the problem.

What Alan Greenspan has in mind when he mentioned the irrational exuberance and excesses of market players is, in fact, a frank remark about abuse of the intellect and how it can disrupt economic stability. In wealth creation, greed and lust have overwhelmed the intellect, leaving man to behave irrationally and making his action difficult to predict. Investments are made less on the basis of market fundamentals but running on rumors and guesswork.

Lastly, truly the intellect (*'aql*) in Islam is supreme. It differentiates man from the other created living beings. According to Ibn Miskawayh, "God created Intelligence (*'aql*), and it is by it that the heavens and earth exists, and that the knowers and the world have been made to exist. Without it (intelligence), wisdom would not exist, knowledge would not be perceived, godhead would not appear, nor would divinity be known."

When one abuses the intellect (*'aql*), he is also abusing public interest. So, when an investor behaves irrationally, it will not only hurt him alone, but also the people and economic welfare.

The stock market in Islam is basically a hybrid of *mudarabah* and *musharakah* financing. Stockholders or investors are sleeping partners, while the firm is the entity that runs the business. However, a corporation, say, Tenaga Nasional, is not a *mudarib* because as a corporation, Tenaga owns capital. As a legal entity, a corporation is neither a manager nor a capital provider.

In Islam, shareholders are expected to put commitment (*iltizam*) to their investments. One of the principles of Islamic contract is *iltizam* i.e., committement of contracting parties to the objective of the contract. They are expected to grow with the firm and help it achieve its objectives. Although in Islam, selling one's stocks is lawful, it is unethical to do so if doing so will hurt the company and its employees.

In a business relationship, according to Shah Waliyullah of Delhi, Islam enjoins the spirit of cooperation and mutual aid (*ta'awun*). *Riba* is created devoid of the spirit of cooperation and mutual aid. According to Shah Waliyullah, "*Riba* constitutes an unlawful gain and is not in keeping with civic spirit (*tamaddun*) and mutual aid (*ta'awun*), for as a rule the borrowers are people fallen into a severe state of indigence, mostly not able to pay the debt in time ... when this way of earning money takes root, it leads to the abandonment of agrarian trades and skilled crafts which are a fundamental means of earning a living in a healthy society."

Likewise, when one invests in shares, the spirit of cooperation and mutual trade must prevail. Otherwise, any profit arising from stock trading depicting the opposite forces will make it unlawful. So, if a company is facing difficulties, should the stockholders dispose of their shares to play safe?

Four
Purification Process

Investing our hard-earned savings may require a considerable amount of research and soul searching. The latter is important, in case the investment turns bad. We may have enough to endure the subsequent stress and anxiety that comes with it.

It is worthy to remember that any investment made without sound preparation is akin to *israf* and *tadrif*, which means wastage. But today, research may have taken the back seat, as nothing tangible seems to lead the economy out from of the currency debacle. No matter how strong our local companies have performed, as claimed, Malaysian stocks are heading for the worst as the ringgit touches a new low from continuous speculative attacks.

One of the badly-hit sectors is the unit trust industry. On the average, unit values have fallen by more than 30 percent from the year high but relatively few have fallen below their respective Net Asset Value (NAV) per unit. For instance, when the stock market is bullish, ASN is worth RM1.62 per unit. Now it is down to RM1.20 with NAV per unit at RM1.25. RHB Capital fund was at RM1.12 per unit in the year high, but the NAV has dropped to RM0.75 per unit.

So why invest in unit trusts? When people don't have time, energy, and skills to buy stocks on the open market, they often resort to unit trust companies that can do the investment, but for a fee. Mostly run by fund managers, unit trust companies usually provide decent earnings at relatively lower risks.

371

Funds are invested in the stock, bond, and money market. Unit trust companies do not provide capital protection. There are no guarantees on earnings as well. But the advantages of investing in unit trusts are numerous. Investors will find their money invested in diversified securities that help minimize losses arising from adverse price movement. Investments can be made in small amounts, with dividends and capital gains automatically reinvested.

Unit trust companies also allow investors to redeem units on call. During a changing investment climate, investors in the open market may switch their funds, but at a cost. However, in unit trust investments, the switching strategy is commonly observed by the fund managers at no cost to the investors.

In Islam, investment in the unit companies requires investors to be mindful about the *Shariah* requirements of investing in the financial assets. There are about sixteen Islamic funds today with about 6 percent market share.

What makes an Islamic unit trust company different from its conventional competitor? One concerns with the "purification process" involving a number of treatments, namely:

- Treatment for shareholding
- Treatment for dividend
- Treatment for capital gains
- Treatment for the effects of interest-based borrowing on dividends
- Treatment for the effects on interest-free borrowing on capital gains.

The purification process was first introduced by Rashid Hussin Bank (RHB). *Shariah* stock screening conducted by the Securities Commission came out later. This purification process is a pioneering attempt by a private company (i.e., RHB) on Islamization of stock investment.

Let's take Telekom stocks to illustrate the purification process in action. Telekom provides basic communication services. As a product, Telekom stocks are permissible (*halal*). It follows that buying Telekom stocks constitutes an act of worship (*ibadat*). But if the company directly and explicitly deals with prohibited goods and services, such as gambling, *riba*, prostitution, pornography, drinking, swine and swine products, it is not a good idea to invest in the company as doing *haram*. This is the activity approach to purification.

In addition, the fund manager must carefully inspect the activities of *halal* companies; the scope of business may change, say, from a recent merger and acquisition exercise. We now see that the role of Islamic fund managers today is not merely to find the best portfolio that can generate maximum returns at the lowest risk, but also the *Shariah* compliant factor.

The above simply looks at the determination of *halal* stocks using the activity approach. However, there is no easy way to single out stocks using to this method. This is because a company, say Renang, is considered *halal* by activity method, but upon reexamination, activities at the subsidiary level are found to contain elements of *riba* and gambling.

The RHB model introduces a technique so that the prohibitive portion of the investment is taken out via a purification process. These portions are supposedly given away to charities as *sadeqah*. On the treatment of dividends, the purification is done by dividing the value of non-Muslim activities (NIA) by the total worth of the listed company (TWC) and then multiplying the ratio with the dividend per share (DPS) or [(NIA/TWC) x DPS].

At the first level, the purification process will not put interest-bearing financial services companies as *Shariah* compliant. These shall include the conventional commercial banks, finance companies, merchant banks as well as conventional insurance.

However, it is impossible to filter out the interest elements from the remaining non-financial services companies operating in this country. For example, although Telekom or Tenaga stocks are *halal* by activity standard, they may have acquired funds using interest-bearing debt instruments such as syndicated bank loans and private debt securities (PDS). It means their respective gearing or debt-equity ratio is positive. In other words, the capital structure consists of both loan and equity. Since the former is *haram* while the latter is *halal,* how would the fund managers apply the purification process?

Since one is dealing with *halal* stocks not directly dealing with *riba*, the purification process looks at the dividend and capital gains, if any. For example, if the dividend per unit is 30 cents, while debt is $30 million and equity is $100 million, then the amount of dividend that should be given out to charity is (30/100) x 30 = 10 sen per unit. Or if capital gain is $1.20, the unit holders can keep (30/100) x 120 or 40 sen per unit.

It is worthy to note that currently, the *Shariah* Advisory Council (SAC) of the Securities Commission has applied *Shariah* stock screening (SSS) to all stocks issued on the Kuala Lumpur Stock Exchange (KLSE). In other words the job is a centralized one. Managers of Islamic funds do not have to do their in-house *Shariah* screening. RHB purification process is still useful as a guide. As mentioned earlier, the purification process was first introduced by RHB bank before the SAC was set up to institutionalize the Shariah screening process..

Five
Call Warrants

The collapse of Baring Merchant Bank gave the public new insights about crime risks in the derivative market. Rules and regulations set by Bank Negara Malaysia (BNM) and the Securities Commission (SC) both play a crucial role to ensure greater transparency, although there is little authorities can do to control human greed (*hirs*). It is lustful greed that often leads people to commit criminal breach of trust (CBT), one form of fraud (*tatfief*).

Although futures trading will be launched this November, the Kuala Lumpur Options & Financial Futures Exchange Bhd.'s (KLOFFE) simulated trading last April was successful. Here equity derivative products, specifically financial futures, were traded based on the KLSE Composite Index (KLCI). In the pilot simulation exercise, many features like month-end price, exercises, margin calls, and contract adjustments were tested.

Unlike futures trading, where contracts are traded on the KLCI, call warrants are traded on a specific stock of a corporation, say Telekom or Tenaga Nasional. The call warrant gives the holder the right to buy the underlying shares.

What is a call warrant and how does it work? Simply, a call warrant is a contract that gives the warrant holder a legal right to buy the underlying shares. The right to buy the shares comes with a price. For example, Mr. Yusof buys a call warrant from TA Securities at $4.00 each for one Telekom share at an exercise price of $25.00. Thus, if he buys 10,000 call warrants, he has to pay the issuing company $4,000.

If price of Telekom shares increases to $30.00 per unit at the expiration date, Yusof will exercise his right to buy them. He makes $5.00 capital gain per share or simply $50,000 profit. His net gain will be $46,000 (i.e., $50,000 - $4,000). But if the share price drops to $20.00, he can avoid losses by opting not to buy the shares.

For when warrants are bought for speculation, Yusof's main intention is not to exercise the right of conversion, but to sell warrant when there is capital gain in sight. Normally, the price of the call warrant increases as the market price of underlying shares rises. For example, when the market price of Telekom shares increases from $25.00 to $28.00, the price of the call warrant increases from $4.00 to $4.50. A speculative trader in this case will not think of conversion, but will sell the warrant at a fifty-cent capital gain per unit.

Likewise, a drop in Telekom stocks reduces the price of the warrant. Yusoff is expected to sell the warrant for fear the price may drop further. If the price of the warrant drops from $4.00 to $3.50, selling the warrant will see him losing fifty cents per warrant. Thus, if he buys 100,000 warrants, his total loss is $50,000.

So, what is the Islamic view on the trading of warrants? Since a warrant is the right to buy the underlying shares, it means the trading of warrants is equivalent to trading of rights (*hak*). Is trading of rights (*hak*) permissible in Islam?

Recall that a contract (*'aqd*) in Islam is built on five fundamental principles, namely:

1. Rights (*hak*) and commitment (*iltizam*) to pursue the objective of the business transaction;
2. Agents of contract (*Tharafayil 'aqdi*);
3. Objective of the contract (*maudlu'ul 'aqdi*);
4. Object of trade in the contract (*mahallul 'aqdi*)and;
5. Pronouncement of willingness to enter into a contract (*shighatul 'aqdi*).

From the five above principles, only the rule pertaining to the object of trade (*mahallul 'aqdi*) is most intriguing, as it requires an answer whether the right (*hak*) to sell and buy warrants is equal to wealth and property (*mal mutaqawwim*).

Before continuing further, recall that a call warrant is the right to buy an underlying share of a corporation. Thus, our focus now is not about the conversion i.e., decision to buy the shares on expiration date, but trading of the rights before the expiration date. The question now is whether a contract involving the sale and purchase of the rights (*hak*) is acceptable in Islam.

Partly, the answer depends on how one understands the meaning of property (*mal*). In a nutshell, can we regard rights (*hak*) equal to property (*mal*)? According to Muslim jurists, wealth or property has two basic attributes, namely *'ainiyah* (an existing object) and *'urf* (being good and useful to mankind). For example, although a corpse is an object (*'ain*) it is not wealth (*mal ghairu mutaqawim*) because it is not useful to mankind.

But what about say, something that is one's own with transferable usufruct (*manafaah*) but that has no attributes of a physical object; for example, the *manfa'ah* or benefit of owning a house?

According to Muslim jurists, it cannot be associated with wealth, but only ownership (*milkiah*). Thus, by definition, they say that wealth is objects that bear three main characteristics, i.e., they must be valuable, tangible, or physical and tradable.

All the above leaves us to further investigate the difference between wealth (*mal*) and rights (*hak*). In a contract of sale (*al-bay'*), we are looking at the sale of an object (*mal*) but the transfer of ownership right (*hak milkiyah*) from the seller to the buyer. Even though both are related, the object of sale is not equivalent to ownership right (*hak milikiyah*) but *mal mutaqawim.*

The question whether a call warrant contract is permissible or not requires serious research and should be closely monitored by the Securities Commission and Bank Negara Malaysia for policymaking. Studies should use both the theoretical and historical approach. The former refers to the techniques of making legal judgment (*fatwa*) while the latter looks into the experience of early Muslim communities in conducting economic activities.

For example, placing a money deposit (*arbun*) in order to secure a purchase is permissible. The transfer of right via *arbun* without a premium is also less controversial. But it is about selling or transfer of *arbun* that at a price that has become flirtous. To find a credible answer, one should investigate whether in the early Muslim history, a trader who places one dinar deposit as a right to buy a horse or camel at a later date, is allowed to sell his right to purchase the animals for two or more dinar, thus making a gain.

Call warrants work along the same line. Again, the issue is not about whether buying call warrants is *halal* or *haram*. The issue is about tradability of warrants. Can one treat a warrant as an object of sale? One who hedges against market volatilities will either use the warrants to buy the underlying stocks or simply abandon the stock purchase.

But as a speculator, a person who buys the warrant has no intention to exercise his right to buy the underlying stocks, but instead sells the warrant to make profit. *Shariah* advisors should take note of this point. It is easy to give an opinion about call warrants as a hedging device, but most of the time it implicates speculative trading.

Six

Does Islam allow short-selling?

The new securities borrowing and lending guidelines (SBL) released by the Securities Commission (SC) was timely in view of the launching of the Malaysian financial futures and options market. The SBL, according to the Securities commission, are expected to facilitate derivatives trading through the provision of prudential standards of safety and soundness for participants authorized to engage in securities borrowing and lending activities. It will open up the capital market while putting the risk due to asymmetric information under close scrutiny.

What exactly the issue is remains a mystery to many, but one can now be assured that this borrowing and lending of securities is essentially about legalizing short-selling. We once heard about it in the Union Paper short-selling scandal. It was technically illegal then, but now the SC has made it a legitimate transaction, under strict SBL regulations.

What really is short-selling and how will it help make a stock market more competitive? Most textbooks will say that short-selling involves the sale of a security (e.g. common stocks) not owned by the investor at the time of sale. In other words, short-selling is about selling what one does not own. But how does it work and what good will it to do investors?

To understand the Islamic position on short-selling would first require a sound knowledge about the practical operation of the stock market and investors' profit-maximizing behavior. It boils down to the principle of buying cheap and selling high. But what really happens in short-selling is that investors do not own the stocks they sell when prices are high or overpriced.

Let us take an example of how this is done in the stock market. Suppose Ameen made a study of Rentung Steel Sdn Bhd common stocks and found it is overpriced at $20 per share. He wants to be in a position to benefit if his assessment is correct. So he calls his broker, Ariff, indicating that he wants to sell 100 shares of Rentung (which he does not own). Ariff will do two things. First, he will sell 100 shares of Rentung on behalf of Ameen. Secondly, he will arrange to borrow 100 shares of that stock to deliver to the buyer.

Let us look at the second option. Ariff is able to sell the stocks for $20 and borrows the stocks from Lee. The shares will be delivered to the buyer. This borrowing and lending activity is now allowed in the Malaysian stock market under the SBL guidelines. Whether this will lead to abuse will depend on how much Ameen can make; and perhaps it will violate the Quranic verse, "Woe betide those who take more than they give." (83:1) and "Do not curtail or diminish what is due to other people" (11:85).

The proceeds from the above sale will be $2,000. However, the proceeds do not go to Ameen, because he has not given his broker the 100 shares. Thus, Ameen is said to be "short 100 shares"—hence the term short-selling. Now, suppose three days later, the price of Rentung Steel declines to $15 per share. Ameen may instruct his broker, Ariff, to buy 100 shares of Rentung Steel, costing him $1,500.

These shares are then delivered to Lee, who has initially lent out the 100 shares. So, he no longer has any obligation to his broker or to Lee; i.e., Ameen has covered his short position. He is now entitled to the funds in the account generated from the selling and buying activities.

He sold the stock for $2,000 and bought it for $1,500, and therefore made a profit of $500. Of course, he will have to pay some fees such as commissions, fees charged by the lender of the stock, and dividends paid by Rentung Steel. But when the share price increases to, say, $27, Ameen will lose $700 when he is forced to cover his short position.

The position of short-selling in Islam is still not clear and requires a commendable response from the Securities Commission as the transaction is said to be in conflict with one Prophetic hadith.

The *hadith* says; *"Ja'far b. Abi Wahshiyah reported from Yusuf b. Mahak from Hakim b. Hizan (who said): I asked the Prophet PBUH: O Messenger of Allah! A man comes to me and asks me to sell him what is not with me, so I sell him (what he wants) and then buy the goods for him in the market (and deliver). And the Prophet said: sell not what is not with you."*

The last statement: *sell not what is not yours,* on the surface may imply that Ameen cannot instruct his broker to sell Rentung Steel stocks, since Ameen does not own the stocks. But really, what is the message in the statement? It is about uncertainty over Ameen's ability to deliver the stocks to Lee. Certainly, it is not about the issue of ownership in its literal sense, because Islam allows *salam* sale which does not require ownership of the asset.

Seven
Islamic Venture Capital

One of the essential features of Islamic financing is the role of cooperation in wealth creation. The importance put to the profit-loss sharing ratio instead of profit fixation in *mudarabah* or *musyarakah* ventures is one good example of Islam's concern for equitable income distribution through equity participation.

But the brave new world of finance theory today envisages a world in which investors are not concerned with individual firms; managers are not interested in shareholders; bondholders and managers are locked in eternal conflict generated by self-seeking interest. Insider dealings by management and others take place to boost share prices artificially in the case of takeover. Tax fraud and manipulating accounting numbers to strike abnormal profits are dealings which are no stranger to the business managers.

The underlying ethos in the above behavior is self-interest, short-term orientation and the relentless focus on deal making, rather than on long-term investment. Finance theorists invest in "opportunities" and not in goods, services, or people. Will Islamic financing today fall into the same trap?

The Quran says, "Woe to those that deal in fraud, those who when they have to receive by measure from men, exact full measure, but when they have to give measure by weight to men, give less than due. Do you not think that they will be called to account? On a Mighty Day, a day when all mankind will stand before the Lord of the Worlds." *(A1-mutaffijin:83)*

383

What we see above is the spirit behind the ban on usury or *riba*. The prohibition of *riba* is therefore not manifested in the legal setting alone, but bears an ethical meaning, namely the spirit of cooperation *(ta'wun)*. Taking *riba* is therefore a fraud because bankers will count to the last cent how much they should pay depositors, while charging borrowers a rate which takes no heed of their ethical and moral strength. What counts is the collateral. More collateral will mean less interest payments. Now the human element is downgraded below the mundane.

This is the danger that Islamic bankers and practitioners should try to avoid. In the legal sense, these products are permissible (*halal*), but from the ethical point of view, the Islamic practice does not seem to be significantly different from conventional norm.

One good example is venture capital financing, which in essence constitute a partnership or *musyarakah* contract. I have reiterated that the main objective of a venture capitalist is to make capital gains from the sale of company stocks they hold upon exit. As such, determining stock ownership is crucial. The deal is the percentage equity he should control in the company.

However, in the *musyarakah* framework, the main element of the contract is the profit-loss sharing ratio (PLSR). It is set on the basis of terms and conditions agreed upon by the participating agents. But in modern finance, it is irrational to say that an investor will not give a look at the expected return on investment of a project, which all venture capitalists will do. So, how are the PLSR and pricing of the venture capital deal related?

One of the methods of pricing a deal in a venture capital project is called the Hockey Stick Method. Let us see whether this method, when applied to *musyarakah,* is plausible. Here, the investor first decides what return on investment he wants when he cashes in on his investment at the end of the project, say three years.

Let's say, from a $1.5 million investment he wants a return on investment (ROI) of 6 or $9 million. Also he envisages the project to make a net profit of $2 million. If he decides on a price-earning ratio of 10:1, he will obtain a 45 percent equity in the company. This is done by multiplying the projected earning ($2 million) by ten and dividing it by his targeted return of $9 million.

What we see here is a deal that a venture capitalist will offer to an entrepreneur. Here the former wants 45 percent equity in the company on the basis of a ROI of $6 or $9 million on a $1.5 million investment. Can this be a genuine case in a *musyarakah* deal in which the spirit of cooperation or *ta'wun* is made visible? Is the fixation of profit ($9 million) in equity investment in the form of equity ownership permissible in a *musyarakah* contract? It is, therefore, inadequate to say that venture capital is by nature *halal* before any substantial research is made on the subject. There is a great deal of work one must do before the Islamic label can be used.

Eight
Blaming George Sorros

When Ivan Boesky and Nick Leeson went to prison for committing illegal business practices, the financial community begun to realize that despite stringent laws and regulations, it is hard to prevent greed from becoming a crime.

In the case of George Sorros, who has been accused of dismantling the Asian currency market, the issue at hand seems to be about ethics and morality; Western observers see Sorros as a man who neither sells nor conceals information for money. He did not violate any law. Instead, he was simply observing the laws of supply and demand. As a speculator, he was only making a plain business strategy where market players seek profits on the basis of arbitrage.

Because we are living in an uncertain world, market players are, in essence, speculators in their own right. A vegetable farmer speculates about future commodity prices and chooses to invest a certain amount of capital and employ a certain number of workers. If he thinks that future prices of vegetables are attractive, he may spend more money and energy to increase produce.

Let's assume that all vegetable farmers feel the same. Come harvest time, the supply of vegetables increases dramatically. Bumper crops do not always mean happy hour. But with stronger demand, perhaps price will increase. What we see here is the market process in action.

Most students today do not have an opportunity to understand the factors governing the behavior of economic agents. Economics in schools and universities is taught like science subjects. Solutions to problems must be strictly based on facts alone, namely what we only see. Economic concepts and solutions are further translated into elegant graphical and mathematical illustrations without putting equal attention to the nature of man who is responsible for giving the market a direction towards equilibrium, say the economists.

Today, the developed countries are giving us assurance that Sorros has abided by the law of supply and demand and should not be implicated in the ASEAN currency turbulence. Accordingly, whatever the impact it will have on ASEAN nations is secondary, as this is only temporary, for the market moves on the basis of fundamentals. The market, through the working of the Invisible Hand, will soon find a new equilibrium, with all players enjoying the "win-win" deal.

But as ASEAN leaders lament on the evil of rogue currency speculators and how their actions have caused loss of foreign reserves and higher cost of imports, we should try to ponder what actually should be done to prevent the same from happening. In 1992, it was the rising yen against the ringgit.

Then, in 1995, it was the falling sterling causing Bank Negara to lose billions. Now we see how badly the ringgit has depreciated due to, according to one theory, heavy speculative selling of the ringgit by Mr. Sorros. To prevent further ringgit decline, Bank Negara has sold huge amounts of its dollar reserves to buy ringgit. Again, what we see here is the market process in full swing.

Economics students will find these changes inevitable. Human sufferings, injustices, and manipulations arising from these processes are too subjective to be considered in their economic analysis. So when the next turbulence comes, we end up telling the same story.

As I have indicated earlier, we utterly despise the people who are directly responsible for the speculative fall of the ringgit. We hate such action because it causes human suffering. The question is, how can we teach the kids to guard themselves against these negative values, particularly in business and commercial transactions pursued for the sake of self-interest? Have our schools and universities gone the extra mile to make courses on ethics and morality compulsory? At least, such exposure can help students prepare for the onslaught of ethical dilemmas in their future careers.

In Islam, the education system is made to provide two types of reinforcing knowledge to mankind. The first is divine knowledge, while the second is knowledge derived from rational enquiry and the senses. In terms of responsibility, the acquisition of divine knowledge is an obligation (*fard 'ayn*). This divine knowledge contains *Quranic* teachings as well as the Prophetic sayings (*hadiths*) about *Aqidah* (faith), *Akhlak* (ethics and morality), and the rituals in worshipping God (Pillars of Islam), such as the five daily prayers, fasting in Ramadan, giving out Zakat and performing the Hajj if one can afford. These are the essential foundations of knowledge in Islam that educators must acquire and be able to impart to the *fard kifayah* knowledge of the sciences such as physics, biology, chemistry, medicine, engineering, computers, economics, military, aerospace, etc.

In other words, to become a medical doctor is a collective responsibility (*fardrd kifayah*) which means that not everybody, but only a few selected ones will be chosen and trained to become doctors in the Islamic tradition. Here, the student must acquire fundamental or divine knowledge such as courses about the Quran and *hadiths,* Islamic history, Islamic jurisprudence, Islamic ethics, and morality of Akhlak, etc.

But also, divine knowledge can be imparted when topics on, say, the process of human reproduction are discussed. Similarly, in economics, the study of human behavior in allocating scarce resources can be done in greater depth based on the Quranic concept of man.

For example, when neoclassical economics talks about man as a rational being seeking to maximize his satisfaction driven by self-interest, Islam can further discuss the concept of the "self-interest" in greater depth, since the word "self" in the Quran is sometimes referred to as the intellect (*'aql*), heart (*qalb*), spirit (*ruh*) and desires (*nafs*). So, if it is true that George Sorros is the one behind the currency turbulence, would his self-interest then be driven by the *'aql* or *qalb* or *ruh* or *nafs*? Using this applied approach to the study of ethics can help pacify unethical behavior in business and commerce today.

Nine
Musyarakah Venture capital

To design niche products for the banking industry today can be a daunting task, but not for Islamic banking. The contracts of *istisna'* and *salam* are viable for trade and contract financing, but have not yet found ready application. Likewise, Islamic equity financing such as *musyarakah* is also in limbo. Islamic banks have stayed away from them too long. This is quite pitiful, since Islamic banks must run on niche products to reflect true label. It needs to exert a market presence that others cannot pierce through.

The emphasis of productivity-led growth in the last Seventh Malaysia Plan has put research and development (R & D) in the limelight. Under the Plan, RM100 million has been allocated to commercialize R & D, especially that used technology-intensive techniques. The upcoming Eighth Malaysia Plan will push R & D even bigger. To do the above, the role of the venture capital industry is crucial in determining the extent to which the commercially viable inventions can be produced large scale. The risks involved can be extremely high and only venture capitalists are willing to take them. It is here we fail to see how banks can play a new role in entrepreneur financing. Logically, when they do it, profits generated from the venture will be enjoyed by many parties, including depositors.

The involvement of the local banking industry in venture capital is mainly through their subsidiaries. A bank would normally set up a venture capital company when it has enough reserves, usually accumulated after five to ten years of operations. The company, now a subsidiary of the bank, is governed by the Company Act 1964. It allows companies to conduct activities formerly not allowed by BAFIA 1989, for example, stock acquisitions or trading. Let's say Company XYZ, a subsidiary of Bank M, should be able to acquire stocks of Company STU through management or leverage buyouts. If the venture capital company is wholly owned by Bank M, profits will go Bank M's shareholders.

But such banking structure tends to limit the role of depositors in Bank M to that of lender alone. They may be given an interest income of 3 percent a year while those who invest in the unit trust industry will get more, say 8 percent. Of course, the latter cannot avoid market risk, but knew well that investments are attended by professional fund managers.

So, will the lower interest income from deposits invite financial disintermediation with money moving from bank deposits to unit trusts? The main issue now is about income distribution. Most depositors are risk-averse individuals, i.e., they prefer high-yielding investment, but at relatively lower or zero risks. But they too know that to earn more, they must take more risk. This is hard to do unless they know that these investments are run by a group of experts. Then depositors do not have to shift their funds to the unit trust industry, since the bank can do the same investment under the same roof.

The problem now is what types of investments an Islamic bank should pursue beyond *al-bay bithaman ajil.* In the case of Bank Islam Malaysia Berhad (BIMB), investments where stocks are involved have been dealt with by subsidiary companies such as Amanah Saham Bank Islam (ASBI) and Bank Islam Malaysia Securities (BIMS). What we see here is the Anglo-Saxon type of banking instead of a universal banking structure, with the two activities running under the roof of the parent bank (i.e., BIMB). Doing so will increase bank's asset size, and reduces cost arising from scale economies.

When BIMB adopts the Anglo-Saxon banking model, it will not be surprising to see her setting up a venture capital subsidiary company later on. It may be the right thing to do, as the banking law does not want to put deposits into danger, thus prohibiting banks from conducting joint ventures. But the public should be given the opportunity to participate in venture capital investments, which today only are confined to the rich people in view of the large amount of capital required there. Banks will say that venture capital is highly risky, and the common investor should not think about investing there, but this is not always true. Venture capital investment is extremely risky only in the seed-stage financing, a sort of hit-or-miss type of investment. But it also deals with relatively less risky financing such as:

- Second-stage financing involving working capital financing required by business for expansion due to growing sales and inventories.
- Mezzanine financing given to established and profitable companies for substantial business expansion.

All of the above require banks to hold ownership in the investee company. It serves to hold control and monitoring rights over company operation. In this way, risks arising from moral hazards can be minimized. In Malaysia's Islamic banking system, such ventures will not come easy, as BAFIA prohibits commercial banks from doing so. It also implies that Islamic banking system banks (IBS) are affected by these BAFIA rulings.

Apparently, Islamic banks too are not keen to apply the venture capital model. As banks by nature deal with credit, venture capital is not their cup of tea. Full-fledged Islamic banks are not an exception. They too have no experience in venture capital investments. Why should they invite trouble when BBA financing has been providing life support without fail?

In essence, venture capital investment is a *musyarakah* transaction, since the contracting parties—namely the venture capitalist and the entrepreneur—supply both capital and value-added inputs. But the venture capital *musyarakah* arrangement can be unique. (See Figure 7.1.) Accordingly, the investee company supplies the least capital and the most of value-addition, while the venture capitalist provides the opposite.

Musyarakah Matrix

Investee Company   Venture Capitalist

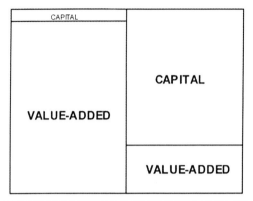

CONTRACTING PARTIES PROVIDING BOTH CAPITAL AND
LABOR INPUTS. MUSYARAKAH VC IS UNIQUE AS THE
FINANCIER USUALLY CONTRIBUTES THE BULK OF CAPITAL
WHILE INVESTEE COMPANY CONTRIBUTINGTHE BULK
OF LABOR.

Figure 7.1 *Al-Musharakah* Venture Capital

Islamic banking should be seen as one vehicle which can help increase the wealth of both Muslims and non-Muslim depositors. When Islamic banks use deposits to finance asset purchases via *murabahah* and BBA, returns to depositors can hardly absorb the inflation rate. In this manner, wealth creation via Islamic deposits is not an attractive option. Likewise, investment in unit trusts implicates higher transaction costs, and the yields are not competitive either. To invest directly in the stock market can be quite tedious, as retail investors must study well the market sentiments and company earnings. Failure to so can mean getting their fingers burnt.

But when Islamic banks participate in venture capital financing via the *musyarakah* mechanism, it means an opportunity opened to depositors to participate in the venture as well. Successful VC projects under professional project monitoring and risk management will mean handsome returns to Islamic depositors, thus increasing their standard of living. This opportunity will not materialize when an Islamic bank opted to set up a subsidiary company catering VC investment.

This is true since the subsidiary cannot collect deposits from the public. Sources of funds are mainly drawn from shareholders limited to few financial institutions and some wealthy individuals. In this way, the common people are left out to share the economic cake. Under the Anglo-

Saxon banking model, "the rich become richer and the poor remain poor." It is worthy to experiment how *Musyarakah* can run under a banking structure. This is the very reason why Muslim economists have for so long believe in the *musyarakah* model.

Ten

Investment In Shariah Stocks – The Moral Factor

Muslim investors are concerned whether the act of buying and selling of *Shariah* stocks is valid (*sahih*) or invalid (*bathil*). People dealing in *Shariah* stocks and Islamic funds such as unit trust and insurance agents should take note as they are supposed to know some basics of Islam. In marketing, one must understand the tastes and preferences of consumers. In this particular instance, the purification process plays an important role in putting *Shariah* legitimacy to *Shariah* stock trading.

A marketer may well ask, "Why are Muslims so concerned with the *halal* and *haram*?" The answer can be simple if one is familiar with Islamic commercial law (*fiqh muamalat*). That is, if the contract of stock trading is invalid (*bathil*), the act of buying and selling of stocks is therefore a sin and brings along with it a sense of regret, helplessness, and loss as the wrath of God is definite. In wealth creation, the Muslim community certainly does not desire this unwarranted stress and grief (*shawqawa*) as opposed to happiness (*sa'ada*) and tranquility.

It seems an explanation is in order to ascertain the desire for *Shariah* legitimacy (that is, the legal factor) via the purification process. The methods of *Shariah* screening constitute Islam's way of purifying the soul (*tazkiyah an-nafs*). These methods i.e., the activity, income and capital structure, are the means by which an individual can attain purification of the self.

In Islam, purification begins from within. This is among the central theme of the Quran. That is, the individual strives to purify him- or herself in a way ordained by the Creator. Purifying oneself is the final objective in this life, achievable by way of submitting one's desires to the Will of God, as embodied in the *Shariah*. In the end, Man shall achieve happiness (*sa'ada*) when the self returns to its true nature.

Submitting one's desire to *Shariah* values requires a driving catalyst that both motivates and excites the individual to do it with conviction. This is because submitting one's desire to a particular value system needs convincing.

Temptations to realize gains through falsehood (*fasad*) such as fraud (*ihtihal*) and corruption are overwhelming as less effort is required to obtain the gains. Income derived from *riba* and gambling (*maisir*) is immoral, as both constitute unlawful gains, since no equivalent countervalue (*'iwad*) is evident from the surplus made. Likewise, allowing ambiguities (*gharar*) in contractual obligations is against mutual and cooperative values.

Islam as *Al-Din* means submission. In fact, one of the meanings of *Din* or the Arabic root word *Dyn* is indebtedness; that gives deeper meaning to the reason for human existence in Islam. Logically, when a person is in debt, he is supposed to settle it.

In Islam man is indebted to God, his Creator and Provider, for giving him life and sustenance in this world. On this point, the Quran states, "Man, We did create from a quintessence of clay. Then We placed him as a drop of sperm in a place of rest, firmly fixed. Then We made the sperm into a clot of congealed blood; then out of that clot We made a lump; then We made out of that lump bones and clothed the bones with flesh; then We developed out of it another creature. So blessed be God, the Best to create." (Al-Mu'minun{23}:12-24).

But how is Man supposed to repay the debt? God the Almighty is in no dire need of anything, as He is the Creator and Sustainer, but the debt that Man owes God must be paid. In Islam, paying or returning the debt means to give oneself up in service or *khidmah* to the Lord and Master, to abase oneself before Him. In this manner, Man sincerely and consciously enslaves himself for the sake of God in order to fulfill His Commands and Prohibitions and Ordinances, and thus to live out the dictates of His Law.

Now it becomes clear that the meaning of Man's existence is related to his indebtedness to God and his subsequent enslavement of His Law.

Man himself is the object of the debt. In fact, the covenant that Man sealed with God in the primordial stage of life, that is, when he says, "Am I not your Lord?" and Man's true self-testifying, answer, "Yea!" requires Man to manifest the Covenant (*Al-Mithaq*) through his submission in absolute true willingness.

The question now is, how can these meanings of indebtedness via the theory of *Al-Mithaq* be of significance in explaining the need for purification, for example in investments? The answer lies in the Islamic conception of the self. The self in the Quran has been mentioned in different level of Man's inner experience such as:

1. Human Spirit (*Ruh*)
2. Soul (*Nafs)*
3. Intellect (*'Aql*)
4. Heart (*Qalb*)

Naquib Al-Attas provides a coherent exposition on how these different modes of the self are seen as the unity:

Thus when it (the human soul) is involved in intellection and apprehension it is called "intellect" ('Aql); when it governs the body, it is called "soul" (Nafs); when it is engaged in receiving intuitive illumination it is called "heart" (Qalb) and when is reverts to its own world of abstract entities it is called "spirit" (Ruh). Indeed, it is a reality always engaged in manifesting itself in all these states.

The self was once pure and clean. Muslims believe in this fact (see Al-A'raf : 175). The covenant that Man, that is, the self, sealed with God in the primordial life implies the self is indebted to the Creator. Man or the self pays the debt by way of submitting his desires to God's Will as embodied in the *Shariah* when Man is born into the physical world.

Man in Islam is the highest creation of God because he is bestowed by the Creator the power of intellect (*'aql*) with which he is able to differentiate right from wrong. At the same time, Man is composed of forgetfulness (*nisyan*), and despite having testified to the truth of the covenant he sealed with God, he forgets (*nasiya*) to fulfill his duty and his purpose. Forgetfulness is the cause of man's disobedience, and this blameworthy nature brings him towards injustice (*zulm*) and ignorance (*jahl*).

Thus, in life (*al-dunya*), the self is inflicted with disturbances that do not allow it to fully submit to the law of Allah as promised. In this manner, the self is surrounded with impurities that further cloud his or her remembrance of the *Al-Mithaq*. These impurities cause the self to lose touch with God and lose the sense of the purpose of existence. Here the self will fall into grief (*shawqawa*). The Quran mentions this very clearly:

> *Verily by declining day, man is in loss (khusrin), except those who believe and do good works, and exhort one another to truth, exhort one another to endurance (Al-Asr 1-3)*

However, when the self strives hard to free itself from impurities (by abstaining from what has been prohibited by God), by way of submitting itself to God's commandment, it will again experience the happiness (saada) it used to enjoy in the primordial stage of life. In this way, cleansing of the self is achievable when the self struggles through life, enjoining the good and avoiding the bad (*'amal ma'afuh nahi mungkar*).

Likewise, investments in *Shariah* stocks are one aspect of man's submission to the Will of God. In wealth creation, a believer is expected to avoid the prohibitions and pursue the alternative means recommended by God. When Man is able to pursue wealth creation in this way, he or she will see that justice is put in place. From the moral and ethical angle, Man will be at ease with himself/herself. This is the level of *nafs muthmainnah* (the contented soul).

In explaining the need for purification of stocks listed in the KLSE bourse, two factors, namely the legal and the ethical factor, can help explain investment behavior of Muslims. The legal factor explains why there is a need to spell out the real nature of *'aqd* (contract) of stock trading.

If the contract (*'aqd*) is valid (*sah*), then the action of buying and selling stocks will receive God's blessing and be rewarded both in this world and the hereafter. These actions are categorized as good deeds (*'amal saleh*). But if the 'aqad is void (*bathl*), investors have committed a sin punishable by God. This desire to secure Shariag legitimacy (the legal factor) is driven by the ethical factor, namely the desire to purify oneself by way of obeying the law of God (*Shariah*). It is an act of submission or enslavement to God as He has given Man life and sustenance. The concept of indebtedness is fundamental to further understand why Muslims desire to purchase stocks that are fully compliant with *Shariah* principles.

Eleven

Can Islamic Unit Trusts buy stock futures index?

The bullish run in the KLSE had many analysts fooled. Many believed the market will break 800, only to see it gone south. However, relatively heavy institutional buying saw the market going up again. It's really hard to say what's going on. Is the economy recovering as claimed? Can we believe in stock indexes and what they imply?

Apart from retail investors, it was institutional buyers who have been hit most by the currency crisis. Unit trust companies for example have seen their investments diminished by more than 70 percent. Many were set up during the economic boom and had their worst day when the index hit the 297 level in September 1997. Although the stock market has gradually recovered, it cannot be taken for granted that it will remain bullish since no one knows what will happen to the economy when the capital control is lifted.

So, how can we prevent our investments from depletion, when no one can accurately predict the future? For example, as the market rises, the question is what stocks to buy? It may look good when the index went up by say, 10 percent but this may have only affected a few blue-chip companies, while the rest remained unchanged or even incurring losses. Is the economic growth driven by these few local companies? Certainly not as economic growth in this country was largely driven by multinational companies with most of their stocks traded in New York, Tokyo, and Hong Kong.

But the essential question will still revolve around risk management. How will unit trust companies protect themselves from making more losses that no one knows how to control?

It is common knowledge that fund managers have long been trying to avoid buying stocks of companies that have weak fundamentals, such as those with poor earning reports, undertaking adverse reshuffling of top management, making unwise restructuring and sales of asset or even reports of union strikes and poor dividends payout. These unsystematic risks in stocks can be avoided through diversification of stock portfolio, although it cannot be eliminated completely.

But it is the avoidance of systematic risk that they could not handle too well. Systematic or market risk refers to the risk of stock price decline as a result of adverse changes in the country's economic or political fundamental, such as volatile interest rate movements, severe trade and fiscal deficits, inflation, etc. In the political front, change in the country's leadership and ruling party also will affect stock prices. Natural calamities also explain the adverse price movement. Without risk management, when stock prices plummeted down, all players will suffer. It is no longer a zero sum game.

In the West, fund managers will usually buy or sell futures contract to protect themselves from systematic risks. Although such a market exists in this country, fund managers are not allowed to trade in futures, even for hedging purposes.

This has exposed them to unwarranted risks that they could have avoided in the first place if they were allowed to trade. However, it was told that many fund managers in Malaysia do not have the knowledge and experience to do so.

Trading in the futures market, for example, in Malaysia normally involves buying and selling an index or number consisting of a basket of 100 stocks represented the Kuala Lumpur Composite Index (KLCI). In a futures contract, the seller and buyer will agree to respectively deliver and take delivery of a commodity, namely the index at a specified date.

It is certainly not the place to describe fully how players gain and lose in index trading, but a short one will do. Let's say Mr. Wan, a fund manager, feels that the stock market will go up and would want to buy more stocks now, but is still afraid to do so, in case prices fall instead.

With the stock futures market at hand, he can protect himself from losses (if indeed prices declined) by buying a future contract today but delivered three months later, say the 15th of August 1999. Let say, the strike price three months later is 760, so Wan will pay $100 X 760 = $76,000. Osman, on the other side a speculator thinks otherwise that prices will fall so he agreed to sell the contract. On the the 15th of August 1999, the KLCI index indeed goes up to say, 800.

So, now the contract Wan is holding is worth $100 x 800 = $80,000. Wan buys low at $76,000 from Osman and delivers to him at $80,000, and thus makes a $24,000 gain. Likewise, Osman losses the same amount, since he has agreed to sell the contract at $76,000. This, in essence, is a classic a zero sum game.

What happens in the above is the hedging exercise has turned into a profit-taking venture. But if prices did fall down, Wan will make a loss, but the actual loss will be relatively big if he went on to invest without using the futures market.

This instrument is indeed very tempting to play with, and Islamic fund managers will find the futures market very useful, especially as a hedging device. However, there are many pressing issues for which they need to find quick remedies, and these are as follows:

1. Can one sell goods that one does not own? This is an important question, since trading of futures contracts involves short-selling. It occurs when one party agrees to sell a future contract consisting of stocks not belonging to him.
2. Is an index or number (namely the KLCI index, say at 720) a commodity and qualify the status of property (*al-mal*)? Does an index constitutes an object of trade (*mahallul 'aqd*) in Islam?
3. The issue of *qabd,* that is taking into possession of the good before resale. In futures trading, a buyer can sell the contract before the expiration or delivery date.
4. Sale of contract before expiration implicates the occurrence of *bay' al-dayn bil al-dayn* i.e., sale of debt for debt. For example, a March contract that expires in July can be exchanged for an August contract that expires in December in the same year.

5. Creation of ambiguities (*gharar*) and manipulation. The impact of the futures market on economies has been on the negative side as it often brings about volatility and instability.

Twelve
Shariah Index and Stock Screening

The religion of Islam allows the sale and purchase of stocks as long as the transaction does not contradict the *Shariah* law. When a company issues a common share, it does so to obtain risk or equity capital from the investing public. Investors who take up these shares are willing to bear the risk of losing their capital in exchange for securing higher returns. Investment in stocks is therefore a profit-loss sharing activity, which Islam rightly enjoins.

There are two types of profit-loss sharing (*'uqud al-ishtirak*) contracts in Islam, namely *al-qirad* or *al-mudarabah* and *al-shirkah* or *al-musyarakah*. Islamic law, therefore, requires investors to participate in risk-taking (*ghorm*) if they wish to earn profits, as doing so prevents the occurrence of economic injustices. Two legal maxims (*Qawaid Fiqiah*) on risk-taking supporting this view are given below:

1. *"Al-Ghormi bil Ghonm"* (No rewards without risks)
2. *"Al-Kharaj bil Daman"* (No guarantee on profits)

Apart from risk-taking (*ghorm*), which also means no guarantee on profit-taking, Islamic principles of investment in stocks require the production process of issuing companies to be free from prohibitive elements, which the Quran has made explicit; namely interest (*riba*), gambling (*maisir*), intoxicants (*qimar*), and pork .

Shariah scholars have prepared guidelines on the valuation of stocks from a legal perspective:

1) Production Approach
2) Capital structure Approach
3) Income Approach
4) Asset Approach

By using the production or activity approach, a stock is declared permissible (*halal*) when the production of goods and services by the issuing company is free from the explicitly prohibitive elements of *riba*, gambling, intoxicants, pork and its derivatives. In Malaysia, the Securities Commission applied the term "*Shariah* consistent stocks" to indicate the nature of Islamic label given to stocks that have passed through the screening system successfully.

To apply the production approach, the output of issuing companies is classified into ten groupings or sectors, namely:

1. Consumer products
2. Industrial products
3. Constructions
4. Trading/services
5. Finance
6. Hotels
7. Properties
8. Plantations
9. Mining
10. Technology

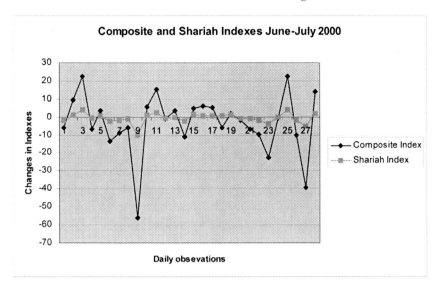

Figure 7.2 *Shariah* and Composite Index

A direct screening will show that almost all finance stocks are not *Shariah* consistent as the main instrument of business is based on the payment and receipt of interest. Consumer products such as alcoholic beverages and pork or pork-related derivatives are also not *Shariah* consistent. Hotel and other service business in which the selling and buying of liquor constitutes a major part of business will also not pass the *Shariah* screening.

The *Shariah* Board of the Malaysian Securities Commission has set up guidelines on Islamic stock investment based on the above information. As of October 2003, 799 listed companies were declared *Shariah* approved. This encouraging development saw the launching of the Kuala Lumpur *Shariah* Index (KLSI) in August 1998 to help investors gauge the performance of *Shariah*-linked counters. The above diagram shows that a positive correlation exists between changes in the Composite and *Shariah* Indexes. That is, ups and downs in the Composite Index are seen in the *Shariah* Index as well. A Pearson correlation = 99.4 percent is found significant, although changes in the Composite Index look definitely more volatile than the *Shariah* Index.

Such behavior is expected, since the numbers of counters that represent the Composite Index is a lot higher than the *Shariah* Index. At this juncture, the *Shariah* Indexes are not much of a help to Islamic portfolio managers who must now look at individual *Shariah* counters for a good buy.

Certainly now, more indicators should be created to help Islamic investors find the appropriate means to diversify their portfolio. Even when stocks traded are *Shariah* consistent, an Islamic view of investment in common stocks does not end here. Islamic investors, especially retailers, are not encouraged to purchase and sell stocks for speculative purposes, since the business of speculation is not their line of work.

In Islam, speculation is an everyday event. People whose life depends on trade and commerce speculate daily. That is, they purchase goods at cost price, hoping or speculating to sell them at a higher price. Speculation in this sense is permissible in Islam, since it fulfills the legal requirement of a sale contract. However, for people whose line of work is not business, the practice of speculation may lead to gambling (*maisir*), because they are simply taking chances.

As such, stock purchases in Islam must be made on the basis of a sound investigative system of stock valuation. This is the *Tabi'* (nature's way) dimension of Islamic stock investment, as a contrast to the *Shariah* dimension discussed earlier.

So, in stock trading, an investor must make proper valuation of the company it intends to partner with. For example, they must make use of financial and company indicators in making decisions to invest.

These fundamentals must be observed closely. Failure to do so ultimately leads to losses and is like committing a sin, since the investor fails to uphold his role of a trustee of God-given bounties.

The basic principle of investment in Islam is that wealth belongs to God, and Man is entrusted, i.e., given the *amanah* (trust), to look after it in the best manner possible on the basis of rules and regulation ordained by God.

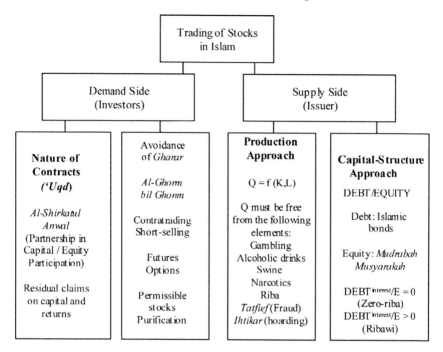

Figure 7.3 Trading of Shares in Islam

In doing so, man must not put wealth to waste by way of unwise investment decisions. He is expected invest wealth in the most efficient manner. The Holy Prophet Muhammad (*pbuh*) once said, "Whenever you make anything, pay special attention to its beauty and finesse." On another occasion, the Prophet (*pbuh*) said, "the best among you is he who when given a task, does it beautifully."

Thirteen
Shariah Stock Screening

Since the incident of September 11, the growing interest on the religion of Islam can mean two things. On one side, it concerns more antagonism against Islam and the Muslim people, while on the other— curiosity about the true meaning of Islam. Either way, the impact of Islam on geopolitics and economics before and after the bombing has been momentous. For example, before September 11, interest in global Islamic investments has been robust, with Dow Jones and London setting up their respective Islamic Indexes. Financial planners are also keen to know how they can advise clients on Islamic investment products such as Islamic stocks, bonds, mutual funds, insurance, money market instruments, and fixed deposits.

However, it is in the investments in stocks that had brought both great excitement as well as enormous grief. It is common knowledge that stock markets have brought tumbles and fumbles in the advanced and emerging economies alike. Usually, the stock market serves as a medium where surplus and deficits units met, thus fueling economic growth from a fresh injection of equity capital. But it can be used by the same people to make bets, thus making the stock market their personal casino.

As a way of life, Islam provides rules and guidelines governing the sale and purchase of equities. However, a systematic understanding of stocks from an Islamic perspective is necessary. This can best be acquired by first looking at contractual aspects of stock trading. But we must begin with a brief look at the *Shariah* before indulging in the mechanics of legal rulings.

Literally, *Shariah* is defined as the "path or road leading to the water" i.e., a way to the very source of life. It is God Who is ordaining the Way where Man is to conduct his life, spiritual, mental, and physical to realize His Will. The submission to the Divine Will includes both faith and practice, from prayer and fasting to legal and social transactions.

When God lays down the law for mankind, it is for a noble purpose. That is, *maqasid al-Shari'a* or the objective of the *Shari'ah* is to preserve five things: the preservation of religion (*din*), of life (*nafs*), of reason (*'aql*), of descendants (*nasl*), and of property (*al-mal*). For example, in preserving the religion, the five daily prayers (*solat*) were made compulsory to the believers (*mukallaf*). To preserve life, providing *nafaqah* (spending on oneself and family) is an obligation on all married man. To preserve reason, man is enjoined by the Quran to seek knowledge (*'ilm*) while at the same time, the Quran forbids the consumption of intoxicants. To preserve the family, the Quran enjoins the institution of marriage but forbids fornication and adultery. Finally, to protect property, the Shari'ah enjoins man to work (*khayr*) for a living while prohibiting wealth creation by way of interest (*riba*), fraud (*tatfief*) and gambling (*maysir*).

To sum up, the Shari'a is built on two basic principles, namely: the removal of hardship (*ra'f al-haraj*) and the prevention of harm (*daf' al-darar*). This has direct bearing to the Quranic verse that, "God never intended to make religion a means of inflicting hardship" (22:78) and "God intends to make easy for you" (4:28). Thus, when the five things (*darurah*) are well preserved, man's attention will not go into disarray, that is one hand rejecting Divine values (hedonism) and the other rejecting the worldly living. On this ground, it is important to recognize efforts to introduce *Shariah* screening on stock and portfolios such that the *darurah* is always preserved and protected.

THE SHARIAH

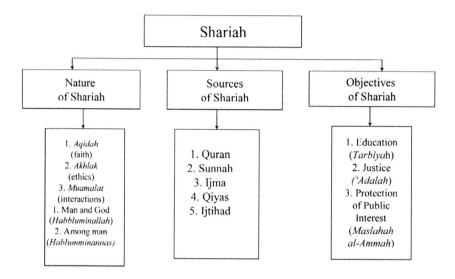

Figure 7.4 The *Shariah*

In general, screening stocks along *Shariah* values can be made in two ways.

a) First, it deals with the nature of contractual agreement taking place between the issuing company and investors.

b) Secondly, it looks at the nature of production and financial activities observed by the issuing party.

On the first approach, the trading of stocks in Islam essentially involves the contract of sale (*al-bay'*) since what is taking place is the exchange of assets (shares) for money. A share certificate is evidence of one's ownership of assets. Although the ownership is only fractional, it gives the owners the right to participate in profit-making, such as determining company policy by way of appointing company directors.

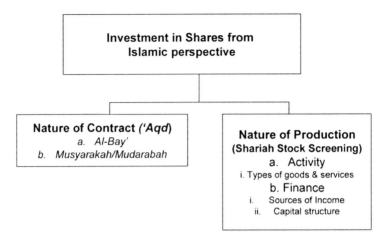

Figure 7.5 Investment in *Shariah* Stocks

Thus, at one point, selling and buying of shares is associated with buying and selling of assets. However, the type of contracts actually applied in stock trading remains unclear. In the above, the contract of *al-bay'* seems fitting, since a share certificate is seen to represent assets or property (*al-mal*) that is taking part the production process. In the contract of *al-bay'* the *al-mal* constitutes the subject matter of contract (*mahallul 'aqdi*). But in stock trading, no physical transfer of assets from the buyer to the seller is evident. In addition, investors do not really know which particular asset they actually own from the share purchases.

Also, a person who purchases a common stock does not resemble an ordinary consumer or merchant who respectively buys goods for consumption or trading purposes respectively. So, using the contract of *al-bay'* may not be an accurate one, to say the least.

Investment in stocks can also be better understood by way of applying profit-loss sharing principle (PLS). When a company issues a common stock, it does so to obtain risk or equity capital from the public. Investors who took up these shares are willing to assume the risk of losing their capital in a hope to obtain higher returns. Investment in stocks is therefore a profit-loss sharing activity, which Islam rightly enjoins.

In share purchases, it seems that the contract of *musyarakah* is more relevant, since it deals with partnership in capital. That is, the investors and issuing companies constitute the equity holders and thus, participate in profit sharing.

When the contract of *musyarakah* is applied in stock investment, the spirit of cooperation (*ta'awun*) requires both investors and issuers to put some degree of commitment in the business ventures. That is, both parties should stay together during ups and downs. To that effect, contra-trading seems to go against the *musyarakah* spirit, since this involves exiting the partnership when an opportunity to enjoy a capital gain is sight.

In this sense, contra-trading has brought some ethical (*akhlak*) implications to the *musyarakah* framework. Even though law and ethics do not mix in legal contract, the contract can become voidable if it explicitly specifies the special covenants pertaining to exit policy.

In profit creation, Islamic law requires people to participate in risk-taking (*ghorm*). Risk is defined as the variation of outcomes arising from uncertainty. In Islamic law, two popular legal maxims (*Qawaid Fiqiah*) are most useful, as they highlighted the constructive role of risk-taking in wealth creation, namely: a) No rewards without risks—*"Al-Ghormi bil Ghonm"* and b) profits must be accompanied with liability *"Al-Kharaj bil Daman."*

Apart from risk-taking (*ghorm*), Islamic principles of investment in stocks requires companies to produce goods and services that are free from the elements prohibited by the Quran. This is where the second approach to stock screening is applied. The prohibited goods and services are given as follows:

a. Interest (*riba*): contractual increase over capital loan.
b. Gambling (*maisir*): speculative or aleatory contracts in which obligations and benefits accruing to participating parties are not fully defined at the time when the contract became effective leading to either winning or losing arising from mere chance instead of work and effort.
c. Uncertainty (*Gharar*): ambiguities in contracts involving contracting parties and the subject matter, which can lead to disputes and unjustified gain.
d. Intoxicants (*qamar*): consumption of alcoholic beverages, which can impair the intellect (*'aql*) leading to irrational behavior.
e. Consumption of pork.
f. Illicit sex (*zina*): sexual relation outside marriage which annihilate the sanctity of the family system (*nasl*).

However, there are a number of *Shariah* approved companies whose activities are not totally shielded from the prohibited elements. To further filter these companies into the *Shariah* approved list, the *Shariah* Advisory Council (SAC) of Securities Commission have applied several additional criteria such as:

a) The *haram* activities must be very small compared with the core *halal* activities.

b) The image of the company in the public eye must be good and well-behaved.

c) The core activities of the company are important to the economy and considered providing general benefit (*maslahah*) to the people.

d) The *haram* element must be very small and tolerated on the basis of common plight (*umum balwa*), custom (*'urf*) and rights of the non-Muslim community acceptable to Islam.

e) The level of contribution of interest income received from interest-bearing fixed deposits and financial instruments such as bonds, bills, and money market instruments must be less than 5 percent of total revenue.

The *Shariah* Advisory Council (SAC) of Securities Commission has set up a guideline on Islamic stock investment bearing the above information. The April 2003 list shows that 81 percent or 704 of the total 804 companies listed on the Kuala Lumpur Stock Exchange (KLSE) are *Shariah* approved. This encouraging development saw the launching of the Kuala Lumpur *Shariah* Index (KLSI) in August 1998 to help investors gauge the performance of *Shariah*-linked counters.

Offshore, the Dow Jones and Islamiq.com Islamic indexes provide a wholesome approach to the screening process. However, the three approaches, although not identical, were able to observe three main areas in the screening process. Here, *Shariah* scholars have prepared a guideline on the valuation of stocks from a legal perspective. The Islamicity of stocks can be determined using the following methods of valuation:

1. Activity or Production Method: By using the production or activity approach, a stock is declared permissible (*halal*) when the issuing company produces output or products that are free from the prohibitive elements of *riba*, gambling, intoxicants, pork, and pornography. *Shariah* stock screening by the Securities Commission Malaysia, Dow Jones Islamic Index, and Islamiq.com follows these guidelines well.

2. *Income Method*: Income derived from reserves and investment securities must be free from interest. One example is placing reserves in interest-bearing bank deposits. Income receivables must not contain interest (*riba*). Income receivables are bills owned by customers who buy on credit, which the firm expects to collect in a relatively short time. First, the credit sale may require the firm to impute interest charges due to the delay in payments. Second, firms seeking loans may use accounts receivable as a security. This is known as the assignment of account receivable, in which the payments and receipts of interest as *riba* has also taken place. The Dow Jones Islamic Index is the most conservative here. Companies that hold cash and interest-bearing securities exceeding 33 percent of total assets are excluded from the index.

3. *Capital Structure Method*: By capital structure we mean composition of debt and equity in capital mobilization measured by the debt/equity ratio. Given a debt/equity ratio, one can know the amount of debt the issuer uses as capital. The bigger the ratio, the more dependent is the bank on debt financing with the payments and receipts of interest fully implicated. Full compliance, however, is not possible today. Islamic scholars have prepared a cleansing or purification system in which the impurities, say, *riba* can avoided by giving it away as charity (*sadaqah*). In this way, stockholders will not be directly associated with *riba* or other prohibitive elements accompanying the dividends and capital gains earned from investments, if any. On the leverage factor, a debt/equity ratio of less than 45 percent will claim Islamic legitimacy while Dow Jones Islamic Index at less that 33 percent.

Apart from capital gains arising from secondary trading, another issue to examine is the types of assets the corporation owns. It is common knowledge that a company holds both current and fixed assets. Current assets shall consists of cash, accounts receivable, inventories, and investment securities, while fixed assets often take the form of company building premises, plant, and equipment. Profits are created out of these assets as the entrepreneur combines them with skills and expertise acquired from labor.

Fourteen
Islamic share-trading and dot-com companies

According to most *Shariah* scholars, the trading of stocks in Islam is permissible, since what is taking place is the exchange of assets for money. A share certificate is a documentary evidence of one's ownership of a company, namely ownership of assets. Although the ownership is only fractional, it gives the majority owners the right to participate in profit-making such as determining the board of directors.

Thus, at one point, selling and buying of shares is comparable to buying and selling of assets. However, the type of contracts actually applied in stock trading is not clear.

In the above, the contract of *al-bay* seems fitting, since a share certificate is seen to represent assets or property (*al-mal*) that takes part in the production process. In the contract of *al-bay,* this is called the subject matter or *mahallul aqdi.*

But the ability to participate, say in the election of the board of directors seems to indicate that a person who buys a stock is not like an ordinary consumer or merchant who respectively buys a particular good for consumption or trading purposes. So, using the contract of *al-bay* may not be an accurate one, to say the least.

However, prevailing discussions on stock trading seem to confirm that *al-bay* is the correct contract to use rather than partnership, namely

419

mudarabah and *musyarakah*. This is because the permissibility of stock trading, among others, is explained by the composition of assets that the stock certificates represent.

As a refresher, *Shariah* scholars have prepared some guidelines on how one can assess the Islamicity of a stock. First, using the production approach, a stock is permissible (*halal*) when the issuing company produces output or products that are free from the elements of *riba*, gambling, intoxicants, pork, just to name a few.

Secondly, any income derived from reserves and investment securities must be free from interest. Thirdly, income receivables must not contain *riba*. On the input side, the debt/equity ratio must comply with some *Shariah* standards.

Certainly, full compliance is not possible today. So, the scholars have prepared some kind of cleansing or purification system where the impurities say, *riba* can be given away as charity (*sadaqah*).

In this way, stockholders will not be receiving any form of *riba* and *haram*-related elements in their dividends and capital gains, if any.

Speaking of capital gains arising from secondary trading, another issue crops up; namely the types of assets the corporation owns. It is common knowledge that a company holds both current and fixed assets. Current assets shall consists of cash, accounts receivable, inventories, and investment securities, while fixed assets often take the form of company building premises, plant, and equipment.

Profits are created out of these assets as the entrepreneur combines them with skills and expertise acquired from labor. *Shariah* scholars have agreed that stocks must contain at least 55 percent fixed assets to justify trading and negotiability. Even though the 45 percent balance is cash, the *qawaid fiqiah* that says the majority has precedence or has chosen over the minority, making it permissible to trade in stocks and common shares.

The main issue here is *riba*. If the company holds no fixed assets but only cash, then the stocks one is holding represent money. When they—i.e., stocks—are traded at a premium or loss, this amounts to *riba* to either party, since money can only be exchanged at par. Since a common share represents an asset and when all assets are held in cash, it follows that trading of shares must only be done at par value. Otherwise the taking and receipt of *riba* will be implicated.

Finally, in stock trading, pricing is influenced by many things. How much reserves, i.e., cash and the value of fixed assets the company holds are two common factors. Another important determinant is the expected cash flows arising from future markets and operations. Often this has to do with intangibles and goodwill.

At this juncture, *Shariah* scholars must address the problems arising from the so-called "new economy," and the trading of stocks issued by the mushrooming dot-com companies. These companies have become successful upon listing in the stock market. Fresh ideas and intelligent logistics help attract investments in a busload. Amazon.com is a good example. Although it has yet to show profits, the company hit a peak of US$13 billion (RM49.4 billion) at one time, although it recently dipped to US$6 billion (RM22.8 billion) as a result of the fallout at NASDAQ.

One common feature of the dot-com companies is the lack of assets, namely plant and equipment. All they need is a space with a computer system plus people who can play around with new and genuine ideas about making a good marketing job. And what they are strong at is the ability to command huge potential future earnings, which often excites investors.

So, when the contract of sale (*al-bay*) is applied in this context, in which the subject matter (*mahallul aqdi*) must consists of fixed assets up to 55 percent or even 51 percent of total assets, the dot-com companies may not qualify at all. Certainly there are a lot of Islamic-based global fund managers who have invested heavily in these dot-com companies recently. Perhaps they can discuss this matter further with their respective *Shariah* panels and let us know the *Shariah* rulings on these dot-com companies.

Fifteen
Islam and Financial Derivatives

Legal opinions on financial derivatives are usually made by Muslim jurists (*fuqaha*). They are responsible for making *fatwas* (legal rulings) on whether investment in derivatives is *wajib* (obligatory), *sunnat* (optional) *makruh* (discouraged), *mubah* (permissible) or *haram* (prohibited). Existing guidelines on financial derivatives generally relates to interest rates and forex swaps. Stock derivatives, financial futures, and options will be soon be introduced, says the Security Commission. Be that as it may, the whole story is about financial risk management—how to protect oneself from speculative risk.

But what action can we take when these derivatives are used by speculators to make money instead? Naturally, there is a need to regulate their activities. Here ethics will take center stage when someone wishes to understand the Islamic viewpoint about financial derivatives. But is that all? What about the legal point of view?

Let's see what financial derivatives can do to us. I will use stocks as an illustration. Two broad stock derivatives are the stock futures and options. They do not have a direct claim on the real asset, but on another security, which is the common stock itself. To understand how they work in the real world requires an understanding of the economic principles that tie the market prices of these derivatives to the underlying asset.

Basically, futures and options are contracts traded on a securities exchange. To evaluate how they stand in Islam requires an understanding of Islamic contract theory (*nadhariyatul 'uqud*). Before that, a brief explanation of the nature of futures and options contract is necessary. This is important because the *muftis* and *ulamaks* need to know what the contracts actually are before making the necessary *fatwas*.

In spot or cash market transactions, which involve both financial and real assets, assets are delivered immediately. In a futures contract, the call for the purchase or sale of financial or real assets is made at some future date, but at a price, which is fixed today. In other words, the owner is obligated to purchase the asset from the seller at the agreed on price and future date. The contract also specifies the agreement to deliver the asset at the agreed on a date normally called the *delivery date*.

In short, a futures contract is simply a delayed purchase or sale of a spot asset. For example, Larry buys a futures contract which obligates him to pay $15 on 15 February, 1995 for one Telekom share. Suppose the spot price is $17. On the delivery date, the share price goes up to $20. So, his gain is $2 per share ($17 - $15). But if the price falls, say to $13, he will lose $2 per share ($15 - $13).

So how one does decide to buy a futures contract will depend on his perceptions about future price movements. Futures contracts are mainly speculative in nature. In fact, most speculators do not trade futures in order to physically receive or deliver the underlying spot asset. This is one problem area in evaluating futures in Islam in which the objectives of the contract (*maudlu'ul 'aqdi*) must be clearly spelled out.

What if the person wants to sell the contract before the delivery date, in view of fear that the price will fall? Here, one can buy an option contract. The option contract allows the person the right—but not the obligation—to buy (a call option) or sell (a put option). Thus, in the present case, he may buy a put option. So, if the price really falls, he will exercise his option not to complete the transaction, which means avoiding actual losses.

To buy the option contract, he pays premium, whether he makes a gain or not. For example, the person buys a call option on a stock index for $100 in March 1995. The current spot index is quoted at $120. The price of the call option contract is $5. What about when the index rises to $130? Surely, he will exercise his right to buy the index, and the option writer is obligated to provide him with one unit of the index. So, his net gain will be ($130 - $120) - $5 = $5. If the index falls on the expiration date, he can exercise his right not to buy the index and his net loss is $5; that is, the cost of the call option contract.

What really happened in the above is a transaction of stock indexes. Does the *Shariah* consider stock indexes as wealth and property (*al-mal*) so that it becomes an object of trade (*mahallul 'aqdi*)? This is another gray area. Indexes are numbers while the underlying assets, namely common stocks, are asset or property (*al-mal*). Lastly, we can see that people who buy options do so to hedge against adverse price movement. Hedging is normally practiced by companies engaged in real production where price changes could adversely affect profits. Will hedging and speculative behavior invalidate a contractual agreement in Islam? This is because although one buys an option for hedging purposes, the selling party is always a trader. Many say that speculators are important to the derivative markets as they provide liquidity. But does speculative buying actually destroy one important pillar of contract, namely the objective of the contract (*maudlu'ul aqdi*)?

Sixteen
Qabd and Futures Contract

Fund managers who invest in futures on behalf of their Muslim clients may want to know the Islamic point of view about futures trading. To the authorities, decision made to set up new and sophisticated systems of wealth creation should at least acknowledge their ethical and moral implications on society.

Since *akhlak* or ethics is a core component of the Islamic faith, the need to know to what extent new financial products would impact the Islamic faith and the Muslim people is logical. This is because in Islam, knowledge about things, as vividly explained by Hussein Nasr, is supposed to increase wisdom, increasing the depth of understanding God's signs (*ayat*) and His creation in relation to Him and the perfecting of the human soul. Any gain of "information" that takes man away from these goals of knowledge would mean taking a step backward against progress.

On the position of futures trading in Islam, the first issue is ownership (*milkiyah*). That is, the seller must own the object of sale (*mahallul 'aqdi*). This will ensure that once the goods are delivered, a buyer become the legal owner of the traded object. The main spirit here is to avoid ambiguities in the agreement, otherwise the contract will be declared void. Owning what one sells removes *gharar* in the contractual obligations.

The second issue is possession (*qabd*). Literally, *qabd* means taking or holding something in one's hand. In its juristic sense, *qabd* implies legal custody and possession in a priority capacity, even if it does not involve the physical act of holding.

427

Thus, a seller may own the asset, but it does not necessarily mean that the object he owns remains in his possession. But one of the requirements of a valid sale is that the seller cannot sell the object he owns until it is in his possession.

In the case of futures trading, the purchaser of the futures contract—who can either be an investor or speculator—can sell the contract before the expiration date. It is evident that he does not have possession of the commodities traded. So, would such practice be allowed in Islam?

A look at two Prophetic *hadiths* may help us see what the subject of *qabd* is about. 'Abd Allah Ibn 'Umar has reported that the Prophet (*pbuh*) said: "He who buys foodstuff should not sell it till he has received it" (Al-Bukhari). Ibn 'Abbas has also reported the following *Hadith* from the Prophet (*pbuh*): "He who buys foodstuff should not sell it until he has taken possession of it." Ibn 'Abbas said: "I think it applies to all other things as well." (Al-Bukhari)

Islam is a simple way of life and it will be so in the conduct of business affairs. Certainly, the above *hadiths* would not mean that physical possession of all types of objects are required to fulfill the requirements of *qabd*.

If one owns a house in Penang and plans to sell it in Kuala Lumpur, would Islam require the contract to be concluded in Penang simply because the house must be in his possession? Or if he owns a delicate instrument that cannot work well if moved, would you insist on the *qabd* or the requirement of physical possession? That is why the Hanafi and Hanbali schools of thought are of the view that possession is not a requirement in the sale of real property as there is no fear of destruction or loss.

In fact, the main message of the *hadiths* is not physical possession per se, but the avoidance of ambiguities (*gharar*) in the contract. This is confirmed by a recent resolution of the Fiqh Academy that the *'illah* or effective cause of the prohibition of sale prior to taking possession (*qabd*) is *gharar* which consists of potential failure to deliver.

The buyer runs the risk of not receiving the goods, as the seller may delay the delivery or wish to revoke the contract. But these may not be the order of the day in both financial and commodity futures trading as the market participants are guided by stringent rules and regulations, thus eliminating *gharar* elements in the delivery system.

SECTION EIGHT

ISLAMIC BONDS

One
Global Islamic bonds worth a look

The economic crisis in Asia is now fast moving into a critical stage, where economic and financial sector restructuring efforts may not bear fruits if the real sector is not pushing hard enough to achieve efficiency.

Earlier, the economic bubbles in Asia caused by hot capital inflows have shown that corporate borrowers do not have to worry about their internal rate of return (IRR), since high liquidity leads to lower cost of capital. Normally, companies will borrow or invest when the IRR is higher than market interest rates. Likewise, if interest rates exceeded the IRR, no investment will take place. With excess funds available to be taken up at any price, the fundamental economic question—"what to produce" is forgotten as a more exciting thing to do then was to produce anything as long as there is abundant cheap capital.

Excess supply of funds, therefore, makes way for complacency. Idealistic entrepreneurs went shopping for new products and technologies in the West and reproduce them at home, as this is very easy to do when cheap loans are easily accessible. Invention and innovation then took a back seat when money seems to be the only precursor to production.

But lack of market research has brought unwarranted corporate failures. Market is found saturated and cash flow is slow. Earnings took a big plunge, easily explaining why enough foreign investors don't stay longer.

Most companies today acquire capital from borrowing as well as equities. In a captive market scenario, project finance firms will look for debt rather than issuing new stocks. Debts are superior to equities, as it prevents dilution. If successful, debtors are able to secure a larger piece of the cake. But when financial disaster hits the economy, say, due to a banking crisis, the remedy was to reduce bank loans; to cut down bank lending. This brings us to the question of bond issues and the renewed attempt by the government to borrow via the foreign bond market.

As Malaysia too has expressed her interest to become Asia's leading Islamic financial center, Islamic bond issuance should be given an opportunity to take a fair share. Opportunities in the Middle East market or even tapping savings of Muslims residing in the U.S. and Europe are wide open. But how much financing does Malaysia really need today?

It is common knowledge today that Danaharta and Danamodal require RM15 billion and RM16 billion respectively. Infrastructure development fund and allocations for the Seventh Malaysia Plan have amounted to RM31 billion. But funds received so far, as reported, were only RM20.18 billion, mostly from Japanese sources.

The Rating Agency of Malaysia (RAM) said about RM18 billion to RM20 billion is expected to be raised using private debt securities. This is possible, given an estimated RM32 billion sitting idle in our local bank deposits. As Malaysian banks today are flush with liquidity, Malaysian entry in the global bond market is seen as a new strategy to test its market value.

Malaysia, as reported, intends to issue up to RM7.6 billion of sovereign bonds initially with a thinner spread, compared with the RM7.6 billion it planned to raise in 1998. Islamic bonds may not be in the national agenda presently, but in case Malaysia finds it difficult to raise any significant amount, it is worth looking at the second best solution.

The *Shariah* allows bond sale and trading at par value, since this is equivalent to doing *al-hiwalah* (debt transfer). However, when a debt certificate (*shahdah al-dayn*), say initially priced at RM1000, is sold for RM900 (in the case of an Islamic zero coupon bond), the extra RM100—according to Middle East jurists—amounts to usury or *riba*. Likewise, bond purchased below par and redeemed at par value also saw the phenomenon of *riba*. So issuance of the Malaysian styled Islamic zero coupon bonds may not be acceptable to these investors.

The second issue is the process of securitization itself that saw an intensive application of the controversial contract *bay' al-'inah*. Again, this is not welcomed by the Middle East jurists and investors alike. So where do we go from here?

One way is the issuance of the *mudarabah* bonds fully guaranteed by the government. But how can this be possible when the *rabbulmal* is given capital guarantee by *mudarib*. This will go against the principle of the *mudarabah*. The development of the government guaranteed *mudarabah* bond requires close and undivided attention, solely to avoid any potential conflict with the prevailing thinking of Muslim investors in the Middle East countries.

Two
Bay' al-Dayn and Islamic bonds secondary trading

Islamic approved investments are not only confined to investment in *Shariah* stocks but also Islamic bonds. These bonds are in short supply in view of the increasing demand for Islamic instruments by newly-formed Islamic mutual funds, takaful companies and the expanding Islamic banking business. In 2002, both government and private corporations have raised RM14.5 billion from Islamic bonds issuances. The term "government Islamic investments (GII)" is associated with government Islamic bonds issued to meet banks' liquidity requirement. Bonds issued by corporations are called "Islamic private debt securities (IPDS)."

KLIA Airport Berhad, for example, issued more than RM2 billion *al-bai-bithaman* ajil notes issuance facility (BAIDS) to finance the construction of the Sepang Airport and the Formula One circuit. The PUTRA light railway is also financed by Islamic bonds.

Since both are mega-projects, it is a worthy way to make Islamic bonds known to the public. What an Islamic bond really is and of what significance it is to national development are some good questions for which the public would want simple answers.

A bond is essentially a debt instrument that carries a contractual promise to pay the lender a specified amount of interest or coupon. An Islamic bond adopts similar features. Since the former is a *riba* phenomenon, in what way does an Islamic bond operate to guarantee both capital and returns but still claim Islamic legitimacy?

Theoretically speaking, a contract of debt in Islam can only guarantee the repayment of capital but not the return; but as a debt instrument, Islamic bonds today are able to guarantee investors some specified nominal returns. The process is rather complex to the layman, but it is worth the time to understand how these bonds are structured. This I will now explain.

First, a bond issue means a sale (*al-bay'*) of a financial asset. A bond is a debt instrument. A debt is a right to future cash payments. When someone sells a bond, he holds the right to collect current payments in return for more future payments. So, bond issuance and their subsequent trading implicate the sale and purchase of debt. Islamic bonds behave in similar fashion. They deal with the selling and buying of debt at par, as well as at a discount.

In Islamic commercial law, debt (*dayn*) can be traded only at par under the purview of *hiwalah* (transfer of debt). To profit from a debt trading, however, it is not logical to sell a bond at par value without any coupon attached. Since Islamic bonds are sold for a profit motive, it is hard to imagine they would be are traded at par value in the secondary market.

One way to guarantee that contractual coupon is to do the following. The mode of payments is made via bond issues. There are two forms of bond issues, namely primary notes (PN) and secondary notes (SN). The former represents the capital component, while the latter the profit component. To qualify the PN and SN as an asset so that it can be sold at any price just like any sale does, the debt must be supported by an underlying asset, say plant and equipment, stocks and land. In other words, if the new bond issues are worth RM200 million, then it must be backed by at least the same amount of underlying assets.

Once this is done i.e., securitizing underlying assets will see the assets turning into notes and certificates (i.e., PN and SN) equivalent to an object of trade (*mal mutaqawwim*). To earn the fixed coupon, investors can redeem the secondary notes at par value on maturity. Likewise, the primary notes are redeemable at par value on maturity. In this way, the Islamic bonds are sold to the issuer at par value on different maturities.

For zero-coupon Islamic bond, if it was initially purchased below par, say $950, then it can be sold again at $980. The $30 profit is considered lawful (*halal*) since what is taking place is not an exchange of money for money but a sale of an asset for cash. Apart from BAIDS, MuNifs (*murabahah* notes issuance facility) are also popular for short and medium term investments. In essence, these are fixed coupon bonds with relatively no attachment to the variation in interest rates.

The *bay' al-dayn* issue is serious to the Islamic banking and finance movement, as it is not about minor details of religious practices (*furuq*) but sadly dealing with the fundamental (*usul*) of religion. This time it is *riba* or usury.

But one who opposes *bay' al-dayn* must not be overwhelmingly brutal to say that it is *haram* outrightly, since some types of *bay' al-dayn* are indeed permissible, while others are not. For this reason, it is critical to put things straight. This means getting back to basics.

In *fiqh muamalat,* debt (*al-dayn*) is a payable right arising from a transaction, services, or loan. This right includes deferred payment of *murabahah* sale, deferred payment of dowry, as well as rental payments to be collected at the end of the month.

First, sale of debt (*dayn*) at par value is permissible since this is equal to the exchange of equivalence for equivalence (*mithlun bi mithlin*). And the debt must be a confirmed debt (*dayn mustaqir*). Sale of debt at par value can take place between the debtor and creditor, or more specifically sale of debt by the creditor to the debtor (*bay' al-dayn lil mad'in*). For example, bond redemption (i.e., on maturity) at par value is permissible. It means sale of debt by the creditor (i.e., bondholders) to the debtor (i.e., issuing company) in return for cash payment is permissible as long as the debt is equal to the payment in cash.

Secondly, sale of debt by the creditor to a third party (*bay' al-dayn lil ghairil mad'ine*) is not permissible. This is because the sale can either be made at a discount or premium. In this way, exchange of non-equivalence in money has taken place. For example, the creditor (i.e., investor) is forced to sell at a discount the bond for liquidity purposes. A bond worth $1,000 was sold for $930 cash. That is, debt ($1,000) is exchanged for money ($930). Since debt is also money, the above sale is said to contain *riba*. This time, the *riba* is the difference between debt value and cash value. However, sale of debt by the creditor to a third party is permissible if it is sold at par value. But no non-debtor will buy debt from the debtor at par value. This is because as a speculator, the non-debtor or the third party will only buy the debt if he can make some capital gain from it.

Likewise, the third party who is a speculator can sell the bond at a profit before maturity. Earlier, he may have bought the bond because he is certain that interest rate is falling. If interest rate indeed declined, bond prices will increase. So, if bond price goes up to $980, he makes $50 in capital gain. On the other hand, if he chooses to hold the bond till maturity, the he can certainly gain from the previous sale. That is, when he buys the bond for $930, he will redeem the bond on maturity at par value, thus making $70 in profit. A speculator will always buy and sell bonds for capital gains. In Islam, capital gain cannot be acquired from the exchange of money for money.

The Islamic jurists (*fuqahas*) at the Shariah Advisory Council (SAC) of the Securities Commission have made the trading of debt at a discount or premium as permissible (*halal*) In 2003, the trading of Islamic private debt securities (IPDS) increased by 59.7 percent to RM60.7 billion from RM38 billion in 2002.

Lastly, the *Shariah* allows sale of debt at a discount between the debtor and creditor. This can happen if the creditor (i.e., investors) is in need of money and would like the debtor (i.e., issuing company) to pay up earlier than scheduled. Under *dhawwa ta'ajal*, the creditor can ask the debtor to pay early but with an incentive i.e., to pay less than the total loan. *dhawwa ta'ajal* means *pay less for early settlement*.

Bay' al-Dayn (Sale of Debts)

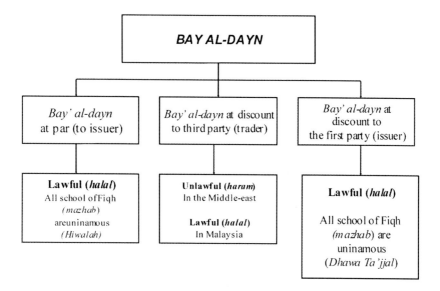

Figure 8.1 Types of *Bay' al-Dayn*

Three
Al-Ijarah Munthahia Bittamleek Syndicated facility

Kumpulan Guthrie Bhd has secured a RM1.5 billion *al-ijarah munthahia bittamleek* syndicated facility from seven banks as bridging finance for its acquisition of Holdiko Palm Plantation in Indonesia. Repayment of the *al-ijarah munthahia bittamleek* will be made from Holdiko's operating cash flow.

Al-ijarah munthahia bittamleek means leasing ending with ownership. A transfer of ownership of the leased asset will take place at a terminal date specified in the contract. *Al-Ijarah munthahia bittamleek* is also sometimes known as *al-ijarah wa iqtina or al-ijarah thumma al-Bay.*

Let us first look at the meaning of *al-ijarah*. It is defined as the ownership of the right to the benefit of using an asset in return for consideration. In the contract of *al-ijarah*, four basic principles must be observed, namely:

1. The agent of contract (*tharafail 'aqdi*)—lessor and lessee must be rational and not acting under duress.
2. The objective of contract (*maudu'ul 'aqdi*)—sale of usufruct (*manfaat* by the lessor to the lessee.
3. The subject matter of contract (*mahallul 'aqdi*)– the consideration (rent) and the benefit (*manfaat*) from the use of the asset.
4. Offer and acceptance (*ijab & qabul*)—expression of the two contracting parties' desire by way of the offer made by the owner of the asset and an acceptance expressed by the lessee.

441

The lessor's obligation includes making the leased asset available, guarantee in respect of defects, and maintenance of leased asset. Prior to that, it is of utmost importance to ensure that the lessor is the legal owner of the leased asset. Otherwise, it will contradict the *Hadiths* of the Prophet Muhammad (*pbuh*), "Do not sell what you do not own." The term "sell" also means the right to use and dispose one's asset and this includes *al-ijarah* as well.

From the above Hadith, it is implied that *al-ijarah* is not a financial lease, but rather an operational lease. In the former, the lessor holds a beneficiary ownership. This is a normal practice in hire-purchase and term financing, where the bank places a charge on the asset bought. What this means is that no transfer of title has taken place from the seller of asset to the lessor. The lessee has no legal right to dispose of the asset and can only do so when full repayment is made. It is purely a term loan where interest is charged on the amount of facility granted.

Al-Ijarah Munthahia Bithamleek
(Leasing ending with ownership)
(Lessor must hold ownership title)

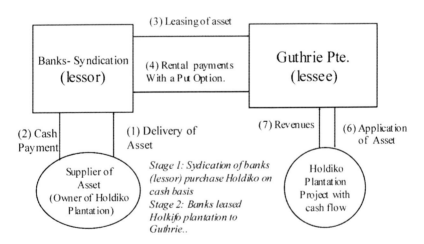

Figure 8.2 *Al-Ijarah Munthahia Bitamleek*

On the contrary, operational or true lease involves outright purchase of asset by the prospective lessor. He will hold the risk of ownership, namely the risk of asset price depreciation.

As a lessor, he is also expected to undertake some maintenance obligation. As such, the rental payments he continuously receives over the leasing term contain the element of *'iwad* (equivalent countervalue).

According to Ibn 'Arabi, "any increase without an equivalent countervalue (*'iwad*) is *riba*." Likewise in *al-ijarah*, any rental collected without *'iwad* is *riba*. The *'iwad* element in *al-ijarah* are ownership risk and maintenance.

Once the issue of ownership is settled, *al-ijarah* can take a new form. For example, the contract of *al-bay'* (sale) can be executed following *al-ijarah*. One well known hybrid is *al-ijarah munthahia bittamleek* or *al-ijarah wa iqtina*, which is a lease in which the legal title of the leased asset will pass to the lessee at the end of the lease.

There are four types *al-ijarah munthahia bittamleek*. The same applies for *ijarah wa iqtina* and *ijarah thumma al-bay'*. The transfer of ownership is conducted through:

1. Gift (transfer of legal title for no consideration).
2. The transfer of legal title (sale) at the end of a lease for a token consideration.
3. The transfer of title (sale) at the end of a lease for an amount specified in the lease.
4. The transfer of title (sale) prior to the end of the lease term for a price that is equivalent to the remaining ijarah installments.

By *Shariah* standards, Islamic hire-purchase via *al-ijarah munthahia bittamleek* is an operating lease. The ownership of the asset remains with the lessor i.e., the owner of asset. *Al-ijarah munthahia bittamleek* is not a capital or financial lease where the lessee is viewed as the owner of the asset and has to show the asset on his balance sheet.

The issue now is finding out whether the Guthrie case has fully observed the above *Shariah* guidelines. Figure 8.2 shows the true version of *al-ijarah munthahia bittamleek* . If the bridging finance provided for by banks to Kumpulan Guthrie fits into the model, then it is safe to say that Guthrie's *al-ijarah munthahia bittamleek* syndication facility is *Shariah* compliant.

Four
Structuring Islamic bonds:
Role of Bay' al-'Inah

In the early years of Islamic banking in Malaysia, people had a hard time understanding—if not pronouncing—names such as *al-bai-bithaman ajil*, *murabahah* and *mudarabah*, but somehow we gradually got used to these unfamiliar terms. Now *al-bai bithaman ajil* is simply called BBA, *sukuk al-ijarah* is known as *Sanif* and so on.

Recently, a few more new names came out, like those mentioned in Bank Negara's guidelines on Islamic money market. These are *bay' al-'inah* and *bay' al-dayn*. Some may wonder what *bay al-'inah* and *bay' al-dayn* really stand for. Non-Muslim practitioners must be having difficulty handling these terms, especially when little is written about them, particularly for the layman.

I now will help explain the meaning of *bay' al-'inah* and *bay' al-dayn*. First, let me say their application in banking and capital market is quite huge. For example, all Islamic personal financing products run on *bay' al-'inah* (INAH). *Bay' al-dayn* is widely applied in money and capital market instruments such as Islamic accepted bills, negotiable Islamic certificates of deposits, Islamic treasury notes, and private debt securities.

So, knowing these two contracts is pretty important, especially when going global is no longer an option. When traditional portfolio investments are fast leaving the country, the reversal factor must come from global Islamic funds.

445

It is worth noticing that international Islamic portfolio fund managers are mostly advised by Middle Eastern Muslim jurists, most of whom belong to the Maliki, Hanbali, and Hanafi schools of thought.

Malaysians are predominantly Shafi'. So, if the Malaysian Islamic system is Shafi' oriented, does it mean our products are also compatible with Middle Eastern standard? This we must investigate. One way is to investigate the nature of *bay' al-'inah* and *bay al- dayn,* as they are among the most popular. Let me explain what they stand for.

Normally, INAH is used to obtain cash, just like getting a loan. Using a plain BBA can only end with a purchase or ownership of an asset. It does not help people who want money. However, cash must be acquired through an interest-free loan (*qardhu hasan*), but not available commercially. As a business entity an Islamic bank seeks to maximize profit, so giving away *qardhu hasan* does not make sense.

Since the bank is willing to finance any transaction at a price and customers are ever willing to pay this price, Islamic banks devise a product that give people access to cash without implicating *riba.*

There is a fairly easy way to do this. Suppose Mr. Salleh wants a $10,000 loan and he is willing to pay a price but does not want to do it via *riba* loan.

ISLAMIC PERSONAL FINANCING
Model 1: Bay' Al-'Inah

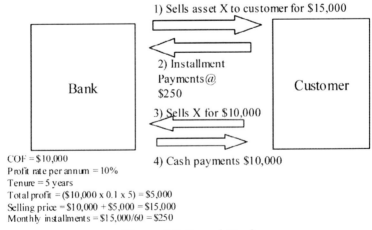

COF = $10,000
Profit rate per annum = 10%
Tenure = 5 years
Total profit = ($10,000 x 0.1 x 5) = $5,000
Selling price = $10,000 + $5,000 = $15,000
Monthly installments = $15,000/60 = $250

Figure 8.3 *Bay al-'inah*

446

To do so, the bank sells asset X to Mr. Salleh at a credit price, say $15,000, which he pays by installment. Then, instantaneously, Mr. Salleh, who now owns asset X, sells it back to the bank for $10,000 cash.

Now Mr. Salleh gets the $10,000 in cash, while the bank makes a $5,000 profit over the period of financing. Both get what they want without implicating *riba*. The deal only applies to a sale and purchase (*al-bay'*) contract, namely a) *al-bay' bithaman ajil*, b) *al-bay mutlak* (cash sale), where the credit sale is followed in sequence by the cash sale. See Figure 8.3 in the above.

Now, let's see what Muslim jurists have to say about this deal. Strictly speaking, juristic opinions can be divided into two, namely those represented by a) Hanafi, Hanbali, and Maliki schools and b) that of the Shafi' school.

According to the first group, what matters most is the implicit or real intention of Mr. Salleh and the bank who were both willing to pay and accept interest respectively but do it using the contract of buy and sell (*al-bay'*). This is because, as the Quran has commanded, *al-bay'* is an alternative to *riba*.

But *al-bay'* under one version known as *Bay' al-'inah*, is used to bypass *riba*. Mr. Salleh is not interested in using asset X for consumption purposes. And the bank knows that very well. On this point, it is worthy to look at the eminent jurist Ibn Taimiyyah, who divided sales into three groups executed according to the buyer's intentions, namely:

i)   that he purchases the goods in order to use or consume them such as food, drink and the like, in which case this is sale, which God has permitted.

ii)   that he purchases the goods in order to trade with them; then this is trade, which God has permitted.

iii)   that the reason for purchasing the goods is neither the first nor the second, then the reason must be dirhams (money) which he needs, and it was difficult for him to borrow, so he purchases the good on credit (with increased dirhams) in order to sell it and take its price. This, then, is 'inah which is Haram according to the most eminent of the jurists.

Based on these arguments, the contract of *bay' al-'inah* is considered invalid (*bathil*). In Middle Eastern countries, it is application of *bay' al-'inah* in the Islamic banking business does not exists.

Five
Islamic bonds: Fixed Coupon and Capital Protection

The positive note of the Capital Market Master Plan (CMMP) on Islamic banking will further boost the growth of the Islamic bond market. A well known megaproject, KL Sentral and Putra Jaya have heavily used Islamic bonds to mobilize capital from institutional investors, Islamic and non-Islamic alike. Certainly, this is only logical. Why should Putra Jaya Holdings opt for interest-bearing bonds, when only conventional investors can buy them?

The question now is why an Islamic bond in Malaysia is well-received by both Islamic as well as mainstream investors. The answer has a lot to do with the structuring issue. On this point, I will further explain the nature of Malaysian Islamic bonds and the role of *bay' al-'inah* and *bay' al-dayn* in making Islamic bond issues a success story in Malaysia.

Recall that the contract of *bay al-'inah* generally involves using two contracts of sale applied in sequence, namely spot and deferred (credit) sale. It is a necessary condition for Islamic bond issues and constitutes a fundamental element in determining *Shariah* legitimacy.

As we also know, a bond is a loan given by a creditor to a debtor. Unlike banking loans, obtaining a loan using bonds is cheaper. Although the transaction cost can be higher, interest rates paid by an issuer are much lower than bank loans. This is because funds are acquired directly from creditors, namely the investing public.

From a bond issue, a debt is created consisting of the principal amount and coupon payments to subscribers. Within the capitalistic financial system, a loan that one obtained has a price, namely interest. A coupon bond is one in which interest or coupon is paid over time as the price of capital.

For example, if the face value of bond X is $1,000 with a coupon rate of 5 percent per annum, then the interest income is $1,000 x 0.05 = $50. For a five-year bond, bondholders receive $50 annually plus $1,000 upon redemption on maturity.

It is now clear that a bond investment guarantees capital protection and a contractual income. An Islamic bond investment also provides the same features. Investors will receive a contractual income plus a guaranteed redemption of capital. How this is possible is interesting to see.

Laymen and market watchers must take note that the term *"al-bay'"* meaning trading or commerce or sale, signifies the alternative to the payment and receipt of interest as *riba*. The Holy Quran says, "God has allowed *al-bay'* (trade/commerce) but forbids *riba*." (Al-Baqarah :275)

Bay' Al-'Inah Islamic Bonds (BAIDS/ABBA) (Sale Buyback)

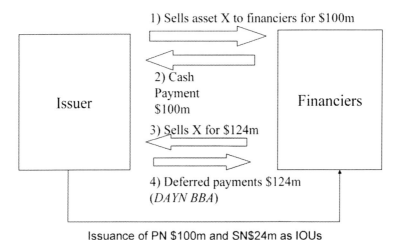

Issuance of PN $100m and SN$24m as IOUs

Figure 8.4: *Bai-bithaman Ajil* Islamic Debt Security

450

Therefore, anything that uses *al-bay'* as opposed to debt in profit creation is lawful; implying that as long as an Islamic bond is free from taking or giving interest or implicating itself with an interest-bearing debt or loan, it constitutes a legitimate *Shariah* instrument.

Using the contracts of *bay' al-'inah* and *bay' al-dayn* for Islamic bond issues is vital to claim *Shariah* legitimacy, at least in Malaysia. Using these contracts will make it possible to guarantee investors a contractual income and capital redemption. The *Shariah* Advisory Board of the Securities Commission (SAC) has approved sale of debt (*dayn*) at a discount.

In principle, structuring Islamic bonds usually involves three main steps:

1. ***Bay al-'Inah* asset securitization**: Here, two sale contracts (a buyback sale) will be applied in sequence. That is *bay' al-inah* = spot sale + credit sale. Firstly, a spot sale (*bay' mutlak*) is executed. If the issuer wants to raise, say, $100 million, assets worth this amount will be identified and subsequently sold to investors on cash basis. By doing so, the issuer gets the $100 million in cash.

   Secondly, a credit sale is concurrently applied. Here, investors sell back the underlying assets to the issuer on credit, with the price no longer at $100 million, but higher. If investors want an 8 percent profit margin per annum with a three-year tenure, the selling price should be $100 million + $24 million = $124 million. The underlying asset can be anything as long it has value. It ranges from plant and machineries to concessions awarded by the government.

2. **Issuance of bond certificates**: The payment by issuer to investors via BBA sale is made through the issuance of debt certificate (*Shahdah al-dayn*). Technically, this simply means a bond sale is underway. But a bond is only a piece of paper evidencing a debt obligation. How could one in Islam sell a piece of paper (i.e., bond certificates) for $1,000?

   The answer lies in the juristic debate on the sale of debt (*bay' al-dayn*). The Malaysian jurists say that these papers are equivalent to property (*al-mal*). This is because they say that the the transaction leading to the issuance of debt papers is supported by some underlying assets via the *'inah sale*. Since property has value, it can be sold at any price.

451

For example, when issuance involves a zero coupon Islamic bond, it is sold at a discount (i.e., less than face value). An Islamic coupon bond, such as the KL Sentral ABBA, is sold at par value. Redemption at face value has been the main attribute of ABBA bonds.

Practisioners have also use the concept of Islamic securitization to justify the legitimacy of Islamic bonds. However, there seems to be some misunderstanding as to what actually constitutes Islamic securitization. At first impression, it looks as if the securitization of underlying assets is conducted by the issuing company for the new Islamic bonds issuance. However, upon closer look, no securitization of underlying asset has taken place. Instead, practisioners and regulators seemed to agree that the new bond issuance is coming from the securitization of debt obligation (BBA receivables) by the issuing company. This seems quite perplexing because asset securitization means securitization of asset by its owner. However in Islamic coupon bonds, Islamic securitization is turned upside down. This time, it allows the debtor to securitize debts it does not own.

It seems what actually happen is the plain issuance of debt certificates by the issuer as an evidence of indebtedness, which is also a norm in conventional coupon bonds. No actual securitization of asset has really taken place as commonly found in asset-backed securitization. Not withstanding the impending controversy on the issue of Islamic debt securitization, it is however important to understand how Islamic coupon bonds are able to guarantee both profits and income. This is discuss below.

The question now is how in ABBA investors are guaranteed profits and capital, a common feature found in conventional bonds. This will be explained as follows:

a) **To guarantee repayment of capital, primary notes (PN) are sold to investors at par value redeemable on maturity**. Primary notes represent the capital component of the bond issues. In our example, $100 million of BAIDS will be sold back to the issuer on maturity for $100 million cash. This is *bay' al-dayn* at par value.

b) **To guarantee payment of profits, secondary notes (SN) are sold at par value, redeemable annually or semi-annually.** For example, $24 million will be paid by installments over a period of three years. With secondary notes maturing every six months, investors will receive $3.98 million in cash. Again, this is *bay' al-dayn* at par value. Redemption of secondary notes at par value is equivalent to *bay' al-dayn* at par value.

Each primary is represented by more than one secondary note. For example, if the ratio of primary notes to secondary notes is 1:10 , then 500,000 primary notes support 5 million secondary notes. In this case, each primary note will cost $1,000 (i.e., $100,000,000 / 100,000) while each secondary note is worth $48 (i.e., 24,000,000/5,000,000).

Al-Bai Bithaman Ajil Islamic Debt Security (BAIDS)

1st Stage

Cost of financing: $100 million
Annual profit rate: 8%
Underlying asset: Land and building
Issue Date :   5th February 2001
Maturity: 5th February 2004

Tenure: 3 years

Total profit: $100,000,000 x 8% x 3 = $24 million
Selling price = cost of financing + profit margin = $124 million

2nd Stage

Number of Primary notes :   100,000 units
Price per unit : $100,000,000/100,000 = $1000
Number of Secondary notes: 50,000 units
Price per unit: $24,000,000/50,000 = $480
Semiannual profit payments: $3.98m approximate $4.0 million

Redemption of secondary and primary notes

1	6	12	18	24	30	36
•	•	•	•	•	•	•
$0m	$4m	$4m	$4m	$4m	$4m	$4m + $100m

Figure 8.5 Primary and Secondary Notes in *Al-Bai-Bithaman Ajil* IDS

It is worthy to note that *bay' al-dayn* at par value is permissible. All *fuqahas* agree on this point, including those from the Middle East. However, the Malaysia *bay' al-dayn* is supported by *bay' al-'inah*. Jurists from the Middle Eastern countries have rejected *bay' al-'inah,* as the contract is considered invalid. In this way, *bay' al-dayn* in Malaysian Islamic bonds are not well accepted in the Middle East, even though these bonds are sold at par value.

3) Bond Trading: For liquidity purposes, the need for trading is vital. Equally important is capital gains arising from trading. Since Malaysian jurists at the supervisory level agree that a bond paper is property (*al-mal*), sale of primary notes at discount and premium is allowed both in trading and initial public offers (IPO) . In other words a debt (*dayn*) can be sold for cash at par or more or less than the face value.

This is the Malaysian view, but we need to appreciate the Middle Eastern outlook as well. Remember, going global on raising fund campaigns must consider Middle East juristic opinions too. Otherwise, we will have to contend with local funds, and thus putting more strain on the economy.

Six
Some viewpoints on Bay' al-'Inah

A bond is actually the present value of future income streams arising from a) coupon interest payment to the maturity dates and b) its par value on maturity. These future income streams are contractual in nature. Apart from selling Islamic bonds at a discount involving *bay' al-dayn*, the Malaysian Islamic bond has yet another problem. It applies *bay' al-'inah* to make the contractual coupon payments lawful.

It may sound academic to discuss *bay' al-'inah*, but rarely it is openly discussed in many Islamic banking seminars held in Malaysia. It is a taboo of some sort. The *bay al-'inah* contract involves a cash sale of a fictitious object by, say, Mr. Ibrahim to someone, say, Mr. Ali, who needs the cash. The same object is then sold by Mr. Ali to Mr. Ibrahim at a higher price payable in the future either by installment or lump sum. Thus, the *'inah* sale may consists of two parts, namely a spot sale as well as a credit sale *(al-bai-bithaman ajil)*.

In the Islamic bond market, repayments are made by issuance of Islamic bonds, one of which represents the contractual coupon profits known as secondary notes. This is only possible by way of the *'inah* sale. However, there is no intention of either party to utilize the object of sale from which some form of usufruct or *manfaat* should be realized. For example, we buy food or medicine in order to protect the family from hunger and sickness respectively.

But we will never buy them for, say, decorations, as this is not a sensible thing to do. In *bay' al-'inah*, the object of sale is made to exist only to fulfill the requirements of contract (*'aqad*) as the buyer has no intention to use the object of sale (*mahallul 'aqdi*). Likewise, the seller too is interested to conclude the deal, as doing so brings profits to the bank. He can only make a loan with a contractual extra payment. However, both will not enter into a contract of debt bearing a contractual returns, but will use the contract of sale (*al-bay'*) to achieve the same end as any profits made from sale is deemed permissible (*halal*) in Islam.

Now, some may say the intention of the buyer and seller is not sincere, as there is no real intention to consume or utilize the object of sale. The object (*'ain* or *'in*) holds a mere fictitious function. This transaction is pursued only to legalize making loans with interest. At least this is what many Middle Eastern jurists have been saying all along.

Whatever suspicion one has about *bay' al-'inah*, the Shafi' school of *fiqh* still considered a legal and valid contract. The Shafi' school says the intention or *niyyah* is not a significant element in determining the validity of a contract. This is the viewpoint taken up by the *Shari'ah* scholars in Bank Negara and the Securities Commission.

However, the *niyyah* element is a crucial factor in the *Hanafi, Hanbali,* and *Maliki* schools. E.E. Rayner summarizes this debate with much grace, some of which is quoted below. Interested observers can find more details about this *'inah* sale in her book *The Theory of Contracts in Islamic Law*.

Rayner said that "although all transactions forming the *'inah* contract are correct in themselves, when put together they merely mask a loan with interest which is prohibited in Islamic law according to the rules of *riba*." Therefore, the *Hanbali*, in accordance with their principles and taking into account of the illegal nature of the contract, condemn the *'inah* contract and regard it as null and void.

The *Shafi's* regard it as perfectly valid on the basis that one has the right to sell an object at a diminished price to that which he himself paid (i.e., Mr. X sells an object worth, say, $1,000 for $800 cash to Mr. Y and buys it again from Mr. Y at $1,000 payable by installment). The *hilah* exert no influence on the validity of acts with the *Shafi's*; accordingly the *'inah* sale is regarded as perfectly valid within the *Shafi's*' school. The *Hanafis* are not unanimous in their decision regarding the *'inah* sale. Abu Hanifa himself admits only the case where the third party buys from the buyer to resell to the seller.

ISLAMIC PERSONAL FINANCING
Model 2: Bay' Al-'Inah

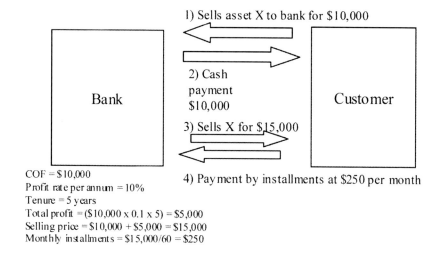

1) Sells asset X to bank for $10,000

2) Cash payment $10,000

3) Sells X for $15,000

4) Payment by installments at $250 per month

Bank

Customer

COF = $10,000
Profit rate per annum = 10%
Tenure = 5 years
Total profit = ($10,000 x 0.1 x 5) = $5,000
Selling price = $10,000 + $5,000 = $15,000
Monthly installments = $15,000/60 = $250

Figure 8.6 *Bay' al-'Inah* Financing

Muhammad al-Shaybani, however, regarded the *'inah* sale as valid, but he categorizes it as blameworthy (*makruh*). The status of the *'inah* contract in the majority opinions of the *Maliki* school is less tolerant; *'inah* sale is not approved of, but it nevertheless forms a valid contract." The central issue here is none other than the distinction between real and declared intentions. Rayner further says, "It may be concluded that the *Malikis* and *Hanafis* give due effect to the real intention or *niyyah* of the parties, but that as regards illicit motives both schools are reluctant to make such an uncertain element as motive a dependent factor of a legal act.

"The Hanbali School however, always gives precedence to real intention over declared intention. Indeed, in the *Shafi'* school, this is not just a tendency but a doctrinal stance. Wahbah Zuhaili reasserted the Shafi' school preference for declared intention over real intention as a means to protect the stability of contracts (*istiqrar al-ta'amul*). If contracting parties are required to put their real intention into writing, it will bring economic transactions into disarray as nobody can know for certain what is contained in the heart of others.

The importance of declared intention over real intention is critical. It is for this reason, we see the contract of *muta'* or contracted marriage as invalid since both parties have declared their intention of divorce or separation after an agreed period of marital life. However, the *nikah* contract of similar marriage in which no declared intention is made is considered valid, even though his real intention is to marry the woman only for a short while, after which he will divorce her.

One good example, of a contract that may look despicably immoral but still valid in the eyes of the *Shariah* is the case of *cina buta* (*nikah muhallil*) as it is called in Malaysia. Here, a man has divorced his wife three times, leaving him with no rights to reconciliation or remarrying her again. However, he can do so only if she is divorced, after marrying another man. This is the only legal way to marry his ex-wife again. To do so, he will assign or pay a man known as the *muhalil* (or the *cina buta*) to marry her, but with a directive to divorce her right away and prohibiting him from exercising his rights as a husband, say in consuming sexual relations.

The real intention in this marriage is not to observe the objectives of marriage but only to play with contract technicalities. This contract is found valid in the *Shafi'* school because no declared intention is evident to invalidate the principles of marriage. The religious officer (*kadhi*) who performs the marriage (*nikah*) has practically no idea what is going on. He assumes the marriage is a normal one. But the contracting parties knew well what is going on!

Many people will definitely find this act disgusting and immoral. The *Malikis* and *Hanbalis* prohibit this shameful contract, as both schools give due effect to the real intention. Having said all this, one can easily see now that *bay' al-'inah* falls in the same category.

Seven
Can local Islamic bonds go global?

Malaysian Islamic bonds have always been under heavy scrutiny by the Middle Eastern jurists. The jurists have been critical on the Malaysian way of doing Islamic finance. The application of *bay' al-'inah* and discounting based *bay' al-dayn* in Islamic bond issuance is one such example.

At a recent conference on Islamic economics jointly organized by the International Islamic University and the Islamic Development Bank, these issues were again raised. But due to time constraints, the matter was left unresolved, which leads many to believe that I have fully endorsed the instrument.

Certainly this isn't my job. We usually rely on the *Shariah* experts to make endorsements. Worse still, some local newspapers seemed to have misunderstood the paper and reported a misleading conclusion.

Let me now explain this one more time. A bond is a debt (*dayn*), defined as the right to claim the money one has lent out. This debt can be traded or transferred at par value—meaning that a bondholder can sell his right to collect payments to someone else without involving a discount or a premium factor. In essence, this is *Al-Hiwalah.*

But, selling or buying debt at a discount or premium is unlawful, since this amounted to a contractual increase or decrease involving money or currency. This is equal to *riba*. The *Shariah* allows the trading of *dayn* at par value since this is similar to exchanging $1 for $1.

459

The principle of equal for equal (*mithlin bil mithlun*), must therefore be observed when an exchange of debt is conducted, whether the debt is in money or in kind. Doing so will free the contracting parties from *riba al-nasiah* and *riba al-fadl*.

The problem now is how to apply this Islamic principle to the arrays of fixed income instrument found in the market today. A bond is one example. So, how can one structure an Islamic bond where issuers and investors expect to receive similar benefits given by conventional bond investments? This can be explained as follows.

Bondholders possess a legal right to both principal and interest earnings. The legal claim on the capital can be traded at any price depending on the level of interest rates. Long-term investors normally make gains from interest income while speculators seek profits from capital gain.

When a company intends to issue an Islamic bond (i.e., to sell a bond to investors) or to redeem a bond (to buy back a bond), there are two major problems it must overcome. First, the selling and buying of bond must also mean the selling and buying of a commodity or property *(al-mal)* since one of the pillars of contract in Islam requires the object of trade *(mahallul 'aqdi)* to hold real tangible features.

But a bond or *dayn* in the modern sense is not a commodity but right to a future cash flow arising from loan repayments. It is only a legal right to a loan represented by a piece of document in the form of papers and certificates.

A legal right in Islam is not a commodity and therefore cannot become a tradable object (*mahallul 'aqdi*) or therefore, sold at any price. According to the Middle Eastern juristic thinking, Al-Shafi'e has only allowed the trading of debt involving debt in kind but not debt in loans.

In addition to this, debt in kind or debt in commodity is tradable but only in the context of *yadin bil yadin* that is at exchangeable par value. This implies that if Ali owes Yusof ten kilos of wheat and Kamil earlier owes Ali the same amount, then Ali can sell or transfer his debt to Yusof. That is, Kamil can pay his debt of ten kilos of wheat to Yusof. No more and no less.

The question now is how to make the *dayn* in loan (i.e., the bond certificates) to assume the role of a commodity *(al-mal)*. And how then can this translate into making the contractual surplus (i.e., periodic profit payments to bondholders) a lawful gain? It is here that the Malaysian jurists and practitioners find al-Shafi'e's viewpoint on *al-'inah* most applicable. And it is well connected with *bay' al-dayn*. Now, *bay' al-dayn* in Al-Shafi'e's school refers to debt (*dayn*) in kind, but none is mentioned by the Shafi'e jurists about the trading of *dayn* at a discount or *dayn* involving money or currency.

It is here the Malaysian jurists need to further convince us why they allow selling of Islamic bonds at a discount. The Khazanah Islamic benchmark bond is one good example where bonds are sold at discounted value.

To allow the trading of Islamic bonds akin to the trading of assets, the securitization process was applied. It is claimed that this securitization exercise will glue the bond or papers to some underlying asset and thus can automatically qualify itself as property (*al-mal*). By doing so, the bonds can be purchased or sold just like any asset or property. In the worst case scenario, since the bond now is an asset ,some even claimed that it can now be sold at any price agreed upon by both parties. This has allowed Malaysian jurists to conclude that an Islamic bond can be sold at a discount.

But the securitization process can only be made in the pretext of applying *bay'al-inah* contract, which again is not acceptable to the Hanafis, Malikis, and Hanbalis jurists. What happens here is a plain sale-buyback mechanism where a special object that the buyer has no intention to use is used as the the object of trade (*mahallul 'aqdi)*. As an example, the issuer will sell his existing assets worth, say, $100 million to the investor on cash basis.

DEBT (*DAYN*) = PROPERTY (*MAL*)
(Malaysian View)

Since debt = property, the debt can be sold at any price

eg. $100 debt can be exchanged for $80 million cash (discounting)

DEBT (*DAYN*) = MONEY (*MAL*)
(Middle-Eastern View)

Money can be exchanged with money of equivalent value

If $100 million (debt) is exchanged for $80 million (cash) then, the surplus is *riba* (usury)

Figure 8.7 Views on *Bay' al-Dayn*

He gets the cash and goes ahead to do his business. Now the issuer must think of a way to make repayments but in a delayed manner. What kind of delayed payment system is most suitable here? Certainly they can apply the conventional coupon bond model, namely payments of contractual income as an incentive to invest. In *riba*-bearing bonds, this contractual income is simply interest earnings, while in Islamic bonds, they are called profits.

The *'inah* sale will further see a buyback system where now the asset is sold to the issuer at a markup price, say $125 million, with payments to be made in, say, three years.

How this $125 million will be paid will require the issuance of papers, which has now acquired the *al-mal* status. It is *al-mal* because the issuer is presently the legal owner of the asset once the buyback sale is concluded. As a legal owner, the issuer can now securitize the underlying asset into notes, i.e., the Islamic bonds.

The security or notes shall consist of two main components. This mode of payments will see the issuance of primary notes to represent the capital component redeemable upon maturity at par value in bullet form. So, no discounting or premium is attached to this bond redemption.

The other one is called the secondary notes. Each represents the contractual profit components. When it is redeemed on maturity, it uses the contract of *bay' al-dayn* a par value. What we can learn from the above is the ability of issuers to pay investors some contractual coupon payments or profits through the issuance of secondary notes via the *bay' al-'inah* mechanism.

The coupon or interest payment, which is not permissible in conventional bonds, is now permissible via Islamic bonds by way of legal gymnastics. The sale of debt at par value is only made possible through the application of *bay' al-'inah*. But *bay al-'inah* remains unacceptable among most Middle Eastern jurists and investors as the contract is deemed invalid.

Structuring Islamic Papers

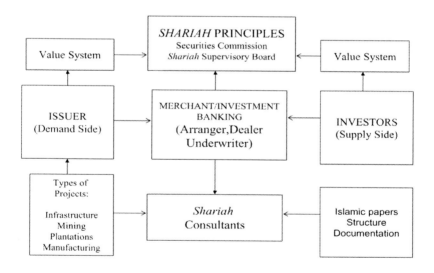

Figure 8.8 Structuring Islamic bonds

Thus, in structuring Islamic papers, practitioners must also think long-term. They must consider possible solutions in meeting new problems when financial liberalization takes off in the coming years. Now, when Malaysia needs to rely on foreign portfolio investments, it must also account for the global Islamic funds. This may imply considering sensitivities of investment preferences arising from differing schools of *fiqh* (*mahzab*).

Eight

Why the Shafi'e School of Fiqh put less importance on Niyyah (real intention)?

Structuring Islamic bonds and their respective initial public offers (IPO) have somewhat relied on *bay' al-'inah*, a contract which is valid according to the Shafi'e school of *fiqh* (*mahzab*). Since the real intention does not count in the Shafi'e' school, *bay' al-'inah* is valid, since nothing explicit on real motive is mentioned in the legal documentations of Islamic bonds. Even though both parties are willing to pay or receive some extra amount on money from a given credit facility (which is tantamount to *riba*), this motive is not put in writing or mentioned verbally. On this basis, the contract remains valid since all principles of contract are fulfilled.

One can relate an infamous example to help illustrate the role of internal (real) and external (declared) motives in contractual obligations. This has a lot to do with the *"cina buta"* analogy (*nikah al-muhallil*).

In Islam, when a man, let's call him Ismail divorces his wife Fatimah three times, he cannot remarry her unless she is married to another man, who later divorces her, or upon his death leaves her a widow. In the case of the former, a legal trick (*hilah*) can come handy. That is, Ismail will pay Iskandar to marry Fatimah but with a condition of divorcing her right after the marriage (*nikah*).

Certainly, the Kadhi (the person who conducts the *nikah*) does not know that Iskandar intends to divorce Fatimah. So, the contract of marriage is valid according to the Shafi'e school since what matters is the external motive rather than the internal one.

But neither one wishes to prolong the marriage, as the real intention of Iskandar and Fatimah is not to live as husband and wife but only to play around with the law in order to get what they want. In this case, Iskandar wants the money and Fatimah wants divorce so that she can marry Ismail again.

If Iskandar declared that he wants to marry Fatimah for only, say a week, then the *nikah* contract becomes invalid since stating so (i.e., declaring his real intention) violates the principles of marriage. It follows that once the real motive that contradicts Islamic law is explicitly made known, the contract becomes invalid. This is the *muta'ah* marriage which is forbidden in Sunni Islam.

However, Imam Shafie does provide a few examples, which invalidate contracts with illegal inner or real motive. One concerns a contract involving the sale of swords by a Muslim merchant to the enemies of Islam. The contract is not a valid one. This has a lot to do with the motive of the buyer who will or can use the swords to annihilate the Muslim people.

Ibn Qaiyyim's Classification of Riba

"Riba is of two categories - manifest, explicit, clear, obvious (*jali*); hidden or implied (*khafi*). Manifest or clear riba has been forbidden for its immense noxiousness an harm. Hidden riba has been prohibited because it is a means (*dhar'ia*) leading to manifest *riba*. The prohibitions of the first is deliberate and intentional (*qasdan*), while the second has been interdicted as a means, *wasilatan*, (leading towards th clear or manifest). Manifest or clear riba is actually riba al-*nasi'a* (in which capital loaned on credit for an increase). In pre-Islamic times, it was of the form in which creditors allowed delay in repayments of loans while debtors increase their loans. The result was that the more repayment of debt was delayed, the more borrowed capital increased, so much so that a sum of one hundred could turn into a sum of many thousands".

(*Ibn Qaiyam I'lam al-Muwaqqi'in*)

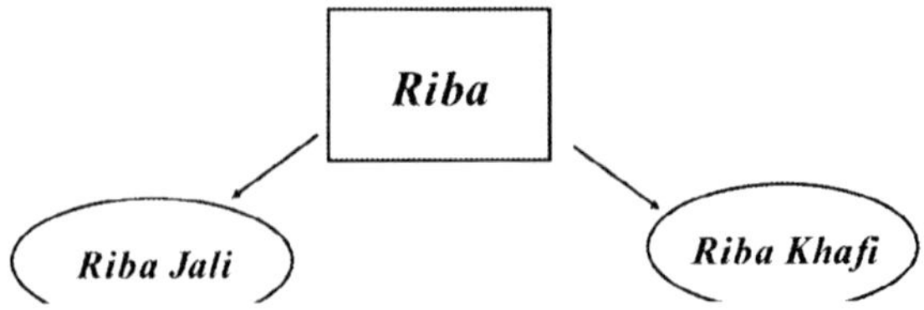

Figure 8.9: Ibn Qaiyyim's Classification of Riba

Similarly, a Muslim cannot sell grapes to a winery, as the grapes will be used to produce a prohibited commodity. Again, the motive element is crucial in determining the validity of a contract.

The only reason why the Shafi'e school of *fiqh* discounted the role of intention (*niyyah*) in sale is simply to provide stability to transactions. The principle of stability or solidarity of contract (*istiqrar al-ta'amul*) that is fundamental in Shafi's *fiqh* methodology. This principle cannot be uphold when contracting parties to declare their intentions for every sale made. When one starts exploring real intentions of economic agents, it will be difficult to ascertain the nature of true motives, since only God knows what is in man's heart. In this way, it will pose hardship to conduct business and economic activities. Even if one contracting party says the truth, there is no certainty what he has said is true in the eyes of the public, since no one except God knows what is in his heart. Must he take a lie detector test to establish that what he put in writing actually reflects his real intention (*niyyah*)?

If the legal system requires that his *niyyah* must be equal to his offer and acceptance (*ijab and qabul*) whether expressed verbally or in writing, the courts must introduce a method of proof to certify them.

How to ascertain that real intention is equal to declared intention? Doing so would be impractical and may introduce more harm than good. It will delay economic transactions and put participating agents into suspicions and anxieties.

For this reason, Imam Shafi'e discounted the role of *niyyah* in determining the validity of a contract, as it may introduce instabilities in business transactions. But in no way is this done by Imam Shafi'e simply to justify *bay' al-'inah*. The *niyyah* factor is made secondary by Imam Shafi'e only to protect the general welfare, i.e., the greater *masalih*. Maslahah is protected when the stability of contract is protected. i.e. the protection of people engaged in business transactions. It is not pursued champion the shameful acts of *tahayyul,* which include *bay al-'inah* and *nikah al-muhallil.* Both constitute a legal device (*hiyal*) that may eventually lead the contracting parties to commit the actual prohibited (*haram*) actions such as *riba* and zina.

For this reason, Ibn Qayyim Al-Jauziah says that the permissibility of *hilah* runs against the principle of *sadd al-dzari'ah* (i.e., blocking the means). Practicing *hilah* will lead the individual to indulge in the actual

SAIFUL AZHAR ROSLY

haram activity (i.e., indulging in *riba*). It does not make sense to see the permissibility of *hilah* when it actually conflicts with the principle of *sadd al-dzari'ah*. This principle aims to block any means or passages that will take the individual to commit the prohibited act. *Bay' al-'inah* is one type of legal device (*hilah*) that serves to make profits without equivalent countervalue and generate income from *riba* without implicating the contract of loan (*qard*).

Nine
Secondary IPDS Trading

With inter-bank rates settling at 3 percent to 4 percent nowadays, liquidity is running high. The three-month fixed deposit, negotiable certificates of deposits, bankers acceptances and treasury bills were all hovering at about 3.4 percent. Therefore, it is not surprising to see the recent three-week bullish run in the stock exchange as investors can find nowhere else to go. With inflation at 4 percent, placing money in fixed income instruments will mean getting negative returns in real term.

Fundamentalists also see the lower interest rates as cost reducing, which means higher corporate earnings. Among other things, this could help explain the surge in the local bourse, not forgetting that herd mentality is also well and here to stay.

At low interest rates, the time is also ripe to shop for cheap credit through bond issuance. ABN Ambro Bank says the market is liquid and the timing is right for corporations and the government to consider bond issues. Naturally, the issuance of PLUS bonds will come as no surprise any time now while improving international ratings on Malaysia's sovereign risks will see new issues of Petronas Yankee bond.

However, when interest rates have finally reached the bottom and started to rise again, bondholders as lenders will find their interest income declining relative to market rates. For example, if today a $1,000 P-Bond pays 5 percent interest or coupon rates per annum, the coupon amounts to $50 per year.

But as market rates increase to 8 percent, alternative fixed income investments, say fixed deposits, will therefore give relatively better yield than the 5 percent fixed P-bond coupon rate. Normally, bondholders who expect further rises in interest rates will sell these bonds at a discount to compensate buyers from the lower coupon payments, thus realizing a loss. This helps explain why bond prices are falling at higher interest rates and vice versa.

But the question is who will invest in bonds when the interest rate is low? Who will lend at low interest rates? Textbook economics says that an inverse relationship exists between bond prices and interest rates. For example, at a market rate of 5 percent, the coupon payment is $50, the bond is selling at $1,000 per unit (i.e., $50 divided by 5 percent). When interest rate rises to 10 percent, the price of bonds drops to $500 ($50 divided by 10 percent). In this way, investors will not purchase bonds when interest rate is falling. No fool will buy high and sell low. What we will see next is who will gain and who will lose when the interest rate is rising.

Normally, if we are looking at a fixed-rate bond issue, the creditor will be the one taking the beating. Debtors have less to worry about because future interest payments are already fixed and safely locked at the old, much lower rate. This is one of the evils of the interest rate system. It takes away wealth from the investors in the most systematic way.

The Quran says, "Do not consume the wealth of the other people by wrongful means" (2:188). The secondary market normally acts as a lubricant to the interest-based system, so that wear and tear is minimized.

Bondholders who want to get out will dispose of bonds at a heavily discounted price, while those who take a long-term view of the market may stay on. In this way, secondary market trading is crucial to supply the liquidity the market needs, but at whose expense?

In the Islamic front, trading of bonds on the secondary market is highly controversial. Even if there is a need to provide liquidity (al-suyulah), it must not be done at the expense of Islamic values. In Islam, it is well known that a debtor can pay the creditor less for early settlement if both parties agree. This is known as Dha'awa Ta'jjal.

For example, Ali gives Yusof a $5,000 loan, payable in two years. But after twelve months, Ali needs the money badly and asks Yusof to pay him back, say only $4,000. Applying the same to bond issues may be problematic because full payment can only be made when the bond matures.

Dha'wa Ta'ajjal (Debt discounting in Early Payments)

Narrated by Ibn Abbas when Rasulullah s.a.w. directed Bani Nadhir to evacuate from Madinah, they said: "there are still debts due to us, then Rasulullah s.a.w. replied: "give discount and asked for early payment"
(Hadiths narrated by Baihaqi)

Figure 8.10 *Dha'wa Ta'ajjal*

Early payments normally do not take place between the issuer and investors unless the bond is callable. So *dha'wa ta'ajjal* cannot be applied between the investors and traders or the third party. Malaysian practices seemed to permit sale of debt (*bay' al-dayn*) at a discount. The over-the-counter transaction requires both parties to agree on the quoted price. Islamic bonds held by investors constitute debts as assets emerging from the BBA transaction. The debt arising from BBA sale was securitized to make way for the issuance of debt certificates (ABBA). The securitization of dayn BBA has entitled the debt certificates to be called property (*al-mal*). Since a property can be sold at any price, ABBA as a property can be disposed at any price agreed upon by the contracting parties. In 2003, the trading of Islamic private debt securities (IPDS) increased by 59.7 percent to RM60.7 billion from RM38 billion in 2002. The higher increase emanated from new issues of IPDS amounting to RM8.1 billion.

Ten
Malaysian Global *Sukuk* Bond

In 2002, the government of Malaysia issued a US$600 million Islamic bond known as *Global Sukuk Al-ijarah* in the island of Labuan. It was an attempt to motivate market players to raise funds via the bond market using instruments readily accepted by global Islamic investors, especially those from the Middle East. The Malaysian issuance was followed by *sukuk* issued in 2003 by the state of Qatar amounting to USD700 million. Next was the USD400 million Islamic Development Bank (IDB) issue in the same year. In 2004 saw the latest issue of USD250 million *sukuk* by the Bahrain Monetary Agency (BMA).

Before getting into the detail of Global *Sukuk,* it is imperative to examine the meaning of *sukuk. Sukuk* is a document or certificate that represents the value of an asset. The Auditing and Auditing Organization for Islamic Financial Institutions (AAOIFI) refers *sukuk* to investment products. It constitutes certificates of equal value representing, after closing of subscription, receipt of the value of the certificates and putting it to uses as planned, common title to shares and rights in tangible assets, usurfructs and services, or equity of a given project or equity of a special investment activity. *Sukuk* is distinguish from shares, notes and bonds as *sukuk* must have an instrinsic value. AAOFI states that investment *sukuk* does not represent debts owed by the issuer or certificate holder. In this manner, *sukuk* cannot be issued from *dayn* or debt receivables. In Malaysia, however the Securities Commission applies all *sukuk* to all securities including shares, notes, unit trusts and bonds, partly because the contracts of *bay' al-'inah* and *bay' al-dayn* are approvd by the Shariah Advisory Board (SAC)

The Malaysian Global *Sukuk* does not apply *bay' al-'inah* and *bay' al-dayn*. No *fictitious* assets were used in the contract. The *sukuk* was structured and arranged by Dubai's Hong Kong and Shanghai banking Corporation (HSBC) and issued in Labuan. The *Shariah* advisory council consists of three prominent *Shariah* scholars (*Fuqaha*). To raise the USD600 million fund, a special purpose vehicle (SPV) is set up as the issuing party. An *al-ijarah* contract (operational/true lease) is applied. The structure is based on the sale plus leaseback model. The government sells a property (i.e. hospital complex) to the SPV. Using the contract of *al-ijarah*, the SPV then leased the property to the government. Rental payments are then collected by SPV and passed on to the investors. The government will buy back the property at the expiration of the lease term and pay SPV in cash. The cash proceeds will be used by the SPV to pay investors upon full redemption of the trust certificates on maturity.

On the supply side, SPV tells prospective investors about the *sukuk* issuance, the structure of the *sukuk*, its risk and return. Trust certificates are issued to investors where they will receive a fixed income arising from the rental (*'ujrah*) payments arising from the leasing business. They will also be given capital protection. This happens when the government purchases the property from the SPV, the proceeds of which will be used to pay investors on redemption date.

The Global *Sukuk* bond is still not free from juristic disputes. One issue concerns the application of *bay' al-wafa* i.e., sale with a promise to buy back. The government sells the property with a condition that the SPV will sell it back to the government at the same price. This is one form of legal device (*hiyal*). In general, the Middle Eastern investors accept the Global *sukuk* bonds, since the disagreements among jurists are not considered serious. A brief summary of the *sukuk* is given below:

Stage 1: Contract of Cash Sale (*Bay' Mutlakah*)
SPV purchases property (hospitals) from the government (1)
(SPV holds ownership right of property)
Government received cash proceeds (2)

Stage 2 : Contract of Leasing (*Al-ijarah*)
SPV rents property to the government (5)
SPV collects rentals. (6)

Stage 3 : During the tenure
SPV passed the rentals to investors (7)

Stage 4: At maturity
SPV sells the property to government (8)
Government pays cash US$600 million (9)

Stage 5: On Maturity - Redemption
Investors redeem the Sukuk (10)
SPV pays investors US$600 million (11)

Figure 8.11 Malaysian Global *Sukuk Ijarah*

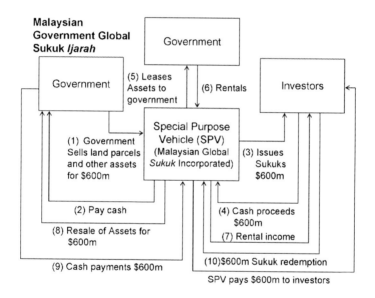

The *Sukuk* is essentially a trust certificate. It serves to mobilize funds to be invested in properties. It is like a property trust fund. The money pooled from investors is used to purchase the property, such as office and residential properties. In the case of the Malaysian *sukuk*, government properties were sold by the government to the SPV. Unlike property trust funds, where incomes are derived from capital gains, the Sukuk focuses on the leasing of property to generate income.

It is common practice to assume that property trust fund is equity in nature. No apparent guarantees are given to income and capital protection. Likewise, the Malaysian *sukuk* is expected to adopt similar risk-return features.

Eleven
Muqarada Bond

In 1983, the government of Jordan via the Ministry of Awqaf, Islamic Affairs, and Holy Places issued an unspecified amount of *al-Muqarada bonds*. The proceeds were used to build shops, offices, and factories on the state *Waqf* land. The properties were rented out to the business population using the *Al-ijarah* contract. The rentals *('ujr)* constitute the profits earned from the venture.

The Jordanian government introduced the Act of the *Muqaradah* Bond in 1983. *Muqaradah* or *qirad* is also known as *Mudarabah*. The latter is a term used by the *Maliki* and *Shafi'e* school of *fiqh,* while the former, the *Hanafi* and *Hanbali* schools. *Muqaradah* or *mudarabah* means an agreement between two parties by which one of the two parties provides capital for the other to work with on the condition that any profits derived are to be shared between them based on a contractual profit-sharing ratio.

The Jordanian *Muqarada* bonds have one unique feature: It provides full capital protection of capital under the *Al-Kafalah* contract. i.e., the government provides full guarantee of the original capital. The Act says that "the Government guarantees the settlement of the nominal value of *muqarada* bonds due to be completely extinguished as scheduled; the sums paid for this purpose become loans to the project given without interest and due immediately after their complete extinction." Further, the Jordanian Law of Muqarada Bonds states that :

1. Documents of definite value issued in the names of their owners against funds they pay to the owner of the project in question

with the object of executing the project, utilizing it and making profits.

2. Entitle the bond owners to acquire a definite proportion of the project's profits, as set out in the bond's prospectus.
3. *Muqarada* bonds neither yield interest nor entitle their owners to make claims.

The salient features of the *Muqarada* bonds which constitute the basic elements of the issuance process are given below:

1. Nominal value of issuance.
2. Description of the project which the issuance proceeds would be used to finance.
3. Project feasibility study.
4. Definition of the grace period required for project implementation.
5. The rate of annual profit distribution between bond extinction and profits due to bond owners.
6. Dates of opening public subscriptions and its closure, as well as payment of profits and maturity of bonds.
7. Any other rule the issuing committee sets up should be added by way of reassuring the investor and safeguarding his rights.

Muslim governments can also consider using the contract of *mudarabah* to finance their deficit. This model is most appropriate for development financing from which incomes generated can be shared among investors. Potential development projects are given below:

a) revitalization of idle lands.
b) revitalization of Waqf lands.
c) construction of residential and business properties for rental purposes.
d) Construction of public utilities (e.g. dams, power stations).

SECTION NINE

ISLAMIC INSURANCE

One
Islam and Risk Management

Risk management is about controlling of the possibility of losses arising from pure and speculative risk. Financial derivatives such as futures and options, as well as commodity trading are the main instruments used today in managing speculative risk. They provide liquidity and hedging mechanism to protect traders and producers from adverse price movement.

Risk management in the insurance business deals with pure risk. It serves to transfer pure risk from the individual to the insurance operator. There are many issues in Islam relating to risk management. One issue concerns the instruments applied in managing risks – whether the application of derivatives and insurance are permissible (*halal*) in Islam. To examine this issue in more detail, a critical observer is expected to understand the meaning of risks and uncertainty in Islam. The same applies to the insurance business.

In *fiqh* literature the term *gharar* is associated with risks and uncertainties in contractual agreements. When this is true, it is rather silly to say that risk management is about managing *gharar*. In fact, *gharar* must be avoided at all cost. Risky or *gharar* sales (*bay' al-gharar*) banned by the Prophet (*s.a.w*) include selling fishes in the ponds and birds in the sky. Managing *gharar* is therefore not an accurate thing to say about Islamic risk management.

Here one needs to look at the issues one at a time. First, one is dealing with forward futures and option trading, i.e., a contract to buy or sell a commodity and financial instrument at some date in the future. What needs to be done now is to see whether *gharar* is evident in these contracts. To do so, one must have knowledge about the principles of contract (*'aqd*) in Islam and to see that no ambiguities or uncertainties (*gharar*) are contained in them. But this is not what modern as well as Islamic risk management is all about.

Like conventional risk management, Islamic risk management deals with risks and uncertainties of business outcomes. Islam condones *gharar* i.e., risks in contractual obligations, but acknowledges the presence of the same in the outcome of business and investment. But this time, the correct term to use is not *gharar,* but *ghorm. Ghorm* comes from the legal maxim *al-ghorm bil ghonm* meaning *no pain no gain.*

Risk (*ghorm*) that one finds in business activity can mean two things, namely market and financial risk. The former deals with price, regulatory, operating, commodity, human resources, legal, and product risks, while the latter refers to credit, liquidity, currency, settlement, and basis risk. Market risks are a law in nature (*hukm tabi'*) whose outcome none other but God can know with precision. Also known as systematic risk, man cannot control market risk. The opposite is true for financial risk, also called unsystematic risk.

Because man cannot predict the future with precision, variation in business outcomes constitutes the risk they cannot avoid. However, man can strive hard to manage these risks to minimize adverse impacts. For example breakdowns in technology, commercial failure of a supplier or customer, political interference, or a natural disaster are additional potential risks all businesses must face.

Islamic risk management must not jump onto the bandwagon to endorse prevailing instruments like commodity and financial futures. It should first identify the type of business where risks are inevitable. As an example, in real production, firms are faced with risks and uncertainties of cash flows. That is, the outcome of the business is not known. The business can either succeed or fail. Failure can be caused by pure as well as speculative risks.

But no company can find a party that can insure it against losses arising from speculative risk. A sole proprietor can buy a life insurance policy to cover his debt in case he dies prematurely. A manufacturer can buy palm oil forward contract to ensure that volatilities in oil palm prices will not affect his profits when production begins in the coming months. But no company will insure another business against loss arising from market risks. Can a RM100 million new business pay an insurance company a certain premium in return for compensatory damages if the business fails to take off?

The question now is twofold. First, protecting oneself against pure and speculative risks warrants the use of instruments that may contain the elements of:

1. *gharar* (risks and uncertainties in contractual agreement),
2. *maisir* (gambling).

Secondly, if the Muslim jurists (*fuqaha*) are prone to endorse the application of commodity futures and financial derivatives, they must confirm that these instruments do not contain the elements of *gharar* and *maisir*.

For example, let us look at one of the principles of contract in Islam, namely the object of trade (*mahallul 'aqdi*) and see at what point the *gharar* element may be present and avoided. One of the requirements of valid sale is that the buyer can only sell the goods he owns. Hence, futures transactions involving short-selling are forbidden. According to the *fuqaha*, the sale has violated the Prophetic *hadith* which says, "sell not what is not with you."

One reason why people are not permitted to sell what does not belong to them has a lot to so with the agricultural produce system in Medina, where there was no guarantee of full delivery. Hence, the advice of the Prophet (*pbuh*) about ownership is geared to eliminate *gharar* in the contract, i.e., the risks and uncertainty of delivery.

Gharar is caused by human choice, but it can be controlled. For example, a deliberate action not to declare a price during a sale can lead a customer to pay more than he should. But the *gharar* can be eliminated when the trader decided to put the price label. Selling fish in the water is a transaction full with *gharar* about delivery and also the true value of the sale. Using *gharar* to serve one's end is therefore destructive, as it can harm others.

Two
Concept of Islamic Insurance

The thirty-third annual report of the Director General of Insurance, Ahmad Don, shows another strong year of robust growth in the insurance industry. Total premium income rose from RM6.5 billion to RM7.82 billion, showing a 20.2 percent increase. The *takaful* business also shows remarkable growth. In 2002, the takaful sector expanded to claim 5.7 percent of total assets and 6.0 percent of total contributions of the insurance industry.

The main complaint has been the high cost of providing service and coverage. The governor said that guidelines on cost control are expected to promote efficiency through reduction in expenses of clients, more professional sales practices, and higher productivity among agencies involved.

The complaints seemed to affect all insurance operators in this country, which may or may not involve *takaful*. It is therefore timely to know what *takaful* is or Islamic insurance is all about, and how it differs from the conventional practice.

Before we spell out their main differences, it is worthy to understand why people buy an insurance policy. An insurance policy is basically a written contract between an individual and an insurance company, transferring financial liability in the event of some loss to the insurance company in return for a fee.

This is because individuals and firms recognize the existence of the various risks and hazards around them, and therefore need to plan ahead to protect their properties and assets from potential damage and losses. Insurance companies exist to do just that.

The insurance business mainly deals with pure risks instead of speculative risks. Pure risks always result in a loss, like car accidents and fire damage. It cannot be avoided, but can be minimized. A speculative risk, on the other hand, is a deliberate act by an individual or businessperson who hopes to gain by that action, but recognizes the chance for a loss instead.

Gamblers and investors are speculative risk-takers. These risks are not insurable. Hence, it is incorrect to say that the gambling factor has been the basic reason to set up the *takaful* business as conventional insurance companies today do not insure gambling activities.

In the insurance business, policies are issued only for insurable risks. To qualify as an insurable risk, the risk must not only be a pure risk, but also meet several other criteria. That is, the insured loss must be predictable, measurable, spread over a large geographical area, and acceptable to the insurance company.

Why are insurance companies willing to run these risks, given the potential losses incurred if they could not cover client loss? The reason is a simple one. As a profit-maximizing firm, insurance companies operate on the basis of the law of large numbers. The ability to make profits stems from the fact that they have many clients paying them for protection against the same loss.

For example, take a housing estate with 5,000 insured houses. Insurers know from past records, that fifty of these houses will be involved in a fire each year with an average damage of $40,000 each. So, companies can expect to pay $2 million to cover the clients ($40,000 x 50).

To earn profits, companies are expected to charge each household $500 a year for the fire insurance. With insurance premiums of $2.5 million ($500 x 500), insurance companies are expected to make $500,000 as profit from the policies ($2.5 million - $2 million). Would Islamic insurance or *takaful* adopt or reject this mechanism?

Is there a better way to cover client losses, such that they get more from the Islamic scheme? What is *takaful* actually? If a *takaful* operation is said to inculcate Islam values in the insurance business, in what way is *takaful* superior to the conventional schemes?

Takaful simply means joint guarantee. It is not a contract but an agreement for mutual help among the group, and can be visualized as a pact among clients who agree to jointly guarantee among themselves against loss or damage that may befall any of them. The basic objective of *takaful* is to pay for a defined loss from a defined fund.

In Islamic insurance, the practitioners often say that *takaful* operators assume the role of *mudharib* while clients are known as *rabbulmal.* What we see here is the application of the *mudarabah* contract to the insurance business. The clients act as investors, while a *takaful* operator assumes the role of entrepreneur. The *takaful* operators will invest the pool of funds and specify how the expected profit generated is to be shared among clients. Mutual help among clients is observed through the concept of *tabarru,* meaning to donate, contribute, or give away.

Here a certain proportion of clients' *takaful* installments or premiums are allocated to pay his fellow participants who suffer from a defined loss. This *'tabarru'* enables the client to fulfill his obligation of mutual help. Hence, the term *takaful* or joint guarantee is used to signify the Islamic elements contained in the insurance scheme.

Mudarabah is used in *takaful* to serve the investment function. That is to mean *takaful* funds are invested in interest-free financial assets. Conventional insurance companies normally buy long-term bonds and stocks of companies that may or many not indulge in non-permissible (*haram*) activities such as gaming, production of alcoholic beverages, interest-based banking, etc.

In the case of life-insurance, upon maturity clients will receive their premiums plus interest earned. Or the family member of policyholder who died may receive insurance payout, say $100,000, that may partly come from non-permissible investment activities.

Muslim clients may not be comfortable with such arrangements and may not desire to buy insurance policies from such companies. As an alternative, the *takaful* operators will use *mudarabah* investment instead, and therefore remove these doubts from clients.

Mudarabah-based *takaful* is mainly applied to the Family *Takaful* Business or Islamic life insurance which amounted to about RM94.2

million in 1995. The general *takaful* business, on the other hand, is a short-term scheme, which covers fire, motor, accident, marine, and engineering cases. In 1998, it accounted for about RM98.1 million. The bulk of the *takaful* fund (61.9 percent) was invested in the interest-free government investment securities.

Three
Islam and Life Insurance

In 1974, the National Religious Council (*Majlis Fatwa Kebangsaan*) issued a legal opinion (*fatwa*) that conventional life insurance is not permissible (*haram*) because it contains elements of 1) *gharar* or risk and uncertainty; 2) *masyir* or gambling and 3) *riba* or interest. To that effect, an Islamic version of life insurance was introduced in 1983, known today as Family Takaful.

The question now is, what was the nature of *gharar* and *masyir* the *ulamak* had in mind when the above *fatwa* was made? Are they thinking about risk and uncertainty arising from human manipulations or are they referring to speculative and market risks?

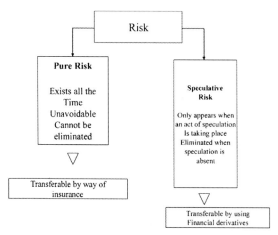

Figure 9.1 Risk and Insurance

If they do, the Muslim jurists may have been ill-advised, since conventional life insurance today does not address speculative risks. In addition to that, an insurance company will not compensate a policyholder if a loss occurs as a result of moral hazard. To attract people to buy Family Takaful, it is good to see this matter clarified by *takaful* companies.

In essence, family *takaful* and conventional life insurance seeks to administer one form of uncertainty in our daily life, known as pure risk. Pure risk exists when there is no potential gain, only possibility of loss. Fires, floods, earthquake, car accidents and thefts are forms of events involving pure risks. The role of an insurance company is to absorb pure risk from the insured through a mutual business agreement. In other words, by way of insurance, pure risk is transferred from the individual to the insuring party.

The speculative risk which insurance does not seek to address is the potential of making a gain as well as a loss. When someone invests his money in common stocks or properties, he is playing with speculative risks. Such a risk has no reason to be prohibitive (*haram*), since Islam enjoins man to seek wealth through trade and commerce, both of which embrace risk and profit sharing principles. The Quran says, "Allah permits commerce but prohibits *riba*" (Al-Baqarah: 278). Speculative risk only occurs when someone undertakes investment activities; that is, when investment is undertaken, speculative risks will surface. If no investment is made, it disappears. In this manner, man can control speculative risk by not investing.

Speculative risk is different from pure risk since pure risk exists all the time. For example, at any moment, man is faced with the possibility of death from fire, car accident, natural calamities, health hazards, etc. Hence, pure risk cannot be controlled by man. Insurance is therefore instrumental in helping man reduce his exposure to pure risk and losses arising from it.

Islam prohibits gambling (*masyir*). In gambling, the probability of winning or making a gain is very remote. Speculative risk in gambling is extremely high and unpredictable, since there is extremely little chance to win.

As most people are risk-averse (for example, they prefer safe investment to unsafe investment), the act of gambling is fact irrational. In the case of life insurance, pure risks exist as the event of death is certain, but when it will occur no one knows. It is the job of the insurance companies to calculate the probability of death or the death rate. It is the probability that an individual will die at a given age.

In gambling, there is no guarantee that everybody will win, but there is a very big chance that most will lose their bets. Insurance is therefore not gambling, as speculative risk only exists when the act of gambling materializes, while pure risks exists whether or not one buys an insurance policy.

Speculative risk in trade and commerce, however, is quite different from speculative risks in gambling. In the former, the outcome of not making profit is highest when the economy is slowing down. However, in gambling, the outcome of winning is still very small, whether or not the economy is doing well. It is therefore interesting to see actually what the Muslim jurists have in mind when *gharar* and *masyir* or gambling are used to argue against the permissibility of conventional life insurance in Islam.

On the *riba* elements, perhaps this is the only way to convince Muslims that conventional life is not *halal* as the *fatwa* has declared. This is because insurance companies invest most of their funds in interest-based securities such as government bonds, private debt securities, and money market instruments.

When a person passes away, the death benefit is taken from the total profits of the insurance company. These profits can be broken into two components, namely underwriting profits and investment profits. Underwriting profits result when the premium collected exceed the expenses of providing coverage plus the losses paid by the company, while investment profits are generated from investments in bonds and stocks.

It is in the latter, then death benefits from conventional life insurance are deemed *non-halal* since they are laden with interest or *riba* derived from investments in bonds. Perhaps, when financial instruments are free from the payment and receipts of interest, all conventional life insurance policies will naturally turn *halal*. But they must also abstain investing in other non-*halal* products as well.

To conclude, the way family *takaful* could be better or superior than its conventional competitor is now only attributed to the *riba* factor. *Takaful* means joint guarantee. Under *takaful*, benefits are given out based on the concepts of *tabarru* and *mudarabah*. *Tabarru* refers to the sharing and cooperative relationship among policyholders. That is, death benefits are taken from a pool of funds consisting of the collective premiums of policyholders and the dividends from their interest-free investments.

The relationship between policyholders and the *takaful* operator is based on the contract of *mudarabah,* where the latter acts as the entrepreneur or *mudarib,* while the former takes the role of capital providers. The *takaful* operator invests the premiums in interest-free instruments, where profit generated will be shared according to the agreed-upon profit-sharing ratio.

What we see in the above is one way to arrive at a death benefit, which is interest-free. Anyway, most of the benefits are taken from the Special Participant Account rather than dividends. As a whole, life insurance as a contract that protects individuals against financial losses resulting from death should no longer be linked to *gharar* and *masyir* elements.

Takaful operators should make this matter clear. At one time, Islamic banking was able to attract customers using the slaughtered-unslaughtered chicken analogy. Should *takaful* companies cherish such ideas by using the *gharar* and *masyir* factor to gain a market share? Are they saying that conventional insurance companies today refuse to tell their customers how and where the company has invested the premiums, thus creating some form of uncertainty and uneasiness among the public?

Four
Islamic and conventional Insurance: A comparison.

The growth of *takaful* business in Malaysia has been impressive, given that more Muslims are aware about the system and government support has been positive. At present, the bulk of *takaful* is handed by four *takaful* companies, namely Syarikat Takaful Malaysia, Malaysian National Insurance (MNI) Takaful, Mayban Takaful, and Takaful Ikhlas. Products range from general and family *takaful* to specialized ones like marine and health. The premiums are invested in *Shariah* compliance shares, bonds, and money market instruments.

A number of *Shariah* investment-linked insurance funds (SILIF) are also available in this country, offered exclusively by conventional insurance companies. Some of these funds are invested into companies with businesses that meet *Shariah* principles, while others are in fixed income instruments such as Islamic bonds (*sanad/sukuk*) and money market instruments. In this regard, their policy to promote Islamic investments via insurance is a noble one.

But to what extent these SILIFs hold Islamic legitimacy remains unclear, since the nature of conventional insurance remains unacceptable by *Shariah* scholars today. In 1974, the National Religious Council issued a *fatwa* (legal opinion) that conventional life insurance is forbidden (*haram*) because it contains the prohibitive elements of: 1) uncertainties (*gharar*); 2) gambling (*masyir*); and 3) interest (*riba*). To that effect, the *takaful* business was introduced in 1983.

A casual look at conventional insurance leaves no doubt that it has implicated both *riba* and gambling. The *riba* factor is quite straightforward since insurance companies invest in interest-based securities such as government bonds and private debt securities.

On gambling, most textbooks on insurance have attested to this point, that insurance is aleatory. According to Emmette Vaughan, the term "aleatory" means that the outcome is affected by chance and that the number of dollars given up by the contracting parties will be unequal. The insured pays the required premium, and if no loss occurs, the insurance company pays nothing. If a loss does occur, the insured's premium is small in relation to the amount the insurer will be required to pay. In this sense, it is aleatory; an insurance contract is like a gambling contract.

When the above is true, it is somewhat strange to see how *Shariah* investment- linked insurance funds (SILIFS) made their way into the Islamic markets via an insurance scheme the *fuqaha* had earlier disapproved. Hopefully, Bank Negara Malaysia will allow conventional insurance companies to open up Islamic windows through which investment-linked *takaful* products (such as general, family, etc.) can be made available to the public.

Table 9.2 : *Shariah* Investment-Linked Insurance Fund (SILIF) in non-*takaful* insurance companies

Shariah Investment-Linked Insurance Funds (SILIF)	Insurance Company (Non-*Takaful*)
MCIS *Shariah* Fund	MCIS Insurance Berhad
Shariah Malaysian Equity	Mayban Life International (Labuan) Ltd.
Dahlia *Shariah* Income Fund	Mayban Life Assurance Berhad
MAA *Dana Assalam* MAA *Dana Alfayyadh*	Mayban Assurance Alliance Bhd.
Prulink *Dana Rasulmal* Prulink *Dana Sanad* Prulink *Dana Idarah*	Prudential Assurance Malaysia Bhd.
Lion Barakah Fund	Great Eastern Life Assurance
AIA *Dana Alistithmar* AIA Dynamic *Shariah* Fund	American International Assurance
HLA Venture Dana Iltizam	Hong Leong Assurance Bhd.
Shariah Growth Fund	AML Assurance Bhd.

As we all know, *takaful* means "joint guarantee." The system of *"aqila"* as practiced among the Muhajirin and Ansar in Medina was often said to lay the foundation of *takaful* since *aqila* implies mutual help and support, which can also mean to guarantee each other on moral ground. However, we must understand that the system of *aqila* is non-commercial in nature and aims to help those in difficulties without demanding contractual payments.

Since the growth prospect of the *takaful* business is promising, it is worthy to examine nature of contract applied when someone purchases a *takaful* policy. For example, Mr. Ismail purchases a family *takaful* policy from a *Ummah Takaful Bhd* (UTB) for $100 per month or $1,200 per year. Here, Mr. Ismail pays UTB the premium, but in exchange for what?

Most writings on *takaful* claim that the basis of the *takaful* business is *al-Mudarabah*. So, when Mr. Ismail pays his monthly premium, he becomes a *Rabbulmal* who stands to lose his investments if the project undertaken by UTB management (i.e., the *mudarib*) fails. Otherwise, he will get back his capital plus some dividends.

But what Mr. Ismail gets from the *takaful* operator is not only the possibility of making profits and losses from his investment, but a promise or guarantee to be paid the actual loss arising from his death or injuries when they occur. Actually, this is the contract of indemnity. The contract of indemnity is in fact the core component of *takaful*, which it heavily borrowed from conventional insurance. It is strange to see why this point was not addressed in the same rigor as it did to the *mudarabah* factor.

Underwriting Surplus in *Takaful*

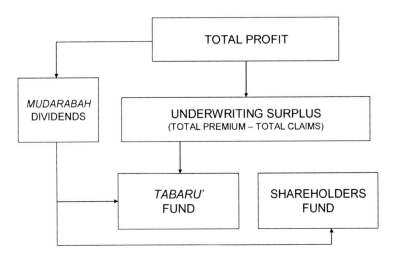

Figure 9.3: *Takaful* profits

In fact, the bulk of *takaful* profits are generated from underwriting surplus, namely the amount of premium collected and the amount paid out as compensations. The issue on underwriting surplus is also a cause for concern. Since takaful uses the concept of *tabaru'* (i.e., give away or contribute) in determining the nature and amount of compensations given to the insured, it readily implies that the surpluses must belong to the *tabaru'* fund. But this is yet to be seen in takaful, as the underwriting surplus constitutes the bulk of takaful profits.

By way of the *tabaru'* system, *takaful* operators have diligently showed customers how compensations are formulated by incorporating the *tabaru'* element. This is done to promote transparency and therefore prevent *gharar* (uncertainties) in the contractual agreement. But in *fiqh muamalat, tabaru'* is not a contract that binds participating parties, as we normally observe in many classical Islamic contracts such as *al-ijarah, salam, kafalah,* or *wakalah*. It is therefore crucial that we fully understand the underlying contract of *takaful* in order to avoid further uncertainty over things that matter a great deal to us today.

First, if the contract called *takaful* exists in early *fiqh* literatures , the concept of *takaful* must truly observe the Quranic and Prophetic injunctions.

There is little doubt that the divine guidance above is associated with the *takaful* business, but we must not discount the problem of moral hazards and deliberate violations by the insured. This is because insurance and *takaful* is a unilateral contract where only one part is legally bound to do anything.

That is, the contract is not enforceable if the insured violates certain conditions. Perhaps this is what the *fuqaha* (Islamic jurists) meant by the *gharar* element of insurance, where the insured are not certain that the insurer will pay compensations in the event of a loss.

Secondly, the *takaful* business must be able to define *takaful* by way of contractual agreement *('aqad)* among which include:

- Offer and Acceptance (*Ijab & Qabul*)
- Subject matter and price (*Mahallul 'aqdi*)
- Competent parties (*Tharafail 'aqdi*)

For example, what is the subject matter (*mahallul 'aqdi*) of *takaful*? Does it mean a client pays a premium in exchange of a compensation guarantee, a physical asset, or even right to future cash flows arising from the *mudarabah* agreement? Some writers say that *takaful* is not a contract of sale (*al-bay'*) but a contract of *mudarabah*. This is quite inaccurate, as reading through the *takaful* documentation shows that indeed the element of price (*thaman*) exists, i.e., the premium. This is because the essence of underwriting, which is a fundamental component of *takaful,* involves risk assessment on which pricing of *takaful* premium is based.

We now should be able to address the following issues, specifically determining the nature of *takaful* contract. First, as mentioned earlier, conventional insurance is a contract of indemnity, which means the insured is entitled to payments by the insurer if he has suffered a loss and only the extent of financial loss sustained. In this manner, the principle of *tabaru* is applied in *takaful,* on which donations from the pooled fund to the insured is based. But the indemnity contract remains operative since a *takaful* operator will not compensate the insured anything more than the loss.

Table 9.4 : *Takaful* and conventional insurance: A comparison

Conventional Insurance (Without SILIF)	Conventional Insurance (With SILIF)	*Takaful*
Contact of Indemnity	Contract of Indemnity	Contract of Indemnity
To transfer pure risk from customer to operator	To transfer pure risk from customer to operator	To transfer pure risk from customer to operator
With *riba* (interest)	Without *riba* (interest)	Without *riba* (interest)
Aleatory Outcomes affected by chance and operator gets underwriting surplus	Aleatory Outcomes affected by chance and operator gets underwriting surplus	Outcomes affected by chance. Depends on who gets the underwriting surplus • *Takaful* operator • Tabaru' fund

To some extent, it is true that insurance is an aleatory contract. This is the *maisir* (gambling) argument that *fuqaha* have raised on many occasions. By aleatory, we mean the outcome is affected by chance, and the number of ringgit or dollars given up by the contracting parties will be unequal.

For example, Mr. Ismail pays $300 per year on his car insurance and will lose his premium if no loss or injury occurs. But in the event of an accident, the size of compensation paid by the insurer is always disproportionately larger than the amount of premium received.

We can see that the element of *'iwad* (equivalent countervalue) is absent in the above example, thus making it difficult to accept conventional insurance as a valid commercial contract in the eyes of Islamic law. This is because insurance is a unilateral contract. But *takaful* is also guilty of the same, whether one uses the *mudarabah* or *tabaru* argument in to legitimize a family or general *takaful* policy.

498

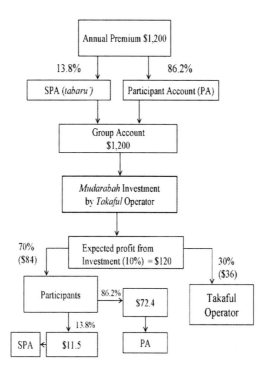

Figure 9.5 *Takaful* distribution system

For example, Mr. Hasan, who took a thirty-year family *takaful* policy, has been paying a $100 monthly premium for a year. According to the *takaful* computation on *manfaat*, the family of the deceased will receive: 1) the accumulated participant account contribution, say $1,000, and 2) the award arising from the *tabaru'* pool, say, $1,200 x 29 = $34,800.

The total *manfaat* is equal to $35,800, which is more than the amount paid for, namely $1,200. Certainly, many would like to know in what way is this "excess" sum (i.e. $34,800) lawful, given that it is created and paid to the insured without him holding any form of risk (*ghorm*) or effort (*ikhtiyar*).

Using the principle of *tabaru'* however has not been able to erase the aleatory nature of *takaful*. The *mudarabah* aspects deal with the investment function and help little to discount aleatory elements.

But the aleatory nature will stay but only to be benefited by the participants as the *tabaru'* component of *takaful* receives all of the unclaimed revenues (underwriting surplus). To ensure that *tabaru* participants actually receive the underwriting surplus, a representation of the *tabaru'* fund owners in the *takaful* board meeting should be made mandatory. This can be done by appointing a trustee whose main task is to protect the interest of *takaful* customers.

This is an issue that the *takaful* business today must address in a professional manner if it desires to insist saying that conventional insurance is similar to gambling (*maisir*) while *takaful* is not. And when people are confused on this issue, an element of ambiguities (*gharar*) starts to creep in, which is also not good for the *takaful* industry. Education is therefore essential to promote greater transparency so that economic justice reveals itself in trade and commerce, and *takaful* is not an exception.

SECTION TEN

SPECIAL ISSUES

This is because the Quran says' "Allah has allowed *al-bay'* but prohibits *riba*" (Al-Baqarah : 275). So, using *al-bay'* would be a feasible solution for Telekom. Usually, Telekom is advised by a merchant bank it does business with, who in turn consult its *Shariah* committee for juristic advice.

The issuance of Islamic PDS implies that it is no longer a piece of document evidencing a debt (IOU) but a commodity, an object of sale (*mahallul 'aqdi*). The IPDS can be sold in the secondary market for liquidity purposes and capital gains. In other words, as an asset or property (*al-mal*), it (i.e., IPDS) can disposed at a discount and premium just like any conventional bonds do.

The question now is how in the first place the IOU—namely Islamic debt papers—can be turned into tradable commodities. This question causes no problem to interest-bearing bonds, since an IOU or a debt certificate is by definition an asset to the creditors. But this is not true for Islamic debt certificates (*sanad*). Any exchange involving *sanad* represents a voidable contract, since it—i.e., the *sanad*—does not qualify as an object of sale (*al-mal mutaqawim*).

To convert *sanad* into an object of sale (*mahallul 'aqdi*), the contract of *bay' al-'inah* has been intensively applied in most Islamic PDS issues. Since Telekom is willing to pay for the cost of funds and investors will only purchase bonds with conventional debt features, the contract of *bay' al-'inah* can made this possible in the following manner:

- Using the contract of *al-bay' mutlak* or cash sale, Telekom sells some underlying assets worth $800 million to the investors and gets the cash injection.

- At the same time, using the contract of *al-bai-bithaman ajil* (BBA), investors will sell back the underlying assets at a price comprising the capital component ($800 million) and the profit component ($20 million) payable by installments. If the coupon or profit rate = 5 percent and n = 5 years, the profit component is equal to $800,000,000 x 0.05 x 5 = $20 million. The capital component is to be paid lump-sum as normally practised in conventional bonds. The BBA debt obligation of Telekom to the financiers is therefore equal to $820 million.

- From the *al-bai-bithaman ajil* sale, Telekom will then securitizes its BBA debt obligation (*dayn* BBA) into Islamic PDS. In other words, the issuance of Islamic IPDS, namely MuNif (medium term PDS) or BAIDS forms the mode of payments to the financiers.

Apparently, the securitization of debt (*dayn* BBA) by the issuer (Telekom) has taken place here. What should have actually taken place is the securitization of underlying assets by the issuer. Only this method would justify the issuance of bond certificates via asset securitization as a means to raise funds and mode of payments.

It is rather strange to see the *Shariah* Advisory Council (SAC) allowing the issuing company to securitize the *dayn al-bai-bithaman ajil* that actually and legally belong to the investors. Telekom has not yet paid up the $820 million debt. It does not make sense that Telekom is allowed to securitize something it does not own.

The debt arising from the buyback *al-bai-bithaman ajil* sale (*dayn BBA*) constitutes an asset to the investors but a debt to the issuer (Telekom). In real terms, securitization of the *dayn BBA* should be performed by the investors (creditors) and not Telekom (debtor).

But this is true only when a merchant bank (i.e., also acting as lead arranger) underwrites the bonds. But this time, the issuing party must sell the underlying assets to the underwriter, who then sells back the same assets to the issuer. As the *dayn* arising from the BBA sale—called *dayn al-bai-bithaman ajil*—is now owned by the underwriter, the *dayn al-bai-bithaman ajil* can now be securitized by the underwriter (i.e., merchant bank), making way for the ABBA/BAIDS bond issuance.

In other words, the securitization of receivables, namely the *dayn al-baithaman ajil* was executed by the merchant bank who owns the *dayn* (*debt*). From the underwriter's viewpoint, the *dayn* constitutes an asset and not a liability. As an asset, the *dayn al-baithaman ajil* can then be securitized into tradable papers. But is this how Islamic debt securitization is conducted? This, however, may not possible because SAC legal opinion on the securitization of receivables is not out yet.

In the early 1990s, securitization of *al-bai-bithaman ajil* receivables (i.e., *dayn* BBA) was conducted by Cagamas Bhd. By using the *bay' al-dayn* contract, BBA receivables were sold at a discount by Bank Islam Malaysia Berhad (BIMB) to Cagamas, which later securitized the receivables to make way for the *Mudarabah* bond issuance. This method seemed more logical, since the BBA receivables were securitized by its owner (i.e., Cagamas).

The other possibility may be the sale of MuNif/BAIDS to the merchant bank that underwrites the paper. The BAIDS are sold at a discount price by the issuer to the underwriter, who then sells the papers to investors at a margin. But such arrangement will still see the securitization of underlying assets (i.e., not the receivables) by the issuing party. What can happen here is: 1) the sale of debt (*bay al-dayn*) at a discount by the issuer to the underwriter, and 2) the sale of debt (*bay al-dayn*) at a premium by the underwriter to the investors.

It looks like the Islamic practitioners and *Shariah* experts at the supervisory level have put new standards on what constitutes asset and debt securitization. In traditional banking firms, the securitization of debt as asset can be made on the loan portfolio. For capital market application, a company can securitize its assets into securities, which it consequently sells to investors.

The Islamic practice today adds a new dimension to securitization, namely securitizing debt (*dayn murabahah*) that belongs to the creditors by the debtor. It defines securitization as the creation of tradable certificates evidencing a debt (i.e., *dayn murabahah*) arising out of a finance facility.

If this is true, then the securitizing party in Islamic securitization (i.e., the issuer) must be none other than the financiers. But surprisingly, in the case of MuNif and BAIDS or BAIDS, the securitizing party turns out to be the issuer (debtor).

The question now is how and why the issuing company is allowed by the *Shariah* Advisory Council to conduct the securitization of debt (*dayn murabahah*) that belongs to the investors. In conventional practice, securitization is the transformation of illiquid assets into a security, an instrument issued out and consequently traded in the secondary market.

But in the Islamic practice, securitization is the creation of securities evidencing a debt arising out of *murabahah* or *al-bai-bithaman ajil* facility and conducted by the debtor. This has been the terms and definitions used by practitioners. They claimed that the debt obligation (*dayn*) can be securitized since it (i.e., *dayn* BBA) is supported by some underlying assets. By doing so, the ABBA i.e., the debt security issued out of the securitization process is considered as wealth or property (*al-mal*). See Figure 10.1 below.

ISLAMIC DEBT SECURITIZATION

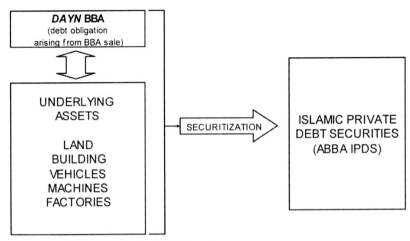

Issuer owns underlying assets after the BBA sale
Issuer securitizes the BBA debt obligation backed by underlying assets

Figure 10.1 Islamic Debt Securitization in Malaysia

The main purpose of this article is only to show that this is possible only when the *'inah* sale is in action. The sale-buyback of underlying assets by the financiers to Telekom via the sale allows Telekom to securitize the underlying asset in order to issue ABBA as a mode of payments.

Two
Islamic Law of Inheritance (Fara'id)

When someone dies without a will, he is said to have died intestate. His wealth and property will be handed over to the authorities for distribution among the rightful heirs, but this will involve complicated and time-consuming legal procedures before they (i.e., the heirs) can receive the property.

In Malaysia, the distribution of property of an intestate estate is governed by the Distribution Act of 1997. For example, when an intestate dies, leaving a spouse and no children or parent, the whole estate goes the surviving spouse. For Muslims, the Islamic law of inheritance (*Farai'd*) automatically applies.

One may be asked what if he wants to reserve some of his wealth for his beloved parents or sisters (who do no have *fara'id* rights on the estate) since his existing wife (wives) and children serve as the legitimate heirs. One can refer to the *wasiya* component involving up to one-third of the estate. "But if at the time of division, other relatives, or orphans or poor, are present give them out of their property, and speak to them words of kindness and justice." (An-Nisaa:8)

In Islam, when one makes a will (*wasiya*), only one-third of his wealth and property can be allotted those he desires, excluding the people defined by the law of inheritance (*farai'd*). These include the poor, orphans, close friends, and other near relatives not mentioned in the *Farai'd* law. The remaining two-thirds must be distributed to the heirs according to the shares prescribed by the Quran given below:

509

"Allah (thus) directs you as regards your children's (Inheritance): to the male a portion equal to that of two females: if only daughters, two or more, their share is two-thirds of the inheritance. If only one, her share is a half.

"For parents, a sixth share of the inheritance to each, if the deceased left children; if no children, and the parents are the (only) heirs, the mother has a third: if the deceased left brothers (or sisters) the mother has a sixth. (The distribution of all cases is) after the payments of legacies and debts. Ye know not whether our parents or your children are nearest to you in benefit. These are settled portions ordained by Allah: and Allah is All-Knowing, All-Wise (*'aliman hakima'*)." (an-Nisaa:11)

"In what your wife leaves, your share is a half, if they leave no child. But if you leave a child, ye get a fourth: after payments of legacies and debts. In what you leave, their share is a fourth, if you leave no child; But if you leave a child, they get an eighth: after payments of legacies and debts." (An-Nisaa:12)

"If the man or woman whose inheritance is in question, has left neither ascendants nor descendents, but has left a brother or a sister, each one of the two gets a sixth; but if more than two, they share in a third; after payments of legacies and debts; so that no loss is caused (to any one). Thus it is ordained by Allah, and Allah is All-Knowing, Most Forbearing' (*'alimunhalima*)." (An-Nisaa: 12)

"Those are limits set by Allah; those who obey Allah and His Messenger will be admitted to the Gardens with rivers flowing beneath, to abide therein forever, and that will be the supreme achievement (*wazhalikalfauzul'azim*)." (An-Nisaa:13)

The Islamic law of inheritance therefore requires the Muslim people to observe the Quranic prescriptions and not to follow their whims and fancies. If no heirs (*warith*) were found, then the property shall be taken over by the *Baitul Mal* (Islamic Treasury) to be spent on the welfare of the general public.

Those who are engaged in the business of estate planning should be mindful of this point. They should not lead Muslim clients to believe that they can leave a will based on their whims and fancies. In Islam, the concept of will or *wasiya* only involves one-third of the estate and not all.

The Quranic law of inheritance (*fara'id*) serves to make the distribution of wealth more equitable. It aspires to prevent the accumulation of wealth among the few, as the law clearly shows that it is against *taqsim murtakiz* or corporate or compact inheritance. It is against primogeniture where the property goes to the eldest son or to one single person by way of making a will.

One practice that defies the Islamic law of inheritance is the *adat perpatih* still practiced by some Malays of Minangkabau decent in Negeri Sembilan and Sumatra. In *adat perpatih*, the daughters become the only rightful heirs to all the property of the deceased. They argue that women do not possess the capacity or ability to create wealth while men who are stronger, always do.

The Quran has clearly warned against disobeying the law of inheritance In Surah Al-Baqaran, the Quran says, "And do not eat up your property among yourselves for vanities (*bathil*), nor use it as bait for the judges, with intent that you may eat up wrongfully and knowingly a little of (other) people's property." (Al-Baqarah:188)

The Quran also says, "But those who disobey Allah and His Messenger, and transgress His limits (*wayata'adahududah*) will be admitted to the fire, to abide therein; and they shall have a humiliating punishment." (An-Nisaa: 14)

It is therefore well understood that those who have consumed wealth and property by way of defying the *Farai'd* law have indeed transgressed God's commandments.

In the Hereafter, not only the deceased are made responsible for their actions but also the heirs (*warith*) and lawyers (will writers) who could have reminded them not to do so. Thus, the role of Islamic education and financial planning in this matter is crucial.

Three
The Islamic Dinar

Ever since the collapse of the gold standard in 1925, increasing turmoil and volatility is evident in world financial markets. It wreaked havoc on the flow of international trade by one-third between 1929 and 1933 and partly contributed to the industrial depression in the United Kingdom in 1926 and the crash of the stock market in the United States in 1929.

The 1997 Asian economic crisis and the Mexican peso debacle in 1991 were two infamous events that mercilessly plunged the emerging economies into near bankruptcy. What actually went wrong is no longer a mystery, but what ought to be done remains an agenda world economies must find common grounds.

At least two factors can help explain why financial volatility persists today. First, it has a lot to do with excessive money creation and secondly, the absence of regulation over the activities of hedge funds. And both are linked to the exchange rate system and monetary order of trading nations.

When major economies adopted the gold standard in 1870, money is created only when enough gold reserves are added to the existing stock. This is because by using a commodity-backed currency, namely money backed by gold, people saw that holding currency is as good as holding gold. The gold standard system allows convertibility of currency into gold. Gold is the basis on which the exchange rates of currency between nations are established.

But when world monetary order places the U.S. dollar in place of gold at Bretton Woods and eventually allows the exchange rate to move according to market forces in 1973, it allows money creation to roam at will, since nations can increase the money supply without any need to increase gold reserves.

Excessive money creation creates inflation, eventually driving up interest rates. In the economics of capital flows, high interest rates attract foreign portfolio funds, which causes the country's exchange rate to increase.

Currency appreciation implies trade deficits when exports become less competitive. A country can overcome trade deficits if it has enough hard currencies to pay for the increasing imports. Otherwise it will resort to borrowing. If nothing else works, devaluation is the only way out.

But devaluing one's currency sapped away the trust and confidence that other nations put on the country. And when one got entangled with the International Monetary Fund for help, it can mean less freedom to meet national economic and social objectives.

Notwithstanding IMF's role, the prospect of devaluation invites hedge funds to their doorsteps as well. By "buying low – selling high," arbitragers seek immediate profits based on exchange rate differentials. Fueled by greed, in the name of market forces they further brought the short-selling the currency.

Excessive money creation earlier landed say the ringgit or bath in international bank accounts. Arbitragers, namely the international speculators, borrow these ringgits to sell them back again. Oversupply of ringgit saw it plunged further down. By buying ringgit at the lower price and paying minimal interest charges on the ringgit loan, speculators make money in the billions, leaving the economy bleeding with corporate bankruptcies, rising unemployment, and production standstill.

Without any remedial international consensus to regulate hedge funds and putting a tight control on money creation, returning to the gold standard is one viable option. As nearly all financial crisis put a blame of money, either too much or too little of it, controlling the money supply must be a basic necessity.

If the power to create money lies in the hands of the state, it can be used as a political tool to garner more power and corrupt practices and when banks are made free to create money by way of deposit creation it can lead to similar evils.

The Asian economic crisis is a clear evidence of banks' destructive capabilities; according to Thomas Jefferson, "The banking institutions are more dangerous to our freedom than the enemies armies. The creation of money has to be removed from the banks' hand."

Under the gold standard, countries agree to define their monetary units in terms of a physical amount of pure gold. For example, if the dollar can buy 1/20 of an ounce of gold and a British pound is defined as 1/4 of an ounce of gold, implicitly it means one British pound can be exchanged with five dollars; or 1 British pound = US$5. Based on mint parities, the exchange rate between dollar, franc, deutschmark, yen, ringgit, etc. can be established.

Central banks should be able to redeem all currencies for the amount of gold they are defined. In this manner, the country's money supply is dependent on the amount of gold reserves the nation's monetary authority has. A ratio of money stock and gold reserves can be then established. For example, between 1879 and 1913, the U.S. money stock was 8.5 times the amount of monetary gold stock. If the supply of gold remains constant, it promotes long-term stability in the money stock and long-run stability in real output, prices and exchange rates.

However, without a gold standard, printing money and deposit creation can run out of control. The Bretton Woods system is one step up to reduce the role of gold in making international trade settlement. Instead the system uses the U.S. dollar to settle cross-border transactions with only a U.S. dollar - gold convertibility.

However, the U.S. abandoned the convertibility of dollar into gold reserves partly driven by the Vietnam War. Financing the war implied printing more money, which is only possible if it has enough gold to do so. The U.S. also feared that foreign governments may sabotage the country by presenting their million dollar reserves for gold.

When President Nixon closed the Gold Window in 1971, he said the U.S. would suspend temporarily the convertibility of dollars into gold or other reserves assets, except in amounts and conditions determined to be in the interest of monetary stability and in the best interest of the United States.

However, with the impending slowdown of the U.S. economy, people may find it less worthy to hold the dollar, as it may lose value over time. The yen also is not spared, with the Japanese economy still in the doldrums after a decade of recession.

In Malaysia, a prospect of the depreciating dollar would also mean a falling ringgit if it persists to peg the currency to the greenback. Malaysia may run huge trade deficits in view of her high dependence of capital and intermediate imports.

What we fear is that no more currency is worth holding because it is worth nothing. Money as legal tender is a promise of payment, but now it is not convertible into gold or guarantees a tangible conversion. Economies may resort to the barter system and even use commodity money to settle economic transactions.

Abu Bakr ibn Abi Maryam reported that he heard the Messenger of Allah, may Allah bless him and grant him peace, say, "A time is certainly coming over mankind in which there will be nothing (left) which will be of use save a dinar and a dirham." (The Musnad of Imam Ahmad ibn Hanbal)

The Islamic dinar is a specific weight of gold equivalent to 4.3 grams. Returning to the gold standard can mean adopting the dinar standard or the mint standard of the early gold exchange rate system. On this ground, the Islamic dinar must take the form of a commodity-backed money rather than a commodity money, although the latter can be used on a limited basis involving cross-border transactions.

The Islamic dinar can help control the supply of money by way of changes in gold reserves, similar to the gold standard. In this manner, the role of the central bank can be made redundant since money supply is no longer determined by size of monetary base but the amount of gold reserves.

An increase in the money supply is a reflection of real growth arising from more exports. No longer did it come into being by way of artificial demand arising from speculative purchases in real estate and shares.

As the *Shariah* serves to protect common interest, the prohibition of *riba* must accompany the dinar system. It is a monetary order that establishes the framework within which individuals conduct and settle transactions. Without an order, i.e., laws and regulations, it is impossible to see how justice can be promoted effectively.

For example, in the Islamic Dinar Order, both debtor and creditor can be protected from the evils of inflation and recession. In the case of inflation, it is normal that a creditor gains while a debtor loses out. In the Islamic Dinar Order, loans given out in currency, say three-year 5,000-ringgit personal loan is peg to the dinar. The contract of loan thus, is based on dinar and not ringgit.

If one dinar is equivalent to $500, then the loan made is 50 dinar which the debtor must pay the same amount on maturity. If the price level increases on payment day to where he has to pay, say $6,000 to purchase 50 dinar, he must do so.

In this manner, the creditor is protected from monetary depreciation since he receives 50 dinar, but a higher amount in currency. This is not *riba*, since the contract is not based on currency but dinar as the Prophet (*pbuh*) says, "gold for gold, silver for silver, like for like." It is a natural process of indexation that serves to protect the creditor in time of inflation.

The call by Mahathir Muhammad to revamp existing international monetary order is timely, and the Islamic Dinar can play a meaningful role, at least among Muslim countries. Before that, it is crucial to determine the mint parity of one dinar for each of the Organization of Islamic Countries (OIC) member countries' mint parity.

To maintain the mint parity i.e., the exchange value of the nation's currency with gold, the country must condition its money stock on the level of its gold reserves. Doing so will see hedge funds unable to find enough money to execute short-selling activities.

In short, the value of a nation's currency is now dependent on gold and not the market forces. In some sense, market forces are necessary to guarantee efficiency, but it is also open to manipulation.

On this point, the eleventh century Islamic jurist Ibn Taimiyyah in his *Fatawa* said that:

"rise and fall in prices is always due to injustice (zulm) of some people. Sometimes its reason is deficiency in production or a decline in imports of the goods in demand.

"Thus, if the desire for the goods increases while its supply

decreases, its price rises. On the other hand, if availability of the good increases and the desire for it decreases, the price comes down. This scarcity or abundance may not be caused by the action of any people; it may be due to a cause not involving any injustice or, sometimes, it may have a cause that involves injustice. It is Allah the Almighty Who creates desires in the hearts of people."

Thus, markets are simply tools to be made subservient to the desire of people. When markets are exposed to skillful manipulation of hedge funds, prices are no longer equitable and this invites volatility.

In the Islamic dinar system, Malaysia can sell palm oil to Saudi Arabia paid in riyals, which Malaysia can convert into the Islamic dinar on call. Thus, there is less to worry about currency fluctuation and the need to hedge against adverse price movements.

Lastly, in the Islamic Dinar System, the role of fiat money as a medium of exchange will be replaced by dinar-backed money. By definition, fiat money is money not redeemable for any commodity, and its status as money is conferred by the government.

In Islamic history, the introduction of copper coins or *fulus* as money by the Mamluks (648/1250) coupled with famine, created a period of high inflation or *ghala'*, leading to its downfall. The *fulus*, unlike the dinar, can easily be produced at will. Without control, excessive supply of copper *fulus* leads to spiraling inflation. The same applies in modern times when excessive fiat money creation created overspending and asset bubbles.

Four
Do profits from BBA contain 'iwad?

As Islamic banking enters the new millennium, attempts to understand how it presently works and equally important how it should work must be pursued with more rigor. Academicians are responsible to create awareness among the public so that their rights as consumers are protected.

We must know the status of our savings in Islamic deposits, whether or not the banks are keeping to their words about the risk-return implications. Likewise, as fund users, we want to make sure the prices are right. Meaning that prices are set on the principle of efficiency and equity.

How much depositors could earn from their *al-wadiah* and *mudarabah* deposits depends a lot on the financial policy of Islamic banks. Today, we know well that more than 90 percent of Islamic banking assets consist of the deferred sale products, namely *al-murabahah* and *al-bai-bithaman ajil* (BBA). How much longer the high dependency will continue remain a question we find remedies as we enter the new millennium.

High-dependency on BBA financing will mean small returns to depositors, and this may lead them to put most of their savings elsewhere. The low interest rate regime will see people turning to the stock market. The same applies to Islamic banking depositors.

The main issue now is not the constant criticism I have about BBA. The issue has to do with distributive justice and income distribution, as we believe strongly that Islamic banking does have a role in reducing income disparities.

BBA-based consumer and asset financing cannot deviate significantly from interest-bearing operations, especially in the pricing issues. So, the margin remains the same and customers in both systems will see no significant difference as far as yields from deposits and financing are concerned.

One good example is product pricing. In loans, the contractual interest rate is the sum of 1) interest rate of deposits, 2) overhead, 3) credit or default risk, and 4) profit margin. In the case of BBA, the *Shariah* can only recognize the overhead and profit margin elements. But normally, they only command about 2 percent and 1 percent respectively. This is in line with Bank Negara guidelines. For smaller banks, the lack of scale economies may see higher overhead cost than larger size banks. Overall, the markup element should amount to about 3 percent.

However, banks must also impute the cost of deposit factor. Since no promise to pay is made on *wadiah* and *mudarabah* is given, this naturally implies that Islamic banks need not worry about determining the targeted rate of return to depositors. But how can this be if they can declare up front how much profit they want from each of the *murabahah* and BBA sales made?

For example, the bank sells an asset for $200,000 on BBA credit term. As customers, the BBA or *murabahah* contract gave us the right to know the cost price. It is then not difficult to see that given the terms of maturity of say, 20 years, the profit rate per annum should amount to 10 percent with a nominal markup of $100,000.

But now, the question is, how should the bank explain the $100,000 profit they make from the BBA sale as legitimate? Recall the *'iwad* or equivalent countervalue is the condition for a lawful sale. Any increase, according to the majority of jurists in the Shafi', Hanafi, Maliki, and Hanbali schools must contain *'iwad*. To benefit from these increases, Islamic banks must be able to provide something of equal value in return. Hence, when someone pays $200,000 on BBA financing at $100,000 cost price, what is the nature of *'iwad* he receives from the bank?

Certainly, if the transaction is made on the spot or cash basis, a problem with the nature of lawful and unlawful gains should not have risen, since no time element is involved here. Which means that the bank purchases the goods at direct or wholesale price, takes the risk of ownership, and sells it later to the customer for $200,000 on cash term.

The legitimacy of the profit made is irrelevant, since the bank has indeed delivered the *'iwad*. This may be in the form of 1) its ability to make the goods available in the market and 2) absorbing market risks and risk of ownership (*daman milkiyah*). In the former, we are looking at the valued-addition (*kasb*) factor, while the latter describes the *ghorm* or risk-taking aspects of sale.

However in the BBA sale, it seems that the $100,000 profit is made on the basis of time factor alone. To some extent, we failed to understand how a profit rate of 10 percent can be determined *ex ente,* when concurrently Islamic banks cannot declare *ex ente* the rates of return on deposits.

Even if we accept the assumption that the 10 percent profit per annum charged on every BBA sale arises from 1) cost of deposits, say 3 percent, 2) overhead 2 percent, and 3) profit margin 1 percent, which only equals 6 percent, what then explains the additional 4 percent stipulated in the contract? In conventional loans, the 4 percent can easily be explained by credit or default risk. This risk premium or spread will vary according to the type and maturity of loans coupled with the credit ratings of borrowers. Normally, a bank will charge a higher spread when risk of defaults is higher. But these can only hold for loans (*qard*) and not sale (*al-bay'*).

So, what can indeed explain these extra profits that Islamic banks took from BBA sales? If the answer is about risk of default, then certainly it is not about *'iwad*. The risk of default is about the game of waiting for payments and problem of collections. It does not concern market risk. It may be easy to say that profit from BBA is *halal,* since BBA is not a loan but a sale (*al-bay'*). But one has been misled to think that BBA is a spot sale. The markup from spot sale is lawful since it contains *'iwad* but can we imply the same for BBA credit sale when no tendency of *'iwad* can be detected there? This is true since the profit created from BBA is a consequence of waiting. In this sense, the *Shariah* advisors seemed to have approved gains arising from time value via BBA financing.

Five
Marketing issues in Islamic consumer financing

One important aspect of marketing is to know what consumers want. Undoubtedly, product design and pricing are vital organs in the marketing mix. But all will go to waste when managers do not know who is buying. Research and development costs end in the drain when the management failed to understand the profile of buying party. It is vital that managers know with whom they are dealing. What is it that consumers want? Do they go for prestige, design, price, or attractive credit facilities?

Focus now is on credit financing. People are prone to think that paying by installments is a good bargain. The more installments the better, since the amount payable is marginal, especially when it is paid by the week. But very few knew they are actually paying more the longer the credit period. Often a good deal will turn sour when many fail to pay up and have their goods auctioned off by creditors.

To find out consumer perception of credit sale, a study was conducted on 100 consumers who made their purchases using installment schemes offered by leading household credit-based retail outlets such as Singer, Catalog-Shop, Courts Mammoth, MOCCIS, and Arastu. The information gathered is entirely based on respondents using interest-bearing credit financing.

Five questions were asked to extract consumers' perception of credit sale. It serves to investigate whether the same facility can be offered using

Shariah principles. The findings should able to tell us what consumers actually want from Islamic financing and how financiers strategize to meet profit targets without compromising Islamic values.

The survey findings should provide practitioners valuable information about the challenges in Islamic consumer financing and the necessary actions for remedy. These main issues are given below:

- Reasons for choosing installment schemes
- Awareness about price differences
- Awareness that the price difference is interest
- Fairness paying above cash price
- Support for Islamic financing

1) Reasons for choosing installment schemes

Thirty-one percent of respondents have chosen credit financing because household durable goods today are becoming more expensive. Rapid economic growth brought along problems of labor shortages, higher cost of raw materials, and interest rates. As a result, prices have increased, with cash purchases no longer affordable. The credit scheme could help consumers meet their household needs. It also helps boost sales as well. Only 9 percent of the respondents will buy on credit because the scheme does not require any down payment.

This indicates that the majority of respondents do not belong to the lower income group. Down payments are therefore not crucial in credit purchases while the demand of easy payment schemes cannot be ignored. Fifteen percent of respondents prefer consumer financing with easy payments alone.

2) Awareness about price differences

Ninety-two percent of respondents knew the difference between cash price and total payments paid when items are bought using credit. This shows that they are willing to pay more using the credit schemes. They are willing spend more in order to purchase goods today. But despite the readiness to pay more via credit, customers are sensitive to factors concerning fairness. More than half of the respondents (56 percent) felt that paying more is unfair. They may have computed the total payments and discovered that they were paying high interest rates. It is likely that many of them opted for a longer easy payment since it will pose a lesser pressure on their budget, but many may not be aware of the credit trap.

For example, 44 percent of respondents felt that it is fair to pay more as they are paying low interest. Not knowing the truth may explain why they felt that the price is fair. In reality, the effective interest rate is punishing.

The above point is crucial to show that Islamic consumer financing can make the extra yard in the credit market. Pricing of *murabahah* or *al-bai-bithaman ajil* products should be made using a pricing model containing of scale and a decent amount of returns to depositors. Failing to do so may result in unfair pricing and may scare away potential customers.

3) Awareness that the price difference is interest

Eighty-eight percent of the respondents are aware that the price difference constitutes interest (*riba*). This may indicate the lack of Islamic schemes offered by the credit retail outlets. Probably the respondents felt that they are not paying exorbitant rates to these interest-bearing schemes.

Hence, it is unreasonable to say that interest (*riba*) is evil. Likewise, it could make them think that interest is not *riba*. These findings should make Islamic practitioners more aware that they can no longer rely on the *halal* factor to do business. Customers may put more weight on the pricing factor and the easy mode of payments.

The Islamic scheme shown to respondents is a short-term deferred sale scheme i.e., a mixture of *murabahah*. Our findings showed that 82 percent of respondents have shown interest in buying goods using the Islamic scheme. Thirty-one percent of them do so because no *riba* was found in the scheme, while 11 percent wish to do so only to support the Islamic scheme—a sympathy factor.

The religious factor, therefore, remains a strong pull-factor to the scheme, although this may contradict finding (4). But the interest (*riba*) factor only commands 31 percent of respondents' support of the Islamic scheme. This is a poor showing of religious commitment. This invites us to highlight the following questions:

1. What are the reasons behind the prohibition of interest (*riba*)?
2. Why are credit sale prices higher than cash prices?

Sixteen percent of respondents do not want to use the Islamic scheme because it is expensive and the rate is similar to the conventional scheme. These findings may require Islamic banks to look loosely at the pricing model used in the *murabahah* and *bai-bithaman-ajil* products.

Six
Product Pricing

With some slight fall of the base lending rates (BLRs), it is interesting to see how customers make their move. When interest rates are rising, customers are expected to choose fixed rate asset (FRA) facilities such as *al-bai-bithaman ajil*. At relatively lower rates, the demand for BBA products is likely to fall. This is because the BBA does not allow any changes to be made to its price. It also implies the annual profit rate locked to a BBA sale must stay put too.

No doubt this is good news to the Islamic banks, but the market normally clears at the best price signal. In this case, customers will favor the conventional banks. They will opt for the relatively cheaper conventional loans. In a dual banking system, changes in the BLRs would reveal optimal portfolio choice pattern among customers.

The question now is, what explains fall in the BLR? This has something to do with lower average three-month Kuala Lumpur inter-bank offered rate (KLIBOR). KLIBOR is the inter-bank interest rate on loans made to borrowing banks. These banks may be short of cash or money to fulfill statutory reserve requirements (SRR) or other liquidity purposes and therefore must find a quick way to acquire funds. These borrowed funds are available overnight or for up to a three month period in the inter-bank money market.

In August 1999, the average three-month KLIBOR was 7.8 percent, and most banks pegged their respective BLRs on this three-month KLIBOR.

Thus, a lower KLIBOR would mean a lower BLR. But what is the BLR, and what does it have to do with the profit rate on BBA facilities?

The point is, when a BBA customer asks the bank on what basis he is charged an annual profit rate (say 9 percent), it will not be easy to give the customer an honest answer. On the contrary, it is easier to quote interest rates, as commonly done in conventional loans. This is because the market interest rate is the sum of BLR and the spread. The spread is an additional interest rate that customers must pay to reflect their respective credit risks.

Hence when interest rate on loans is 12 percent at 9 percent BLR, the spread is 3 percent. Lower BLR means lower lending rates, while the risk profile of customers remains the same. Since the BLR now is pegged to the KLIBOR, changes in KLIBOR are expected to affect market interest rates, and therefore the demand for loans.

The notion of a base lending rate is alien to Islamic banking, simply because they do not make interest-bearing loans. Profits are created using credit sale payable by installments. The public should be informed about profit rate fixing as it is best to eliminate unwarranted ambiguities (*gharar*) in the BBA sale.

There are some variables in the BLR that are considered *tabi*'elements. By *tabi*'elements, we mean an action or situation that is nature's way. It can be sorted out by reason and experience. One does not need the Quran to confirm what value it stands for. For example the base lending rate shall include the following items:

- Cost of funds or cost of deposits.
- Resource costs i.e., staff and other overhead costs.
- A statutory profit margin at a prescribed rate of 0.25 percent per annum.

In Islamic banking, the cost of deposits is not interest paid to customers but the *hibah* and dividends they received from Islamic deposits. But Islamic cost of funds often reflects the KLIBOR . In Islamic banking system however, the cost of deposits consists of the *hibah* and dividends paid to the *al-wadiah* and *mudarabah* investment depositors respectively. These are not interest rates on deposits since deposits in Islamic banks mobilized via the *al-wadiah* and *mudarabah* contracts and not through the contract of interest-bearing debt. But the question now is on what basis are these *hibah* and dividends formulated?

To answer the above question, more research must be done to highlight the pricing policy of Islamic banks. To arrive at a "just" profit rate, it is important that bank's operation is efficient such that resource cost is minimized. Islamic banks should also able to differentiate the good paymasters from the bad ones such that the former would not be penalized for the sins of the latter.

Seven
Marketing Islamic Banking Products

Marketing in Islam is a *tabi'* phenmenon, meaning that it is a universal value. It is nature's way that one must market in order to make sales. It must be conducted by the selling party, Muslims and non-Muslims alike, if both want to see sales to go up. People who neglect this aspect of production will end up as losers, even if their products are deemed *halal*. The legal value of marketing is *mubah* (permissible). Islamic banking business must see this point straight without doubt as faith (*iman*) alone will not compel Muslims to become instant Islamic banking customers.

Marketing can be defined as the process of planning and executing the conception, pricing, promotion and distribution of ideas, goods, and services to create exchanges that satisfy individual and organizational objectives. Managers generally rely on four principal elements of marketing, namely: 1) Product, 2) Pricing, 3) Promotion, and 4) Place.

However, a marketing strategy using a marketing mix involving the product and its respective pricing, promotion, and distribution techniques would not guarantee success unless the managers are well informed about the environmental factors affecting consumers, such as 1) psychological, 2) personal, 3) social, and 4) cultural.

Even though managers may be able to gather information and knowledge about the above, they also need to understand how consumers make decisions to purchase products. They are expected to understand what elements are involved in the consumer buying process. Scholars who studied consumer behavior have given various models to explain the process.

In general, the buying process includes a) problem recognition, b) information seeking, c) evaluation of alternatives, d) purchase decision, and e) post-purchase decisions.

Based on the above guidelines, to market an Islamic financial product, one is required to conduct marketing research. This is the efficiency argument. Even if observing *Shariah* principles guarantees equity and fairness, Islamic banks must be mindful of the efficiency criterion. This is where marketing plays a vital role in Islamic banking.

The Prophet (saw) once said, "the best among you when given a task, will do it in the best possible manner." In this *hadith* lies the principle of efficiency in Islam. That is man must not put God's given resources to waste. As a trustee and vicegerent (*khalifa*) of God on earth, a believer is expected to look after His bounties in the best manner possible. This means fulfilling the efficiency requirement.

One way to achieve efficiency is by conducting research and investigation about the market. The research process would include the following: 1) study of current situation, 2) selection of research method, 3) data collection, 4) analysis data, and 5) preparation of a report.

In line with the objective of the banking firm, namely profit maximization, the main objective of marketing is to get the product to consumers. Concerning the profit objective, a bank's profit is the difference between cost and revenues.

In conventional banking, *bank's profit = interest income from loans* (i_L) *– interest cost of deposits (i_D)*. Since an Islamic bank operates on the basis of trade and commerce (*al-bay'*), *bank's profit = profits from investments of assets (p_A)- profits paid to depositors (p_D)*.

With profit maximization as the fuel to the banking business, the main objective of the financial system is to channel funds from the surplus sector (household) to the deficit sector (firm) such that all savings are injected as investments. This will create an equilibrium level of output with aggregate demand equals aggregate supply.

The banking sector is one of the many financial intermediaries that channel these funds from the surplus unit to the deficit unit. In similar fashion, the function of the Islamic banks is to channel surplus funds from the household sector to be used as investment in the production sector without the implication of interest as *riba*.

As a business entity, banks will compete for the surplus funds. They must be efficient to ensure that the funds mobilized from depositors are invested with an objective of making profit. But how does an Islamic bank make known their products to potential depositors and fund users?

Bank customers need to be informed what the products represent? In a plural society like Malaysia, a market segmentation study is necessary to ensure that accurate information is made available to Muslims and non-Muslims alike.

To the non-Muslim community, the *halal* (permissible) attributes of the product may not the main attraction, but these products are the only alternative available to the Muslim market and therefore Islamic banks are expected to educate them about the new products.

Apart from the *halal* attribute, Islamic financial products should also be proven to be more *equitable*. Product users should be informed that using Islamic financial products should improve income distribution and economic stability. The latter means that depositors would stand to receive higher returns while fund users will have greater opportunity to generate profits. The economy is expected to be stable since Islamic banking products will not create oversupply of financing and undersupply of deposits.

This factor should make a positive impact to people who do not favor interest-bearing system on both philosophical and economic grounds. These are the ethical investors. Thus, Islamic banks should pursue a proactive campaign to educate the public about the nature of the Islamic banking products. For example, to attract funds, a number of Islamic deposits are now available, two of which—namely current and savings account products—are based on the principle of safe-keeping called *al-wadiah yad dhamanah*. No interest is given on these deposits. To Muslims, it may not been a significant factor, but the non-Muslims may see this as a step backward, i.e., scraping away the benefits available in conventional banking deposits.

Islamic bank marketing managers should inform potential long-term depositors that these deposits are not similar to fixed income deposits.

For instance, managers are expected to enlighten *mudarabah* investment holders that:

1) they have contracted a partnership arrangement with the bank according to which no fixed returns and capital protection are guaranteed. To earn more requires them to assume higher risks;
2) if they desire capital protection, *al-wadiah dhamanah* is a suitable alternative. But here, banks do not hold any legal obligation to distribute profits.

Hence, the marketing from the liability side must look into the needs of the depositors, their religious allegiance, and their philosophies on investments and wealth creation. Effective marketing research should be pursued to further investigate the behavior of depositors, especially at the micro level, using statistical tools such as factor and discriminant analysis. Parametric testing such as regression analysis is helpful to extract evidence about how psychological, moral, and cultural factors affect supply and demand of Islamic banking products.

Eight
Full Financing via BBA

A move to offer 100 percent *al-bai bithaman ajil* (BBA) home financing is a positive step to make the credit sale contract (i.e., BBA) more wholesome. Before conducting a BBA sale, the bank as the selling party purchases the property from a developer or vendor at market price. If the market price is $250,000, the bank will sell the property to the customer at a credit price, consisting of the market price and a profit margin. When this happens, it implies that banks should have provided customers a full-financing scheme, since it purchases the property from the vendor at full price, i.e., the market price.

But to observe the safety principle, end financing is a practical way to safeguard the bank against bad debts caused by moral hazard. Customers will not attempt rather deliberately to default on a loan if they have put up a sizable sum as a down payment. It serves as a deterrent to potential bad paymasters.

In end financing, the amount of loans given out is always lower than the value of the mortgage. In a contract of loan such as housing loans, it is vital to observe the end financing rule. But applying the same rule on BBA sale has forced Islamic banks to finance only part of the purchases. It apparently distorted the BBA concept altogether.

In a genuine BBA sale, an asset worth, say, $50,000 at cost price must be entirely taken up by the purchasing bank. The BBA contract is misleading if the customer is required to come up with a 20 percent down

535

payment, leaving the bank only to finance the remaining $40,000. A BBA facility should provide 100 percent financing.

Certainly the Banking and Financial Institution Act (BAFIA) guidelines would not allow conventional finance companies to take up the 100 percent financing scheme. Even those that operate under the Islamic banking division (IBD) are not spared. But banks such as Bank Islam Malaysia (BIMB) and Bank Bumi-Muamalat Malaysia (BBMM under the governance of the Islamic Banking Act 1983 (IBA)) can virtually do so. Bank Rakyat is also capable of doing the same, since the Cooperative Act 1948 allows cooperatives to provide full financing to members. But doing so can be risky too. Such outing, although done with good intention, can hurt Islamic banks.

But why? The end financing scheme works well for conventional loans. The asset will serve as collateral and securities exceeding the amount of loans given out. This measure is pursued on safety grounds for fear of deliberate default if loans are given in full.

For example, if Farid does not have to pay any down payment on a $60,000 car, he will not mind skipping payments the first three or four payments and eventually defaulting the loan. It is similar to the problem of moral hazards in the insurance business. Motorists often become reckless, since insurers cover damages. In the case of Farid, his money is not at stake, so why must he be worried about making prompt payments when hard pressed by other commitments? Certainly, if Farid is required to put up $15,000 as down payments while the bank finances the remaining $45,000 he will think twice about defaulting, since he has his own money at stake. So, moral hazard is checked well under the end financing policy.

As the technique, a BBA transaction is similar to conventional loans; and it is not surprising to see a half cut BBA contract in action with end-financing rules. Since BBA is a credit sale, the credit-like nature will make no compromise with safety. It will therefore be suicidal if Islamic banks went on to offer full BBA financing, as customers may be tempted to dishonor payment obligation.

The same cannot apply to government BBA vehicle financing in which full facilities are granted today. Public servants will have their income deducted automatically to pay for these purchases by installment. Therefore, moral hazards will be kept to a minimum. Moreover, who would want to default payments when the government BBA sales are heavily subsidized?

Currently, the official annual profit rate is still 4 percent, compared with 7 percent to 8 percent offered by private banks.

So, should Islamic banks go ahead and make full BBA finance? The answer is "yes" if the intention is to make it nearer to the "real classic BBA transaction." But to do so can be mind-boggling, as this will endanger depositors' money when many BBAs become non-performing.

It is a desperate and risky measure if the scheme is intended to kill the market by taking advantage of the Islamic Banking Act in a recessionary economy like ours when moral hazards run wild. How will such a scheme help increase bank's earnings when the prospect of defaults is imminently higher?

The solution now lies not in BBA financing but something that captures the credit scheme in a more equitable manner. Leasing ending with ownership (*al-ijara wa iqtina*) should gradually take over BBA finance, as it allows full financing.

But this must work on the basis of operational lease so that the banks hold ownership claim. Unlike BBA financing today, this *al-ijarah* contract is closer to justice (*'adalah*) since an Islamic bank as the genuine owner leases out the vehicle to the customer.

However, in the present BBA setup, by virtue of the Charge Document, the bank holds the right of disposal until the customer completes his payments. This seems a bit weird, since all contracts of sales in Islam intend to transfer ownership of asset from the seller to the buyer, even if this means a deferred one. Again, as BBA financing tries to emulate loans for safety purposes, it has not been able to fully observe the "true BBA contract" that most *Shariah* scholars had readily approved.

Nine
Islamic Fund Management

Our first look *musyarakah* must be where it is made for, namely the non-banking firms. The problem at hand is how to apply *musyarakah* in the banking business. This can be tedious, since a significant change in the banking laws is in order to allow equity participation in the banking business

It is, thus, a little too soon to deal with this issue, as the unit trust industry is just around the corner. Moreover, unit trust companies are governed by rules and regulations that are essentially *musyarakah* oriented.

Looking at the nature of unit trust business from an Islamic angle has been quite monotonous today. It seems that it is all about *Shariah* stock screening, which the Securities Commission (SC) updated from time to time. A visit to the Securities Commission's website (www. securitiescommission.com.my) helps explain the fundamental of Shariah screening process.

What it does is identify companies whose direct operations involve *riba*, pork and pork products, gambling, and alcoholic beverages. Companies that put too much cash in interest-bearing fixed deposits are also sorted as *Shariah* non-compliance.

As of October 2003, 799 companies were categorized as *Shariah* compliant. Once done, individual Muslim investors and Islamic Unit trust companies will find these *Shariah* compliant companies most useful, as any capital gains and dividends obtained from investments in stocks and bonds of these companies are deemed lawful and permissible (*Halal*).

In Islam, this material gain is a spiritual one as well. It is capable of showing that the worldly life and the hereafter are inseparable. That's how the Islamic worldview is meant to be. *Shariah* stock screening is therefore most significant when a unit trust company is licensed to sell units with *Shariah* compliance features. However, there are other aspects needing further examination, such as:

1) the contractual relationship between the unit trust company and investors,
2) the contractual relationship between investors and the underlying companies they invested in the stock market, and
3) ethical principles in marketing unit trusts.

Since a unit trust company sells units to investors, one may wonder what is the Islamic contract applied to the transaction. It is agreed by the *fuqaha* that the contract of agency or *al-wakalah* is the most suitable one, since no profit sharing scheme is taking place between the company and investors.

The management fee (*ujrah*) associated with the skilled professional management supplied by the unit trust company is the intermediation cost that investors pay. By investing in unit trusts, the larger funds pooled from investors has made it possible for the managers to invest in many companies in order to spread the risk associated with equities.

The Islamic unit trusts business in essence displays a consolidation of a number of Islamic contracts. It begins with *al-wakalah,* followed by an indirect *musyarakah* system between investors and companies traded the stock and bond markets by way of units issued by the unit trust companies.

Units are equities, whether or not the underlying assets consist of money market instruments, bonds, shares, or the mixture of both. When the market is down, investors will see the decline in the net asset value (NAV), but this will not affect the value of shareholders' wealth of unit trust companies. Thus, issuance of units by these companies to investors does not constitute a *musyarakah* contract between them.

In this way, it is relatively difficult to identify the exact classical contract explaining the risk-taking dimension of unit trust investment. This is because the unit trust companies do not serve as investment partners, but rather service providers as units constitute shares issued by them (i.e., unit trust companies) to the investors who will assume market risks related to capital protection and returns.

The unit trust company is somewhat shielded from losses due to price movements. But it can suffer too, rather indirectly, when slow transactions translate into smaller commissions. When the operating costs exceeded commissions and fees collected, the company will soon get into trouble.

From its intermediation function, the company charges a fee that investors must pay for every purchase and sale of units it helps execute. Any losses incurred by investors due to adverse market movement will not affect the shareholders' wealth in any way.

The last but least-mentioned issue is the ethics in marketing unit trusts. It has a lot to do with honesty (*amanah*) in dealing with goodies often offered to the prospective investors. These include a promise to give away double-digit dividends, bonus and split issues, often without ascertaining how they are made. There are two possible outcomes if these incentives are realized.

First, the NAV per unit remains the same and secondly, it may become smaller. What concerns us most is the latter, as it has to do a lot with ethical conduct. Unlawful behavior in most cases is punishable as there are punitive laws to deal with them. But this is not true with unethical behavior. An individual can cheat or lie, but as long as he does not cause any physical injury or harm to the community, he is innocent in the eye of the law.

Likewise, unethical behavior can lead a person to commit a crime when the outcome of his immoral action transgresses the law. This is evident, for example, when man who is driven by greed (*hirs*) may indulge himself in corrupt practices, hence committing the criminal act. Unit trust agents too may fall into this trap, as less is done to see that it is wrong to make promises about capital protection and guaranteed returns, as if these were real and contractual in nature. For example, when double-digit dividends were promised at year end, investors were made to think that it is given away due to the fund's superior performance.

Instead, it may turn out that the dividends were taken out from the sale of assets, thus diminishing the asset value and consequently a decline in NAV per unit. In the final run, investors receive zero net gain, while unit trust companies profited from the fee they charge for every new transaction made.

Even if investors expected to read the prospectus before committing the purchases, they must be informed by the unit trust companies and their agents what impact it has on the NAV per unit. This is what ethics is all about. You don't play by the rules when information is not symmetrical.

As such, the role of *akhlak* is most important to promote the welfare of investors. Islamic unit trusts should be mindful of this point as they are made to do just that, namely to project the Islamic spirit of observing the good (*ma'aruf*) and avoiding the bad (*mungkar*).

Legal issues in Islamic unit trusts have been rather straightforward, namely determining the *Shariah* compliance stocks and also how to deal with problems of purification when companies whose direct activities are *halal* but *non-halal* in the indirect operations as investments in conventional fixed deposits and money markets.

On this point, Islamic funds that fail to comply with the given rules will have to abandon their business by legal dictum. However, this may not hold for unethical practices committed by unit trust agents who may not be too well informed about Islamic ethics.

Ethics is a study of human conduct. It serves to explain why people conduct themselves in a particular way. It looks at the value of human action and explains why some actions are considered good while others are bad. In Islam, the study of ethics and morality falls under the purview of *Akhlak*, which is one of the three constituents of the *Shariah*, the other two being *Aqidah* and *Muamalat*. The *Shariah* dimension of unit trust investments thus must not undermine the *Akhlak* aspects once the *Muamalat* component—namely *Shariah* stock screening—is fully put into application.

Islamic unit trusts companies should not allow any bonus and split issues by way of depleting the net asset value per unit. Prospective investors may be lured by offers promising a year-end bonus issues once a purchase is made. Instead, the bonus issue is given out by way of increasing total units without a proportionate increase in net assets made. As this will reduce NAV per unit, investors stand to lose out, while the company earns more commissions.

Ten
Islamic Trade Financing for SMIs

Lack of collaterals and guarantors seem to plague most Small and Medium Industries (SMI) today. And banks find it difficult to make loans. Without capital, SMIs cannot find space to survive even if they have the expertise and captured markets. Unlike the big conglomerates, SMIs cannot stand alone. They can easily perish when failed collections and accumulating receivables would mean failure to pay suppliers on time. Cash flow problems will make it hard for SMIs to maintain the product line, and its adverse impact on employment is obvious.

In financial matters, SMIs normally look for overdraft facilities. Standalone letters of credit (LC) are relatively less popular than trust receipts, bills of exchange, and export credit-refinancing schemes. With an exception of LCs all of the above facilities run on interest-bearing debt contracts.

Loans to the SMIs are given with guarantees normally granted by the Credit Guarantee Corporation (CGC). As guarantors, the CGC will back the bank loans for a fee. Project appraisal and credit assessment are conducted by the lending banks often made in the most conservative ways to guard against defaults.

Today, banks can obtain loans at subsidized rates from Bank Negara Malaysia to help fund many SMI operations. But still not enough loans were given, as many banks are still afraid to make commitments. To avoid more non-performing loans, more cash is lying idle in the banks, as more and more SMIs are deprived of getting the much-needed loans. Is there is a way out?

The growth of SMIs is crucial for economic development, as it represents the backbone of the manufacturing sector. It supplies essential parts and components to large manufacturers, which in Malaysia is run under the Vendor and Umbrella program. So the role of the banking sector in providing the necessary financial support must continue despite the economic slowdown.

Islamic banking, too, must be proactive to the needs of SMIs. It was reported recently that a special fund for SMIs was set up by Bank Islam Malaysia Berhad (BIMB) and Bank Rakyat Malaysia. It will be interesting to see the types of financing available and in what respect these instruments can indeed help increase the supply of Islamic financing for SMIs.

So, the question now is no longer about the demand for loans or financing. Rather it looks at the supply factor. That is, how can Islamic banks guard themselves against potential credit risks, as most Islamic trade financing products are based on debt. Table 10.1 below shows leading instruments of Islamic and conventional trade financing. Other than the *halal* and *haram* principles, it should be noted that both profit and interest-bearing products do not deviate significantly from normal credit valuation and appraisal. That is, even though Islamic banks will not extend trade finance facilities to companies involved in the production of non-permissible goods and services, it will still have to observe the profitability, safety, and liquidity principles of banking.

Table 10.1 Trade Financing Products

TRADE FINANCING FOR SMALL AND MEDIUM SCALE INDUSTRIES A COMPARISON			
Islamic trade financing VS Conventional trade financing			
•	*Al-Naqad* Overdraft (profit based)	•	Overdraft (interest-based)
•	*Murabahah* Letter of Credit (profit-based)	•	Letter of Credit (fee-based)
•	*Murabahah* Trust Receipt (profit-based)	•	Trust Receipt (interest-based)
•	*Bay' al-dayn* Islamic Accepted Bill (profit-based)	•	Bankers Acceptances (interest-based)
•	*Kafalah* letter of guarantee (fee-based)	•	Letter of guarantee (fee-based)
•	*Murabahah* export credit refinancing (profit-based)	•	Export Credit Refinancing (interest-based)

So, in what way do existing Islamic trade financing facilities make the difference? For example, making *mudarabah* letter of credit will involve the same valuation process. Pricing is made using conventional formulas with premium attached on the basis of current banking norms. The same is applied to overdraft, trust receipts, and banker acceptances.

It is interesting to see how Islamic banks can supply more funds to SMIs when they have no powerful tool to work with. To relax credit assessment is certainly not the remedy, especially when moral hazards are running wild these days. The next alternative is profit-sharing, which Islamic banking can pursue without too much worry about accompanying legal inhibitions. In principal, the Islamic Banking Act 1983 allows an Islamic bank to own shares of companies, as doing so is in line with the *Shariah*. In this way, Islamic banks can participate in joint ventures. Finally, existing *murabahah*-based Islamic trade finance is undoubtedly interest-free, but still heavily based on collateral. But under the current economic recession, how can SMIs provide the collaterals they don't have? Will Islamic banks turn down SMIs that do not have enough collateral? What, then, is the role of Islamic banks in economic development?

Islamic banks should pay heed to the fact that current facilities do not make the difference. What they need is some new way that can put them at the forefront of SMI financing. If Islamic banks are not confident with *mudaranah* and *musharakah*, the *salam* and *istisna'* model can be more appealing.

In *salam* and *istisna'* financing, the letter of credit is still relevant. But using the overdraft, trust receipt, and bankers' acceptances is no longer relevant. In other words, there is not need for the entrepreneur to be in debt, as he is paid in advance over the goods sold. The bank has a new role to take and this is the marketing job. Even though this is rather alien to the banking business, making a breakthrough demands new sacrifices and risk-taking.

Eleven
Khiyar al-'Aib: An option to cancel the contract

It was reported recently that a housing developer of the Bandar Puncak Alam at Bukit Cerakah will meet buyers to resolve their complaints about structural defects in their new homes. Obvious cracks and sunken floors have made it dangerous for them to move in. To ensure safety, repairs must be made, but who shall foot the bill?

To some extent, it is assumed that some of them may have used the Islamic mode of *financing*, namely *al-bai bithaman ajil* (BBA). This is because Shah Alam is a predominantly Malay area and Muslim township.

By definition, a BBA contract is a markup credit sale sale with payments made by installments. Theoretically, in a BBA transaction, the bank purchases the house from the developer at the prevailing market price. Then the bank sells the house to the customer, at a markup price consisting of the cost price plus the profit the bank wants to make over a specified financing period, say 20 years.

The question now is who should chase the developer to see the house delivered according to its true contractual specification. Is it the bank or the customer? If we look at the financing documentation of BBA, there are some good lessons to be learned.

In the case of Bandar Puncak Alam, we are dealing with the sale of uncompleted houses. In fact, using BBA has not been accurate here since the delivery of these houses is not made on the spot but in the future. To some extent, Islamic practitioners should think of using *Istisna'* plus BBA i.e., a sale in which future delivery is based on either spot or deferred payments.

There are three main agreements in most BBA home financing documentation involving uncompleted houses, namely:

1. Property Purchase Agreement
2. Property Sale Agrement
3. Deeds of Assignment

In the above case, we know that the document title has not been issued, since the house is not yet ready.

In the early years, the Novation Agreement is used to the transfer of property right to the bank. This tripartite agreement is made between the bank, the customer, and the developer. Here, the bank purchases the house from the developer (usually based on the outstanding amount, say 80 percent of the total price) and therefore secures the right of ownership. But currently, the property purchase agreement (PPA) is used instead since the bank must own the asset prior to the property sale agreement. This is because the customer via the sale and purchase agreement (S&P) is the legal owner of the property. Only after the property is sold to the bank that the PSA can be executed.The Property Sale Agreement (PSA) sees the bank selling the property to the customer at a stipulated selling price with definitive repayment period and monthly installments. The PSA contract signifies the BBA sale between the bank and the customer.

For property under construction, the Deed of Assignment spells out the rules whereby the customer assigns the property to the bank as a security. This property will serve to secure repayments within the specified financing period. If the property is a completed one, the charge document is used instead.

Now that some defects are found in the new houses, should the customer go after the developer, or should they leave the matter to the selling party, i.e., the bank? In conventional financing, the latter is true, but should Islamic banking do the same thing?

By virtue of the BBA documentation, particularly the Property Sale Agreement with the bank acting as the selling party, it is apparent that the bank must take responsibility for property it sells.

It is here that the customer must be informed about their Islamic rights of option (*khiyar*). The right must be exercised on the seller, namely the bank, rather than the developer, since this represents the *'iwad* (i.e., risks and value added) factor that must exist in all trading activities.

The issue at hand is *khiyar al'-ayb* or option of defect. It is about the option given to the customer to cancel or annul the BBA contract when a defect on the goods sold is found.

To ensure that the agreement remains valid, the bank is expected to take forceful action on the developer and ensure that the defects are removed. The *khiyar al-'ayb* or the option of defect is a legal right. This means the customer does not need to stipulate a special clause or provision of the option at the time of contracting. It comes automatically with the BBA sale.

According to the *Mejelle*, "any buyer in Islamic law has an automatic implied warranty against latent defects in the goods purchased." According to Kasani, "the buyer is also permitted to expressly renounce a defect which might develop in the goods during the restrictive period after having been taken into possession by him."

The term "latent" here must be well understood to avoid unsound claims leading to the right to cancel the contract. The Hanafi School defined a "latent" defect as "everything, which results in a diminution of value according to commercial custom, whether this diminution is gross or minimal."

The Malikis term this option as *Khiyar al-Naqisa* and state that the defect must be of such a nature as to cause a "discernible" diminution of value of the goods, or to render the object less suitable for the use to which it was intended to be put.

The question now is who the customer should turn to in order to receive protection. They have paid at least 25 percent of the total price and cancellation of contracts requires a lengthy and expensive court process. In the Islamic sense, the BBA mode of financing must show that it can no longer restrict itself to conventional norms. They must take an active role in putting things right and help the customers to get what they have paid for. Doing otherwise will disappoint customers, and tarnishes the image of Islamic banks.

Twelve
Islamic Unit Trusts

Understanding Islamic unit trusts or mutual funds is not an easy concern, as many may not see what actually Islam wants from the contracting parties, namely the unit trust companies and investors. For example, unit trust agents and financial planners may simply place the *Shariah* requirements top in the agenda. They usually resorted to the *Shariah* Advisory Council (SAC) for the latest information on *Shariah* stock listing. The SAC has a definite approach to stock screening. Unit trust management companies (UTMC) do not have to conduct their own. The *Shariah* issues and problems are left to the SAC for corrective measures and remedies. In this way, UTMCs need only to do one thing i.e., investing the funds wisely and act professionally in conducting business.

But it seems that Islam's role is put in a tight jacket, as if it has less to do with the act of investing itself. Likewise, *Shariah* advisors are confined to making opinions about *halal* and *haram* alone, and not about how UTMC is running the business and managing the funds.

Before indulging further into the *Shariah* issue, it is worthy to explain the difference between Islamic unit trust management companies (UTMC) and Islamic funds. A unit trust company is a financial intermediary that sells new shares to the public and redeems their outstanding shares on demand at a price equal to an appropriate share of the value of their portfolio. The money collected from the sale of new shares is pooled into a unit trust fund. The fund will then be invested by the unit trust management company in diversified portfolio consisting of authorized investments such as stocks, bonds, government securities, money market instruments, fixed deposits, and also in unquoted shares via direct business ventures.

In this way, one can see that a UTMC may offer several funds. Funds can be categorized into two. First, they are classified according to objectives and risk-return features. For example, growth funds put more focus on capital gains while income funds are concern about dividends, rentals, and interest.

Secondly, funds are categorized into what fund managers want to focus on as a strategy to maximize performance. Thus, in a bull market, equity funds are popular or when interest rate is low, bond funds are better options. For relatively risk-free investments, money market funds should be the best bet. Derivative funds and property trust funds should do the trick when the time is right. Lately, Islamic funds appeared in almost all UTMCs. These funds are invested in *Shariah*-approved financial assets such as *Shariah*-approved stocks, Islamic bonds, Islamic deposits, and money market instruments.

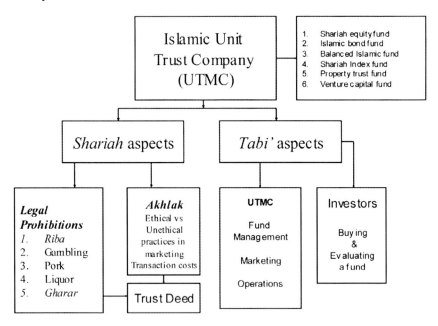

Figure: 10.2 Islamic Unit Trust Company

An Islamic UTMC is one that offers only *Shariah*-approved funds. These can be equity, bond, or balanced funds. Most UTMCs in Malaysia, however, offer both conventional and Islamic funds. Thus, as a company, these UTMCs do not bear an Islamic label. But they do carry an Islamic label on the Islamic funds offered.

As mentioned earlier, investment in Islamic funds is not about investing in *Shariah*-approved financial assets alone. This is the *Shari'* dimension. The *Shari'* aspect is a God-given rule. *Shariah* advisors are trained to acquire, understand, and interpret these divine rules to help people live and conduct economic activities according to the Will of God.

But their job should not end there. Equally important is to ensure that people are able to earn decent returns from the investment. This is where people tend to forget about investment in Islamic unit trusts. We used to think it only deals with *Shariah* stock screening and identifying the *halal* products from the *haram* ones. When people start believing the same, they are, in fact, compartmentalizing Islam.

My main point is that investing wisely is the main thing. To be a wise and intelligent investor, first one must truly observe the *Shariah* principles. Secondly, he must know well the art of investing. This is the *Tabi'* dimension in Islamic investment. The art of investment cannot be ignored. It is a law in nature, irrespective of the funds he invested in— Islamic or conventional. Once ignored, the implication can be punitive.

But investing in Islamic funds means that one does not have to do the actual investment. He need not conduct fundamental and technical analysis or make tedious forecasting exercises in order to make the right buy and know when to exit. That job belongs to the fund management team. They will set the asset allocation policy and keep track of investment values. In fact, the UTMC charges investors a lot of money for these services. This *Tabi'* aspect of investment falls on the shoulder of UTMCs.

For these professional services, investors pay UTMCs fees and commission. Let's see what kind of fees and commissions customers must pay to invest in Islamic funds. Basically, there are three types of fees, namely:

1. Entry load – this is the initial service charge on the value of the fund bought. The entry load = [Selling price – NAV / NAV) x 100
2. Exit load – this is the fee customers pay when they sell off their units. The exit load = [NAV – Buying price/NAV] x 100
3. Management Expense Ratio (MER) – this represents the administration fees of the UTMC for running the unit trust business.

The fee includes the UTMC's overhead, trustee fees, and audit fees. The MER actually reports the fund's total annual operating expenses as a percentage of the fund's asset. If the expense ratio is 1 percent, for a given $50,000 investment, the investor will pay $5,000 in annual fees.

Now what is the Islamic view about these charges? To the answer the question, one must now examine the nature of contract between a UTMC and investors. Since the latter pays the former fees and commissions, the contract cannot resemble an equity one, such as *mudarabah* and *musyarakah*. It looks like the UTMC is appointed by investors as an agent (*wakil*) to manage the funds. In this way, the contract of agency (*wakalah*) seems more accurate.

But a UTMC does not serve as an agent (*wakil*) who is allowed to manage the funds without control and supervision. To prevent moral hazards, a trustee is appointed to safeguard the interest of investors. The trustee will act as a custodian to the funds and will ensure that investments are properly run according to true label. This includes conducting due diligence and making sure that all transaction and distribution of dividends are recorded. For the services rendered, investors will pay the trustee some fees. In this way, it is correct to say that the trustee business runs on the contract of *wadiah amanah*.

Regarding the trust deed—the trust deed is a tripartite agreement that binds the UTMC, the trustee, and the unit holders as one unit or family in the unit trust scheme. It is a covenant that spells out each party's role and obligations in the scheme. Among others, the covenant implies the following:

1. UTMC – the services of marketing and fund management in return for fees and commission.
2. Trustee – the services of custody in return for fees.
3. Investors – investing their money via UTMCs fund managers but without guarantees on income and capital protection.

What can be seen in the above is the interdependent association of the three parties to make the scheme achieve its objective, but in no way does the same apply to the fees and income that each party gets. For example, when investors make losses, the trustee and UTMC still collect their fees, though they are lower. As long as NAV remains positive and people buy and sell units, there is money to be made. The trust deed is therefore an interesting subject in Islamic law. There is no single and definite contract (*'aqd*) that one can relate to the trust deed.

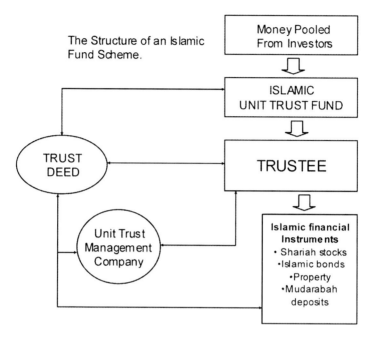

Figure 10.3 Islamic Unit Trust Company (UTMC)

Finally, investment in Islamic unit trust should put investors in a position to ponder over their decisions to invest. This is because wealth (*al-mal*) is a trust (*amanah*) from God. As a trustee, a Muslim investor must see the investment conducted along Islamic values. One of them is the *Shariah* values. It means fund portfolios must be *Shariah* approved. This work is undertaken by the UTMC and the SAC of the Securities Commission.

But although investors have paid some fees on the investment services rendered by UTMC, they are still not free from an important obligation. That is, they must know how to buy and evaluate Islamic funds.

The above constitutes one more aspects of *Tabi'* investments. Buying an Islamic fund among others requires the investors to know the net asset value (NAV) or share price of the units. The NAV = Fund Asset / Fund shares. For example, if the value of the fund (say, dinar fund) is \$50,000,000 and investors own 1,000,000 shares, the NAV = \$50,000,000/ 1,000,000

= $50. Likewise, investors should also be mindful about the transaction costs, namely the loading fees and management expense ratio.

To evaluate the funds is by no means easy. It requires investors to know: 1) changes in NAV, 2) the yield, 3) risk and return, 4) tax, 5) cost, and 6) the how the fund has so far met its objective. This is where most investors are in the dark. They can engage a financial planner to help out, but this means more fees to pay. By no means a UTMC with whom a person does business with is willing to do this work, since they are competing with other UTMCs as well.

Thus, it boils down to doing one's own work and research. This *tabi'* dimension of investment cannot be ignored. If ignored, capital losses are inevitable whether one is investing in Islamic or conventional funds. To ignore the *tabi'* aspect of investment means he has neglected his role as God's trustee, and therefore has committed a sinful act. It is sinful because putting money in a business venture without knowledge is akin to gambling (*maisir*). In this way, the *al-akhira* (*Shariah*) and the *al-dunya* (*Tabi'*) aspect of investment is made inseparable. This is what an Islamic worldview actually means.

Thirteen
Is there a limit to profits in Islam?

Keynesian economics today seemed to dominate policy direction to further stimulate consumer spending. High liquidity means that people are not spending enough. Credit card promotion has been highly competitive. Glut in the non-landed property market saw the home ownership campaign with $5 billion worth of property up for grabs. To what extent this is possible will very much depend on the demand side, as supply is already glutted.

The demand for property usually depends on prices. It is also influenced by the level of disposable income and wealth of household. For example, if companies begin to cut wages and lay off workers, disposable income declines. The demand for housing will fall too. Likewise, a bear market will see less capital gain and thus, less wealth creation. In both cases, people will be less inclined to purchase houses.

Consumers also look at interest rates. Lower cost of fund rates means lower installment payments. So it helps a great deal if lower discounted prices offered came with lower interest rates.

In a market economy, the forces of supply and demand are expected to govern the allocation of scarce resources. In this manner, oversupply of property must translate itself into lower and affordable prices. Lower interest rates alone will not help when loans are contracted on a floating rate basis. Consumer will soon pay more when interest rate eventually rises.

The government may be doing a noble job to make housing more affordable by lowering interest rates. But it has to do more. The main storyline is how to get rid of the unsold apartments and condominiums. The construction industry has relatively ignored landed properties such as low-cost single-story and medium-cost two-story houses. They have put aside the Malaysian lifestyle and opted instead to ape densely populated urban economies such as Hong Kong and Singapore. Both have adapted well to the flat-living lifestyle.

A cursory look at landed property in the Klang Valley showed that there is hardly any attractive offer for double-story houses. The price of a basic 22-foot x 75-foot unit today is not within the reach of the middle class. These houses, costing between $200,000 and $300,000, are obviously overpriced. But why?

There seem to be two plausible explanations: 1) excess demand and 2) a flagrant misrepresentation of value. The first factor can be overcome through policy. To build more landed properties, the government can award larger tax breaks to construction companies. The supply of these homes should increase, thus putting pressure on demand and prices.

But what people fear more is the absence of policy to check cases where a flagrant misrepresentation of value in pricing is evident. It is rather strange to see how a developer can sell at such high prices, given that resources in this country are abundant. The government must see that developers quote reasonable prices.

Apartment lifestyles are definitely not suitable for the average Malaysian person. At one time, the government encouraged Malaysian couples to raise seven children because bigger families mean bigger markets. It means more consumption and this helps stimulate sales and increase business profits. As profit increases, investment will go up and so does economic growth. But ironically, there seems less consistency in this policy move, as most developers are keen to build apartments and condominiums that can only accommodate a family of three.

But people cannot afford to purchase two-story houses that can support at most nine family members. The prices of these properties do not make sense. Could it be caused by overpricing? Is there a flagrant representation of price?

In Islam, flagrant misinterpretation of prices is called *ghaban al-fahish*. In the Mejelle, *ghaban al-fahish* is defined as "excessive deception in the value of goods." By excessive deception, the Mejelle implies not less than one-twentieth of the total price in respect to goods, one-tenth in respect to animals, and one-fifth in respect for real estate. For real estate, this will imply the following: if a developer builds a house at a cost of $100,000 and sells it at $120,000, (i.e., earns 20 percent margin) he is not committing *ghaban al-fahish*. However, if the property is quoted at $200,000 or any price above that, then *ghaban al-fahish* is said to exist in the sale.

However, *ghaban al-fahish* is not at all condoned unless it is caused by fraud (*taghrir*). Excessive profit created from sales when demand is rising is allowed in Islam. According to Ibn Taimiyah, this is a bounty (*rizk*) from God. In this case, the person who feels deceived for putting a high price cannot annul the contract. Only when the *ghaban al-fahsh* is accompanied by fraud can the person who is deceived annul the sale.

One can also wonder whether pricing in *al-bai-bithaman ajil* (BBA) sales constitute *ghaban al-fahish*. A house at $100,000 market price can be sold at $200,000 based on a ten-year BBA installment scheme at 10 percent profit rate annually. For this reason, it is crucial that the BBA model is replaced with an Islamic hire-purchase scheme (IHP). The latter is more flexible and warrants the bank to practice true leasing to collect rentals. The IHP is a floating-rate product and does not solely run on a sale and purchase model.

Fourteen
Islamic banking and credit risk

Since the early 1960s, Muslim economists have been propagating the idea of profit-loss sharing (PLS) in the banking business. The main philosophy is distributive justice. More attention was given to the asset side of the balance sheet, namely financing while deposit mobilization received relatively less focus.

Making profit via interest (*riba*) is banned by the Quran and considered unproductive since it is created without risk-taking. Sometimes, Muslim economists tend to use the Marxian argument that interest and capital have no value, since value is only created by labor. As such, any gain where labor is absent is illegitimate. Thus, capital is impotent without labor. Capital becomes productive only when labor is applied to it. No production can take place without labor.

In contemporary Islamic banking business, profits derived from *al-bai-bithaman ajil* and *murabahah* are considered lawful because in trading (*al-bay'*), capital is combined with labor. In contrast, *riba* is an unlawful form of profit because it is created from "capital divorced of labor." That is, the bank is not taking an active role in converting capital input into final output. There is no value addition coming from the bank side.

But as a financial intermediary, a bank may find it too demanding to get itself directly involved in production, say in manufacturing and agriculture. The risks in production are too overwhelming and new to banking operations. Banks have refused to combine their capital loan with labor, out of fear that the business entity in which both capital and labor are combined may suffer losses.

As a consequence, Muslim economists further argue that *riba* is prohibited because the bank refuses to assume risk in conducting business. However, this view may not be so accurate. In 1998, troubled financial companies such as Sime Bank and Abrar Finance will find such views both naïve and arrogant. If the banking business is risk-free, how can one explain the $1.53 billion loss by Sime Bank in 1998?

The answer is quite simple, something that early Muslim economists did not attempt to clarify. To that effect, lesser attempts were made to explain why Islam prohibits interest as *riba*. Non-Muslims too may find it paradoxical upon seeing that a BBA contract is lawful while a loan contract is unlawful even though both generate the same contractual profit.

The main argument lies in the type of risks taken by the Islamic banking firm. What kind of risks an Islamic bank actually holds. In principle, risk can be divided into two, namely 1) general risk, and 2) specific risk. General risk is also known as market risk. In finance, it is called systematic risk. It is something that human beings cannot control.

If one looks at an interest-bearing loan as a financial asset, systematic risk includes a wide range of factors exogenous or outside to the security. These include recessions, war, structural changes in the economy, and also changes in consumer spending preferences. Like it or not, the buyer of the security—namely the borrower—cannot escape this part of risk, because no matter how well he or she diversifies, the risk of overall market cannot be avoided. In Islam, market risk is therefore part of the *tabi'* law (i.e., law in nature).

Non-Performing Financing (NPF)
2003

- Islamic banks (BIMB, BMM)   = 10.8 %
- Commercial banks^{Islamic}   = 6.9%
- Finance companies^{Islamic}   = 2.7%
- Merchant bank^{Islamic}   = 13.2%

- Conventional banks   = 7.7%

Source: Bank Negara AnnualReport 2003

Figure 10.4 : Non-Performing Financing in the Islamic banking business

However, banks as issuers of loan have no part in taking on market risks. Instead, they are exposed to what is known as specific or issuer risk. It is also known as non-systematic risk in finance. Non-systematic risk includes default or credit risk, interest rate risk, liquidity risk, business risk, exchange rate risk, and crime risk. Through diversification or best known as risk management, these risks can be eliminated. For example, default risk can be minimized by issuing more equity products or cutting down on loans. In the case of Islamic banking, equity products are based on the *mudarabah* and *musyarakah* principles. Interest rate risk and forex risk can be avoided by hedging in the financial futures market.

Thus, the objective to avoid non-systematic risk has become the main task of conventional banks' risk management today. Costs incurred in risk management are borne by borrowers and not banks' shareholders. Also, personal costs (staff salaries, overtime, refreshment, entertainment allowances, training expenses, performance awards, etc.) can easily account for about 50 percent of a bank's overhead. So, if banks fail to do their job properly due to negligence and complacency, they have nobody except themselves to blame.

This is, however, also true for Islamic banks that run on credit finance via *al-bai-bithaman ajil* (BBA) contracts. They are shielded from market risks if ownership (*milkiyah*) of traded assets prior the BBA sale is not evident. Islamic banks driven by BBA without ownership risk (*daman milkiyah*) are only exposed to non-systematic risks, just like any conventional bank does. This time, it is default or credit risk. To mitigate credit risk, Islamic banks can readily apply conventional risk management tools to minimize risk arising from the defaulting BBA payments. Given that Islamic banking is predominantly credit-driven, credit risk can be worrisome. In 2003, non-performing finaning was 10.7 percent for Bank Islam Malaysia and Muamalat. This was much higher than the 7.7 percent non-performing loan in conventional banks

On the contrary, businessmen who made purchases of machinery and equipment via BBA are exposed to bankruptcy risk. If business goes wrong due to a recession or political unrest, there is no way the company can find protection. This is the market risk that no business can avoid. It is not controllable. Losses incurred as a result of market risk will find business unable to meet debt obligations.

The legal maxim (*qawaid fiqiah*) that says "no rewards without risk" (*al-ghorm bil ghonm*), is positive about risk-taking. The legal maxim is definitely not referring to credit risk because the meaning of *al-bay'* as the Quran implies is not credit driven but overwhelmingly pointing towards general trading and commerce. Because Islamic banking is credit driven, focus on risk management issues will always revolve around mitigating credit and default risk. It will no longer find the above legal maxim applicable as products prone to market risks such as *salam, istisna, mudarabah,* and *musyarakah* are not viable to the banking business.

Fifteen
Currency trading in Islam

Currency trading today can mean three things, namely sale and purchase of currencies, a) to settle international payments, b) to hedge against market volatility, and c) to make profits. In Islam, the exchange of currencies for the purpose of international trade is called *Al-Sarf*, or the sale of price for a price, also known as *bay' al-thamab bil thaman*. For example a Malaysian company orders machines from the United States valued at US$10 million (RM38million). It is only logical for the U.S. firm to accept payments in its own currency. At the current exchange rate, the Malaysian company needs RM38 million in exchange for US$10 million.

What is evident is not the exchange of commodities but an exchange of prices. As the demand for U.S. imports increases, there will be greater need to exchange ringgit for dollars, leading to changes in the exchange rate. In this case, the ringgit may depreciate against the dollar. But normally, this will not happen easily, since U.S. companies also purchase Malaysian goods and pay Malaysian companies in ringgit. Automatic adjustment of the exchange rate is largely market driven.

However, when there is a heavy selling of ringgit, Bank Negara Malaysia (BNM) may step in to stabilize the local currency. To push up the ringgit, BNM uses its foreign reserves to sell, say, U.S. dollars in buying ringgit. In this case, the selling of dollars and the purchase of ringgit is no longer meant to settle international trade, but to protect the local currency. Failure to stabilize the ringgit will result in severe trade imbalances.

In Islam, this intervention is made to protect the *daruriat,* i.e., the basic needs of the people. One of the objectives of the *Shariah* is to protect the public interest (*maslahah al-ammah*). That is, it is in the public interest that the *daruriat* is protected. The *daruriat* has five components: religion (*din*), life (*nafs*), intellect (*'aql*), family (*nasl*), and property (*mal*).

An as example, in preserving the religion, the five daily prayers (*solat*) were made compulsory (*wajib*) to the believers (*mukallaf*). To preserve life, providing *nafaqah* (spending on oneself and family) is an obligation on all married man. To preserve reason and the intellect, man is enjoined by the Quran to seek knowledge (*'ilm*), while at the same time, the Quran forbids the consumption of intoxicants. To safeguard the family, the Quran enjoins the institution of marriage and prohibited fornication and adultery. Finally to protect property, the Shari'ah enjoins man to work (*khayr*) for a living while prohibiting wealth creation by way of interest (*riba*), fraud (*tatfief*) and gambling (*maysir*).

So when a central bank intervenes in the market process to protect the local currency, Islam viewed it as a means to protect life (*nafs*) and property (*mal*). In this, Islam finds no evil in currency trading by the government as sales and purchases of ringgit are made in the spot market. It is pursued not for profits, but to protect national interest.

As the term "trading" (*al-bay'*) constitutes a profit-seeking activity, how does Islam look at currency trading involving individuals and private property? As an example, the purchase price of imports is quoted in U.S. dollars. The Malaysian firm fears that at the time the machines were delivered, the ringgit may fall against the U.S. dollar, say to RM4. Now the company has to come up with an extra RM2 million in exchange for US$10 million. Without a doubt, the cost overrun may hurt the company.

Today, firms hedge against such price volatility. Hedging against foreign exchange risk is not a new thing. There are four instruments an investor can use to protect against such risk, each of which constitutes one form of currency trading. They are:

a) currency forward contract
b) currency futures contract
c) currency options
d) currency swaps

As mentioned earlier, the *Shariah* serves to protect wealth (*al-mal*), both public and private. In protecting private wealth, does Islam allow an individual or private institution to hedge against foreign exchange risk? Let's take currency forward contracts and ignore any changes to interest rates and taxes.

For fear that the ringgit may drop to RM4 against the dollar, the Malaysian firm purchases currency forward contracts to lock in the desired exchange rate, say at the spot rate RM3.8 to the dollar. By doing so, the firm foregoes the opportunity to gain if the ringgit appreciates instead. If this happens, the gain does to the buyers of the forward contract, most of whom are speculators.

If the ringgit indeed depreciates to RM4 against the dollar, the firm that sells the forward contract at RM3.8 per dollar is protected from forex losses. The speculator who buys the contract at the prevailing spot price will be squeezed dry.

In the above case, two parties are taking part in forward contract. The buyers constitute the genuine merchants and manufacturers. These are the hedgers. The other party has no interest in trading real goods, but only to make money out of speculation. They have no intention of using the currency for import and export, but rather buy and sell currencies for profits on the basis of market movement.

The main argument against currency forward contract has been the *riba* (interest) factor. Spot exchanges do not involve exchanges of unequivalence. But the same is not true in forward contract. Given the prevailing value of ringgit at RM3.8 per U.S. dollar, a purchaser of forward contract practically agree to exchange RM3.8 for RM4.0 since the strike price (i.e., RM4 per U.S. dollar) is contracted on the spot. Although the conversion will only take place near or on the expiration date, the forward contract has locked in a certain price, which is equivalent to the exchange of RM3.8 for RM4 on the spot. Here in an effort to eliminate downside risk, it has implicated the taking and receipts of interest (*riba*).

The *Shariah* scholars (*fuqaha*) at the supervisory level may have a hard time rationalizing forward contracts, especially for Islamic banking applications, notably that involving Islamic export credit refinancing (IECR) and similar products. In the case of IECR, it provides financing of export prior to payments by importers. It helps exporters obtain early payments via bank financing.

When the export bill is contracted in dollars, the ringgit value tends to move with the currency market. The Islamic bank charges the facility in ringgit but the customer receives payments in dollars. If the dollar depreciates, upon conversion, the customer (exporter) receives less in ringgit. Likewise, if the dollar depreciates, he will gain instead. But the exporter is not keen to speculate in this way. All he wants is to avoid foreign exchange risk.

In the above, should the customer be allowed to purchase a forward contract in order to safeguard his ringgit export value from market volatility? If allowed, the Malaysian exporter who will receive US$10 million in 180 days, and be assured of receiving RM4 per dollar from the currency conversion. But this means implicating *riba,* since the forward contract specified the exchange of RM3.8 per dollar for RM4.00 per dollar.

Avoiding foreign exchange risk can best be pursued using the Islamic dinar system. It constitutes an avenue in eliminating the use of currency forward contract for Islamic trade financing involving cross-border settlements. In the Islamic dinar system, an export of RM38 million can be contracted and quoted in Islamic dinar (say, 10 million Islamic dinar), but payments settled in ringgit. That is the exportables are sold for 10 million dinar, say, payable in three months.

In case some volatility in the dinar system does take place, the following method can be used. If after the expiration date, the 10 million dinar is worth RM40 million, the exporter will pass the RM2 million surplus to the buyer as a discount (*wadhiah*) Likewise, if the dinar is worth RM36 million, the exporter shall be awarded an additional RM2 million as an *ibra.* These special provisions are only voluntary in nature and in no way defined on contractual basis. The above illustration can only be a special case when the value of gold suffers some volatility. But for centuries the value of gold is relatively stable. As such, it may not suffer from market volatility as commonly seen in the currency market.

To conclude, Islam allows the sale and purchase of currency to meet cross-border transactional needs. It also recognizes the need for hedging but not via forward currency contract. Instead the dinar system is readily available for application. The *riba* (interest) factor in forward contract holds heavier weight than the protection private wealth, thus rationalizing currency forward contract for Islamic banking application, if any, is considered short-sighted.

Sixteen
Islamic Corporate Governance

Studies on corporate governance have gained momentum with the reported misconducts of Enron and WorldCom on accounting practices. Back in 1999, corporate governance has gained prominence, as attested by the Organization of Economic Cooperation and Development's (OECD) definition of corporate governance as the "set of relationships between the company's management, its board, its shareholders and other stakeholders." In the same year World Bank indicated that the purpose of corporate governance is to create "fairness, transparency and accountability" to all stakeholders. It is only when the world was shocked by the Enron scandal that corporate governance was put in high gear, but now with punitive policy measures.

There seems to be a contrast how the Americans and the Europeans look at the issue. The former runs under the Anglo-Saxon model that says corporate governance intends to maximize profits, i.e., to maximize its shareholders' value, and nothing else is more important. This is the shareholder value-centered view of corporate governance. It is based on agency relationship between the shareholders and the manager, with the protection of shareholders' interests as the main objective.

The opposing European version, as confirmed by the Franco-German model, aims to protect a wider circle of stakeholders and incorporates each stakeholder's claims, rights, and obligations. Stakeholders may include customers, suppliers, providers of complementary services and products, distributors, and employees. This model says that corporations should be managed for the benefit of all who have some stake in the firm.

The scandals at Enron and WorldCom seem to have put the stakeholders' theory of corporate governance to greater focus. The shareholder-value concept of profit-maximization is too narrow a view. And the disadvantages imposed by profit maximization choices on other stakeholders can further damage society if left unattended.

The evolving thinking of corporate governance from the shareholders' to stakeholders' models proved one thing: People do learn from mistakes and theories evolved from observing how people behave both in good conducts and misconducts. Things are getting better as people guilty of corporate misconducts paid a heavy price. The irony is that laws are often enforced after total damage is done.

The Islamic view of corporate governance boils down to one thing: accountability. As simple as it sounds, the study of accountability as a principle of human action in a corporate environment can be very complicated. This is because men do not seem to agree on one thing, namely accountability to God.

In the pre-Islamic (*Jahiliya*) era, the secular Meccan pagans did not believe in life after death. There was no such thing as day of judgment (*khiyamah*) or ideas about resurrection or final accounting. Whatever they did was supposed to end in this world alone. But when Prophet Muhammad (*pbuh*) says that man is accountable to God, that man will rewarded for their good deeds and pay for their sins in the Hereafter (*akhirah*), it struck the Meccans hard like a rock. Their material worldview was severely threatened. They revolted against this idea and put the lives of Prophet Muhammad (*pbuh*) and his followers under constant danger.

The Meccans do not want to help the poor and orphans, to protect the women, and conduct business with honesty and fairness. This is because there is no legal obligation to do so. The Meccans may have to observe certain tribal laws, but nothing significant to check them from oppressing the poor, slaves, and women, or manipulating business transactions. Clamping down these gross injustices is the main mission of Prophet Muhammad (*pbuh*). The teaching of Tawhid and monotheism will leave man accountable for his deeds in this world.

The concept of *formal contracts* and *informal contracts* as readily found in corporate governance literatures, can help see how the concept of accountability is linked to the requirement of law and ethics. In a *formal contract*, each stakeholder is required to fulfill his contractual obligations. Failure to do so bears serious legal implications, often with punitive damage. This is because man is accountable to society and there are penalties and punishment imposed upon people who break the law. In this way, individuals will stay away from unlawful practices that implicate penalties and sanctions. This is what the law intends to fulfill.

As for *formal contract,* both secular and Islamic law are quite similar when penalties are concerned. Although in the former, man is accountable to society, while in the latter he is accountable to God, failure to observe the law comes with punitive sanctions and punishment in this world. For example, in the secular system, people found guilty of evading taxes go to jail. In an Islamic government, the same applies under a category of penalty called *ta'zir.*

But Islamic law is not a legal system *per se,* but also a religious and moral one. No doubt the Quran laid down penalties (*hadd*) for theft, murder, and robbery, but the Quran is not a book of law alone. It is a book of Divine Guidance, carrying many themes such as God, Man, Society, Nature, Prophethood and Revelation, Eschatology, Satan, Evil, etc.

The central aim of the Quran is to establish a viable social order on earth that will be just and ethically based. It is here the concept of *informal contracts* among stakeholders bears importance. For example, managers can draw a lucrative salary package for them and subsequently approved by the directors. They have every right to do so. But doing so may trigger overhead cost overrun, but now the burden is put on the consumer in the form of higher prices. They have readily observed the *formal contracts,* but to the *informal contract,* they have not.

Informal contracts invokes ethical obligations that warrant no worldly rewards and punishment. In the western environment, ethical and unethical actions are rationally induced behavior. It is reason that says whether an action is virtuous or not. There is no fear of legal penalties when one commits an immoral act such as lying, breaking promises, or turning down a beggar. Man is accountable only to himself i.e., to reason on which his conscience is based.

However, in Islam, man is made accountable to God both in his legal and ethical conduct. As mentioned earlier, the Meccan pagans find it hard to accept the concept of monotheism and revelation, what more the idea of resurrection. As a consequence, the idea of moral responsibility is as dead as the idea of the Hereafter, where the final accounting is to take place. To observe the requirements of *informal contracts* brings no material reward. Likewise, ignoring them too will not incur legal punishment.

People who are prone to violate *informal contracts* are often tempted to commit corporate crimes like insider trading and manipulating financial statements were described by the Quran as "gravitating to earth" (*wa la kinnahu akhlada filal ard*). This is because it is easier to do so than ascending to the heights of purity. It is easier to follow one's lust and self-seeking ways than to struggle to attain purity, says Fazlur Rahman. "So, for him who gives of this wealth, guards against evil and confirms goodness, We make good easy for him, but for him who is niggardly, thinks he is self-sufficient and gives lie to goodness, We make evil easy for him." (92:5-10)

The study of Islamic corporate governance should be an interesting one, given that many untrodden paths are yet to be explored. On the legal side (*fiqh*) side, it requires the *fuqaha* (Muslim jurists) to take a serious look at the nature of the corporation and joint-stock company. Undoubtedly, examining the nature of the human-self and factors affecting his actions falls under the domain of philosophy (*falasafah*) and mysticism (*tasawuf*).

Seventeen
How Islamic banks handle bad "loans"

Islamic banks do not make loans on commercial basis but offer credit sale products such as *al-bai-bithaman ajil* (BBA) and *al-ijarah thumma al-bay'*(AITAB). They will do well when scheduled collections of BBA and AITAB receivables are met; but how can one account non-performing BBAs and AITABS? Are both treated like bad loans in traditional banks?

In traditional banking, bad loans are often written off using the bank's own capital. If bad loans are larger than capital, the bank will cease to operate. In the olden days, bank closures saw depositors scrambling for their cash. Usually the government will intervene and lends the bank a hand. Government bailout is a norm. In the United States, for example, to reduce the fiscal burden the Federal Deposit Insurance Corporation (FDIC) was set up to insure deposits. So when a bank closes down, depositors can rest assured their money is reclaimable.

It is interesting to see what an Islamic bank would do when some BBAs and AITABs turned bad. Theoretically, it will use capital reserves to write off both. Let's say total BBA and AITAB receivables amounted to $200 million, with 10 percent or $20 million non-performing. With a capital of $25 million at hand, the bank can absorb these non-performing assets and still has $5 million left as capital. How it restores capital requirement is interesting to see.

Usually, traditional banks will not put deposits in distress, since deposits constitute legal claims. Deposits are placed on debtor-creditor terms. As a debtor, a bank promises depositors two things, namely capital

573

protection and guaranteed interest income. If loans are not performing, the bank cannot use deposits to write off the bad loans. Doing so is against the banking law.

But the nature of Islamic deposits may allow Islamic banks to clear non-performing BBAs and AITABs without using capital reserves alone. If they indeed want it, *mudarabah* deposits are next in line. It is common knowledge that *mudarabah* deposits are neither structured on loans (*qard*) nor safe-keeping (*wadiah dhamanah*). It does not guarantee fixed earnings as well as capital protection. Earning prospect can be tempting, but risk can be high as well.

In principle, Islamic banks hold the right to use *mudarabah* deposits to write off bad BBAs and AITABs. But it must be proven that *mudarabah* funds were indeed invested in these two credit sale products. Transparency is therefore critical. For example, assuming the *mudarabah* portion of RM200 million deposits is 60 percent or RM120 million. Usually an Islamic bank differentiates a general *mudarabah* account from a specific one. But no one knew how much *mudarabah* funds are put into BBAs and AITABs. Likewise, Islamic bank financial statements do not reveal whether *mudarabah* deposits are invested in Islamic securities such as Islamic bonds and money market instruments either; and no one knows how much *mudarabah* deposits landed as idle cash balances.

The *mudarabah* investment account is based on trust, so the label *trustee partnership* must mean something tangible, i.e., transparency, otherwise *gharar* (ambiguities) is implicated. Islamic accounting standard must see that *mudarabah* deposits are not for window dressing, as the risks put on depositors are overwhelming when non-performing financing (NPF) hits the red light; with Islamic banks wanted badly to exercise their right as *mudaribs*.

There are two main things Islamic banks do to mitigate NPF. One is the general provision for doubtful debts. Higher provision would mean lower bank earning; and this is bad news for shareholders. Using the provision is truly workable when the *al-wadiah dhamanah* constitutes the bulk of Islamic deposits. Since Islamic banks provide capital protection to *wadiah dhamanah* deposits, they are shielded from capital depreciation arising from NPF.

However, when a large amount of NPF (i.e., bad BBAs and AITABs) implicates *mudarabah* deposits, the provisions for bad debts both specific and general cannot be applied as it will only affect shareholders. In true color, *mudarabah* deposits should be accounted for NPF since it (i.e., *mudarabah*) runs on profit-loss sharing principle. When BBAs and AITABs turned bad, it directly implies that the *rabbulmal* (i.e., *mudarabah* depositors) must take the brunt.

But the bank acting as the *mudarib* must provide evidence that the loss is not caused by negligence. Otherwise the beating falls purely on the bank, i.e., the shareholders. And it is worthy to note that credit risk predominate BBA and AITAB financing. In this way, failure to collect these receivables may imply the bank's own deficiency for not being prudent in credit valuation and debt collection.

The problem now is what kind of risk are the *mudarabah* participants (i.e., *mudarabah* depositors as *rabbulmal* and the bank as *mudarib*) actually exposed to. Debt instruments such as BBA and AITAB are mainly ridden by credit and interest rate risks. The bank should be able to minimize these risks by pursuing prudent risk and asset-liability (ALM) management policies.

The question at hand can be mystifying in view of the NPF burden put on *mudarabah* depositors. Islamic banks in Malaysia, especially BIMB, have put an additional provision charged against the profit payable to depositors, and the balance is shared between the Shareholders' Fund and the *mudarabah* depositors. It says that the basis of apportionment between *mudarabah* depositors and the shareholders is the proportion of total deposits in *mudarabah* fund, in relation to the total deposits from customers.

The above provision is said to have conformed to Bank Negara Malaysia GP3 and AAOIF standard. Truly, NPL in conventional banks are a liability of the shareholders alone, since loans are debt and not equity instrument. To comply with AAOIF standard must imply also full compliance to the *mudarabah* principle, where *mudarabah* depositors acting as *rabbulmal* must know what kind of risk (*ghorm*) they are actually accountable for.

The basis of sharing NPF should thus be made transparent to deter ambiguities (*gharar*) in the *mudarabah* contract. *Mudarabah* deposits allow the investing public to exploit opportunities not found in unit trusts and other equity portfolios. Which means that they can participate in say, contract financing and even real production that may yield handsome profits if things run in the right direction. But it also means that market risks can trigger capital loss.

However, Islamic banks today have opted to use *mudarabah* deposits to finance BBA and AITAB purchases. In this way, deposits are not exposed to market risk but credit and interest rate risks. As depositors have given a green light to the bank to run BBA and AITAB operations, there must be some basis on which the sharing of loss is attributed to the risks associated with debt (*dayn*) and not equities (*mudarabah/musyarakah*). The legal maxim *"al-ghorm bil ghonm,"* meaning *no reward without risk,* must now explain the nature of risk (*ghorm*) that Islamic commercial law actually recognizes in wealth creation, especially when the *fuqaha* (Muslim jurists) have overwhelmingly endorsed debt financing under the BBA and AITAB labels.

BBA and *AITAB* Risks

- *Liquidity risk* – risk from deposit outflow
- *Interest-rate risk* – changes in value of BBA and AITAB caused by movement in interest rates
- *Credit risk* – risk that capital and profit not paid as promised
- *Capital risk* – how much value of share capital may decline from NPF
- *Structure risk – loss due to changes in the market cost of funds*

Figure 10.5 Risk associated with BBA and AITAB

Eighteen
Financial Planning in Islam

Since the establishment of the first Islamic bank in Malaysia in 1983, awareness about Islamic financing has gained more ground, but only among practitioners, academicians and to a lesser extent, policymakers. The general public is more fascinated with investments in the stocks and unit trusts. The spectacular growth of the Islamic bond market recently also has not benefited household investors as bond purchases require larger amounts of investment, which only large corporations and rich individuals could participate in.

Now, the latest fad in town is financial planning. It is about putting our personal finances in order with some help from people who are Certified Financial Planner (CFP). They help suggest how and where to invest our money, whether we need a fine-tuning or a major overhaul. It looks like asset allocation with a realistic view of time horizons.

As people in different age brackets deal with different financial issues, the decision to save for emergencies and long-term goals such as child's education and retirement are thus critical. Unlike asset management companies, financial planners usually earn introducer's fees by making referrals. They don't manage funds. They simply advise us what asset to buy and recommend where to get them.

For example, after carefully studying our risk-return profile, a financial planner may recommend us to invest our EPF money in KL Mutual or purchase an investment-linked life insurance policy from Prudential. By making these referrals, they will earn commissions.

Financial planners also give advice on estate planning. They can help us write a will and recommend a legal firm to execute it. In a nutshell, financial planners help those who cannot do everything alone since it really gets tricky when we have to make decisions about our banking, retirement, insurance, investments, taxes, and wills all by ourselves.

In Islam, financial planning can be examined from two perspectives, both of which are inseparable. The first aspect deals with *Shariah* matters, that is, the divine rules governing human actions such as spending, saving, and investment. It sees that relations between economic agents such as contractual obligations are dutifully observed. It assumes that economic choices were made on the basis of faith (*iman*) and knowledge (*'ilm*) such that the objectives of equity and efficiency are met.

For example, the role of financial planners is a *tahsini* – adopting what conforms to the best of customs where efficiency is a virtue. Certainly, people can plan their own personal finances, but engaging someone to do so would be comforting.

On human action, the legal rule (*hukm shari'*) in giving financial advice is permissible as it helps in protection of wealth and property (*al-mal*) of people. The appropriate contract is *Al-Wakalah* (agency) where the financial planner (*wakil*) is paid a fee (*'ujr*) for the service rendered. However, the *wakil* is not responsible for the outcome of the investments, which only the customer and fund manager are held responsible.

The role of financial planning in Islam should not be construed as merely distinguishing the permissible (*halal*) from the prohibited (*haram*) financial assets. More importantly is to understand the motive and incentive to plan ahead. Here, knowledge in Islamic economics is vital, since it deals with the study of choices made by people. Choice must be made on knowledge, which financial planners must acquire if they wish to advise customers on *Shariah* matters. This is also true for non-Muslim financial planners whose contact with Muslim customers cannot be discounted.

The concept of *infaq* (expenditure) is key in understanding Islamic financial planning. In Islam, *infaq* means to spend one's wealth for the sake of God. It includes spending for the family (*nafaqah*), meeting *zakat* obligations and giving charity (*sadaqah*). In the Quran, *infaq* is mentioned several ways such as *anfaqa* (he spends), *anfaqta* (you spend), and *anfaqtum* (they spend). Islam enjoins spending (*infaq*) as opposed to hoarding and wealth accumulation (*ihtikar*).

In modern economics, spending and expenditure is the natural path to equilibrium. The only obstacle has always been people who refuse to spend, thus constricting the circulation of money.

Spending in Islam certainly does not mean lavish and extravagant living, but to put money and wealth in their proper places. Here again, financial planning is critical. We need to know how to spread our expenditure over time. This time frame includes the short term, medium term, and long term. This is the second aspect of Islamic financial planning. It deals with using reason and experience to get the job done. For example, the obligation of *infaq* requires Muslims to set their financial goals, and identify priorities, targets, and costs.

Infaq does not imply undertaking current spending alone but also meeting future spending, such as making down payments on mortgages, children's college education, and retirement fund. It is here that savings and investments appear in financial planning. People set aside the surpluses for future consumption by way of investing them wisely. In this manner, we can see how the rule of God (obligation to observe *infaq*) and rational action of human beings, that is, planning, remain inseparable in Islam.

In a nutshell, *infaq* or spending, which involves making a decision to purchase an asset, includes the financing decision as well. As assets can be tangibles such as property, automobiles, and home appliances, as well as bank deposits, stocks and bonds, financial decisions involve looking for the best mode of finance and investment.

When one is looking for *al-bai-bithman ajil* home financing, the financial planner is expected to know the best yearly profit rate in town. He is expected to know which bank has outperformed the rest in *al-mudarabah* account dividend payout. Or which Islamic unit funds one should buy and when is the best time to do so. In this manner, a financial planner who intends to deal with Islamic finance and investments is expected to know a great deal about Islamic economics, Islamic jurisprudence, and commercial transactions, as well as modern-day financial market operations.

Islamic financial instruments in Malaysia range from bank deposits to stocks, bonds, and derivatives. It follows that financial planners are expected to know well the concepts and operational aspects of *Shariah* compliance products as some may be controversial. Giving the wrong advice for the sake of earning commissions is not only unethical but will earn the wrath of God.

As customers rely on a financial planner for advice at a price, the service rendered must be free from *gharar* (uncertainty). That is, whether or not financial planning aims at beating inflation, managing the unexpected, and meeting retirement expenses, the means to do so must comply with *Shariah* principles.

Certified Financial Planning (CFP) examinations in Muslim countries should therefore include the Islamic aspects of financial planning. In Malaysia, this is relatively easy to do, since Islamic financial instruments are readily available in the market. What financial planners add on is exploring the philosophical aspects of Islam, since they will be dealing with Muslims more intimately.

Understanding the value system that motivates them to invest is vital. This is because financial planning in Islam does not put importance to success in this world only but more importantly, life in the Hereafter. It is here that Islamic financial planners must see well what Islam has to say about wealth (*al-mal*) and property rights. Giving advice on wealth creation and management is the fundamental duty of the financial planner in Islamic financial planning.

Not all services rendered is translated into a fee earned. The financial planner needs to have, and to impart to the Muslim customer, various religious obligations like *zakat* (Islamic tax) and *farai'd* (Islamic inheritance) obligations, or reminding them of the virtues of charities (*sadeqah*) via the system of *waqf* (endowment) and *wasiya* (wills). This the financial planner should provide free of charge.

Nineteen
The Economics of Zuhud

Mahathir Muhammad has called on all Malaysians to sacrifice for the country in view of the hard times to come. The same message haunts Thailand, Indonesia, the Philippines, and South Korea, all of which received International Monetary Fund (IMF) aid. In these countries, the sacrifices will be real because the IMF conditions require the closure of weak financial institutions.

Companies with low earnings and troubled with high debts will be forced into bankruptcy, while the trimming of growth rates to 1 percent or 2 percent or even less will cause severe unemployment and poverty.

In Malaysia, the only thing that Malaysians are called to do is to increase their savings in the local banks, knowing that these savings will fall in value relative to the dollar the ringgit keeps on falling.

The depreciation of the ringgit will make imports more expensive to buy. So, Malaysians who are used to buying imports may find it tough to keep up, as their savings now could buy less. Fears of the incoming recession have caused many of us to take austerity measures in case some may lose their jobs. The fear of food shortages and inflation has also brought about the need not to delay spending.

Inflation would erode our purchasing power, and to postpone consumption may not be a good idea. The call to increase savings will not be a popular one and will be tough, for the well-to-do in particular.

And when things are becoming so uncertain, spending decisions become less rational and savings cannot be easily predicted.

Any student of economics can explain easily what the Mahathir Muhammad had in mind when he called on Malaysians to increase savings. In the general eclectic terms, savings are influenced by the interest rates and the level of income. Higher level of income and interest rates are expected to increase savings.

However, the cut in annual salary increment, promotions, and bonuses implies that less savings are expected from these sources today. So, even if interest rates are higher, they may not increase savings dramatically, except among the rich, who can convert investment in shares into fixed deposits.

The only way now to increase savings is by eating less, and cutting down on entertainment and vacations. Since income is not increasing, more savings means less consumption. People can make the sacrifice only when they possess reliable information about how well their money is utilized by the banking sector.

If the bankers take our money and lend them to fund less productive ventures such as real estate or saving troubled companies that can go bust anytime, our money will be in jeopardy when these banks cannot recover loans from the failed businesses.

More bad loans would create bank panic when banks have little left to honor deposit withdrawals. Only when there is transparency in bank lending policy or when bankers are required by the law to hold more capital to prevent investments in unproductive projects will people consider the sacrifice a worthy one to do.

The question remains to be our ability to increase savings, particularly voluntary savings.

In Japan, high savings rate is attributed to cultural element, where Japanese put their money in banks, even with negative real interest rates. For example, if the market or nominal rate is 3 percent while the rate of inflation is 5 percent, the real interest rate is 3 percent– 5 percent or -2 percent.

In Malaysia, the high national savings rate is largely sourced from forced savings into the Employees Provident Fund (EPF). To what extent

Malaysians can curb their current level of consumption voluntarily to help the economy reduce its current account deficit is yet to be tested. The question now is, what will motivate people to save?

Muslim economists have often cited the concept of moderation as one important principle of consumption, where man is enjoined not to go the extreme even if he is allowed to do so. For example, the Prophet (pbuh) once said about moral and ethics (*akhlak*) during eating: "The best among you is he/she who stops eating before he/she feels full."

Another concept is righteousness, which describes the types of goods and services to buy.

Here, the goods and services must be permissible (*halal*) and pure (*taib*) while the income spent on consumption must also be free from the prohibitions (*al-bathil*) such as those found in *riba*, gambling, liquor, swine, and fraud elements.

However, the concept of moderation and righteousness in consumption seems to be a bit too general to describe what actually can be done to generate the desired level of consumption in Islam. This is because the law governing consumption behavior is not free from questions about values and spiritual experience. That is, the decision to consume or not to consume is controlled by our knowledge (*'ilm*) concerning how such spending can affect our lives and make us happy or otherwise.

In *Tasawf*, a subset in the study of Islamic theology, the term *zuhud* can also be used to deepen our understanding of consumer behavior and consumption. *Zuhud* means to reject anything "worldly" (*al-dunya*).

According to Fazlur Rahman, *al-dunya* is not "this world" but the lower values, the basal pursuits which appear so immediately tempting that most men run after them most of the time at the expense of higher and long-range ends. This is akin to the Meccan merchants' skill in making money but to neglect the higher values of life or the ends of life.

The Quran says, "They [Meccan merchants] know well the externalities of this life but are heedless of the higher ends" (30:70). *Zuhud* is, therefore, an ethical concept. It is not about rejecting basic necessities and convenience of life. It is a moral conduct a believer should observe in his or her daily spending activity.

To further explain the concept of *zuhud*, al-Palimbani for example, described three stages of *Zuhd* that man can experience, namely:

> ➢ *Zuhd* for the beginners (*mubtadi*), namely those who want to fight their desires (*nafs*) even so his heart is still inclined to *al-duniya*;
> ➢ *Zuhd* for the intermediate where he/she has easily rejected the *al-duniya* and is no longer in love with it; and
> ➢ *Zuhd* for the *muntahi*, that is he/she who puts no value to *al-dunya* since his/her heart is already deeply attached to the *al-akhirah*.

When consumer behavior has embraced the *zuhud* morality, the consumer is less likely to indulge in extreme spending that often leads to wastages (*israf*). This does not mean that aggregate spending is made lower. It only implies that *zuhud* consciousness should be able to generate more voluntary savings available for capital investments. In this way, lower consumption does not readily imply excess liquidity, since the Islamic financial system via risk-sharing mechanism will see that idle balances are automatically removed from the financial sector.

Twenty
Islamic Project Financing

There are a number of things one should look for to properly understand what exactly is Islamic project financing. Some are interested to examine closer the nature of Islamic bonds issued by the project company. Structuring an Islamic bond is becoming more challenging and popular among investment bankers. Most common are the *al-bai-bithaman ajil* bonds (ABBA) and *murabahah* notes issuance facility (Munif). Only a few use *al-ijarah* and *istisna'*. Latest are the Global *Sukuks* issued by Malaysian and Qatar governments. The bond proceeds are used to pay for many things. Some are used for refinancing purposes, while others to finance infrastructure projects. Some infrastructure project finance examples are given below:

1. **Kuala Lumpur International Airport (KLIA)**: This RM2.2 billion *al-bai-bithaman ajil* (BBA) notes issuance facility is fully guaranteed by the Malaysian government. In essence it uses *bay' al-'inah*. The issuer sells an underlying asset (i.e., contract concession evidencing equipment and machineries) to the investors in return for the RM2.2 billion cash payment. Using BBA, the investor simultaneously sells back the underlying asset to the issuer inclusive of the profit margin.

2. **Hub River power project**: This US$92 million project uses *istisna'*. The financier purchases turbines on *istisna'* and sells them to the project company on *murabahah*. Funding was provided by Al-Rajhi Banking & Investment Company of Riyard.

3. **Equate petrochemical plant in Kuwait**: The Equate project uses both conventional and Islamic financing. Of the total US$2,000 million financing requirement, US$200 million was structured along Islamic contract, namely *ijarah* (leasing). Equate is jointly sponsored by Union Carbide Corporation, Petrochemical Industry Company, and Bubiyan Petrochemicals Company.

However, there are also other aspects in project financing that the *Shariah* must be vocal and decisive about. Before doing so, let's look closer at the definition of project financing. Project financing can be defined as financing of a particular project in which an investor is satisfied to look initially to the cash flows and earnings of that project. This cash flow constitutes the source of funds from which the financing can be repaid, while the assets of the project are used as collateral for the financing.

It is when the goal of project financing is put in place that the *Shariah* must provide clear rulings on certain aspects of project finance. In project financing, the goal is to assemble funding for a project whose benefit will go to the sponsor. However, the sponsor wants to be protected from recourse, so as to shield its credit standing or balance sheet. To do this, the sponsor uses a third to support the transaction.

In this way, studies on Islamic project financing can be categorized into two main components, namely:

a. **Concept and structure of Islamic instruments**: Here the underlying principles are clearly stated in Islamic law, that the instrument must be free from interest (*riba*), ambiguities (*gharar*), and gambling (*maisir*). The requirement of ownership (milkiyah) is paramount to see that ownership risk (*daman milkiyah*) is rightly observed by the selling parties and lessors. The contract of *murabahah* and *ijarah* are usually applied in Middle Eastern countries, while in Malaysia most financing is based on the *bay' al-'inah* and *bay' al-dayn*.

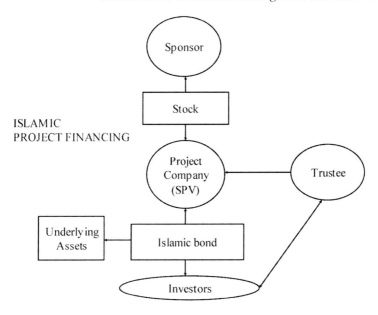

Figure 10.6 Islamic Project Financing

b. Participants of project financing: In general participants of project financing consists of the following:

1. Contract Awarder: In infrastructure project financing, the government awards project by open tender. The project can be based on build- transfer (BT), build-operate-transfer (BOT) and build-own-operate (BOO), build-lease-transfer (BLT). Sometimes the government provides guarantees to debt obligation of the issuing party.

2. Sponsors: A party interested in supporting a project financing. It can be both individuals and corporation who provide credit enhancement to support the project. They prepare the financial modeling, negotiate finance documents etc. Sponsors include consortium of interested parties such as contractors, suppliers, purchasers or users of the project's products or facilities.

3. Special Purpose Vehicle [SPV]; A company that will operate the project and issues the securities. This project company is also a bankruptcy remote entity. It is legally distinct from its sponsor with a purpose to immune itself from any problem and risks faced by the sponsor. The Shariah perspective of the SPV must deal with both issues. Firstly, how SPV serves the

interests of investors and secondly, how it serves the interests of sponsors. It is important to note that not all IPDS issues implicate the formation of SPV.

4. Issuer: A company seeking capital to undertake the project.

5. Trustee: The trustee serves to protect the interest of investors. Acts for and behalf of the financiers and ensure that the issuer truly observed the trust deed. The trust deed is a contract defining the obligation of the issuer and appointing a trustee to represent the interests of financiers. It will conduct reasonable diligence to ascertain no breach of the covenants, terms and provisions of the Trust deed has taken place.

6. Financiers or Tender Panel Members (TPM): Investors who tender for debt or equity papers in return for flexible or fixed income with or without capital protection. Financiers usually consist of institutional investors such as banks, insurance companies, mutual funds, corporations as well as high net worth individuals.

7. Underwriters: Purchasing instruments directly from the issuer before disposal to the investing public in case the issuance is undersubscribed. In the case of Malaysian Islamic bonds, it may implicate *bay' al-dayn* since bonds are purchased at a discount prior in initial public offers. Underwriting common shares is permissible (*halal*) since shares are considered property (*al-mal*) and not debt (*dayn*).

8. Guarantors: The contract of *al-rahn* is applied here. For *muqarada* bond, *al-rahn* is applicable to provide capital protection in case of negligence inflicted by the *mudarib*. Guarantors and collaterals are essential requirements in Malaysian Islamic private securities (IPDS) although the securities are supported by some underlying assets equivalent to the value of the facility.

9. Rating agencies: On Islamic debt issues, rating agencies serve to assess the likelihood of timely repayment of principle and payment of profit over the term of maturity of such debts.

10. Regulatory authorities including Shariah Supervisory Board : In Malaysia, issuance of IPDS must conform to section 32 of

the Securities Commission Act 1993 (SCA 1993) where IPDS are considered synonymous to debentures.

11. Arrangers and Dealers : administer the issuance of the securities. They coordinate paper documentations with the lawyers. They also coordinate the underwriters, guarantors and trustees. All these work are fee-based. The contract of *wakalah* (agency) is relevant here.

Recent issuance of the Global *Sukuk* is a refreshing beginning to secure the application of *ijarah* in project finance. In the Malaysian case, the project does not entail investment and construction of residential and business properties. Rather, it resembles a property trust model with an objective to earn rental incomes rather than capital gains.

The Securities Commission of Malaysia is instrumental in putting Malaysia in the forefront of Islamic project finance. It is currently working on hard to introduce *musyarakah* bonds in project finance and doing so requires amendments to the Securities Commission Act 1993 to exclude Islamic bonds from debentures.

Twenty-One
Low interest-rate regime – Impact on Al-Bai-Bithaman Ajil Housing Financing

A lot have been said about the impact of rising interest rate on BBA financing. Usually, the fixed rate BBA financing is Islamic banking greatest headache especially when interest rate is on the rise. BBA customers stand to gain since their BBA contracts have locked in a fixed BBA profit rate over the BBA tenure. So, unlike conventional loan users, BBA customers don't have to worry paying more as interest-rate rises. It is not surprising to see the demand for BBA to increase as interest-rate increases.

But rising interest rates as evident in the 1996 financial crisis, has adversely affect Islamic banking profits in Malaysia. This is well documented in Bank Negara's 1997 annual report. To prevent a repetition, Islamic banks have struggled to offer a floating rate BBA. But none is evident as the economy moves into 2000.

The 1997 financial crisis saw many unwarranted business failures. One badly hit sector is the construction business. Abandon housing projects loomed over the property sector. The Malaysian government's orchestrated low interest-rate environment is set to revive construction and the production sector. The lower cost of credit serves to increase the demand for housing loans. The same applies for business and corporate loans.

Unfortunately, the interest-rate regime seems to have hit BBA customers rather badly. As an example, on 25th May 1998, Ismail purchases a property for $187,960 using BBA mode of financing with a 15 year tenure. The cost price of the property is $100,000. The $187,960 BBA selling is based on a 9.5 percent annual profit rate declared on the same date. Let's assume that the monthly installment is $1,044.2 As interest rate declined over the years say to 6 percent per annum, Ismail is still paying a monthly installment based on the 9.5 percent annual profit rate. He pays $1,044.2 per month while others using conventional loans are paying less. This is true since BBA is a fixed rate asset (FRA) while loans is a adjustable rate asset (ARA).

As explained in the earlier articles, BBA contract is based on one selling price. Any attempt to change the profit rate to reflect changes in the cost of funds will alter the exisiting selling price and deemed the BBA contract invalid. But customers are not happy how Islamic banks are handling the problem. The differences can be staggering. Paying $1,044.2 per month and $700 per month does make a huge difference especially when the property is not delivered on the spot. In the case for housing under construction, it is a norm that Islamic banks collects payments even before the property is delivered.

Customers who are not satisfy with current BBA system may want to seek early settlement on their debt obligation. They may opt for a refinancing scheme or even aborted the idea of buying the property in view of the higher cost of BBA financing. What can happen next is obvious. The demand for BBA home financing may decline when people choose to use conventional loans.

The next issue is rebate (*ibra'*), which is a waiver to claim the unearned profit. How much should Ismail pay the bank if he wishes to make an early settlement?. Suppose he has paid $37,591.2 over the three years and decided to quit. He asks the bank the outstanding balance he is required to pay up. Accordingly, Ismail assumes he will be given a rebate on the profit. However, this may not materialize since the BBA contract says that Ismail owes the bank $187,960. Since he has pay up $37,591.2, the outstanding balance must be $150,368.

But the $150,368 outstanding balance is now even higher than the amount he had asked for, namely the cost price of property. Ismail must look for a buyer he is willing to pay him $150,368 for a property that is worth $100,000 three years ago. He will be very lucky if someone is crazy to buy his property but this cannot hold for all cases. But it helps if the Islamic bank gives him a rebate *(ibra')*. Doing so, should reduce the outstanding balance and may help him sell the property more easily.

There seems to be degree of uncertainty about the rebate (*ibra'*) policy since the rebate is not automatically given to the customer on his early BBA settlement. The conventional practices on rebate are less worrisome since it is customary (*'urf*) to give customers the rebate as the contract is based on a creditor-debtor relationship. The same does not readily applies for Islamic banking. A legal precedent is found in the case between Bank Islam Malaysia (BIMB) and Adnan Omar where the defendant was required by the court to pay the whole amount of the BBA outstanding balance. Only on appeal the High Court judge ordered BIMB to give the defendant the rebate on the accrued or unearned profit.

It is critical to see that a convincing policy about the rebate (*ibra'*) on unearned profit is deliberated and acted upon by market players. The National Shariah Advisory Council (NSAC) should be put to task to ensure that the welfare of customers are protected by standardizing the *ibra'* as a customary practice (*'urf*) . In this way, customers will not be penalized heavily for wanting to make early settlement. Uncertainy about the *ibra'* policy will only bring undue stress and anxiety to the customers. The consumer friendly *ibra'* policy will help relieve customers who are often victims of abandon housing projects. They should not fear to do so even if early settlement is pursued solely for refinancing purposes.

Twenty-Two
Islamic Interbank Money Market

The demand for and supply of short-term credit generally occur for two main reasons. First, it serves to provide liquidity. For example, companies at certain time need cash to pay for wages, office supplies, repairs or some other unexpected expenses. Immediate cash is also needed when personal and corporate income taxes are due. Government too looks for cash when not enough funds are available to finance current expenditures. Hence, the money market i.e. market for short-term loans is designed to meet short-term cash requirement of corporations, financial institutions and government. Maturities of loans range from overnight to one year.

The money market is also designed for investment purposes. The surplus sector will find holding temporary idle balances unprofitable. When revenues exceeded expenditures, idle funds often swell up. Placing these funds the money market will entitle them i.e. investors and companies to earn some interest income. Otherwise potential income is lost. The money market therefore serves to meet these short-term investment and those who need short-term borrowings.

However, investment in the money market brings along with it many risks. Fluctuations in interest rates may affect profitability especially when prices of these money market instruments fall arising from increases in interest rates. The risk of default must not be discounted while inflation risk can reduce the real value of their interest income and capital investment. When money is invested in the international money markets, investors are exposed to two additional risks, namely currency risks and as well with political risks. Thus, just like long-term investment, short-term investment is not an easy matter.

Choosing money market instruments is therefore crucial in determining the type of risks investors are likely to hold and returns they expect to make. These instruments include treasury bills, certificates of deposits, repurchase agreements banker's acceptances and the inter-bank money deposits. Conventional money market is therefore associated with the use of fixed income instruments, in which the payments and receipts of interest are implicated. The Islamic money market also serves similar functions and covers a larger spectrum of financial instruments and institutions. Of greater importance is the Islamic interbank money market (IIMM) since banking companies in Malaysia remained the backbone of the financial sector.

The IIMM is both designed to fulfill the need for liquidity (*al-suyulah*) and investments. It runs on the basis of Shariah principles derived from the Quran, *hadiths* and legal opinions of the Islamic jurists by way of *ijma* (consensus), *qiyas* (anology) and *ijtihad* (independent thinking). Based on the above, three main principles will form the basis of Islamic money market operation namely , a) the prohibition of interest as *riba (b)*The requirement of *'iwad* (risk-taking and value-addition) in profit and income generation (c) The removal or avoidance of *gharar* (uncertainty) in contractual obligations.

Much of Islamic money market operation is taking place to serve the liquidity need of Islamic financial institutions. These include the Islamic banks, *takaful* companies and Islamic unit trusts. With large surpluses, they must find an avenue to get rid of idle funds by way of Islamic investments. Those experiencing cash deficits must find an outlet to obtain the necessary funding. All must observe the Islamic commercial law (*fiqh muamalat*) exhibited by way of the three principles cited above.

The size of the Islamic interbank money market instruments in Malaysia is fast expanding given the length of time it was given to develop. When Bank Islam Malaysia Berhad (BIMB) was first set up in 1983, an Islamic interbank money market was less urgent until in 1989, when Malaysia first introduced the Islamic windows concept of banking. Prior to 1989, liquidity needs by BIMB were met by way of the sale and purchase of the *Mudarabah* Government Islamic securities (GIS) also known currently as government Islamic investments (GII). However the liquidity is only meant for meeting statutory liquidity requirement rather than investments.

For investment purposes, in 1994, the government introduced Islamic treasury notes. These are zero coupon bonds traded on the *bay' al-'inah* and *al-bay' dayn* principle. Pricing is determined by way of auction and public tender (*al-munaqasa*) where bids from investors were made. For more detail on the size of transactions and yields kindly refer to Bank Negara's website at www.bnm.gov.my.

The following provides a brief account of the Islamic instruments made for the Islamic Interbank Money Market (IIMM)

a. Al-Mudarabah Interbank Investment (MII)

Al-Mudarabah Interbank Investment provides an investment opportunity for surplus banks to place their money from overnight to 12 months. With a minimum amount of RM50,000, profit-sharing ratios (PSR) varies according to maturities. For example, for periods of less or equal to one month, the PSR is 70:30 while for periods exceeding three months, the PSR is 90:10. To illustrate the mechanism of MII, assume Northern bank has a surplus of RM40 million and Bank Shariah is short RM40 million. Bank Shariah will bid for RM40 million through a broker or directly contact Northern bank. Suppose Bank Shariah is able to secure the RM40 million facility for a period of 3 months at 80:20 PSR, the profit Bank Shariah should pay Northern bank is calculated as follows:

Profit = [RM40,000,000 x 6 x 90 x (0.80)] / [365 x 100] = RM473,424.65

The *mudarabah* contract does not specify the rate of return (i.e. 6 percent) upfront but only to declare it at maturity. The rate is based on Bank Shariah's profit rate for 1 year investment. On maturity Bank Shariah will return the principle amount and the profit as well. In 2003, the *mudarabah* interbank investment recorded a moderate increase of 14.9 percent totaling to RM283.8 billion. In 2002, a new mechanism for Islamic interbank deposit was introduced under the *al-wadiah dhamanah* (guaranteed custody) principle.

b. Government Investment Issue (GII)

The Government Investment Issue (GII) is a financial instrument serving to provide Islamic banks a Shariah complaint approach to meet the prescribed statutory liquidity requirement. The Government Investment Act 1983 was enacted to empower the Government of Malaysia to issue Government Investment Issue (GII). Since GIIs are regarded as liquid assets, the Islamic banks could invest in the GII to invent their surplus funds. The GII was initially issued based on *qardhu hasan* (benevolent loan) basis. In *qardhu hasan*, the purchase of GII by any institution or individuals will be considered as a benevolent loan to the Malaysian government to undertake developmental projects for the benefit of the nation. The government is obliged to return the principal amount to the providers of funds at maturity. The *qardhu hasan* contract does not specify any upfront returns, thus any return on the loans (if any) is at the absolute discretion of the government. In 2001, the basis of GII's issuance was further enhanced to accommodate the need to develop further the secondary market activities of the Islamic money market. In June 2001, an alternative concept of GII based on sell and buyback (*bay' al-'inah*) was introduced. Under this arrangement, the government will sell its identified assets at an agreed cash price to the buyer and subsequently buy back the same assets from the buyer at an agreed purchase price to be settled at a specified future date.

Table 10.2: Islamic Interbank Money Market (IIMM) 2002-2003

Instruments	2002 RM billion	2003 RM billion
Mudarabah Interbank Investments	247.0	283.8
Government Investment Issues (GII)	5.9	36.1
Bank Negara Negotiable Notes (BNNN)	2.2	8.8
Short-Term Bills	24.8	34.8
Negotiable Islamic Debt Certificates (NICD)	0.8	4.2
Green bankers Acceptances & Islamic Accepted Bills	24.8	
Total	280.7	367.7

Source: Bank Negara Malaysia Report 2003

The GIIs are offered through a tender process. Banks and investors may place their orders to purchase the government's assets through participating financial institutions (PFIs). Using the contract of *bay' al-'inah*, the government will sell its asset to the PFIs's assets at a purchase price for cash and subsequently, the government will buy back the assets from the PFIs at a selling (i.e. credit) price, which will be settled at maturity. The difference between the selling price and the purchase price represents the profit of the PFIs. The obligation of the government to settle the purchase price is securitised in the form of GII and issued to the PFIs. GII however does not apply the concept of asset or debt securitization. The government in principle, issues GII as an evidence of indebtedness. At maturity, the Government will redeem the GII and pay the nominal value of the securities to the GII holders. In 2003, GII increased substantially by 511.9 percent (RM30.2 million) amounting to RM36.1 billion

c. Bank Negara Negotiable Notes (BNNN)

The most recent public sector Islamic bond issue has been the Bank Negara Negotiable Notes (BNNN). Using the contract of *bay' al-'inah*, the Central Bank of Malaysia (BNM) will identify and sell certificates if BNM assets on a tender basis at a discount to Islamic banking institutions. BNM will then buy back the certificate of assets at par value to be paid on credit terms, i.e., 92, 182 or 364 days. On tendering, only Islamic banks are allowed to tender for the BNNN, with minimum bidding denomination being RM5 million (US1.3 million). Both conventional and Islamic banking institutions are allowed to trade BNNN in the secondary market. In 2003, BNNN recorded an increase of 300 percent (RM6.6 million) totaling to RM8.8 billion

d. The Negotiable Islamic Certificate of deposit (NICD)

The application of Shari'a principles to CDs is crucial to reduce dependency on variable rate deposits. To do so Islamic banks, such as Bank Islam Malaysia Berhad, has applied *bay' al-'inah* to produce the Islamic version of the NCD. Known as the negotiable Islamic certificate of deposit (NICD), the procedure applies the contract of *bay' al-'inah* .

The price of an NICD can be computed as follows:

Price = RV/ 1 + [Tenor x YLD]/ 365 x 100

where,

RV = redemption value per RM100 nominal value

Tenor = number of days from settlement date to maturity

YLD = yield in percent p.a.

Conceptually, the sale and buyback mechanism is explained as follows. Company A wishes to put RM1 million in NICD with an Islamic bank. The bank sells its asset (i.e. its company shares) worth RM1 million to Company A. The bank now secures a RM1 million new deposits. Now, Company A sells back the share certificates to the bank at a deferred price, which is based on a profit rate, say 7.5 per cent for a duration of six RM37,500 in profits. The bank pays Company A issuing NICDs worth RM1,037,500 as the nominal value. The issuance of the NICD is undertaken as evidence of the RM1,037,500 debt that the bank owes Company A. At maturity, the NICDs are redeemable at par value where Company A gets back the RM1 million deposit plus RM37,500 profit. In actual practice, the selling price = nominal value set at RM100 per unit. Thus, NICD is issued at a discount. For example, the price of an NICD with 6 months to maturity and trading at the yield of 3.05 percent is computed as follows:

$$\text{Price} = 100/\ 1 + [181 \times 3.05]/365 \times 100 = 98.5101$$

In the above, the bank NICD sold to depositors at 98.5 and repurchased it at RM100 payable in cash at maturity. In 2003, trading of NICD remained relatively small with current volume amounting to RM4.2 billion.

e. Islamic Accepted Bills (AIB)

Introduced in 1991, Islamic Bankers' Acceptances (AIB) is in essence a time draft drawn on a bank by an exporter or an importer to pay for merchandise. They are used especially in import and export trade because most exporters are uncertain of the credit standing of the importers to whom they ship goods. It is an instrument designed to shift the risk of international or domestic trade to the third party, namely a bank who is willing to take on that risk for a defined cost. IABs are tradable which give them an edge over a letter of credit. The seller or exporter will receive cash payments when the IAB matures but can obtain payment earlier by selling the IABs at a discount in the money market. It is here that the contract of *bay' al-dayn* is applied. In 2002, total issuance of AIB amounted to RM7.6 billion. IAB for import and local purchases is explain below:

For import and local purchases, the contract of *murabahah* and *bay' al-dayn* are applied. For example, customer A looks for a working capital financing to purchase goods X from Customer B. Under the AIB mechanisms, customer A purchases the goods on bank's behalf. The bank pays the supplier in cash and concurrently sells back the goods to Customer A at the *murabahah* price. The *murabahah* sale constitutes the creation of debt (*dayn murabahah*). Accordingly, the *dayn murabahah* is securitized in the form of AIB (i.e. Islamic bills of exchange) drawn by the bank on and accepted by the customer for the full amount of the bank's selling price payable at maturity. For liquidity purposes, the bank can sell the IAB to a third party at a discount via the contract of *bay' al-dayn*.

The main issue of *bay' al-dayn'* in the trading of IIMM products lies on discount trading rather than *gharar* (uncertainty). According to the Shariah Advisry Council of the Securities Commission (SAC) resolutions, the Shafi'e mazhab allows the selling of debt to the third party if the *dayn* is *mustaqir* (guaranteed) and was sold in exchange for *'ayn* (goods) that must be delivered immediately. The SAC also says that Ibnu Qayyim has permitted *bay' al-dayn* although he prohibited *bay' kali bi kali* (sale of debt for debt). However, the SAC should have also said that both the Shafi'e *mazhab* and Ibnu Qayyim were referring to the sale of debt (*bay' al-dayn*) at par value under the purview of *hiwalah* and not sale of debt at a discount or premium.

Finally, the Islamic Interbank Money Market will not be complete without mentioning the Islamic Interbank Cheque Clearing System (IICCS). When a buyer writes a check, it goes to the seller's bank, which forward that check eventually to the bank on which it was drawn. Funds transferred by check are called clearing house fund. The two banks will choose a place where they exchange bundles of checks drawn each other every day. In this local clearing-house checks and other cash items are delivered and passed from one bank to another. In case, if total surplus is less than total deficit, IIMM participants can obtained funds from Bank Negara Malaysia as well as the banks of their choice. Under the IICCS, the calculation of profit for day 1 is 70:30 (i.e. 70 percent for the provider of funds).

Twenty-Three
Islamic Asset-Backed Securities (IABS)

A security is a legal document that shows an ownership interest of financial assets such as stocks and bonds. Securitization is the process of converting an asset or collection of asset (i.e financial as well as real assets) into marketable securities. It is a new financing technique where underlying assets such as real estate loans, automobile loans and credit card receivables are securitized into marketable securities called asset-backed securities (ABS). Other underlying assets for securitization purposes can include corporate leases, lease receivables, mutual fund fees, health-care, prescription drugs or insurance premium receivables, structured legal settlement awards, lottery winnings, royalties, tax liens, municipal parking fines and delinquent tax receivables.

The Securities Commission defined "Asset-Backed Debt Securities (ABS) as private debt securities that are issued to a securitization transaction. Securitization transaction means an arrangement which involves the transfer of assets or risks to a third party where such transfer is funded by the issuance of debt securities to investors. Payments to investors in respect of such debt securities are principally derived, indirectly or directly, from the cash flows of the assets".

A simple process of asset securitization first begins with the sale of underlying asset by its owner to the prospective issuer of ABS. The true sale of underlying asset means that the issuer of ABS has no right of recourse i.e. holding the original owner responsible for loan defaults or failure to collect the total receivables. Once the true sale is completed, the new owner of the underlying asset will securitize the asset i.e. converting the asset into marketable asset-backed securities.

The Shariah Advisory Council (SAC) of the Securities Commission defined asset securitization as a process of issuing securities by selling financial assets identified as an underlying asset to a third party. Its purpose is to liquidate financial assets for cash, or as an instrument to obtain new funds. Financial assets which have a future cash flow is sold by a company that needs liquidity or as a new fund to a third party known as a special purpose vehicle (SPV) for cash. To enable the payment for the purchase of the assets, the SPV will issue asset-backed debt securities to investors, based on the future cash flow of the asset. Investors will then gain returns through a future cash flow managed by the SPV.

The SAC agreed to include cash flow in the category of *mal* (property) if its origin is *halal* (permissible) according to Islamic law. The SAC also believed that cash flow is equivalent to debt (*dayn*). Any *dayn* (debt) without *gharar* (ambiguity) is considered as *haq maliy* which is included as *mal* (property).

The first Islamic asset-backed debt securities (IABS) in Malaysia worth RM986 million were issued on 26th June 2003 by Ambang Sentosa Sendirian Berhad (ASSB) with Abrar Discount Berhad acting as lead arranger. Ambang Sentosa is a special purpose vehicle (SPV) whose main purpose is to raise funds from investors by the issuance of *al-bai-bithaman ajil* Islamic debt securities (BaIDS). Under the transaction, the Originator, namely Maxisegar Sdn Bhd sold its right, title and interest over the Balance Purchase Price or receivables (the "Asset") arising from a selected pool of sale-purchase agreements (SPAs) entered between the seller and the end-purchasers to the issuer. The payment to Maxisegar originated from the proceeds of BaIDS issuance by Ambang Sentosa. Ambang Sentosa (ASSB) was able to issue BaIDS to the investors from the sale and resale of the receivables it acquired previously from Maxisegar by way of gift (*Hibah*). The sale and resale of the receivables is based on the contract of *bay' al-'inah*. A hypothetical example is given below:

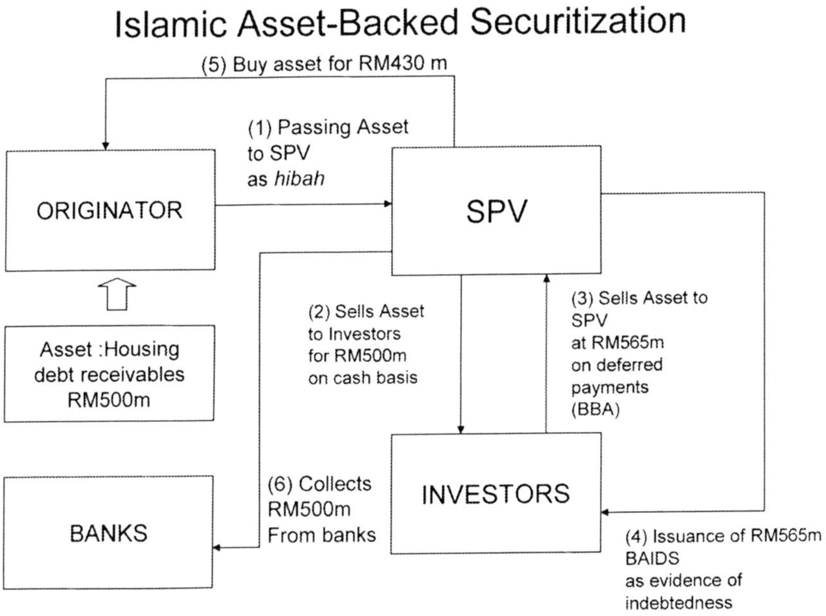

Islamic Asset-Backed Securitization

Figure 10.7: Islamic Asset-Backed Securitization

Let's assume the value of Asset is RM500 million. ASSB sells the Asset to the investor for the same amount on cash basis. Given a 5.5% profit rate per annum, the investors sell back the same Asset via *al-bai bithaman ajil* to ASSB at a RM565 million selling price with RM65 million in profit. The debt arising from the second sale (i.e. *dayn* BBA) is then securitized for the issuance of BAIDS. The SPV issues RM500m worth of BAIDs primary notes and RM65m secondary notes. The proceeds of the BAIDS (i.e RM500 million) are used to purchase from the Originator its rights, title and interest over the said receivables at discount. The purchase of the receivables by ASSB is conducted via the contract of *bay' al-dayn* at a discount. Assuming ASSB purchases the receivables for RM420 million, it pays investors RM65 million in profits via redemption of secondary notes. By using the asset-backed securitization technique, ASSB is able to net RM15 million in profits. The SPV collects the receivables from the banks over the financing period and pays the investors RM500 million at maturity as investors seek redemption on the primary notes.

CITED BIBLIOGRAPHY

Accounting and Auditing Organization for Islamic Financial Institutions. "Accounting, Auditing and Governance Standards for Islamic Financial Institutions." 1423H-2002.

Agnides, Nicolas P. *Mohammedan Theories of Finance.* New York: AMS, 1916.

Al-Amine, Muhammad Al-Bashir. *Istisna'in Islamic Banking and Finance,* Kuala Lumpur A.S. Nordeen, 2001.

Al-Attas, Muhammad Naquib. *Islam: The Concept of Religion and the Foundations of Ethics and Morality.* Kuala Lumpur: Muslim Youth Movement of Malaysia (ABIM), 1976.

Al-Baraka, *Resolutions and Recommendations of Al-Baraka Symposia on Islamic Economy, 1981-2001.* Jeddah: Al-Baraka, 2001.

Al-Hadad, Sayid Abdullah. *Risalah Mu'awanah* (translation), Kuala Lumpur: Pustaka Jiwa, 1997.

Al-Suyuthi, Jalaluddin Abdul Rahman. *Kaedah-Kaedah Hukum Islam Mazhab Shafi'i,* Kuala Lumpur, Darul Iman Publicaton, 1999.

Annuar, Hairul Azlan Annuar, Saiful Azhar Rosly, and Hafiz Majdi Abdul Rashid. "The Impact of the *Wakalah* System on the Performance of *Takaful* Business in Malaysia," *Proceedings of International Conference on Islamic Economics*, Bahrain, January 2003.

Bank Negara Malaysia. *Money and Banking.* Kuala Lumpur, 1994.

Bank Negara Malaysia. *Annual Report.* Kuala Lumpur, 1997-2003.

Bank Negara Malaysia, Guidelines on Islamic Interbank Money Market, Kuala Lumpur, 1993

Bank Negara Malaysiam Guidelines on Islamic Negotiable Instruments, Kuala Lumpur, 1998

Baye, Michael R., and Jansen, Dennis W., *Money, Banking, and Financial Markets*, Houghton Mifflin, Boston, 1995.

Beaver, W.H., and G, Parker. *Risk Management – Problems and Solutions.* New York: McGraw-Hill, 1970.

Chapra, M. Umar. and Tariqullah Khan. *Regulation and Supervision of Islamic Banks.* Islamic Research Institute and Training Center, Islamic Development Bank, 2000.

Clifford, M.L. and P. Engardio. *Meltdown – Asia's Boom, Bust and Beyond.* London, Prentice- Hall, 2000.

Cole, D.W., "A Return-on-Equity Model for Banks," *The Bankers Magazine,* Summer 1972.

Damodaran, A. *Corporate Finance.* New York: John Wiley and Sons, 1997.

Den Berg, L.W.C, and E.C. Howard (translation). *Minhaj At Talibin, A Manual of Mohammeden Law according to the School of Shafi'.* London: 1914.

Duncan, Richard. *Islamic Infastructure Project Financing : The Issues and the Solutions.* Seminar on Islamic banking and finance, Asia Business Forum, Kuala Lumpur, Malaysia, 1987.

Dillon, W.R., T.J. Madden, and N.H. Firtle. *Essentials of Marketing Research.* Boston: Irwin, 1993.

Faboozi, J.F., F. Modigliani, and Michael G. Ferri, *Foundations of Financial Markets and Institutions,* New York, Prentice-Hall International, Inc, 1998.

Goldsmith, R.W. *Financial Structure and Development*, New Haven, Yale University Press, 1969.

Griffin, Ricky E., and Ebert, Ronald J., *Business*, Prentice Hall, New Jersey, 1989.

Hamilton, Charles. *The Hedaya – Guide and Commentary on the Mussulman Laws.* Lahore, Pakistan: Primier Book House, 1975.

Hamouri, Qasem. "Rationality, Time, and Accounting for the Future in Islamic Thought," *Essays in Islamic Economic Analysis*, edited by F.R. Faridi, Delhi, Genuine Publications, 1991.

Haque, Ziaul, *Riba – The Moral Economy of Usury, Interest and Profit.* Kuala Lumpur: Ikraq, 1995.

Hasan, Ahmad. *Analogical Reasoning in Islamic Jurisprudence.* Delhi: Adam Publishers, 1994.

_____. *The Principles of Islamic Jurisprudence.* Delhi: Adam Publishers, 1992.

Hasan, Zubair. "Determinants of Profit-Loss Sharing Ratio in Islamic Finance." *Journal of Research in Islamic Economics.* Vol. 3, No. 1, 1983.

Hassan, Abdullah Alwi. *Sales and Contract in Early Islamic Commercial Law.* New Delhi: Kitab Bhavan, 1997.

Heffernan, Shelagh. *Modern Banking in Theory and Practice.* New York, John Wiley and Sons, 1996.

Homoud, Sami Hassan. *Islamic Banking.* Beirut, Arabian Publication, 1983.

Ibnu Qayyim Al-Jauziyah. *Panduan Hukum Islam (I'lamul Muwaqi'in).* Jakarta: Pusta Azzam, 2000.

Ibrahim, Ahmad. "Resolution of Legal Disputes in the Financial Sector in Accordance with Shariah Principles." Seminar on Islamic Banking and Finance, Pan Pacific Hotel, Kuala Lumpur, 1989.

Idris, Hamdan and Saiful Azhar Rosly. "Salam as a Mode of Agricultural Finance in Malaysia: An Analysis of Risk-Taking Behaviour of Contracting Parties." *Proceedings of International Conference on Islamic Economics.* Bahrain, January 2003.

Iqbal, Zamir and Abbas Mirakhor. "Stakeholders Model of Governance in Islamic Economic System," *Proceedings of International Conference on Islamic Economics.* Bahrain, January 2003.

Islahi, A. Azim. "Ibn Taimiyah's Concept of Market Mechanism," in Sayyid Tahir (eds.), *Readings in Microeconomics*, Kuala Lumpur, Longman Malaysia, 1992.

Jaffee, D.M. *Money, Banking and Credit.* New York: Worth Publishers, Inc., 1989.

Jomo, K.S. (ed.). *South-East Asia's Misunderstood Miracle*, Colorado: Westview Press, 1997.

Jones, Charles P. *Investments – Analysis and Management.* New York: John Wiley and Sons, 1996.

Kabir Khan, M. Fouzul, and Robert J. Parra. *Financing Large Projects.* New York: Prentice Hall, 2003.

Kamali, Muhammad Hashim. *Principles of Islamic Jurisprudence.* Kuala Lumpur, Pelanduk Publication, 1995.

Khayrullah, Walid Al-Muqaradah. "Bonds as the Basis of Profit-sharing." *Islamic Economic Studies.* Vol. 1, No. 2, 1994.

Kinner, T.C. and J.R. Taylor. *Marketing Research*, New York: McGraw Hill, 1996.

Lipsey, R.G., P.N. Courant, D.D. Purvis, and P.O. Steiner. *Economics.* New York: Harper Collins Publishers, 1993.

Mankiew, N. Gregory. *Principles of Economics.* New York: The Dryden Press, 1997.

Masud, Muhammad Khalid. *Shatibi's Philosophy of Islamic Law.* Kuala Lumpur, Malaysia: Islamic Book Trust, 1995.

Mejelle-Majallah el-Ahkam-i-adliya (translation) by Tyler, C.R. and D.G. Demetriades,. Effendi Ismail Haqqi , Kuala Lumpur, The Other Press, 2004.

Muhammad, Ariff. "The Malaysian Economic Experience and its Relevance for the OIC Member Countries." *Islamic Economic Studies*, Vol. 6. No. 1, 1998.

Morris, V. B., and B.D. Ingram. *Guide to Understanding Islamic Investment.* New York: Lightbulb Press, 2001.

Muhammad, Jaafar, Hendon Redzuan, and Rasidah Mohd Said. *Insurans Untuk Anda*. Kuala Lumpur, Fajar Bakti Publication, 1995.

Munawar, Iqbal. *Distributive Justice and Need Fulfilment in an Islamic Economy,* London, The Islamic Foundation, 1988.

Muwatta Imam Malik, Shiekh Muhammad Ashraf Publication, Lahore, Pakistan: 1980.

Nevitt, Peter K. *Project Financing*. London, Euromoney Publications, 1983.

Nik Hasan, Nik Mustafa (ed.), *Ekonomi Islam dan Perlaksannya di Malaysia.* Kuala

Lumpur, Malaysia: Islamic Institute of Understanding (IKIM), 2002.

Quzwain, M. Chatib, Mengenal Allah. *Satu Kajian Mengenai Ajaran Tasauf Syeikh Abdul Samad Al-Palimbangi.* Kuala Lumpur, Malaysia: Thinker's Library, 1996.

Rahman, Fazlur. *Islamic Studies and the Future of Islam in Fadhil Lubis* (ed.), *Introductory Readings on Islamic Studies*. Medan: IAIN Press, 1998.

Rahman, Fazlur. "*Riba* and Interest." *Islamic Studies*, Vol.III, No. 1, March 1964.

Rayner, S.E., *The Theory of Contracts in Islamic Law*. *1ˢᵗ edition.*New York, Graham and Trotman, 1991.

Robert, Cooter and Robert Ulen, Thomas. *Law and Economics*, New York: Addison Wesley, 1977.

611

Rosly, Saiful Azhar. "*Al-Bay' Bithaman Ajil* Financing: Impacts on Islamic Banking Performance," *Thunderbird International Business Review*, Vol. 41 (4/5), July- October 1999.

_____. "Economic Principles in Islam: Some Methodological Issues." *Journal of Islamic Economics*, Vol. 1, No. 1, July 1991.

_____. "*Iwad* as a Requirement of Valid Sale: Application of *Al-bay* as a Mode of Finance." *IIUM Journal of Economics and Management*, Vol. No. 2, 2001.

_____. "Welfare Implication of Interest-Free Bank Asset Management," *Journal of Islamic Economics,* International Islamic University Malaysia, Vol. 2, No. 2, 1989

Rosly, Saiful Azhar, "Al-Bay' Bithaman Ajil Financing: Impacts on Islamic Banking Performance", *Thunderbird International Business Review*, Volume 41 Number. 4/5, July -October 1999.

Rosly, Saiful Azhar and Sanusi Mahmod. "Application of *Bay' al-Inah* in Malaysian Financial Markets." *Arab Law Quarterly*, September 2001.

Rosly, Saiful Azhar, Sanusi Mahmod, and Norhashimah Mohd Yasin. "Does a *Shariah* Compliant Product Automatically Result in a Valid Contract Under *Shariah*?: A Study of Legal Documentation of Islamic Financial Products in Malaysia." *6th Harvard Islamic Finance Forum,* Harvard University, Cambridge 8-9 May 2004.

_____. "*Khiyar Al 'Aib* in *Al-Bai'-Bithaman Ajil* Financing," *International Journal of Islamic Financial Services*, Vol. 2 No. 1, February 2001.

Rosly, Saiful Azhar, and Azizi Che Seman. "Juristic Viewpoints on *Bay' Al-'Inah* in Malaysia: A Survey." *IIUM Journal of Economics and Management*, Volume 11, No. 1, December 2003.

Rosly, Saiful Azhar and, Emad Rafiq Barakat. "The Economic Thought of *Al-Maqrizi:* The Role of the Dinar and Dirham as Money." Proceeding of the 2002 International Conference on the Viability of the Islamic Dinar, August 19-20, Putra World Trade Center, Kuala Lumpur, International Islamic University.

Rosly, Saiful Azhar and Affendi Abu Bakar. "Performance of Islamic Bank and Mainstream Bank in Malaysia." *International Journal of Social Economics*, Vol. 30, Number 12, 2003.

Rosly, Saiful Azhar and Sheikh Ahmad, Mohd Parid. "Islamic Venture Capital- Determining Ownership Share." Proceedings of 2nd International Conference on Law and Commerce, 8-10 December 2003. Victoria Law School, Victoria University, Melbourne, Australia.

Rosly, Saiful Azhar and Mohd Azmi Omar. "Islamic Convertible Bonds: An Alternative to *Bay' al-'Inah* and Discounted *Bay' al-Dayn* Islamic Bonds for Global Islamic Capital Market," Proceeding of the Third Harvard University Forum on Islamic Finance, Harvard University, Cambridge, Massachusetts.

Sanusi, Mahmod and, Saiful Azhar Rosly. *Fiqh Muamalat for Islamic Financial Practisioners*. International Islamic University (unpublished) 2003.

Saud, Abu Mahmod. *Money, Interest and Qirad, Studies in Islamic Economics*, International Centre for Research in Islamic Economics, King Abdul Aziz University, Jeddah and Islamic Foundation, United Kingdom, 1980.

Saunders, Anthony. *Financial Institutions Management*. Boston: IRWIN, 1994.

Securities Commission, *Resolutions of the Securities Commission Syariah Advisory Council*, Kuala Lumpur, Malaysia, 2000.

Seong, Lim Yuen. *Estate Planning in Malaysia and Singapore*. Kuala Lumpur, Malaysia: Brains & Talents Publication, 1999.

Schiffman, L.G., and L.L. Kanuk. *Consumer Behavior.* New Jersey: Prentice Hall, 2000.

Shanmugam, B., C. Turton, and G. Hempel. *Bank Management*, Sydney, Australia: John Wiley & Sons, 1992.

Shim, J.K., and J.G. Siehel. *Source – The Complete Guide to Investment Information*, Kuala Lumpur, Golden Books Center, 1994.

Siddiqi, Muhammad Nejetullah. *Teaching Economics from Islamic Perspective*. Islamic Economics Research Series, Scientific Publishing Center, King Abdul Aziz University, 1996.

Shiddieqy, Teungku Muhammad Hasbi Ash. *Fiqh Muamalat.* Semarang: Pustaka Riski Putra, 1980.

_____. *Hukum-Hukum Fiqh Islam.* Semarang: Pustaka Riski Putra, 1997.

Umaruddin, Muhammad. *The Ethical Philosophy of Al-Ghazali*. Lahore: Sh. Muhammad Ashraf, 1970.

Vaughan, E. J. and T.M. Vaughan. *Fundamentals of Risk and Insurance.* New York: John Wiley and Sons, 1996.

Wan Daud, W. Mohd Nor. *The Educational Philosophy and Practice of Syed Muhammad Naquib Al-Attas*, International Institute of Islamic Thought and Civilization (ISTAC), 1998.

Wan Mohamed Ali, Wan Abdul Rahim. "Securitization of Debt Financing : The Islamic

Alternative." Seminar on Islamic Private Debt Securities (IPDS), Securities   Commission Malaysia, September 2001.

Warde, Ibrahim. *Islamic Finance in the Global Economy*, Edinburgh,Edinburgh University Press, 1998.

Yaakob, Abdul Monir and Wan Roslili Abdul Majid. *Mufti dan Fatwa di Negara-negara.*   Kuala Lumpur, Malaysia: ASEAN, Islamic Institute of Understanding (IKIM),   1998.

Vadillo, Umar I., *The Return of the Gold Dinar: A Study of Money in Islamic Law*, Madinah Press, Madinah, 1996.

Index

ABOUT THE AUTHOR

Saiful Azhar Rosly is Professor of Economics at the International Islamic University Malaysia. As a teacher he has taught various courses, including Islamic economics, Islamic banking and finance, money and banking, economic development, microeconomics, macroeconomics and principles of economics. He obtained his undergraduate and masters degree from Northern Illinois University, DeKalb, USA and Ph.D from the National University of Malaysia.

Professor Saiful has published his work in academic journals including International Journal of Social Economics, Arab Quarterly, Thunderbird Business Review and IIUM Journal of Economics and Management. He has also written for magazines and newspapers such as the KLSE Investors Digest, AmInvest, ZoomFinance, DataNiaga and the Sun.

On the area of Islamic economics, banking and finance, Saiful as a consultant in Islamic banking and finance has advised several institutions, including Ministry of Finance, National Economic Advisory Council (NEAC), Permodalan Usahawan Nasional Berhad (PUNB), EON Bank, Commerce International Merchant bank (CIMB) and Silverlake Malaysia. He has also conducted courses on Islamic financial markets in Singapore, Brunei and Indonesia. In addition to his teaching, research and consultation, Saiful is currently an independent director for the Federation of Malaysian Unit Trust Management (FMUTM).

Professor Saiful lives in Taman Tun Dr. Ismail, Kuala Lumpur with his wife, Faridah, and their children, Anas, Nur Iman, Ameen, Ariff and Nur Ilham. To unwind and relax, Saiful enjoys playing golf.

Lightning Source UK Ltd.
Milton Keynes UK
UKOW051925230812

198006UK00001B/27/A